THOMAS AQUINAS

A Historical, Theological, and Environmental Portrait

DONALD S. PRUDLO

Paulist Press
New York / Mahwah, NJ

Photo credits:
Roccasecca: Shizhao/Wikimedia Commons
Montecassino: Mattis/Wikimedia Commons
Averroes: Hameryko/Wikimedia Commons
Orvieto: Schieber/Wikimedia Commons

Cover image by HIP / Art Resource, NY
Cover and book design by Lynn Else

Library of Congress Cataloging-in-Publication Data
Names: Prudlo, Donald, 1976– author.
Title: Thomas Aquinas : a historical, theological, and environmental portrait / Donald S. Prudlo.
Description: New York : Paulist Press, [2020] | Includes bibliographical references and index. | Summary: "This biography explores the most significant thinker of his time in his various contexts, including his family, his education and formation, as a mendicant and Dominican friar, as a mystic, as a saint"— Provided by publisher.
Identifiers: LCCN 2019023979 (print) | LCCN 2019023980 (ebook) | ISBN 9780809153862 (paperback) | ISBN 9781587687587 (ebook)
Subjects: LCSH: Thomas, Aquinas, Saint, 1225?-1274. | Theologians—Biography. | Christian philosophers—Biography.
Classification: LCC B765.T54 P78 2020 (print) | LCC B765.T54 (ebook) | DDC 230/.2092 [B]—dc23
LC record available at https://lccn.loc.gov/2019023979
LC ebook record available at https://lccn.loc.gov/2019023980

ISBN 978-0-8091-5386-2 (paperback)
ISBN 978-1-58768-758-7 (e-book)

Published by Paulist Press
997 Macarthur Boulevard
Mahwah, New Jersey 07430
www.paulistpress.com

Printed and bound in the
United States of America

To Eamon
Bos mutus noster

Everything will be denied. Everything will become a creed. It is a reasonable position to deny the stones in the street; it will be a religious dogma to assert them. It is a rational thesis that we are all in a dream; it will be a mystical sanity to say that we are all awake. Fires will be kindled to testify that two and two make four. Swords will be drawn to prove that leaves are green in summer. We shall be left defending, not only the incredible virtues and sanities of human life, but something more incredible still, this huge impossible universe which stares us in the face. We shall fight for visible prodigies as if they were invisible. We shall look on the impossible grass and the skies with a strange courage. We shall be of those who have seen and yet have believed.

—G. K. Chesterton, *Heretics*

CONTENTS

CONTENTS

ACKNOWLEDGMENTS

This present work owes its genesis to Fr. John Vidmar, OP, who kindly suggested it to the editors at Paulist Press. I am grateful not only to him for his support, but also to Dr. Nancy de Flon, who has been an extremely active and supportive editor, accomplishing things with a speed and grace unusual for academic publishing. I am indebted to all my colleagues who have taken time to read and critique the manuscript, especially Fr. Augustine Thompson, OP, and Fr. Brian Mullady, OP. It is to my Dominican friends that I owe my interest in their order and in the life and work of our Common Doctor. As usual my friend Russ Lemmons, Distinguished Professor of History at Jacksonville State University, has generously commented on my work. To have such a perspicacious and careful colleague has been an immense benefit for all of my academic work. I am grateful to Dr. Gordon Harvey, my former department head, for his willing support for scholarship and am thankful to JSU, the DAAD, and the Earhart Foundation, all of whom have contributed with research support for this project. The many fine librarians on both sides of the Atlantic who work so hard to preserve the knowledge of the past are also due significant thanks. I would also be remiss not to mention the inspiration and support of my subject, Thomas Aquinas. It is a pleasure to write about the saints, particularly one who is proposed by the church as a model for one's own vocation. I realize too that in this project I have been assisted by a "cloud of witnesses," those teachers and authors who have labored to bring Thomas and his teachings into clearer light. Their patient industry has made Thomism one of the most dynamic theological and philosophical schools in the Christian tradition. When I think of the patient labors of Dominican scholars in particular over the centuries, it is a humbling privilege to be able to employ the fruits of their erudition. It is to be hoped that this book contributes in some way to their efforts. In the end, as always, I thank my family, which has again patiently borne the difficult parturition of a book, including the extended periods of research that necessitated time away. Their support has been foundational and critical for everything I have done. I do it because of and for them.

ABBREVIATIONS

Acta Cap. Gen.	*Acta capitulorum generalium Ordinis Praedicatorum.* Edited by Benedict Maria Reichert and Franz Andreas Frühwirth. 9 vols. Rome: In domo generalitia, 1898.
AFP	*Archivum Fratrum Praedicatorum*
Calo	Peter Calo. *Vita S. Thomae Aquinatis*, in *Fontes*, 17–55. Citation will be by chapter.
Chart.	*Chartularium Universitatis Parisiensis*. Edited by H. Denifle, OP. Paris: ex typis fratrum Delalain, 1899.
Ferrua	*S. Thomae Aquinatis vitae fontes precipuae* (sic). Alba: Edizioni Domenicane, 1968.
Fontes	*Fontes Vitae S. Thomae Aquinatis.* Edited by D. Prümmer and M.-H. Laurent. 6 fascicles from *Revue Thomiste*, 1911–1937. Citation will be by fasc. and pagination, which is continuous.
Fossanova	*Processus canonizationis* (Fossanova), in *Fontes*, 409–510. Citation will be by chapter.
Foster	Kenelm Foster. *The Life of Saint Thomas Aquinas: Biographical Documents*. London: Longmans, Green, 1959.
Gui	Bernard Gui. *Vita S. Thomae Aquinatis*, in *Fontes*, 161–263. Citation will be by chapter.
Hinnebusch	William Hinnebusch, OP. *The History of the Dominican Order*. 2 vols. New York: Alba House, 1973.
Libellus	Jordan of Saxony. *Libellus de Principiis Ordinis Praedicatorum*. Edited by H. C. Scheeben. Monumenta Ordinis Praedicatorum Historica 16. Rome: Institutum Historicum Ordinis Fratrum Praedicatorum, 1935. Citation will be by chapter.
MOPH	Monumenta Ordinis Praedicatorum Historica

Mulchahey	M. M. Mulchahey. *"First the Bow Is Bent in Study..."*: *Dominican Education before 1350*. Toronto: Pontifical Institute of Medieval Studies, 1998.
Naples	*Processus Canonizationis* (Naples), in *Fontes*, 265–407. Citation will be by chapter.
Porro	Pasquale Porro. *Thomas Aquinas: A Historical and Philosophical Profile*. Translated by R. W. Nutt and J. G. Trabbic. Washington, DC: Catholic University of America Press, 2017.
Rashdall	Hastings Rashdall. *The Universities of Europe in the Middle Ages*. Edited by F. M. Powicke and A. B. Emden. 3 vols. Oxford: Oxford University Press, 1936. All citations are to volume 1.
SCG	*Summa contra Gentiles*
STh	*Summa Theologiae*; parts cited as follows: Prima Pars, I; Prima-Secundae, I-II; Secunda Secundae, II-II; Tertia Pars, III.
Tocco	*Ystoria sancti Thome de Aquino de Guillaume de Tocco (1323)*. Edited by C. Le Brun-Gouanvic. Toronto: Pontifical Institute of Mediaeval Studies, 1996.
Torrell	Jean-Pierre Torrell, OP. *Saint Thomas Aquinas: The Person and His Work*. Rev. ed. Vol. 1. Translated by Robert Royal. Washington, DC: Catholic University of America Press, 2005.
Tugwell	Simon Tugwell, OP. *Albert and Thomas: Selected Writings*. Mahwah, NJ: Paulist Press, 1988.
Weisheipl	James Weisheipl, OP. *Friar Thomas d'Aquino: His Life, Thought, and Work*. New York: Doubleday, 1974.
VF	Gérard de Frachet, OP. *Vitae Fratrum Ordinis Praedicatorum*. Edited by Benedict Maria Reichert, OP. Monumenta Ordinis Praedicatorum Historica 1. Louvain: Charpentier, 1896.

NOTE ON NAMES AND TITLES

Most of the names in this work have been anglicized for ease of reading and because of their familiarity. Thomas is called by his Christian name and not by his loconym, "Aquinas," which would have been quite unfamiliar to him and to his confreres. When speaking of Thomas's family members, since they were not familiar, I left their names in Italian (including turning Lombard names into Italian) to help distinguish them from other similarly named contemporaries. Most other names, with few exceptions, are rendered in standard English.

There is a multiplicity of similar titles in the text, which has led me to adopt a somewhat unconventional capitalization. This is particularly the case with the various uses of "Master." When "Master" occurs by itself, I use it to refer to Thomas after his becoming professor at Paris. "Regent Master" refers to those professors who occupied teaching chairs at the universities. "Secular Master" refers to those clerics who had university chairs, but who were not members of the new religious orders. When I simply refer to "Masters" it refers to professors in general. I also use the terms "Master General" for the elected head of the Dominicans, and "Minister General" for the elected head of the Franciscans, though these titles are somewhat anachronistic. I do this in order to distinguish these leaders both from Thomas, and to underline their authority. I will explain the various academic terms used at the medieval universities in the text.

I refer to the orders in several different ways. For example, I use the "Dominicans," "the Preachers," and the "Order of Friars Preachers" interchangeably to describe the same group. Similarly, I employ "Minorites," "Franciscans," and the "Order of Friars Minor" to refer to that order. When I refer simply to "Friars," I am usually describing all the members of the mendicant orders as a group.

In some cases I consciously adopt anachronisms, for example referring to "Conventual" and "Spiritual" Franciscans, which was not a contemporary usage. These are meant to indicate moderate and radical approaches to the question of poverty, respectively. I try to explain in the notes whenever I bring these concepts up, for instance, in the difficult questions surrounding medieval "Augustinianism."

INTRODUCTION

The life of Tommaso d' Aquino (1224/6–1274) spanned the very core of the thirteenth century. This was an age of contrasts and of transformations, of stunning achievements and bitter losses. Thomas (as we ought to call him, not "Aquinas") set his stamp powerfully on the course of that epoch, partaking of its extraordinary dynamism. We see in that period a study in contrasts. Outwardly, it seemed to be the culmination of Christendom. Everywhere mighty cathedrals arose, universities thrived, and the power of the papacy waxed. The 1200s were the home of some of the most beloved saints and most perceptive thinkers in the entire history of Christianity. The pope at the start of the year 1200 was the energetic Innocent III, one of the most competent leaders in church history. The beneficiary of far-seeing predecessors over the previous 150 years, Innocent set his own reforming stamp on the church with the significant Fourth Lateran Council in 1215, whose echoes continue to be felt by Catholics to this day. Yet this vitality masked sources of concern. Innocent's successors engaged in strength-sapping conflicts with secular powers. Although the papacy seemed victorious by the 1250s, in the latter half of the century its power ebbed due to the decreasing quality of its officeholders and the contemporary rise of nation-states. By 1300, Boniface VIII attempted to make claims of supremacy similar to those maintained by Innocent III and failed miserably. The German Empire, founded by Charlemagne and later called the Holy Roman Empire, was on the other side of that struggle with the papacy. It found its strength broken by the battle. The ensuing power vacuum was filled by the new nation-states that presaged the coming of the modern world. In the intellectual realm, the renaissance of the twelfth century—one that continued in the magnificent scholarly achievements of Thomas and his fellow academics—was running out of steam. Though Thomas and his

1

contemporaries would not have admitted a decline, it remains that, after his death, Scholasticism entered a slow death spiral. Focusing on narrower and narrower topics, it would finally be overcome by reactions as diverse as nominalism, voluntarism, Renaissance Platonism, and a new mysticism. These movements effectively ended the great Scholastic project and bore witness to the philosophical exhaustion of the maturing universities.

For all that, it was still a profound age of faith. This is not in the thoughtless and fideistic sense that some historians in the past used the phrase, but rather in a robust consensus concerning the core of Christian belief and practice across all social classes. This faith included within it a hearty commitment to rationality. No one more than Thomas gives lie to the myth of an irrational Middle Ages. Indeed, this astonishing confidence in reason exceeded that expressed in any other age of the church. One only needs to point to a figure such as St. Anselm, archbishop of Canterbury (1033/4–1109), who speculated that even those most mysterious aspects of belief—the Trinity and the incarnation—could be established rationally. The age was also one of humanism: a renewed appreciation of the significance and worth of the human person, born of increased meditation on the humanity of Christ and honed by an encounter with the aggressively antimaterialist ideas of many medieval heretics and reformers. Indeed, along with the fantasy that the age was antirational goes the fable that Christianity was a spiritualizing religion that hated the body and earthly life. The revolution that the Jewish tradition bequeathed to the church was that of a humanity "created in the image and likeness of God." In Christianity this was underscored by the incarnation, when the transcendent Deity became an immanent part of his own creation, assuming to himself a human nature identical to ours. This God-man commanded that his grace be transmitted not through spiritual gnosis, but by bread, wine, oil, water, and human bodies. Medieval Christianity positively basked in materiality and the possibilities for the sanctification of matter, as indicated by Francis of Assisi's promotion of the Christmas crèche, and Thomas's own remarkable devotion to the new Feast of Corpus Christi.

The age was one of beginnings and of endings. It bore witness to the first shadows of the waning of the medieval project that could date itself back to the laws of Constantine and Augustine's *City of*

God. The old consensus was beginning to fail. The idea of political unity—always tenuous in the West because of the separation of spiritual and secular powers—was effectively abandoned with the neutralization of the empire. Religious harmony was also beginning to degenerate. Though the church had been successful against small groups of ardent medieval heretics, the fourteenth and fifteenth centuries would see the rise of movements that would not be so easily pacified: the Hussites and the Lollards, both of which can indeed be called precursors of the Protestant Reformation. The cultural world was seeing new beginnings as well. The poetry of Dante betokened new vernacular possibilities, though in his worldview he was firmly a medieval (and even an imperfect Thomist). The first signs of the approaching Renaissance stirred imaginations, though many have placed an overemphasis on a transition that was really a flowering of medieval humanism fed by the discoveries of new or forgotten ancient texts. The thirteenth century also saw the birth of what would become modern science. Men including Roger Bacon and Thomas's own teacher, Albert the Great, made startling advances. This empirical scientific progress was made possible only in Christendom, which maintained that God was a God of reason who had created a natural order that could be discovered by our own rational participation in it. Indeed, as these early scientists realized, traces of God himself could be found in nature, establishing natural science as a path to the transcendent. Furthering this was the empiricism of Aristotle, mediated through Thomas himself. Aristotelian thought forced thinkers to turn first to the world before considering immaterial realities. He and his interpreter Thomas insisted that the senses are necessary and communicate real and reliable information to us. Underscoring all this was the incarnational necessity of holding faith and reason together, affirming them both, no matter how difficult it might seem. Without these ideas any semblance of a scientific revolution would have been stillborn. Yet the 1200s witnessed other new beginnings, perhaps not as beneficial. The rise of the nation-state as a locus of political action and social identity was to have profound repercussions for the future. As Christianity began to lose its hold over Europe, the exaltation of the nation-state was to have significantly deleterious effects. Further, the radical philosophy of nominalism led to a dissolution of understandings of community and the concept of philosophical nature. This presaged the modern advent of a radical individualism that can be seen in both the Prot- estant Reformation and the Enlightenment and that finds its sum- mation in the hypernominalism of postmodernity. With all the achievements of the thirteenth century, seeds were being planted that would bear fruit in the coming ages. Thomas would live through, and affect, many of these changes.

Still, in the midst of all this, Thomas himself possessed a priv- ilege that few other theologians have enjoyed. He was given space to *be* and time to *think*. His life came after the short-lived erup- tions of medieval heterodoxy. Indeed, while he lived, his breth- ren were busy pursuing the remnants of heretical groups, pushing them to the far margins of European society. He also died well before the occlusion of the papacy, the transfer to Avignon, and the trauma of the Great Western Schism. He did not survive to see the rise of aggressively nominalist and voluntarist philosophers, nor the coming of the religious reformers of the 1300s and 1400s. Though he would encounter challenges from many individuals and engage in numerous polemics, Thomas was largely free from having to commit the whole of his intellectual life to settling ques- tions of pitch and moment. He had the leisure to examine issues in an atmosphere of relative calm (although punctuated by periodic excitement). This was the *otium* or "learned leisure" demanded by the philosophers of the ancient world. Because of this freedom he could investigate the ramifications of theology and philosophy truly *ex corde ecclesiae*, from the "heart of the church." In this he was very much like Augustine of Hippo. Many of the fathers of the 300s and 400s had to spend their lives on the vital issues of heresy emerging at that time—burning questions about the Trin- ity and the person of Christ. Augustine's period of tremendous activity lies after the conclusion of the trinitarian controversies of the fourth century, while he died before the manifestation of the christological conflicts of the fifth. This meant that Augustine was free to explore the contours of the Christian mysteries and enter deeply into introspection without having to apply all of his energy to pressing claims of the moment. Even Augustine, however, was hard put by the manifold duties of being a bishop and was occu- pied with the refutation of the rather pesky heretic Pelagius at the end of his life. Thomas, for his part, was a member of an order founded for the express purpose of freeing men like him from external duties, even the traditional monastic obligations of the choir. Such leisure can be productive of works such as the *Confessions* and the *City of God*; it can also come out in diverse forms such as the *Summa contra Gentiles* and the *Summa Theologiae*.

It will be the purpose of this book to attempt to understand the life and times of this Dominican thinker. It investigates his historical context, his family, his order, his influences, and his character in order to present as comprehensive a picture as possible of the man who became the "Common Doctor" of the Catholic Church. In situating Thomas in this way, perhaps we can once again see how astonishing his achievement was, a feat that was in no way foreordained, for the forces arrayed against him were many. It will demonstrate the characteristics that led later ages to claim him as a saint. In a certain manner, it will be a meditation on the interrelationship between scholarship and sainthood, written at a time when those concepts sometimes seem at a far remove from one another. In particular it seeks to be an "incarnational life" that explores what German scholars call the *Sitz im Leben*, or the setting of his life and work. This approach to Thomas seeks a balance that avoids both Platonic idealization and an exercise in recounting historical minutiae. It also seeks to understand the thinker as a man, and the man as a thinker—and indeed, how a man, by thinking, became a saint. To view him in this manner, it is vital to position him in the world he inhabited. As such, this effort will begin with a consideration of the world in which Thomas— scion of a noble family, relative of the German emperor, yet born into an atmosphere possessing profound papalist inclinations— found himself. I will attempt to lay out a picture of the Italian and European society at the time of Thomas's birth that will include an overview of the papacy, an institution that Thomas later served with such distinction. It will also cover the vicissitudes of the German Empire, in particular those of the Kingdom of Sicily, which was the earthly home of our subject. Born on the border of papal-imperial territory, Thomas experienced power politics firsthand, as well as the devastation of war that often followed. The first chapter will show this by laying out what we know of Thomas's family, whose members would play such a significant role in his story.

In chapter 2, the account turns to the early religious life of the young man. Destined by his family for a powerful position in the church, Thomas was first sent to the Benedictines of Monte-cassino. We will see what kind of religious and educational formation he received there. Still, it was not the sons of Benedict who finally received Thomas, but the upstart mendicant order called the Friars Preachers. In this chapter, I want to explore some of the reasons that the noble Thomas would have given for choosing the life of those founded in humility and transience, an effort that will involve a general overview of the religious movements of the twelfth century. These led to various responses on the part of the church, turning gradually from a negative assessment in the 1100s to the approval of the Franciscans and Dominicans by the 1210s. A brief outline of the life and intentions of Dominic will follow an explanation of the order he founded, and its short twenty-five-year history before the admission of its most famous member. The chapter will return to the effect of Thomas's decision on his family and broader society, for such momentous life choices never happen in a vacuum.

Chapter 3 describes the intellectual life of the early Dominicans, as well as the general scholarly situation in the middle of the 1200s. For too long Thomas has lived in the shadow of his works, hindered by the perception that he was an utterly original polymath. Anyone who has read Thomas's books, even superficially, knows how deep he is in the sources. An overview of the intellectual world of the ancient Greeks, particularly Plato, will give way to an analysis of the use of the Bible and the fathers by the medievals. Then I will describe the intellectual renaissance of the twelfth century, discussing some of its main figures and the inheritance it left for later generations. After that, I will highlight the specific influences on the early Dominicans, so as to see the intellectual world in which the order moved. Others have produced masterful meditations and compendia on Thomas's brilliant theology and philosophy; this present book prioritizes the person and his milieu. I want, however, to give some space to the intellectual precursors and teachers of Thomas in the order itself. It is one of the unfortunate effects of the printing press, as well as of the loss of Latin, that it sometimes seems that the only great medieval theologian was Thomas, whereas in reality he was preceded and followed by a host of notables who influenced him and mediated him to future generations. It is critical to place Thomas within the context of these brilliant men who made him what he was, even if Thomas ultimately outshone them. This chapter will also introduce Aristotle and his rediscovery by the West. In particular it will address the challenges and excitement that attended his arrival. It will also acquaint the reader with Thomas's great interlocutors, the Muslims Avicenna and Averroes and the Jew Maimonides. Rarely in history has there been such a deep and fruitful dialogue. Pagan and Christian, Jew and Muslim: all were read because of the possibility that they might lead to truth, which, for the medievals, was ultimately one—and not many. Its traces could be found everywhere. Such shards could be taken up and made whole under the light of Christian revelation. Truth was the pearl of great price, which was to be purchased even if it meant abandoning everything one had to acquire it. The chapter will end with the initial education of Thomas, his studies in Germany, and how he came under the influence of Albert the Great.

The medium that Thomas moved in was that of the university. The universities were born from the medieval church and populated by churchmen. An overview of these institutions will begin chapter 4. Following this I will explain what life was like at a university, particularly that of Paris, in the 1200s. This will include an analysis of the composition, customs, procedures, and functions of the schools. Understanding the atmosphere in which his thought developed is critical to realizing what exactly Thomas was doing in many of his writings. Since Thomas stands out as the prototypical and patronal university professor, it will be instructive to see how he went about his profession. This will lead to a discussion of Thomas's maturation in the university, his activities as a Bachelor and his inception as a Regent Master, holding one of the two chairs in Paris allocated to the Dominican order. I will describe the contents of Thomas's first works, illustrating how foundational they were for the rest of his career. A significant aspect of this effort will be a presentation of the escalation of the long-running dispute between the "Secular" clerical Masters of the University and the upstart mendicants. This conflict had many roots: labor disputes and lack of mendicant solidarity, social unrest within the university, the contest over the appropriation of Aristotle, and traditional critiques of new forms of religious vocations. Resentment turned to open and violent conflict in the mid-1250s, just as Thomas was beginning his first regency. The defenses Thomas made of the mendicant state and the rights of religious orders are especially significant, demonstrating how he could engage in polemics as well as in dispassionate inquiry. This conflict lays bare the presuppositions of many groups in the thirteenth century and would be resumed periodically throughout the rest of his life. Indeed, in many ways Thomas's answers to this debate provided a fundamental basis for his later canonization.

Chapter 5 sees Thomas at the height of his powers, having become a seasoned debater and Master. Here we will consider what Thomas's life was like within the context of the Dominican order. To live in a convent of the Friars Preachers in the thirteenth century was to encounter a life of strict adhesion to a religious rule, all subordinated to intellectual activity directed toward the final end of the salvation of souls. We will see how Dominican houses differed from other contemporary religious orders, and how those differences paved the way for the enduring achievements of Thomas and his confreres. This will allow us to understand Thomas's attitudes toward work, toward his students, and toward his own order. In addition, his stance toward the church will be made plain in his uncomplaining departure from Paris, the intellectual center of Europe, to take up a post in tiny Orvieto. There he would be faced with the task of running the small *studium* in the city where the Roman curia later came to reside. Thomas took this as an opportunity and did some of the best work of his life in the small convent. Indeed, while the small Umbrian town is known for its eucharistic miracle, one could point to another "miracle": that in such a small town some of the finest minds of the time gathered—not only Thomas, but also Bonaventure, Albert the Great, and the Dominican cardinal Hugh of St. Cher, among many others. During this period another Dominican, William of Moerbeke, was regularly supplying Thomas with new and improved translations of Aristotle to incorporate into his work, which sped the maturation of Thomas's thought.

The sixth chapter traces the life and career of an innovator who had by this time become quite well known. It will recount his assignment to Rome in order to set up a *studium*, which—refounded in later years—has borne his cognomen "the Angelicum" to the present day. This position allowed him full liberty to design a curriculum according to his own understanding of the intellectual needs of his students. In 1259, Thomas had been appointed to a committee to reform the order's studies, and now the Friars granted him plenipotentiary power to create a *studium* from the ground up. Perceptively noting weaknesses in received systems, the Dominican Master began a whole new approach that would culminate in his most famous work: the *Summa Theologiae*. But Thomas was not to be left in peace. Storm clouds were again gathering in Paris. The Seculars had been humbled but not defeated. Between 1268 and 1271 they mounted a major counteroffensive against the mendicant orders. Tied into this was the vexing appearance of a new group of radicalized Aristotelians who later earned the name "Latin Averroists." Most unsettling for the order, however, was that this headstrong group of young Arts Masters intimated that Thomas was on their side. These issues resulted in the recall of Thomas to the university to assume his second Paris regency. During this time he battled the antimendicants and fought off the Averroists, knowing that a radicalized Aristotelian interpretation was just as dangerous to his tenuous project as a traditionalist reaction. When one has considered all of these activities, the character of Thomas Aquinas comes better into focus.

The final chapter deals with the end of Thomas's life and an examination of his personality and legacy. The sources confront us with the narrative of the vision that caused Thomas, already feeling the oncoming of death as he neared the age of fifty, to stop working. In spite of that experience, Thomas remained an obedient religious and answered the call of the pope to prepare for the Second Council of Lyon in 1274. Dutifully he set out from Naples, where he had returned to teach in his last years. He did not make it far. Falling ill, he sought hospitality at the Cistercian abbey of Fossanova. After a short illness, Thomas died. The man who had traveled hundreds of miles, from Rome, to Germany, to France, and perhaps beyond, expired only a few miles away from his birthplace. The chapter will continue by tracing the rise of a modest but well-established cult, centered around his tomb in the abbey. Parallel to that was the great struggle to recognize Thomism as a safe and orthodox theological and philosophical school. Thomas's innovations had meant that many challenged his theology during his life, and even more so after his death. Even members of his own order publicly censured him. Yet the patient labor of dozens of committed Dominican academics and preachers slowly met the challenges, and within twenty years Thomism was recognized as reliable, and within thirty had become the official system of the order. This accomplished, Thomas was finally in a position to be presented for canonization. He achieved this honor in 1323, nearly fifty years after his death, and near the hundredth anniversary of his birth. Having considered the whole of the life of this famous professor, this chapter ventures to make some remarks on his extraordinary character, and what the "life of the mind" really meant for St. Thomas.

The book will conclude with some remarks on the world that Thomas left. It would be difficult to overestimate his effects on his own religious order, on the Catholic Church, and on the history of theology and philosophy. We will make a brief investigation of the later history of Thomas's thought and cult, proceeding through the Middle Ages, to see the theological authority that was accorded to him by the Council of Trent and his appropriation by other orders, such as the Carmelites and Jesuits. The evolution into Baroque Scholasticism will be discussed, as will the pivotal encyclical *Aeterni Patris* of Leo XIII. The book will end by noting the many varieties of contemporary Thomism, all united by his original theological vision, and all convinced of the incarnational necessity of preserving the balance between faith and reason, even when this seems most difficult.

I do not exaggerate when I say that thousands of works have been written on the thought of *Divus Thomas*. Indeed, dozens of biographies have also appeared, many exceptionally valuable in presenting new insights and helping us to know the Angelic Doctor better. What, then, is the purpose of yet another book? It has been my wish to navigate between the two most common types of biographies: the popular (sometimes uncritically hagiographic) and the exceptionally academic (works by renowned scholars such as Simon Tugwell, Jean-Pierre Torrell, and James Weisheipl). These scholars have been my lodestars throughout this effort, not to mention the constellation of other researchers who have tangentially touched upon Thomas. This book does not replace this careful work; but even these fine biographies have limitations. Much of their scholarship is inaccessible and overly academic. The brilliant insights of the Leonine commission—the 130-year-old project to edit all Thomas's works into modern editions—is particularly difficult for the general public to access. Tugwell's keen observations are scattered over a number of books and articles. Weisheipl's exceptionally useful biography has been out of print for a long time, while Torrell's books, quite valuable in themselves, alternate between exaggerated attention to minutiae or an excessive focus on theological and philosophical issues. Though I do not wish to stress this aspect, it also remains that all three of the above scholars are themselves Dominicans, men of St. Thomas's own order, bound not only by adherence to Thomistic principles, but also by fraternal feeling. While this in no way compromises their outstanding scholarship, it does sometimes color their emphases (for instance, in the case of interorder conflict with the Franciscans and in their insistence that he was canonized as a teacher). Further than this, I would venture to say that many of the fine studies of St. Thomas have a particular downside. They are really more about Thomism than about Thomas, simply preferring to use a chronological framework as an organizing principle to drill into his thought. In this I include the fine recent works by Denys Turner and Pasquale Porro. None of the above efforts really gives a genuine feel for Thomas's thirteenth-century context (though Weisheipl often comes closest). Still I am absolutely indebted to their scholarship, and their work is deeply woven into these pages.

In the words of the Dominican motto, I have sought *contemplata aliis tradere* (to bring the fruits of contemplation to others). Thomas knew that the final end of the truth he sought was the salvation of souls and the good of humanity. It is why he taught, and why he constantly wrote responses and introductions to topics. It was not enough for him to write abstruse academic books, works written over the course of years that would be read by only a handful. Therefore, I want to present Thomas in an approachable manner, yet interwoven with the best of contemporary scholarship. This means that occasionally some beloved and often retold stories are revealed as unhistorical. I include at the end an appendix with a commentary on the sources, in order to make plain the principles I have used in assessing them, and as much as possible, I have relegated academic questions to the notes. Likewise, I want to caution that this will be no hagiography. Thomas had faults, often masked by his early admirers as virtues. He was certainly a saint, but not a saint represented in a treacly nineteenth-century holy card. He was a man of his times, engaged in academic battle, just as real and significant as worldly combat, indeed perhaps more so. He had blind spots and did not always comport himself in the best manner possible. This is not to denigrate his sanctity; rather, I am firmly convinced that the ways in which Thomas handled his own limitations enhances claims regarding his holiness.

A further motive for producing this book has been the growing gap between theology/philosophy and history. Though such a dichotomy was present in the Middle Ages, Descartes exacerbated it. The gap then widened into a chasm as each side tried to make itself the sole master of knowledge in the nineteenth century (only to find empirical science outstripping them both). History needs ideas, and ideas are rooted in history. This book, while not a formal intellectual history, hopes to situate the thoughts of Thomas in the environment in which they developed. This does not mean that those ideas do not then take on a life of their own in the minds of people; rather, it means that the Christian philosopher must always be *rooted*. He or she must dwell not in a Platonic/Cartesian dualism that separates mind and matter, but rather in the sometimes dirty reality of a transcendent God—called Logos or Subsistent Reason itself—becoming intimately present within his own creation. Christian thought, whether historical, theological, or philosophical, must at its heart be incarnational. So much historical scholarship today is interested only in minute details of social or economic realities without reference to the difficult and controversial confrontation with ideas. So much theological and philosophical scholarship is Cartesian and dualist, devoid of contact with reality, in particular with rooted, incarnational Christianity. In that I must unfortunately implicate much Thomistic scholarship. This book is meant to be a humble effort to reconnect those often disparate fields and, in so doing, to hearken back to the medieval pursuit of harmony: that all truth, ultimately, is one.

Chapter 1

THE WORLD THOMAS FOUND

Italy, the Church, the Empire, and the Conflicts of the Thirteenth Century

Since the time of the Punic Wars, 250 years before Christ, the Italian peninsula has been at the center of history. It is a verdant and productive land, of mild climate and with an abundance of resources. Yet Italy—spoken of in a geographical sense, for there was never a nation of that name until 1861—is also in one of the most strategic locations in the world. It lies directly in the middle of the Mediterranean, extending five hundred miles into the heart of that sea. Halfway between Spain and the Holy Land, it found itself of necessity as a center of trade and conflict. Further, it represents an extension of Europe, pointing directly at Africa: at times it was a bridge between north and south; at others, an obstacle. While occasionally an avenue for invasion, by and large the sea was its protection. Surrounded on three sides by water and to the north by Alpine mountains impassable for months at a time, Italy was in a generally secure position. It was not only fortunate in its location—history too contrived to make Italy central to the story of the West. After its unanticipated victory over the Carthaginian Empire of Africa, the city of Rome rose to a place of dominance in the Western world. Eventually it embraced every shore of the Mediterranean, with Romans going so far as to call it "Our Sea"— *Mare Nostrum*. It expanded farther, into Gaul and Germany, occupying much of Britain and Dacia (Romania), occasionally taking areas as distant as the Persian Gulf. With this dominion it brought unity: of language, of culture, of law. The shadow of the Roman Empire stretched far beyond its own historical epoch, and its effects are still felt today.

Within the bosom of the empire a new religious movement was founded: Christianity. Finding Palestine inhospitable, and possessed of a mandate for missionary expansion, the early followers of Christianity dispersed through the empire's territories, traveling roads made secure by Rome's legions, and finding many willing listeners among the pagan Gentiles. Eventually the two most significant of the apostles of Christ—Peter and Paul—made their way to the eternal city and found their martyrdoms there. As time went on, Christians began to turn to the Roman church—seen as sanctified by the blood of the two leaders of early Christianity— for guidance and security of doctrine. Even as the political authority of Rome waned, the religious authority of the city increased. Theological disputes in the East aided this development, and the coming of Islam hastened it, as other ancient Christian centers fell to the new religion, first Antioch, then Jerusalem, and finally Alexandria. The Muslim expansion eclipsed much of the East, which resulted in Christians in these areas becoming second-class citizens, not allowed to evangelize or worship publicly. Byzantium— representing the remnants of Roman imperial authority in the East and centered in the city of Constantinople—was embroiled by religious disputes while at the same time scrambling for survival against Islam. Gradually a division formed between the Roman West and the Greek East, one finally consummated in 1054 and sealed by the Crusades. Yet the Greek East was in serious decline. Rome herself had long since turned to the West, to the peoples of the "barbarian tribes" upon whom the Roman church began to exercise a civilizing influence, leading to the formation of Europe.[1] As a result Rome remained the center of European activity well into the Middle Ages. Even while the population of the city dwindled, the position of the Roman bishop became increasingly secure. Italy remained at the center of history.

By the eleventh century, the peninsula could be roughly divided into three distinct regions. In the north were the provinces of Lombardy, the Veneto, Emilia, and Tuscany. These had been incorporated into the Carolingian Empire in the 700s and 800s, but as disorder increased following the death of Charlemagne, these cisalpine territories were left to fend for themselves. For centuries they did not experience any direct interference from the Germanic imperial government. Left to their own devices, they began to govern themselves. In the first place were the mighty merchant seafaring cities of Venice, Genoa, and Pisa, which had become rich, powerful, and independent by the year 1100. These cities maintained contacts with the rich cultures of the East, both Islamic and Christian. Significant developments also occurred inland. The cities of the Lombard plain, though developing later than the seaports, began to experiment with communal democracy. Finding that the bulk of the cities was made up of craftsmen, and having largely turned their backs on the aristocracy, they formed civic constitutions that had not been seen since the days of ancient Greece. At the same time these democracies were fundamentally Christian, economically prosperous, and protective of their freedom. The seaports and the inland cities began to innovate economically, forming the basic tools of protocapitalism and ushering in what would be called the Commercial Revolution.[2] But there was trouble brewing. The German Empire, stabilized under the Ottonian dynasty, again began to grow in strength in the mid-1100s. Having secured the German-speaking territories, the emperors had turned their attention to the south and reawakened their ancient claims to the cities of the Lombard region. Conflict was not long in coming.

The middle of the Italian peninsula was in the hands of the church. The Papal States could legally be dated back to the time of the Donation of Pepin—the father of Charlemagne—in 756. However, the popes' de facto control over the territory could be traced back much further, perhaps even to the reign of Gregory the Great (r. 590–604).[3] Following the power vacuum occasioned by the loss of Roman imperial authority, the popes had, as a matter of course, assumed the functions of day-to-day government. They were the last recognizable authority, and they had no interest in letting their people starve. These states would continue in existence until their annexation by the new Kingdom of Italy in the year 1870. In this area, subdivided into several different counties and duchies, the pope was the earthly or temporal sovereign, though government was usually in the hands of selected proctors. This possession of his own territory secured his independence from secular interference and undergirded his claims as the religious authority for all Christians, irrespective of affiliation or cultural differences. The proximity to the German imperial claims in the north often led to friction between papacy and the empire, which at times broke out into open war in the 1100s and 1200s.

The southernmost third of the peninsula had an altogether different history from the two others. For years the southern tip of Italy had been one of the only remaining areas of Byzantine influence, meaning that the effects of Greek Christian culture continued to be felt. Even today pockets of Greek Catholics and the Greek language still exist in this area. Further, positioned as it was close to Islamic northern Africa, it was the subject of raids on one hand and of trade and cultural contact with the Arab world on the other. Indeed, in the 800s North African Muslims completely conquered the island of Sicily. For two hundred years Sicily was ruled by Islam.[4] Further adding to the multicultural mix were the marauding Normans. As Byzantine authority weakened in southern Italy, and local communities began to rebel, the Normans saw an opportunity. These Normans, called after Normandy in France—which itself took its name from "Norsemen"—were the Christian descendants of the Viking raiders who had pillaged Europe for generations. While they had given up their paganism, it seemed that raiding was still in their blood. After having successfully occupied England after 1066, some Normans began to pursue new opportunities for expansion. The chaos of southern Italy gave them the opening they needed.[5] At first only a few Norman families came, but as the eleventh century progressed, larger numbers appeared. Over the course of several decades, the Normans, led by the warlord Robert Guiscard, first displaced the Byzantines and then wrested Sicily away from the divided Muslim lords of the island. By 1139 the conquest had been completed, and the fine port of Naples had been incorporated into the new Kingdom of Sicily. This Norman rule provided a sizeable amount of religious and ethnic toleration, with Roman Catholics, Eastern Orthodox, Jews, and Muslims all being represented in government. The brief period of Norman occupation resulted in a burst of cultural activity. Yet it was not to last.

There was still one element left to be added to the astonishing ethnic-religious mix that was being created in the southern third of the Italian peninsula. The nephew of Robert Guiscard, Roger II, had chosen to support the antipope Anacletus II over Innocent II in the 1130s.[6] This led to long simmering tension between the papacy and the Sicilian monarchy. The Roman church had long been wary of the Normans in the Italian peninsula; they were not above threatening and even abducting the pope himself, an event that happened on several different occasions. Faced with similar threats in northern Italy from the German Emperor Frederick Barbarossa (r. 1155–90), the popes began to look for ways to destabilize the Norman ruling house.[7] In spite of the tension, Norman Sicily prospered economically, though rocked by periodic revolts throughout the kingdom. Eventually the last Norman king, William II the Good, died in 1189 without a male heir. He had named his daughter Constance as successor, but as she was married to the Holy Roman Emperor Henry VI, local nobles raised a rebellion, not wishing to be ruled by Germans. By 1194 Henry had quelled the revolt and enforced his wife's claims. In 1197, the three-year-old son of Henry and Constance was crowned as King of Sicily. His name was also Frederick. The Norman ruling class found itself displaced as the Kingdom of Sicily entered into the power of the House of Hohenstaufen. The Germans had added the final piece to the ethnic and religious mosaic of south Italy. Constance herself died in 1198, and the guardianship of the young king passed to the powerful Pope Innocent III (r. 1198–1216).[8] After another decade of struggle, largely an effect of the royal minority, Frederick's crown was at last secured by 1208, when he came of age.

In 1209, the pope had crowned Otto of Brunswick as Holy Roman Emperor, attempting to deflect the throne of the Germans away from the house of Frederick Barbarossa. Innocent was unsuccessful in this, as Otto later betrayed his trust by mounting an invasion of the Kingdom of Sicily, seeing an opportunity to back the barons who resented Hohenstaufen rule. For this act Innocent relieved Otto of the imperial title. The power to absolve subjects from allegiances to their rulers was a right claimed by the popes since the time of Gregory VII in the 1080s. The popes used this with varying degrees of success over the next 150 years, though Innocent III had enough charisma and power actually to enforce it. He essentially effected a change (or, in this case, a reversion) in dynasty. Frederick, then only fourteen years old, was elected as the new Holy Roman Emperor.[9] Innocent III, as Frederick's guardian, and having provided his education and secured his crown, was certain that the young man would be an ardent papal supporter. It was to be one of the gravest mistakes of an otherwise success-ful pontificate. Frederick had ideas of his own. The pope's main concern was that Frederick now ruled both Sicily and the empire. A glance at a map now demonstrated that, even though Freder-ick was considered an ally, the Papal States were now surrounded by the territories of the Hohenstaufen, the same family that had threatened the pope's safety on several past occasions. Innocent extracted a promise from the young man to make sure that the two titles were separated and that there would be no personal union that permanently united the two territories. Having done this, the pope, nearing the end of his life, was satisfied.

Frederick proved to be an effective, if self-serving, monarch of the Kingdom of Sicily. In 1224 he chartered the University of Naples. Fearing that his subjects would be drawn to the pro-papal schools of the north, he decided to have his own university in the chief city of his kingdom. In addition, Frederick issued influ-ential laws called the "Constitutions of Melfi" for Sicily.[10] These were a thoroughgoing and centralizing administrative reform that paved the way for modern techniques of governing. Yet all was not well. Frederick had broken his promises to go on crusade and had renewed his claims over the independent northern Ital-ian city-states. These resulted in excommunication and eventual war between the papacy (allied with many city-states) and the empire. While Frederick was on the sixth crusade (1228–29), he had ordered his adjuncts to attack papal holdings in Italy in his absence. This resulted in a papal retaliation and an invasion of the Kingdom of Sicily. Armies marched up and down the Via Appia and the Via Latina, and fighting raged between Naples and Rome, only ending in 1230. Many of Thomas Aquinas's first experiences may have been of this war that occurred on his very doorstep.

THE CHURCH

The church and papacy that Thomas served so faithfully had also experienced many trials and changes in the ages before his birth. After the brief fireworks of the Carolingian renaissance, the church began to slide into corruption. Many bishops were themselves warlords and landowners, some of whom had acquired their ecclesiastical titles through purchase, a practice known as simony. In plenty of cases they were more beholden to their local lords and their own estates than to their spiritual duties. In addition, ancient laws on clerical celibacy were often honored in the breach. While clergy were canonically prevented from marrying, many circumvented this custom by various types of concubinage. Monasteries, formerly the engines that had preserved civilization and spread the faith throughout Europe, had become relaxed, with the choice of leadership often devolving upon the local nobility. This descent accelerated after the reign of Nicholas I (r. 858–67), the last strong pope of the first millennium. After his pontificate the papacy degenerated into the plaything of Italian noble families who imposed a series of unworthy men upon the see during the 900s. This was the age known as the *saeculum obscurum* or the "shadowy times." By the year 1000, however, some green shoots had begun to sprout. A new monastic movement was growing by leaps and bounds—the reformed Benedictines of Cluny, dedicated to strict observance of the rule and the solemnization of the liturgy. As happens so often in church history, it was the stricter orders that attracted novices while the relaxed orders died off, one by one. The papacy aligned itself with this reform movement, and a symbiotic relationship resulted that extended both the Cluniacs' reach and papal authority. The political order of Europe also began to stabilize, with the return of strong Holy Roman Emperors in the Ottonian line and the conversion of the Vikings to Christianity. The borders of Europe were at last secured to the north, east, and south. Now was the time for a purification of the church in head and members.

A circle of churchmen dedicated to the reformation of the papacy began to gather around the monk Hildebrand in the 1040s. Included in his circle were such men as Peter Damian and Humbert of Silva Candida. In order to purify the Roman church, the German emperor Henry III intervened in several papal elections in the 1040s and finally imposed the German Leo IX as pope in 1049 (it was only after this—in 1059—that rules creating a conclave to elect the successor of Peter became established, which limited the influence of outside forces on elections). The reform group quickly coalesced around Leo, who gave his full energy to the enforcement of clerical celibacy and the abolition of simony. This movement gained momentum when Hildebrand himself was elected as Pope Gregory VII (r. 1073–85). The new pope and his allies quickly moved to complete the reforms and began attempts to liberate the church from secular domination. Though this process would take decades, by the middle of the 1100s, the church—particularly the Roman curia—was largely independent of secular princes and had assumed a significant position of political leadership itself in Europe, a trend that would only accelerate for the next one hundred years. The contest between church and state had an intermediate resolution in the Concordat of Worms in 1122. As a result of this agreement the spiritual investiture of bishops—or the handing over of the symbols of their spiritual rule, which descended from God alone—was separated from their temporal investiture as secular lords. Though this certainly did not end church-state struggles, it did provide significant breathing room for the church.

Much of the centralization of the modern papacy dates from this period.[11] The Gregorians began a process of centralization that would mold the institution into the unitary power and source of authority that would reach its zenith in the early modern period, and in many ways continues to the present day. During the first millennium of Christianity, Rome had indeed possessed an honored place as the first see. The undivided church viewed it as the court of final appeal in Christendom. Rome served as an arbiter of doctrinal and disciplinary disputes during those years. While theological controversies ravaged the Christian East, many saw Rome as a depository of the faith of the apostles, particularly the most significant of them, Peter and Paul. However, the pope was a remote figure to most Christians in the first thousand years of the church. The limits of premodern communication and the breakdown of political authority hemmed in the effectiveness of the papacy. A period of 170 years in which a series of bad, incompetent, or indifferent popes reigned between ca. 880 and 1049 only made this situation worse. When the Gregorians came, they arrived with a theory in which they envisioned a reformed papacy as the center of a wheel that could turn Christendom itself. In their conception, the purification of the Holy See would trickle down to all of the local churches. In many cases this model worked during the Middle Ages. The Gregorians and their successors promoted a series of exceptionally successful initiatives that centralized authority in the see of Peter. During this period, the papacy called councils to meet at Rome. Prelates from all over Europe attended councils in the eternal city, surrounded by the memories of Christian triumph and centered on the person of the pope. The papacy extended its reach into foreign countries by appointing plenipotentiary legates who, with papal authority, could overrule even the primates of different regions. Simultaneously the papacy began to appropriate the right of canonization of saints, meaning that people had to appeal to Rome for the public authorization of new cults. The Gregorians streamlined the institution of the cardinalate, which had the effect of promoting the pontifical court, allowing representation of the different nations of Christendom before the pope, and securing papal elections from outside interference. Popes began to assert (sometimes successfully) the right of moral supervision of secular princes. The practice of excommunication and interdict—essentially the excommunication of a whole territory—once again began to be effective.

In a development that would later significantly benefit the mendicant movement, in the 900s the papacy began to experiment with granting the privilege of exemption. This meant that religious orders possessing such a privilege were exempt from any local interference from either church or state. Bishops, who were often beholden to secular princes or corrupt themselves, were disintermediated. Any supervision or judgment of such an exempt religious order was reserved to the pope alone. This created a marvelous symbiosis between the reformed orders and the papacy. The new religious groups received nearly total freedom of movement, supervision, and governance. The popes enhanced their prestige by having elite bodies of religious spread throughout Christendom, promoting papal policy and extending the reach of the Holy See. The Benedictines of Cluny would be the first group to profit from the concession of papal exemption, using it to grow dramatically even when confronted by intractable lay lords and corrupt bishops. As one can imagine, this privilege led to much resentment on the part of those who found their authority impaired. Indeed it was this opposition to this very privilege that would lead to disturbances during Thomas's career, challenges he would have to meet on more than one occasion. Yet this mutually beneficial relationship caused the rapid spread of the ideal both of ecclesiastical purification and of papal supremacy.

All through the post-Gregorian period the church continued to purify itself. At the beginning, such impulses dovetailed with lay desires for increased purity, as indicated by the Pataria faction in Milan in the 1070s.[12] This popular movement, backed by the papacy, drove out all the simoniacal clergy along with those who had violated their vows of chastity. A laity becoming increasingly well-off, urban, and literate was hungry for a renewed religious life, a desire with which the Gregorians allied themselves. The twelfth century saw an efflorescence of religious and intellectual movements.[13] Education migrated outside the confines of the monasteries, to which it had retreated following the decay of imperial order and the upheavals of late antiquity. An urbanization of learning developed, called Scholasticism.[14] This trend spread rapidly, animated by the rediscovery of the logic of Aristotle and made possible by the stabilization of the European geopolitical situation. Bishops formed cathedral schools that attracted famous Masters, who gathered students around them. The students who attended these new institutions subsequently became the leaders of Christendom in both religious and civil affairs during the latter half of the twelfth century. They brought with them incision, erudition, and a rigidly logical system of argumentation (dialectic) that they had learned in the schools. Improved education and the dissemination of learning connected with the desire for reform transpiring both inside and outside of the cloister.

By the 1100s the Cluniac order had become comfortable with its own impressive success. Even if not actively corrupt, the Cluniacs had settled into a prosperous existence. But the religious life had never been about comfort and prosperity. As the lamp of Cluny dimmed, a new religious force, animated by St. Bernard of Clairvaux (1090–1153), launched a new reform: the Cistercians.[15] This group stressed simplicity and the interdependence of religious houses under centralized control, making it perhaps the first recognizably modern "religious order." In what would be influential in the later life of Thomas, they produced the innovation of the canonical novitiate, a period of testing to see whether a young man was suited for the order and could bear up under the austerities of its rule. If he could not, after a set period he was free to leave. This distinguished the Cistercian novitiate from the older Benedictine tradition that accepted *oblates*, that is, children donated by their families to the monastery for training and education. While the Rule permitted a child to make a free choice to undertake final vows, in reality most oblates stayed in the monastery. The Cistercians also adopted an innovation from the eremitical Camaldolese order: the lay brother. These were to be laymen affiliated with the monastery who undertook all the physical labor in a life of penitence and mediated between the monastery and the broader world.[16] This left the monks free for their primary duties in prayer and in choir. These figures would be critical to the mission of the later Friars Preachers, for they liberated the professed Dominican fathers to pursue the intellectual life without compromise. While this did indeed create a two-tiered system in which the brothers were subordinate, in reality the institution arose from lay desire itself for opportunities to live lives of penance in service to God. The Cistercians also created a delicate balance of centralization and independence. The abbot of Citeaux was to be supreme in the order and each house be obedient to him, with the meetings called "Chapters-general." At the same time, each house was free to order its internal life (in accordance with the rule) and to elect its own abbots.[17] Finally, in the interests of simplicity, Bernard's monks celebrated a very simple liturgy, which came to be known as the Cistercian Rite. This simplification and purification would pave the way for Dominican liturgical rules that would serve as a complement to those dedicated to a life of wandering, preaching, and learning. Indeed, the Cistercians offered a model of which later Dominicans would partake. All of these renewals coincided with an increasing emphasis on a new devotional ideal: the imitation of the apostles.

NEW CHALLENGES

As people sought to reform the church, they began to seek new models for imitation. The laity—newly awakened by the ideals of the Gregorian reform and increasingly wealthy, leisured, and literate—began to move beyond older models of lay involvement. During the early Middle Ages, a spiritual division of labor had arisen whereby the laity supported the monks monetarily, and in exchange the monks prayed for them. Such a model was fraying by the 1100s. A new hunger for penitential holiness began to reverberate through Christendom, not least because the Christian people, not used to the possession of wealth, began to worry about the state of their souls.[18] Medievals began to generate an astonishing amount of wealth as a result of their development of the tools of protocapitalism, but their deep commitment to Christianity left them with ambivalent attitudes toward such riches. If it was "easier for a camel to go through the eye of a needle than for someone who is rich to enter the kingdom of God" (Matt 19:24), then who among this new entrepreneurial middle class could be saved? Many rich men, particularly after the deaths of their wives, entered religion, or gave their wealth to the poor or to the church, in the hope of securing their place in heaven. It was similar with widows, who adopted penitential and charitable forms of life dedicated to Christ. Some took the ideal even further. People began to reflect on what types of life made the road to salvation most assured. For nearly one thousand years, the answer had been simple: join a cloistered monastic order, die to the world, do penance for your sins and those of humanity, and choose the better part of Mary, instead of the active life of Martha.[19] By the twelfth century, an alternative model finally appeared.

Candidly, it is hard to find monks in the New Testament. The early followers of Christ had indeed shared all things in common, yet they lived in the world, not apart from it. In addition, had not the last thing Christ said to his disciples been a missionary mandate? How did the cloistered brothers and sisters live out the commandment of evangelization? Indeed, some of Christ's own apostles had even been married. People began to draw novel conclusions: in order to follow Christ more closely, one should follow his earliest disciples and use them as models for imitation. It did not yet occur to early and central medieval Christians that Christ, the God-man, was a proper object of imitation; such a suggestion would have seemed faintly blasphemous until the *Devotio Moderna* of the fifteenth century. These new thoughts meant that people began to conform their lives not to monasticism, but to the life of Christ's closest associates. That meant a life of wandering preaching out in the world. The apostles had not become cloistered monks, they had evangelized and traveled. These "new" apostles did, however, share one thing with the monks. They agreed on the importance of poverty. Still, the partisans of the apostolic way of life took the profession of poverty further. Monks indeed professed individual poverty, yet often lived in the midst of corporate plenty. The monastery had substantial holdings, which provided an income that permitted monks to pursue their life of retired contemplation in stability and security. Those who wished to follow the apostolic path demanded something further: absolute corporate poverty. This meant that, beyond giving up all one's material goods, a religious group must not hold any goods in common either. There was to be no provision for the morrow, but rather a genuine common indigence that surrendered wholly to divine providence, for they imagined that this was precisely the way the disciples had lived in the Gospels. This led to a controversy about apostolic poverty, and indeed about the poverty of Christ himself, that was to last nearly two hundred years (and to which Thomas, as in so many other cases, would have much valuable to add).

The institutional church had difficulty integrating these new tendencies. In some cases, it could think of nothing other than to mainstream the "new" apostles into monastic communities, situating them in the broad tradition of the cloistered life. This happened to Robert of Arbrissel (ca. 1045–1115), an early and popular wandering preacher. Accusations of impropriety followed him in his travels, particularly as the sexes mingled indiscriminately among his followers. This resulted in the church's insistence that he bring his movement into a more traditional disposition. Thus, his movement became shoehorned into a monastic community at Fontevrault.[20] Sometimes such tendencies toward apostolic poverty coincided with those who enjoyed distinction in the institutional church, demonstrating its appeal to those in a wide variety of social conditions. One such instance was the case of Norbert of Xanten (ca. 1080–1134).[21] Norbert, formerly a rich and noble clergyman (indeed, almoner to Emperor Henry V himself), forsook everything in order to pursue a life of wandering preaching. His orthodoxy certified by the pope himself, Norbert typified the best of the movement: appealing to the laity directly not only through strong and orthodox preaching but also matching this with uprightness of life. In the end Norbert could not escape promotion and became the Archbishop of Magdeburg. Nonetheless, he attracted followers. As with the devotees of Robert of Arbrissel, the church gradually formed them into abbatial communities. However, the Order of Prémontré—later known as the Norbertines—had a difference. Instead of formal monastic profession, it adopted the manners of a more flexible form of religious life known as the "canonical state." St. Augustine of Hippo himself had conceived of the canonical life, at least in an inchoate way. Seeing the loneliness that could develop among secular priests, particularly in towns, he decided to form them all into a community around himself, as the bishop. They would live a semimonastic lifestyle, dining, lodging, and saying the Divine Office together, while during the day they would spread throughout the city for their pastoral duties, taking with them the reserve of spiritual energy that had been strengthened by the community life. Such a model appealed to the Norbertines as they worked to modify monastic tradition. The monks, whether Benedictine, Cluniac, or Cistercian, in a flight from the world had sought rural wastes to form their convents. The Norbertines founded their houses in or near cities, living the conventual life but going out during the day for pastoral and liturgical duties. Norbert innovated constitutionally by making the Abbot General subject to the General Chapter, which meant that his rule was supervised by the community as a whole. In addition, Norbertine abbots were required to consult senior members of the community when there was a decision of significance for the house. While the Norbertines were not technically wandering preachers, they had opened up a new religious front in the twelfth century: the urban ministry. The old secular clergy could not keep up with the influx of people in the burgeoning cities of medieval Europe; reinforcements were desperately needed. Norbert had taken the religious life into the towns and squares; he brought the reform to the cities. All of these advances would be appropriated by the Dominican order of the thirteenth century.

Not all movements of this sort ended with successful integration. Not content with being personally poor, many preachers of poverty began to declaim the accumulated wealth of churchmen.

They cultivated popularity among the people by their self-denial, which placed the riches of bishops and monasteries into stark contrast. Little by little the popular anticlericalism of the preachers—a leitmotif in any Christian age—became theological. They began to preach that the church had erred when she accepted wealth and land from Constantine (by this time over eight hundred years in the past). They claimed that the church's possessionate nature was *prima facie* evidence that Catholics could not embody the true church. Puritanical movements of various shades began to manifest themselves. At their most benign they were simple outbreaks of anticlericalism, often with political or sociological undertones. At their most serious, such movements began to coalesce around an ancient idea that long predated Christianity, which the church had struggled to shake off from the very beginning: the concept of dualism.

Whether one is a Jew, a Muslim, or a Christian, he or she professes belief in a single, omnipotent, and transcendent God who is the origin of all that exists. At the same time, people live in a world surrounded by the experiences of both moral evils such as sin and physical evils including sickness and death. To reconcile the two is one of the most difficult and pressing questions of the monotheistic faiths. Of course, the brilliant thinkers of all three religions have come up with skillful and subtle theodicies to explain how an all-good God could permit suffering and sin (particularly notable in this respect is St. Augustine). Yet these brilliant explanatory models, no matter how internally coherent, tend to lose their luster at the bedside of a dying child. Far easier to defend is the ancient idea of dualism, adopted by any number of groups throughout history: Zoroastrians, Daoists, Gnostics, and Manichaeans. Simply stated, their doctrine is that evil is a direct creation of a malevolent deity, generally of equal power with the good god. These two are locked in an eternal struggle of good against evil, a simple idea that reappears with periodic regularity in human history. Dualism extended its reach into the Christian Middle Ages as well, a period in which sickness, infant mortality, and other natural and human dangers menaced people on a daily basis. Since evil was most directly experienced on the material plane, it was a short step to attribute all material reality to the bad deity. It was far easier to attribute sin, pain, suffering, and ugliness to an evil principle rather than

27

to a loving God. Such a position neatly dovetailed with critiques of church wealth. Desire for the acquisition of material things—the creations of a malevolent god—was by its nature evil. This was far more than a traditional Christian critique of greed. The philosophical and theological judgments against avarice were that it was merely a moral failure to order goods correctly, preferring the less perfect to the more perfect. For the dualist, however, the world and the flesh were themselves products of the evil god; to desire to acquire them was the definition of sin and perversion itself.

The critique of its wealth certainly drove the institutional church to action. Challenged in such a way, it was natural that churchmen were interested in preserving their wealth and power. Indeed, there were political concerns involved in the persecution of these heretical tendencies, and many recent historians have followed the contours of that power struggle.[22] But the Catholic reaction went much deeper than mere desire for retaining control. A dualist vision imperiled the Christian worldview in unique ways. Since its beginning, the church had been immersed in materiality; it had been, as Robert Wilken puts it, "an affair of things."[23] The "materialism" of Christianity had been the fundamental characteristic that set it apart from the spiritualizing doctrines of Gnostics, Platonists, and a host of competing religious cults that sprang up in the Roman Empire. The church not only emphasized the goodness of the original material creation by God, but also stressed the reality of the incarnation, suffering, death, and bodily resurrection of Christ. Because of this, a host of other conclusions followed. God had not only created the world but had physically inserted himself into it, sanctifying everything he touched. Christ had used material elements as the conduits through which to mediate his grace: water for baptism, bread and wine for the Eucharist, a physical laying of hands for orders. Early Christians eagerly embraced this materiality. Quickly the cult of the saints grew up, and relics and tombs of holy men and women proliferated. The dead bodies of saints became privileged links to heaven, for these very bones would with certitude be raised up to glory on the last day. The signal Christian belief, which set it apart from all other religions, was the sanctifying power of all material reality. A dualist vision implied the destruction of the entire Christian superstructure of lived religious practice: sacraments, hierarchy, works of charity, and the physical networks of holiness represented by the shrines and churches of the world. But dualism did not stop at a mere critique of material Christianity. In its dark vision of reality, the whole of the material world was corrupt and evil, including human bodies, for the evil principle had created them. Souls, spirits, and angels were the products of the good god. As a result of some unspecified "original sin," the good god had permitted human souls to be imprisoned in material bodies as punishment. The goal, then, of this dualism was liberation from materiality and a return to the world of spirit. In this worldview the worst thing that could be done was to produce more souls locked in bodies, which occurred in only one way: through sexual union. Dualism thus attacked not only Christianity, but human nature as such. It condemned family and marriage, the very basis of premodern society. It went so far as to denounce the consumption of anything born out of sexual union, which included animals, meaning the medieval dualists were vegetarians as well (they did, however—in line with contemporary beliefs about aquatic biology—eat fish). These beliefs rarely, but occasionally, produced a resolution to commit suicide by slow starvation.[24] In addition, dualists condemned oaths outright, breaking down another essential bond of society in a premodern and preliterate world. Such beliefs damaged the social fabric and presented a clear and present danger to the existing order and threatened the whole basis of medieval Christian society. As a result, both church and state reacted accordingly, launching inquisitions and crusades in order to control these heterodox beliefs. There were a variety of levels of commitment to such beliefs; indeed, the heretics themselves had categories such as the elite "perfect" versus the mere "hearers" or sympathizers. Heresy was a fluid phenomenon in the Middle Ages, and theologians tried their best to systematize often disparate beliefs. While they sometimes created overelaborate reconstructions, it remains that such unorthodoxies were really abroad and, from the perspective of the church, endangered not only human society but the very eternal salvation of the Christian people, a belief that animated the church's response at its core.[25]

Not all movements were as radical as the dualism that came to be called Catharism.[26] One group that would have far-reaching influence was founded by a man named Peter Waldo of Lyon (ca.

1140–ca. 1205). In the 1170s, the gospel call to evangelical poverty struck him powerfully, and he sold all that he had and gave it to the poor.[27] This was laudable in itself—similar stories had played out since St. Anthony of the Desert in the late 200s. Peter's wife, however, who was entitled to half his property, was intensely unimpressed. She accused him before the bishop, who ordered Peter Waldo to make restitution. Having received her due—and probably glad to see the back of him—they mutually agreed on a separation and he began to lead the life of a wandering preacher, gathering disciples to his novel way of life. Waldo even petitioned Rome for recognition. He and his followers appeared before the Third Lateran Council in 1179. There churchmen mocked the "Waldensians" for their lack of learning and their absence of canonical mission (the formal permission to preach extended by the church). Using dialectic, the learned members of the council demonstrated how easy it was for an uneducated person to fall into heresy. Waldo left, fuming and humiliated, and began to be convinced that God had called him to preach, and that one ought better to obey God than humans. He pursued his calling and, for contravening the decision of the council, was excommunicated. This led to a rising tide of Waldensian denunciation of the institutional church; by the beginning of the 1200s, the Waldensians had indeed crossed over several lines into heresy (yet it is interesting that the Waldensians opposed the Cathars, and indeed debated with them on occasion). To its credit, the institutional church learned from the incident, and when the opportunity came to enroll other, later wandering preachers of penance, it would not make the same mistake again. It was into this political and religious crucible that Thomas Aquinas was born.

THE FAMILY

The Aquinas castle at Roccasecca (Dry Rock) is today in ruins, accessible only by a rickety and rotting deck staircase that precariously clings to the side of the mountain. Once one achieves the summit, the panoramic view is commanding. Clearly one of the most strategically located castles in the region, it is surrounded on three sides by nearly sheer cliffs. Accessible only by a narrow

The ruins of Roccasecca, the Aquino family's castle and Thomas's birthplace

ridge spine to the east, Roccasecca dominates not only the town, but the entire countryside around it. While only one hundred meters or so above the medieval village, the ruined castle surveys a mighty vista stretching for dozens of miles. The valley of the meandering Liri River sets itself before the gaze of the castle, running through the green, productive land, called the Terra di Lavoro (the readily cultivable land). To stand on the summit is to see why, among mountains and plains along the most ancient Roman roads, this has always been one of the key conduits of trade and travel in central Italy. Whoever controlled the castle also controlled the towns and valley below. Yet historical conditions made the stronghold even more significant beyond a merely favorable location. It was perched nearly halfway between Rome and Naples, just inside the Kingdom of Sicily and on the border of the Papal States. Families who lived there stood in the epicenter of the most significant struggles of medieval Europe. The beauty, fertility, and strategic situation of the area had drawn people to it from the beginning. The fruitful region was the birthplace of famous writers of the ancient world, producing Cato the Elder, Cicero, Juvenal, and Ovid. Such famous associations continued into the age of Christendom. It was in close proximity to St. Benedict's seminal foundation of Montecassino, the towering fortress of sanctity that commanded the valley further to the southwest. Long after the time of Thomas, Roccasecca would remain significant. In World War II, because of its status as a critical Italian rail junction, the town became the headquarters of the German 14th Panzerkorps on the Gustav defensive line. Because of this it suffered relentless Allied attacks in 1943 and 1944 that destroyed much of the town. Certain locales have an importance that endures.

For the reasons enumerated above, Manso, abbot of Monte-cassino, built the castle of Roccasecca in 994, as an outpost to guard the approaches to the mighty monastery farther up the Liri valley. Two years later, the castle fell into the hands of Adenulph III, a noble from a Lombard family seeking his fame in the south. He was to be the ancestor of the aristocratic family that established itself as lords of the county of Aquino. The Lombards were a tribe that had migrated into northern Italy in the sixth century and that caused no end of trouble for the papacy, until their power was broken by the Carolingians. While generally driven out of the north, many Lombard nobles managed to retain holdings in the rural south. They added to the marvelous diversity of the Italian peninsula in the central Middle Ages, and from them the family of Thomas took its origin. In 1137, at the death of Count Landolfo IV, the family holdings were divided between his elder son, Pandolfo, who founded the line that would later hold the title of Counts of Acerra, and the younger Rinaldo, who became Rinaldo I, Lord of Roccasecca. He also retained one-third of the county of Aquino, as well as the town of Montesangiovanni, which he had obtained in an exchange with the pope.[28] Our Thomas was descended of this second, lesser line of nobles, a point made clear by the fact that his father, Landolfo, was designated in all the sources as *miles* (a simple knight) rather than the superior title count, which was the prerogative of the senior line. There is no dispute, however, that Thomas descended from aristocracy. Whereas many other hagiographers attempted to associate their subjects with noble lines (usually for political purposes), the aristocracy of Thomas's family and his genealogy are well established. He was, most assuredly, "to the manor born."

Some disagreement exists over whether Thomas's father, Landolfo, married once or twice, with the likelier case being the latter. It is clear that there were three sons of a certain Landolfo who did not derive from his second wife, Theodora (Thomas's mother). While it may indeed be the case that we are confronted with a second Landolfo of the family of Aquino, I think that a less likely possibility. It was certainly not unheard of in an age of young marriages and mortality in childbirth that a first wife might have died very young, nor would it be unusual for a young husband to marry again to help raise his children, and indeed to have the chance at an advantageous second marriage. As further evidence, given that Landolfo was likely dead or incapacitated around 1240 and that his second wife lived long afterward, the plausibility of a first family is even more likely.[29] In any case, he did marry Thomas's mother, the formidable Dame Theodora, and they had at least nine children. Dame Theodora was a Norman Neapolitan from a branch of the noble Rossi family, known for its devotion to the church in political matters. The union with an urban noblewoman from the metropolis of Naples was a judicious alliance for Landolfo, uniting the new, noble families of the city with the older Lombard nobility of the rural countryside. However, her devotion to the church perhaps led to uncomfortable situations. Landolfo was beholden to Frederick II as his monarch in Sicily. As the subsequent history of the family demonstrates, however, a fissure was growing between the junior branch of the Aquini and its king. The elder branch of the family, ruled by Count Tommaso II d'Aquino (a titular coincidence that has flummoxed historians; he was perhaps only Thomas's fifth or sixth cousin), was firmly in the emperor's camp. This Tommaso was a passionate partisan of Frederick, close enough indeed to marry one of the emperor's own daughters in 1247.[30] Older historians had speculated about a much closer blood connection between Thomas's family and the emperor, but it is likely that this is the closest that they were related: the in-laws of a distant cousin. While Tommaso II was a devoted client, in Landolfo's family the bonds of loyalty were not as clear. The emperor did appoint Landolfo as a royal official in 1220 in the Terra di Lavoro, and he seems to have been devoted to Frederick his whole life. He certainly trained his older sons to be faithful retainers of the king. The eldest son, Aimo, had gone on crusade with Frederick, was captured, and then ransomed by Gregory IX (r. 1227–41). Because of the pope's generosity, he changed his allegiances and became a stalwart supporter of the church.[31] Another son, Rinaldo, had served as a page at the emperor's court.[32] Yet in 1246, after Innocent IV (r. 1243–54) attempted to depose Frederick II at the First Council of Lyon the year before, Rinaldo rejected the emperor, even to the extent of joining a conspiracy to assassinate him. Frederick captured and mercilessly executed him. The Aquino family cherished his memory, and they came to consider him as a martyr for the church. Thomas himself reported a vision of his sister Marotta claiming that Rinaldo was in heaven.[33] This Marotta later became abbess of the nearby convent of St. Mary of Capua. His other sisters, Mary and Theodora, contracted advantageous marriages and remained close to Thomas during his life. It was from them and their progeny that many of the family stories regarding Thomas had their source in the early biographies. It is not hard to imagine the knife edge that such a family found itself upon. Both geography and genealogy had created a familial political dilemma.

At this point it is not out of place to describe the various political tensions that afflicted medieval Italy, and to discuss how they related to the religious life of the medieval world. Since the beginning of the thirteenth century, factions had emerged in Italy that had gone under the name Guelf (pro-papal) and Ghibelline (pro-imperial).[34] These indicated political allegiances that had descended from various claimants to the German throne, and both terms were Italian attempts to get their tongues around the German language. *Guelf* came from the Welf dukes of Bavaria, while *Ghibelline* was a corruption of Waiblingen, a castle of the Hohenstaufen family. In very broad strokes, in the first decades of the 1200s, Guelf had come to denote those generally supportive of the church's political independence from the empire (including the civic freedom of the Italian communes). Ghibelline was shorthand for a supporter of the German emperor's political program. While it is difficult to conceive of today, a Ghibelline who defended the emperor's politics could and often did remain a good and practicing Catholic. One did not have to support the political efforts of the papacy to remain in good standing with the church. It was similar with anticlericalism. One could be an ardent critic of the clergy—its practices, its vices, its indolence—and yet remain a devout Catholic. To call someone a Ghibelline was to identify a *political* orientation, not a religious one. With that having been said, it was often very difficult to make this theoretical distinction work on the ground. Too often the political and the religious got mixed up together. By the 1230s and 1240s, suspicions were growing within the church party that those who opposed the pope's political programs also, ipso facto, opposed the faith. Frederick's personally casual attitude toward Christianity and the irreligion of some of his close advisors did not help the cause of the Ghibellines in this regard. While most of the lower-ranking Ghibellines were still devoted Catholics, their leader's reputation had rubbed off. When one added this to the issue of actual religious heterodoxy (in the case of Waldensians or Cathars), the issue became even more cloudy. These movements occasionally used Ghibellinism as a smoke screen for their own heresy, leading the church (sometimes justly) to lump Ghibellinism in with heresy. When one compounds this with the myriad personal and communal loyalties then interacting in medieval Italy, the issue becomes even more opaque. By Dante's time, the terms *Guelf* and *Ghibelline* had become almost meaningless in relation to their founding principles. Yet by the death of Frederick in 1250, and the seeming ascendancy of the papacy, it was clear that the lesser branch of the Aquino family had switched its allegiances and was wholeheartedly (to use a disputed term) Guelf.

TOMMASO D'AQUINO

Scholarly debate about the year of Thomas's birth has occurred for years, with most historians settling on either the year 1224 or 1225 (though 1226 cannot be wholly excluded).[35] This issue arises for several reasons. In the first place, medievals really did not celebrate birthdays; they considered one's baptism day or patronal saint feast far more fundamental. Further, dating is often approximate, with individuals themselves often not knowing their exact ages. Finally, in many cases birthdates have to be reconstructed from ages reported at death. It is by this final method that Thomas's age happens to be calculated. Even his early biographers were not entirely clear on the exact date of his birth. Based on his death date (March 7, 1274), they gave several estimations for his age that ranged from forty-eight to fifty.[36] In the final analysis, though, his exact birth year remains unclear, but given the fact of his death and rather notable activities, we can come to the probable conclusion that he was indeed born.

Our sources report several legends about Thomas's youth and infancy. In many biographies of saints there are often premonitions and foreshadowings of the future greatness and sanctity of the person in question; it is a hagiographical commonplace. For instance, the biographies of St. Dominic report that his mother had a dream of a dog with a torch in his mouth who, as he ran, set fire to the earth. These legends, related years after the fact, confirm what the world had already come to know: that God, who is "wonderful in his saints" (Ps 68:35 RHE), would not permit the holy man or woman to be unknown. As John the Baptist was the forerunner of Christ, so, too, would there be signs and wonders that preceded the birth of a saint. Thomas has stories of this kind told about him. In one, a passing hermit prophesied his birth to his mother, and mentioned a vocation first to the Benedictines and then the Friars Preachers. The story was given in a deposition at his canonization hearings by his niece Catherine, then an old woman who reported hearing the story from her grandmother. As we shall soon see, Theodora spent much of her life editing narratives of her early relationship with her son. While such a visit is not inconceivable, it is unlikely that the hermit would have given details about the Dominicans.[37] Another story relates that after his birth, Theodora, as a native Neapolitan, made periodic visits to the city. During one of these trips the infant was taken to the public baths of Naples with his nurse and his mother. There he found a scrap of paper on the ground and promptly stuck it in his mouth. Every time the nurse tried to remove it, the baby Thomas pitched a fit. When his mother had finally extracted it, she found it read "Ave Maria."[38] As Fr. Weisheipl wisely points out, "Such an episode is quite normal with children; they will pick up almost anything and put it in their mouths."[39] Indeed, they become enraged when such a prized acquisition is removed, a common human experience for those who know babies. It seems that the infant Thomas had this not uncommon habit.[40] There is no reason to doubt the story, but the hagiographers extrapolated the contents of the parchment into a prophecy of the saint's devotion to Mary and his predilection for holiness.[41]

The vast majority of our sources for the life of Thomas fall into the category of saint's lives, all of them written by devoted followers from his own order. These men are called hagiographers: devotional writers whose subject is the lives of the saints. Though employing historical data, these authorities write with different purposes in mind than modern secular historians. They have a further intention beyond the recitation of facts.[42] In the first place, they write with an eye to allegory and deeper meaning. Whereas a secular historian would have been little interested in such a story about a baby with an oral fixation—or merely have reported it as part of the historical record—the hagiographer sees something different. To take an example, medieval theologians saw four levels of meaning in each biblical story.[43] For them each tale had a fuller meaning that was rooted in the literal sense. Particularly in an age of Protestant literalism and Enlightenment critiques of the Bible as an ancient text, this is the meaning we are most familiar with. In this understanding, if a story is about Jerusalem, then the Bible is speaking about the actual, physical city of Jerusalem. But the fathers of the church and the medieval theologians went deeper. It was their conviction that the Bible had a meaning and purpose beyond that merely conveyed by the human authors. It had implications and messages given unity by a single divine author, which meant that all parts of the texts—both Old and New Testaments—had a mysterious central meaning summed up in the person of Christ. Therefore they discerned three other spiritual senses of the text. The first was allegorical. Of course, Jerusalem was a physical city, but in an allegorical sense it was the "city of God," which under the new dispensation stood for the church. Therefore, in any passage dealing with Jerusalem there was a potential prophecy about the "New Jerusalem," or the church of Christ. Beyond that there was a moral sense. In this way Jerusalem might be seen to stand for the human soul, giving us a glimpse into what an integrated, graced, and saved humanity might look like. In this way, when these writers spoke about Jerusalem, they saw it as an image of the moral life. Whenever the Scriptures condemned Jerusalem it was because it had become disordered. When it was praised, it was correctly ordered and directed toward God. Finally, there was an apocalyptic sense, which pointed to the end of the world. In this sense, when the Bible mentioned Jerusalem, it directed attention to the heavenly Jerusalem, the city of God perfected forever at the end of time. The biblical scholars of the Middle Ages had what might be called a "hermeneutic of providence," focused on the idea that God's messages were too big to be held in the literal text alone, and that consuming such texts with the eyes of faith would open up whole new mysteries to the reader.

The hagiographers shared this providential view of the saint's life. Things that from a literal perspective were uninteresting—a baby sticking a paper into his mouth—all of a sudden became charged with meaning when looked at *sub specie aeternitatis*, or when viewed in relation to the providential plan of God. We have to read these stories with an understanding of the lens they were employing. Another issue that arises is the similarities of many saints to the lives of other, earlier saints. The hagiographer, from the earliest days of Christianity, was convinced that a definitive pattern of holiness existed: the life and actions of Jesus Christ on earth. When the Christian looked at a saint, what he or she was supposed to see was an image of Christ lived out at a particular time and place. This meant there would be *mimesis*, or the subject reflecting the exemplar. The saint would, of necessity, do Christ-like things and so would be conformed to Christ. This had become quite routine in writing about saints. Many saints do seemingly identical things: there are similar prophecies, similar miracles, and similar activities according to the social and cultural status of the saint. Such writing can begin to appear repetitious at best, or a false type of stock filler at the worst. We must remember that medieval people saw such similarities not as disingenuous, but rather as guarantees of sanctity. Of course the saint would do similar things to Christ and to other saints! He or she was a saint, after all, and for medievals, both truth and goodness were one, not many. These repetitions are called *topoi* and are familiar to any-one who has read saints' lives. Historians need to approach them with caution, but they should be used and interpreted according to their form, seeing as they are an integral part of the genre of hagiography.

Even through the lens of hagiography, we can see that Thomas was born into a position of significant privilege. His fam-ily was able to travel, as evidenced by the aforementioned story. His father and brothers were (at first) honored retainers of the most powerful man in Europe. Thomas was to have a nurse (or a nanny) even when he was sent to the Benedictine house at Montecassino. While not part of the highest echelons of aristocratic life, Thomas's family was more than comfortable, able to arrange advantageous marriages and to give substantial offerings for their children who entered the religious life. His father was not only a knight but also a royal official, and for at least the first ten years of his son's life, the family enjoyed the singular favor of King Frederick. The house of Aquino was significant enough that the transfer of their loyalties in the 1240s was noted at the top echelons of political power. The young Thomas then had every advantage. One can imagine that this was even more the case after a stunning incident regarding his younger sister. While the two small children lay in their bedroom one night—as his nurse slept nearby—a tempest arose that struck the nursery itself with a bolt of lightning, killing the infant girl as Thomas and the nurse lay close by.[44] As in similar cases, the family showered the surviving child with additional attention and consideration. When Catherine of Siena's (1347–80) twin sister died in infancy, her parents' fondness and partiality toward her significantly increased. The latitude granted such children may have generated an orientation toward a religious vocation as well as engendering a sense of independence, for the inclinations of such children are often indulged. But as is shown in the case of both Thomas and Catherine, privilege is not the intrinsic problem; it is what one does with it.

Chapter 2

BEGGARS OR CHOOSERS?

The Genealogy of a Vocation

In late 1230 or early 1231, a doubtlessly nervous young boy made the arduous mountain trek that wends its way toward the towering ramparts of the fortress-monastery of Montecassino.[1] Probably accompanied by his parents and his governess, he was to be offered as an oblate to the Benedictines of the house. The practice of oblation was an ancient one found in the Rule of St. Benedict,[2] and indeed one that has survived, in much modified form, into the present. The early Benedictine houses accepted oblates as virtual donations of their parents, perhaps in the fulfillment of a vow or as options for younger sons who would not inherit responsibilities of nobility. As early as the 600s, however, the church recognized that such a religious profession must be freely chosen. When the oblate reached the age of majority, he was able to leave the monastery if he wished. By Thomas's time, the practice of oblation had changed still more. Most oblates in these cases were from aristocratic families, who made substantial monetary endowments to the religious community at the time of their entrance. In Thomas's case his parents contributed the considerable amount of twenty ounces of gold to the monastery. In exchange for such considerations, the nobility sought lodging, education, and—hopefully—a career for their sons. In addition, through such offerings, the nobility of the Middle Ages also sought access to preferment. It is probably unhistorical to say that Thomas was destined to be abbot of Montecassino by some sort of agreement, though his parents may have harbored hopes in that respect. Such stories were embellished to dramatize his later conversion to the Dominicans—the more dramatic the renunciation, the deeper the heroism of the choice.[3] Yet Thomas would have lived an exceptionally comfortable life, in an atmosphere of security and learning, and could conceivably have risen to the leadership of the monastery. His piety and family connections would certainly have suited the Benedictines in the 1230s. In any case, Thomas's position as the youngest son in the family encouraged his vocation. All his elder brothers were in the service of the emperor, while only the oldest would inherit Landolfo's title.

Even though junior members of a noble family tended to be directed toward the religious life, such a path could still be considered an analogue to secular aristocracy. The Benedictines had many advantages in the eyes of Thomas's parents. They had an immaculate pedigree stretching back seven hundred years. Montecassino itself was one of the jewels of the monastic world; membership in such a fraternity would add luster to the house of Aquino. Thomas's family was also close and affectionate—something made clear by his warm relations with some of his siblings and their children in later life. Thus the abbey also had the inherent advantage of being exceptionally close to home, easily able to be visited on short notice. On top of this, the abbot of Montecassino was himself a distant relative of the counts of Aquino; the young boy would be looked after by a powerful relative and patron. Thomas would receive one of the finest primary educations available and the family would be relieved to have found a position for him. In addition, Landolfo probably realized that in many ways such an oblation acted like a strategic marriage. Connections to the proximate and powerful abbey could aid the political fortunes of the family at a later date.[4] Thomas and the Benedictines seemed a "match made in heaven." The Treaty of San Germano on July 23, 1230, made this arrangement possible.[5] This accord provided breathing space both for the nobility of Sicily and for the church. Frederick and Pope Gregory IX made peace—albeit temporarily—with the emperor, promising not to violate the sovereignty of the Papal States, and the pope lifting the emperor's excommunication. This thaw in relations enabled Landolfo to execute his plan.

So little Thomas was trundled off to Montecassino, probably not unwillingly. There he was permitted to keep his governess

The Benedictine Abbey of Montecassino

with him, at least for a few years, and probably found an atmosphere of relative comfort in an environment that was to prove congenial to his development. Life would have been pleasant and regimented for the young boy. For nine years he would live out the Benedictine life without having to commit himself fully to the austerities of the rule. Though there is clear agreement that he never made profession as a monk, it is evident that while he was within the confines of the monastery, he followed the rule and became acquainted with the rigors of religious life. Fundamental to Benedictine existence was the celebration of the liturgy and the Divine Office. While Thomas, as an oblate, would not have been compelled to attend the formal hours of the monastic day, nonetheless, many found it easy to slip into the rhythm of the Office, particularly when all around observed it. Thomas probably went to morning Lauds and evening Vespers, the hinges of the Benedictine day, at the very least. There he was introduced to the weekly recitation of the Psalter and a spiritual and meditative atmosphere that impressed the sacred texts deeply on the heart. The average monk would sing the Psalter in its entirety over 2,500 times during his life.[6] The Benedictine practice of *lectio divina*, or meditative reading, deepened one's acquaintance with sacred texts, and was enhanced by constant oral lessons at meals while the monks ate in silence. Thomas's facility with the Bible probably dated from this monastic experience, where the day was spent in aural immersion in the idiom of the Sacred Scriptures. The tempo of such a life seems suited to the Thomas that we will come to know later. I would propose that Thomas's early formation parallels that of St. Dominic. Both of them had an advantage that most early Dominicans did not: religious formation in an older, more traditional monastic setting (Dominic had been a canon before founding his own order). This rich liturgical and personal development gave their lives a stability and a weight that anchored them in the most trying of circumstances. Dominic's serene temperament is clearly evident in all biographies about him. In that, Thomas was a good imitator of the founder. His imperturbable calm was legendary. Such stability is missing from many other Preachers, who belonged to an order that was dedicated to public, mobile preaching, disputation, and urban ministry. Thomas, as will be seen, was as happy in the silence of the convent as in the bustle of academic life. It is not too much to think that his Benedictine training had much to do with that.

In addition to liturgy, Thomas would have been under the supervision of an experienced monk who would begin to teach him the rudiments of his education. Interestingly, Thomas's stay at the monastery was contemporary with the scholar Erasmus of Montecassino, a monk who had studied at Paris.[7] Some historians make the claim that this scholar was his teacher, but without strong foundation.[8] In any case, it is unlikely that the bright young pupil and the well-known scholar would have failed to come to know each other. Erasmus was a student of Plato and Aristotle, even within the more traditional atmosphere of the convent. He was a student of natural philosophy and wrote a commentary on the *Sentences* of Peter Lombard. Whoever was the boy's schoolmaster, Thomas would have been instructed in the Benedictine Rule and in his basic catechism.[9] Together with this he began his education with the trivium. These were lessons in the basics of grammar, rhetoric, and logic. Such elementary education was essential in acquiring the tools necessary for higher study. Together the three provided instruction in how to read correctly, how to speak clearly, and how to think well (it is no mistake that our elementary institutions were once called "grammar" schools). Fundamental to this was mastery of the Latin language, for Latin was the necessary tool for any advanced form of education. This was still the age before the flourishing of vernacular literature. To be a literate person was to know Latin. Latin was the universal language in a manner that exceeds even English today. It was the language of every church service in Western Christendom, but more than that, it was the normative idiom of church and state. All official writing was done in Latin. When people corresponded across vernacular linguistic divides, Latin provided the universal means of communication. It had the advantage of not prioritizing any particular culture, while at the same time grounding its speakers in a language with clear meanings, fixed for over one thousand years. It was the language of culture, giving access to the treasures of Western civilization. Knowledge of Latin accorded access to the wisdom of the patristic period, most notably Jerome's Vulgate translation of the Bible. The works of Cicero and Caesar, Sallust and Virgil were there for the taking. It was the language of the schools. Scholars from Sweden to Spain, Iceland to the crusader colonies of the Levant could communicate, learn, teach, and study in one common tongue. Richard Southern has spoken of this as one of the critical components of a true unification of Europe, not in political or economic terms, but on the deeper levels of religion and culture.[10] Latin was the key to this world, and Thomas quickly became proficient. He would have learned from the common texts of the ancient grammarians Donatus and Priscian, and would begin to construe sentences, then chapters from the Vulgate. In addition, Thomas probably learned the basics of mathematics and had lessons in chant as the basis both for prayer and the higher academic subject of harmonic music. The sacred texts and the proper use of Latin were planted into the young man's mind, seeds that would blossom fully over the course of his career. Thomas's biographers say little regarding the progress of the boy among the Benedictines, probably because they are eager to get him made a Dominican. There is one story from a later biographer named Peter Calo, written in the 1340s, that tells a charming tale, though it may have more to do with Thomas's later career than with the boy himself. Apparently learning his subjects with swiftness, Thomas was passed from one monastic tutor to another as they tried to keep up with his agile mind. To each one he asked the same question, "Quid est Deus?" "What is God?"[11]

Yet even in the realm of a cloistered monastery—meant to be an antechamber of heaven—the world sometimes made its voice heard. Thomas was not alone among the oblates; others, too, were there, many perhaps uninterested in learning or a life of religion: in other words, normal boys. His biographers say that Thomas did not make a habit of associating with them, preferring to focus on spiritual and intellectual matters. Of course, it is a commonplace in hagiography that the young saint disdained the concourse of his or her playmates.[12] Writers intended it to be a signal that, even in youth, the ways of the world had no attraction for the chosen one of God, for such were destined from the beginning to the path of righteousness. It also might suggest to the modern reader a certain priggishness (indeed, perhaps the feelings were mutual), but to a medieval reader schooled in the language of hagiography, it would have seemed a confirmation of Thomas's elevation above the mundane concerns of the world. It also indicates that the status of oblate was not always a direct avenue to a religious vocation, but simply another path for noble adolescents of the time to follow. A further complication arose in 1236 when Thomas's relative, the abbot Landulfo Sinnibaldo, died. For reasons that are unclear, the abbey held no election until 1239, meaning that the monastery was without a head for three years. Likely the business of the house went on as usual, but such a lack of leadership weakened Montecassino in the face of external threats. The deteriorating relations between the pope and the emperor only complicated matters.

In 1237, Frederick attempted to make good the ancient imperial claim over northern Italy, something that the German Empire had been endeavoring to do in vain for over one hundred years. He invaded in force and defeated the cities of the Lombard plain. Sensing the threat to the church, the pope renewed Frederick's excommunication in March of 1239. It seems that Frederick had been awaiting this step from the pope because as soon as it was proclaimed, he launched simultaneous attacks on the Papal States from north and south. His army occupied much papal territory. The emperor expelled those known as the allies of the pope, such as the Franciscans and the Dominicans. He attempted to exile them from territories he controlled, while his troops began to take over strategic areas governed by the church in the Kingdom of Sicily. This included Montecassino, which was occupied in April of 1239. Frederick's troops ordered all foreign monks to leave, not without violence. After the occupation only a skeleton crew of eight local religious was permitted to remain. In such a situation it was impossible to continue to support and educate oblates. Thomas's idyllic period of early education came to an abrupt end. Were it not for Frederick's aggression, Thomas might have remained buried in the cloister of the Benedictines for his whole life.

Thomas was now approximately fifteen years old. He had been under the tutelage of the monks for nine years. In reality, he had probably reached the end of what the Benedictines were capable of teaching him. Thomas returned to his family. At this point his father, Landolfo, still commanded the trust of Frederick II. Thomas and his parents likely conferred and agreed that—given his aptitude for study—his education should continue for whatever career might await him in the future, including the possible reopening of Montecassino. Following the recommendation of the new abbot, his parents sent Thomas to the fledgling University of Naples. It is significant that Tocco mentions that both his parents consented to Thomas's new endeavor, probably indicating that Landolfo was growing quite old, and that Theodora was possessed of significant authority in the family. Such a move would also flatter the emperor, who at that time was attempting to get the school off the ground. Indeed, in any case, Frederick had forbidden his subjects to go anywhere for higher study but Naples. There Thomas would be able to continue onto the higher Arts, which would enable him to have a career in either church or state, though it is clear in what direction the boy wished to go. Further suggestive evidence comes from Thomas's reputed Master at Cassino, Erasmus. The Cassinese scholar apparently was in the confidence of Frederick II, who asked him to go to Naples to reinforce the faculty. It is possible that the young Thomas accompanied Erasmus to Naples, in order for both of them to undertake their respective positions at the University.[13] While there, Erasmus was especially concerned to bring the theology of William of Auxerre to Naples. It is clear that William's theological methodology later highly influenced Thomas, and he used it extensively early in his career.[14] One can speculate that this was due to the influence of Erasmus, but it would only be a guess. We are more certain about Thomas's studies in Naples under other Masters.

Frederick II had founded the University of Naples in 1224 in order to blunt the influence of other academic institutions, primarily Paris and Bologna, which were seen as more pro-papal (or at the very least anti-imperial). As noted above, Frederick had decreed that all his citizens must attend the new University at Naples in order to avoid being "tainted" by papal propaganda. The further purpose of the school was to train an elite corps of civil servants of proven loyalty who would take up offices in Sicily and in the empire. However, Frederick faced hurdles in launching this new school. Other foundations such as Paris had grown organically over generations, maturing from a local cathedral school into the primary center for theological study in Christendom. Bologna had been a center of legal studies, both canon and civil, for over one hundred years. Naples was created *ex nihilo*. Compounding the difficulties faced by the young school was its proximity to the University of Salerno. This institution had been founded as far back as the 1100s and was the leading European center for medical studies. On occasion Frederick tried to usurp Salerno and combine it with Naples, but universities can be jealous of their privileges, even in the face of imperial power. In addition, the emperor also had to contend with a shortage of faculty, who were far more interested in more prestigious institutions. He attempted to rectify this situation by poaching prominent scholars with promises of large salaries. Using all of these strategies, the infant university took its first tentative steps.[15]

In a certain sense Naples was the first "secular" university, founded by a monarch for the civil good of his kingdom.[16] As a result, Naples had a unique atmosphere. Being beyond the supervision of the church, it was able more easily to integrate new influences into its curriculum. Even though the newly rediscovered works of Aristotle and his commentators were circulating in the north and being employed in scholarship, they found suspicious audiences there. On several occasions the works of the Greek philosopher were censured, though there is clear evidence that Masters were reading and meditating upon his writings anyway. There was no such reticence in Naples, for indeed southern Italy had remained a meeting place for Mediterranean cultures in the early Middle Ages. It had maintained links to the Greek-speaking Christian East, and there was free concourse among the three monotheistic religions and an exchange of ideas similar to what was happening in the Iberian peninsula. The schools of Salerno and Naples eagerly sought Arabic editions of Aristotle and the writings of his commentators. A scholar at Frederick's court named Michael the Scot was instrumental in bringing many new scientific and philosophical works into circulation, bringing these new intellectual movements to Naples long before they arrived in the north. Michael was an early European speaker of Arabic, and in particular his mediation of Ibn-Rushd (1126–98; known as Averroes to the Christian Middle Ages) was critical for the development of high Scholasticism. Because of him, Weisheipl can say that "the whole breadth of Aristotelian science, Arabic astronomy, and Greek medicine flourished in Palermo, Salerno, and Naples prior to their assimilation in the northern universities."[17]

When Thomas arrived, he was placed under the mastership of a scholar named Martin for study in grammar and logic. We know nothing of substance about this Master Martin, though we can make some guesses about what Thomas studied. Having completed the basics of his elementary education, he would have undertaken advanced studies in each branch of the trivium. This would have exposed him to classical sources, particularly for rhetoric and grammar, especially the works of Cicero (known to the medievals from his second name as "Tullius"). Thomas plainly had an affinity for the philosophy of Cicero, finding Plato, Aristotle, and Stoicism communicated through the Latin rhetor's eclectic prism.[18] Yet it is abundantly clear that the elegant style of Cicero left no impression. Thomas cared little for style; indeed, one of the reasons many in the Renaissance turned against him and his Scholastic brethren was their "barbarous" and specialized Latin. The things that would remain with him from his study of grammar were clarity, exactitude, and terseness. The Latin language was Thomas's technical toolbox: a means for elucidating the truth, and not an end in itself. What the Renaissance later found barbarous in

Thomas and the Scholastics was their dry, technical terminology and their lack of attention to form and style. In essence, the difference was one of perspective; the scholars of the Renaissance saw language as an aesthetic end in itself, whereas Thomas considered it the means to achieve the end of knowledge of God and the salvation of souls.

The second study he would have delved into was formal propositional logic.[19] Logic had dominated the curriculum of the trivium for much of the central Middle Ages and was formative for the entire Scholastic movement. Aristotle was the first to outline logic as a science of using clear terms in accurate propositions to establish truths. The six fundamental works of the Greek thinker on logic were arranged in the ancient world and came to be known as the *Organon*. Much of this corpus of logical works slowly disappeared in the Latin West, with the surviving ones being mediated by the Christian philosopher Boethius (ca. 480–524). At the dawn of Scholasticism, a revival of interest in formal logic drove the study and translation of existing texts on the subject and encouraged the search for the lost ones. By the year 1200, the "New" Logic, consisting of the lost parts of *Organon* (in particular the *Posterior* and *Prior Analytics* and the *Sophistical Refutations*), was recovered and translated into Latin, spurring their installation at the center of scholarly formation and preparing the foundations of high Scholasticism. Thomas was a primary beneficiary of this New Logic and demonstrated thorough familiarity with this complex system. This exposure certainly began in Naples.

Apparently, Thomas quickly mastered the advanced trivium and was sent to another Master to begin studies in the natural sciences. These natural sciences were not interchangeable with what today we would call the empirical sciences or the "hard" sciences. Medievals were more concerned about the theories of such sciences rather than with their experimental application (St. Albert was an exception, as we will see). These natural sciences were the medieval *Quadrivium* of Arithmetic, Geometry, Music, and Astronomy. By this time Aristotle's *Physics* and *Metaphysics* were often added to courses in the natural sciences. The scholar to whom Thomas was sent for training in the natural sciences—Peter of Ireland—is better known than Master Martin.[20] Peter was a confirmed Aristotelian; several of his commentaries discovered over the last one hundred years establish this fact (indeed, Thomas later in life would have one of Peter's commentaries at hand).[21] In addition, he was also committed to bringing the observations of Averroes to bear as well. While Peter would later condemn Averroes's positions regarding Aristotle, he nonetheless engaged the Arab's thought aggressively while Thomas was his student. So we find Thomas in a milieu that was energetically delineating the outlines of Aristotelian philosophy. In particular the scholars of the time were trying to untangle the inheritance of Plato, mediated through Augustine, as well as the Arabic commentator Ibn-Sina (Avicenna; 980–1037), from the new philosophy brought by Aristotle and Averroes. The older models whereby Aristotle was seen as a mere scientist-pupil of Plato, or in which the two essentially agreed on all points (a position principally derived from Boethius), were being turned on their heads. As a result, the young Thomas had a crystal-clear vision of the differences between Plato and Aristotle, well before he was apprenticed to St. Albert the Great. Albert was a powerful mediator of the Aristotelian tradition, but, like many of his contemporaries, he still confused the teachings of the two Greeks with regularity.[22] Though we know little of Thomas's actual course of studies at Naples, it was undoubtedly axial for his formation. The advantage in studying there was that he had begun years ahead of many of his colleagues in understanding and appropriating the Peripatetic philosophy, able clearly to distinguish differences while many of his contemporaries muddied the waters with leftover Platonism, a topic addressed in chapter 3.

THE COMING OF THE FRIARS

Thomas studied in Naples for five years, from 1239 to 1244. There he was exposed to a multitude of new intellectual and spiritual experiences. At some point during his studies, he came to know the Order of Friars Preachers. This in itself was remarkable, since Frederick had decreed the banishment of the Preachers from his territories—an unsurprising move, since the friars had shown themselves to be his inveterate opponents in his struggle with the papacy. The Preachers were founded by a Spanish Augustinian canon named Dominic of Caleruega.[23] They were the product of a long maturation in the thinking of the church about the inter-relationships among concepts of poverty, purity, and heresy. In a certain sense, the rise of the Dominicans was the final fruit of the Gregorian purification. We have already seen how the tumult of apostolic poverty movements and heretical tendencies had convulsed the church during the twelfth century. Far from cooling off, such trends were gaining steam by the year 1200, and the institutional church had been floundering in its attempt to find a coherent response. Fortunately, at that time the church found itself under the rule of one of the most powerful and farsighted popes in history, Innocent III (r. 1198–1216). With the authority that had been carefully assembled for him over 150 years of strong and careful predecessors, he intended to bring about nothing less than a wholesale revivification of Christian life.

Innocent intended to use all the tools at his command to finish the purification that the Gregorians had begun. In this he had two aims: to underscore the supremacy of the papal office and to effect the salvation of souls. To reduce his aims to either one of these is reductivist. Modern historians emphasize the former, while confessional historians focused on the latter. In reality, the two were intimately connected in the mind of Innocent. The pope genuinely wanted a reformation of the Christian world, moral improvement, dignified liturgy, and worthy reception of the sacraments so that the Christian people might attain the joys of heaven. In Innocent's Christian worldview, power betokened responsibility. If he was truly going to claim to be the Vicar of Christ (a title first used regularly by him), he knew that the flipside was the care of souls (*cura animarum*) for all the members of the church. A purification of the church would mean a simultaneous increase in papal authority. The pope was happy to have both. Innocent took this responsibility with complete seriousness.

Innocent was convinced that there were two fundamental roots of the problems in the church: the poor foundations of the lay faithful in terms of catechesis and practice and the rise of heterodox movements that sought to take advantage of this fact. He was determined to correct both of these. He created much legislation to improve the spiritual direction of the laity and to purify corruption from the clergy, yet he could not do everything alone. There needed to be orthodox popular movements that guided the people in right belief and practice and that shielded them from heresy. Law would never be enough; it could provide the skeleton for a just Christian world, but it needed to be enfleshed by the lived holiness of committed preachers of the gospel. However, wandering preachers in the past had come under suspicion. Innocent surmised that by giving preachers papal authorization, he could sway those who were tempted by Cathars and Waldensians back to the straight path. To this end he began to commission men who would go into heretical lands and preach the purity of the Christian faith. The chief target for this would be the areas of Provence and Languedoc, in the Mediterranean region of modern-day France. There Innocent began the *predicatio*—the preaching—in order to counter heretical wandering holy men.

Policies of reform were emerging throughout Christendom. One diocese in northern Spain, across the Pyrenees Mountains from the areas of heretical activity, corresponded perfectly to Innocent's ideas about renewal. This diocese was headed by a bishop named Diego de Acebo (d. 1207), a man after the pope's own heart. Diego was single-minded in the pursuit of a well-run and holy diocese. He accomplished his task with zeal and care, and his local church became a model for others. In particular, he invited the Cistercian order to provide a monastic presence, while organizing his own cathedral canons according to the rule of St. Augustine. The one thing that made Diego somewhat unsuitable for the episcopal office was his wanderlust, an attraction for evangelization and apostolic activity that often drew him away from his see. On one occasion he eagerly accepted the charge of King Ferdinand VII of Castile to travel to Denmark to arrange for the marriage of his son. As a companion he brought along the young subprior of his reformed canonry: Dominic of Caleruega. After they crossed the mountains, they lodged at an inn near Toulouse. There they encountered theological heresy on the ground for the first time. The innkeeper was a committed Cathar. Dominic and Diego were moved to pity, and Dominic stayed up all night trying to convert him.[24] In the modern world it is difficult to understand the motivations for this pity. One must remember that Dominic and Diego considered that the willful embrace of heresy by a baptized Catholic could send him or her to hell forever, eternally to be without God or happiness. What was worse, a heretic could spread his ideas, endangering the eternal welfare of others. Beyond this, a heretic was a traitor before God, a traducer of vows, and by that very fact a corrupter not only of the church but of society at large. So moved was Dominic by this pity that he dedicated the rest of his life to converting people and ensuring that they had every chance to live out their baptismal promises and retain the free gift of grace they had received from God. One needs to understand this motivation to comprehend how Dominic—and later Thomas—lived their lives. For them there were not multiple spiritual paths to the same destination, but rather there was only one Savior, Christ, who was head of one Body, the visible church. Only in the church could a person be saved. Though Dominic and Diego returned to Spain, their experiences marked both of them and were never far from their minds in the coming years.

In 1205, the king of Castile again dispatched Diego and Dominic to Denmark. On their way back they detoured to Rome (detouring was a favorite pastime of Diego's). There the bishop begged Innocent to be released from the see of Osma so he could become a missionary. Innocent refused outright; he needed bishops like Diego exactly where they were. While the pope did indeed tell Diego to go home, the bishop as usual interpreted the command rather loosely. The pope had not told him *how* to go home. The two travelers diverted to Burgundy, where Diego was clothed with the Cistercian habit. They then began, slowly, to head back to Spain, but on the way Diego found yet another excuse to tarry. They met Innocent's authorized preachers at Montpellier and found them despondent at their lack of success. All their efforts had been thwarted by the heretics who mocked the ignorance of the local Catholic clergy and the riches of the church's prelates. Diego was inspired by another new idea. In the first place he would seek to study the heretical doctrines themselves. This was an innovation. The papal preachers had apparently assumed that the simple assertion of orthodoxy and calls to obedience would be enough. Diego's method was Scholastic. If you cannot understand the rationale of your enemy, how can you argue with him? Such an attitude would become a hallmark of Thomas and the Preachers, who sought diligently and earnestly to understand their interlocutors, in every case letting them speak first, making every effort to comprehend them, and only then offering counterarguments. With this in mind, Diego went out to debate with the heretics. He then ran into another problem. One heretical interlocutor mocked him, not for his doctrine, but for the fact that he traveled about with retainers and wealth, as was only natural for a bishop, while the preachers of the Cathars and Waldensians embraced the wandering poverty of the apostles.[25] People hearkened to them because they were not hypocrites; they actually lived out the apostolic life. Chagrined at this, Diego made a momentous decision. Putting off the trappings of his state, he and Dominic traveled the back roads of Languedoc in tatty clothing, carrying no money, and begging for their meals and lodgings wherever they went. This was fighting fire with fire. Now their actions matched their words; Diego had pioneered the practice of orthodox mendicancy. The papal preachers followed his example, and positive results began to appear. Later Dominicans saw this innovation as a true turning point.[26] Stephen of Bourbon (d. ca. 1261) would say, "This was the cause for instituting our order. I heard this from the first brethren, who were in that territory with Blessed Dominic."[27]

In 1207, Diego finally had to return to his see, but he left Dominic in charge of the preaching in the area. Innocent III, at first shocked by the spectacle of his bishops begging, slowly began to embrace the idea.[28] That same year, a group of Waldensians under the leadership of Durandus of Huesca came to Rome for reconciliation, and Innocent could see the concrete fruits of the new method. Innocent was determined not to make the same mistake that the Third Lateran Council had in dealing with the apostolic poverty movement. He permitted the Waldensian group to rejoin the church, and to keep their way of life. They would be known as the Poor Catholics.[29] Innocent introduced several innovations. In the first place he gave them a document certifying their orthodoxy, so that they could defuse questions about their loyalties while on the road. He also then ensured that they became tonsured clerics. With the clerical state came not only legal protections for the men but, most significantly, the canonical mission to preach. Innocent made a distinction between two types of preaching. The first was the preaching of penance and conversion, which were central duties of all Christians, and open to all regardless of state in life. The second was preaching on doctrinal matters.[30] This was to be reserved only to those who had canonical mission: the clergy. With that, the Poor Catholics could continue their lives of itinerant poverty, now from within the heart of the church. Many of the innovations of Innocent here would be later incorporated into the foundation of the mendicants.

Meanwhile, Diego died in December of 1207, leaving Dominic to continue the *predicatio* alone. Dominic's situation was made even more precarious when a month later one of the papal preachers, Peter of Castelnau, was murdered by Cathars. It became painfully clear that the Cathars had powerful political protectors in the region, and that a peaceful preaching would not be enough to dislodge them. Because of this act of brutality committed against his legate, Innocent III called for a crusade against the Cathars and their abettors, and the combined forces of church and state worked over the next twenty years to grind the political power of the heretics into submission.[31] Alongside this crusade Dominic continued the preaching while overseeing a convent of converted noblewomen at Prouille. He began to attract a modest following. During this period Dominic became fast friends with the leader of the crusade, Simon de Montfort (ca. 1175–1218). As Simon went from victory to victory, Dominic followed in his wake with solid preaching. Dominic was kind to all he knew, yet he supported the crusade. Simon was a pious man, known as the "Father of orphans," yet he led a brutal war machine. How could one account for this from a Christian perspective? Once again context is vital. For Simon and Dominic, as for Diego and Innocent, heretics had traduced their own baptismal vows, cast off the free grace of God, and were in danger of perishing eternally. Worse than that, they were leading others to treason against both God and the state, planting a primrose path to damnation. In the minds of men like Simon and Dominic, "the sufferings of this present time are not worth comparing with the glory about to be revealed to us."[32] For modern people, for whom the care of bodily life has reached such astonishing proportions, it is difficult to comprehend a system that underscores the priority or superiority of the spiritual life. This is not to say that medieval Christians considered the body evil; indeed, that is the very doctrine they disputed with the Cathars. Rather, the Catholics argued that the body, while good, was necessarily *inferior* to the soul. For premoderns, the body and the whole of the material world was passing away. It did not matter if one met sufferings in this life, particularly for the sake of truth, for in exchange one was offered a crown of immortality. Similar attitudes existed about bodily discipline: better to discipline the heretic for his own good. If the body of the evildoer was harmed in the cause of his eternal salvation, this was considered good and salutary, much as the punishment of a child was meant to save him or her from further error. In modern materialist terms, since only the body exists, then it is horribly immoral to harm it in such a way. These premodern attitudes are not pathologies of sadism or masochism, or greedy power seeking. At least in cases such as Dominic's—and as strange as it may sound to modern ears—love inspired them. It should not surprise us that many, heretic and orthodox alike, were ready to give their lives for their causes. On both sides men and women laid down their bodily lives because they took a message seriously: "For what will it profit them if they gain the whole world but forfeit their life?"[33]

DOMINIC'S VISION

Dominic had characteristics of single-mindedness and mental focus that Diego lacked, and because of these gifts he was able to maintain his mission intact all through the dark years of the crusade. He began to unpack the ideas that Diego had left to him in embryonic form. The *predicatio* would have two fundamental orientations. The first was to a life of penance and austerity, in order to match the conduct of the heretics it sought to convert. In this sense Dominic employed poverty as a means that was to be subordinated to his zeal for souls. A living example was necessary for people to be convinced of the truth of one's life and message. That message was the second, critical part of the mission of the *predicatio*. Given the example of the previous one hundred years, Dominic knew that preaching was the key to the apostolic way of life. Preaching needed, however, to be rooted in learning, for the Scylla of unorthodox cunning and Charybdis of theological error were ever menacing. Dominic began to fashion an order for which the fundamental purpose was the solid theological training of elite preachers of the word of God. Like poverty, learning, too, was to be directed toward the end of the salvation of souls. Dominic recognized that both poverty and learning must be directed primarily to the good of charity for one's neighbors, a charity meant to provide primarily for their eternal welfare.

The leader of the *predicatio* was also convinced that such a group of preachers must spring from within the heart of the church. He had seen the results of previous movements that had rejected ecclesiastical control. Lack of supervision led them to critiques of the church, which easily spilled over into heresy. Dominic knew there must be deference to ecclesial authorities. Learning from the experience of his rapport with the papal delegates, he began to cultivate close relations with prelates in his area, particularly the redoubtable Bishop Fulk of Toulouse (ca. 1150–1231). Fulk recognized the good that Dominic's little band was doing, and he made sure that it had lands and revenues that would free it up to accomplish its mission. Indeed, Dominic made Fulk's job easier. Fulk could not rely on his partially educated clergy. External help such as the Preachers provided was necessary for the reconstruction of his diocese after the cataclysm of war. Dominic saw his female convent at Prouille stabilized in 1212, and in 1215, he accepted Fulk's invitation to move with his ten or so companions to the city of Toulouse itself, where they were given a church and established a quasi-canonical life. There they had the stability to pursue Dominic's ends further. Once settled into their church at St. Romain, the first thing they did was to begin attending lectures at the University of Toulouse under Master Alexander of Stavensby.

Good relations with the local episcopacy were not enough. Fulk wanted to take the opportunity to go to Rome and—in light of the upcoming Fourth Lateran Council of 1215—to secure papal approval for the fledgling order. As noted earlier, Innocent, too, was willing to innovate for the good of souls. He had already commissioned the community of the penitent Francis to become papally authorized preachers in 1209 (probably to Francis's chagrin).[34] Here again an opportunity presented itself to regularize a group doing much good in evangelization. The pope agreed to approve the order providing it accept an established rule. Dominic perceptively selected the rule he knew best, that of St. Augustine. This rule was exceptionally useful because it was a series of guidelines rather than a formal, legal constitution, thereby enabling serious flexibility in implementation. Under its umbrella Dominic was free to form the kind of order that he knew could be fitted for his mission. In choosing Augustine's Rule, the Preachers acquired a dual advantage. First, they were to be a community of clerics, unmistakably recognizable within the hierarchy of the institutional church. Flowing from this clerical orientation came the right to preach. Second, they avoided the monastic rule of St. Benedict, which demanded stability: lifelong residence at a single house. The stage was set for them to be a regularly established order of wandering preachers, with fidelity to Dominic and to a rule, rather than to a fixed abode. The myriad travels of Thomas Aquinas are but one example of the working out of this flexible plan.

The Dominican Rule that Thomas would profess was one of the most stunningly original in the history of religious constitutions. At the same time, it was deeply rooted, in that it flowed from the treasury of Christian reflection on the religious life. This strong foundation, coupled with its innovations, enabled it to become one of the most durable of all religious charters. To the Rule of Augustine, Dominic added many prescriptions from the customs of the Norbertines. In particular, Dominic emphasized the urban character of the order for several related reasons. Fundamentally, the people who lived in the cities were the very ones who needed the pastoral attention, especially since the secular clergy was foundering in attempting to deal with their spiritual needs. In addition, the cities were the locations of the centers of learning. Further, the cities were also hotbeds of heterodox sentiment, the natural focus for an antithetical preaching order. In these new urban convents, Dominic maintained the centralized Norbertine system of government, which provided oversight but preserved flexibility in local matters. Yet it was his innovations that proved the most significant. He discarded one of the cardinal principles of all religious life: manual labor. Since the very beginning, the religious had sought to avoid the accusation that they were merely fleeing from the work of the world, enjoying a life of comfort and ease. Had not Paul said, "Anyone unwilling to work should not eat"?[35] From Benedict, to Bernard, to Norbert, manual labor had been part and parcel of religious life. Indeed, even Francis of Assisi, Dominic's spiritual confrere, had envisioned his life as one of religious, laboring penitence. Dominic omitted it entirely. Perhaps more shocking was the rejection of

Benedictine *lectio divina*, or sacred meditative reading. It is true that the Dominicans were to celebrate the liturgy in common, but it was to be performed "briefly and succinctly." The reason for this was so that not even the Divine Office would impair the fundamental orientation of the life of the Preachers: sacred learning for the sake of the salvation of souls. Dominic added other relief valves to the Constitution to promote further study. Dominican superiors could dispense from any part of the rule— saving only those parts that were of divine law—for any reason, if the needs of the order demanded it. This was most on display as it applied to students and Masters in the order. Much like the discipline of poverty, the rule itself was only a means to the end of the salvation of souls. For example, a Master involved in study could be dispensed from common meals, and from the attendance at the choral office, if his work demanded it. Perhaps most revolutionary was that, unlike every other order, the Dominican Rule bound only under pain of penalty, not under pain of sin. To break the rule would result in canonical punishment or penance, but it did not involve the subject in moral guilt. This brought with it an astonishing level of freedom not possessed by the older monastic or canonical orders, and enabled the brethren to pursue their tasks with clearer consciences. Not only did Dominic liberate his brothers from stability to a place, he even delivered them from profession to a rule. When one was received into the order, one professed obedience to Dominic or his successors, in the person of the immediate superior. There were to be no local ties or canonical obligations to a church or a shrine. The Dominican was a liberated religious who could freely be sent wherever the order needed him.[36]

Another extraordinary achievement was the delicate balance of democracy and aristocracy in the order. Given the power of superiors to dispense from the rule, the danger of autocracy was real. Dominic defused this by an exceptionally clever constitutional structure. Of course, executive power had to be present. This was to be located in the person of the Master General, who was to have full control over the order. Every year, however, there was to be a General Chapter at which the Master General had to give an account of his governance. If a Master General died, then the chapter proceeded to the election of a new leader. The

General Chapters were on a three-year rotation. Two of the years, the chapter was comprised of delegates elected at the provincial assemblies, but the third year it was made up of the provincial priors themselves. This ensured that every third chapter would be run by experienced leaders, while the elective chapter ensured democratic representation. This was especially critical because a law could only come into force if it had been passed by three successive chapters. This meant that the representative democracy of the order would always be involved in passing legislation. The provincial chapters copied this procedure. Houses had the right to elect their own priors, and the prior was supposed to cooperate with the elder brethren in the management of the household. But in the midst of this remarkable democratic ethos, the Dominicans also preserved an element of aristocracy. In an order dedicated to education and to preaching, two categories were permanent ex officio members of the chapters. These were the Preachers General (men granted the authority to preach without permission from the local prior wherever they went in the province)[37] and the University Masters. This ensured that the intellectual elite of the order would have a permanent voice at the chapters and in the legislative activity of the order. All in all, it was a marvelously balanced document, exciting admiration from constitutional scholars and proving itself to such an extent that, in eight hundred years, it has not undergone substantial modification.

Having accomplished all this, Dominic traveled to Rome to obtain definitive confirmation. He impressed the new pope, Honorius III (r. 1216–27). Dominic proved exceptionally adept at navigating the intricate processes of the Roman curia. He deemed a first authorization bull (*Religosam Vitam*) as too vague and constricting.[38] It seemed that the pope considered the brethren simply to be another canonical order, a decision that would have bound its members to service at their local church in Toulouse. Dominic labored through the winter to achieve a more flexible document. On January 21, 1217, he obtained *Gratiarum Omnium*.[39] For the first time the pope addressed the brethren by Dominic's preferred title: Preachers. From that point on they would be the Friars Preachers, the official title they bear to the present day. This bull essentially liberated the brothers from their limited horizon in Toulouse. Having confirmed his leadership and secured papal approval, Dominic returned for the Pentecost chapter of 1217.

Rather than resting and celebrating the confirmation of his band, Dominic shocked his confreres upon his return. Instead of consolidating in Toulouse and planning for the future, Dominic sent them away, as wandering preachers, abandoning their comfortable lodgings in the town that had been his center of operations for nearly a decade.

> Dominic assembled the brethren and announced that, in spite of their small number, his heart's desire was to send them throughout the whole world and that they would no longer live together in the present domicile. Although they were all surprised at the announcement of this unexpected plan, yet, because of his evident authority of holiness animated them, they easily agreed to it in the hope that it would result in a good purpose.[40]

One needs to step back a bit to see the revolutionary nature of this seemingly impulsive decision. This was not yet the order of famous theologians, preachers, and University Masters. This was perhaps a dozen men—among them some lay brothers barely literate—being sent two by two to the intellectual centers of Christendom, far from their community and far from the religious base to which they had grown accustomed. In addition to that, they were not there primarily to study, but to set up a base of operations in the hearts of the universities that would effect a wholesale religious revival. The pope had acceded to Dominic's demand and released them from canonical obligation. He had given them the title and the mission of preacher; now they needed to be sent (Rom 10:15). In order to prevent their looking back, over the next year Dominic renounced all his revenues and temporalities and embraced the communal poverty of the apostolic life. Dominic and his brethren became mendicants (beggars), dependent upon the alms of the faithful for their support. So the brethren dispersed, first to Paris and Bologna, the two most influential intellectual cores of Christendom. From that day those two convents would be the centers of the life of the fledgling order.

EARLY DOMINICAN LIFE

After a difficult time, the brethren finally took up residence at the convent of Saint-Jacques. This would be the home convent for some of the most famous scholars in the history of Europe and the intellectual heart of the order. From this convent they took the name Jacobins. Very different from the eighteenth-century radicals who expropriated the house and the name, the Dominicans of Paris had a much different revolutionary path to take. The friars brought the apostolic poverty movement—now under papal authorization—into the city and into the university. The religious movement that had been coursing through Europe for the previous century had not had a prodigious effect on the intellectual renaissance of the 1100s. In truth there was as much an ivory tower mentality then as there is in any age. Yet both the scholars and townsmen of the new cities had the same religious desires as the rural faithful, needs that were being underserved by the local secular clergy. In particular, the scholars wanted a union of intellectual content with their religious devotion. Waldensianism or Catharism never penetrated deeply into the minds of the University Masters. Even the Franciscans at first made little impression—that is, until the university had converted the Franciscan order itself to the life of the mind.

From the beginning, the Preachers combined a life of intense study with their penitential practices. To say that they were successful in the scholarly environment is an understatement. They created an atmosphere of spiritual renewal. Instructors and students alike began to take an interest, and many started to come to the Dominican houses to hear the preaching. Both in Paris and in Bologna the friars proved irresistible. Hundreds of young men came to profess and take up the Dominican habit over the next several years. Occasionally faculty would try to prevent their students from going to the sermons of the Preachers, usually to no avail. Often the professors themselves were seduced by the lure of the apostolic life. Reginald of Orleans, a famous canon lawyer, was converted to the brethren and was appointed prior of Bologna. There he and Dominic oversaw astonishing growth.[41] Dominic habitually visited students individually in their rooms to encourage them in the spiritual life. In so doing he effected the conversion of many.[42] Reginald oversaw the conversion of famous Arts Masters such as Roland and Moneta of Cremona, both to become intellectual lights of the order. Reginald was so successful there that Dominic sent him to Paris for a repeat performance. After Dominic's death, Jordan of Saxony succeeded him as Master General (r. 1221–36). Jordan was almost as effective at converting scholars as Dominic had been, and the order continued its massive growth, spreading out from the university towns.[43] Paris and Bologna were similar to the hubs of wheels, with spokes extending to the corners of Christendom. It was under the influence of Jordan that the Parisian Master John of St. Giles came into the order and—significantly for the future—brought with him his university chair, which afterward would remain in the hands of the Dominicans. The friars had come to stay in the schools of Europe.

From these humble beginnings new foundations began to dot the map of Christendom. Like the Franciscans, the Dominicans quickly established themselves in the urban centers of the continent. The reason that men were attracted to the Dominicans was the same as when Dominic and Diego had tramped the back roads of Languedoc. The Friars Preachers not only preached, but they lived out the gospel. They answered the devotional ideal of the time: the practice of apostolic poverty. They lived lives of absolute, single-minded dedication to the life of virtue, exercised in community, for the good of others. The laity responded to this with spontaneous outpourings of support. Here was a community, dedicated to a life of holiness, abandoning all worldly goods to take care of them. In response to the begging of the mendicants, the laity answered with overwhelming material offerings. Conscious of the moral weight of their newfound wealth, the middle classes of medieval Europe placed high value on the charity offered to the begging brothers. The Franciscans and Dominicans, by and large, were urban, they were middle class, they were neighbors. A symbiotic relationship grew between the mendicants and urban laity (a relationship that engendered considerable jealousy on the part of the existing local ecclesiastical establishments). On the strength of such endowments, the mendicants reared mighty edifices in the cities of Europe. Men and women sought spiritual direction, counsel, confession, and even burial at these new foundations. The laity packed the convents not only with vocations but also with offerings that, over the course of a generation, essentially ended the need for questing (begging), and led to serious tensions about the practice of poverty, particularly among the Franciscans.

But that was all in the future. For their part, the vocations the Dominicans gained were certainly attracted by the strictness of the life. It is an irony of church history that young men and women pursue strict orders and disdain relaxed ones—a pattern that repeats itself regularly. Yet it was more than that. When young men went to a Dominican church, they heard preaching: solid, antiheretical, biblical, and—above all—intellectual preaching. The sermons of the Dominicans were their most powerful recruitment tool. Men considering an intellectual and religious vocation had no interest in homiletic pablum. The reaction of these young men must have paralleled that of Augustine when he heard the heart-stirring, intellectual preaching of Ambrose.[44] Too often Dominican historians have tried to identify poverty as the fundamental draw of the primitive order (I believe this stems from Minorite envy, and the enduring popularity of the Franciscan movement).[45] Poverty, while practiced rigorously, was secondary, and indeed many of the practices associated with possessionless life (e.g., the practice of begging by clerics) disappeared quite early in the order's history. Poverty, as both Dominic and Thomas recognized, was merely a bodily means to a spiritual end.[46] What dazzled the converts to the order was the exaltation of truth in charity. Particularly in the universities, to see a combination of intellect and holiness was the clinching factor. For in truth, potential vocations could go to many congregations and live a life of holiness, but it was only among the Dominicans that they could combine their intellectual lives with a community seeking virtue and sanctity. It was only in the Dominicans that their studies could bear fruit, not simply for secular gain, but for salvific purpose: the salvation not only of themselves, but of others as well. The Friars Preachers had turned Scholasticism into an apostolate. For students, professors, and intellectuals throughout Europe, this heady mixture proved irresistible.

The life of the Friars Preachers was contemporary with the excitement coursing through medieval Europe as travel and trade began to take off. In essence, the Dominicans were a spiritual counterpart to the commercial revolution then sweeping Christendom.

Like the merchants, the Dominicans were relentlessly itinerant. In the absence of the old monastic *stabilitas*, the friars were free to move about wherever the needs of the apostolate demanded. The friars and the middle classes established a symbiotic relationship. The friars could "spiritually launder" the gains of the merchants, who could set aside a portion of their own profits for their salvation. The friars also provided an outlet for the brilliant children of the laity. Joining the Dominicans gave clever youths the opportunities for advanced schooling and study that they might not have otherwise received. It gave established scholars sanction for their studies, a purpose beyond mere academic achievement. The lives of the friars were lived out in the streets and squares of the city. Their preaching quickly became a central social event in medieval Europe. Their mobility, their fidelity, and their learning quickly brought them to the attention of the papacy.

The mendicant orders and the papacy enjoyed an interdependent and reciprocal relationship that enabled both institutions to thrive and grow throughout the Middle Ages. Much like older papal alliances such as those with Cluny and Citeaux, these new mendicant orders had the privilege of exemption from local ecclesiastical control (this would be another flashpoint in the resentment that was beginning to build against the mendicants). This made the friars exceptionally loyal to the Holy See, from whom all their privileges derived. For its part the papacy had at its disposal an elite army of educated preachers, disintermediated from local interests and ready to spread papal policies wherever they went. Quickly the papacy began to appoint Dominicans to positions of power and influence. Though Dominic had repeatedly refused episcopal office (an example later followed by Thomas), his brethren were not so reticent. Quickly Dominicans were appointed papal delegates, inquisitors, and bishops throughout the Christian world. This brought benefits to the order. Friends in high places never hurt, and the friars soon had many. It also added to contemporary jealousies about the new orders. All in all, however, it was healthy for Christendom to have these men who were so dedicated to the apostolic life as advisors to kings and popes. Within sixty years of their founding, both the Dominicans and Franciscans respectively had one of their own in the very Chair of Peter itself. The Preachers' learning and holiness served the church throughout the century and helped to establish the intellectual dominance of the order.

The mighty Church of San Domenico in Naples today belies the modest foundation of the order there nearly eight hundred years ago. The order first authorized the priory in 1231, though it is likely that friars came to the city as early as 1227.[47] It was natural that the brethren would make a showing there, since a *studium generale* (the normal medieval name for a university) was erected in 1224.[48] Probably the growth of the convent was sporadic, advancing with fits and starts, much like the university to which it was attached. Some have suggested that the friars provided the Theology Master for the university, though this seems unlikely, both because there are no records of such a Dominican Master, and because of the rising mutual mistrust between Frederick and the mendicant orders. The friars, particularly the Dominicans, were becoming the papal vanguard for the struggle against the empire. Rightly or wrongly, this raised the ire of Frederick II. To have Dominicans in his territory was, from his perspective, tantamount to having an established fifth column and actively tolerating it. He finally lost patience and in 1235 ordered the mendicants out of his territories, with a definitive expulsion in 1239. In Naples only two Dominicans were left on duty to minister to the needs of the church, by permission of Frederick. The first was Thomas Agni of Lentini, a Sicilian. He was perhaps permitted to stay because of his native background (Frederick gave similar concessions to the Sicilian monks of Montecassino). Thomas Agni had an illustrious career in the church, eventually writing the authorized biography of St. Peter of Verona and ending his life as the Latin Patriarch of Jerusalem. The second was an aged friar named John of San Giuliano. He was perhaps left because of his age, or so that Thomas Agni could take care of him. In any case he was one of those characters of whom we know almost nothing, a hidden presence, yet one who was assuredly critical to the history of Thomas. He was one of the silent movers of history. He made no other impression on the history of the Dominican order, yet his mentorship of Thomas became one of the most crucial in the history of the church. It is likely that Thomas had become acquainted with the friars during his time at Naples and, like St. Dominic and Jordan of Saxony before, received personal spiritual direction from the experienced John. Thomas, drawn by the example of holiness and the intellectual climate of the Dominicans, had made up his mind. Sometime in early 1244 he made his profession in the order of St. Dominic.[49] He had presumably passed the qualifying evaluations required by the constitutions: mental stability, strength of purpose, and knowledge of Latin.[50] The next phase would have been submission to the chapter of the priory. Given that only two monks were there, the first and second step of the process probably simply entailed a conversation between John and Thomas Agni. Thomas was then permitted to make his profession. While it is probable that Thomas received the habit from Thomas Agni (following Bernard Gui), I am not certain that we can dismiss the hypothesis that he received the habit from Johannes Teutonicus (Master General, 1241–52), given his presence in the city.[51] In any case, Thomas knelt before the Master or his representative, who asked the question, "What do you seek?" The postulant replied, "God's mercy and yours." At that point they clothed him in the Dominican habit: a white tunic and scapular (a long cloth hanging down both front and back, with a small white hood). Over that friars wore the black cape with a black hood (from whence the English designation "Blackfriars" was to arise).[52] Thomas of Aquino from that moment was thereby canonically a Friar Preacher. It is not clear if Thomas immediately professed religious vows. Sometimes the early Dominicans practiced this (particularly in the foundational days of the order). At the time of his entrance, the church and the constitutions required a six-month novitiate, but that could be added to or subtracted from by order of the prior.[53] I propose that Thomas had only received the habit as a postulant, because the haste of the brothers in attempting to move him out of the city coupled with his family's attempts to win him back imply that he had not undertaken final vows. If he had, the efforts of his family were entirely in vain, for such vows were unbreakable.[54]

Now that the Dominicans had such a prominent and aristocratic vocation, what was one to do with him? Neither his family nor the emperor was calculated to be pleased. Thomas's profession could not be made secret, so the news quickly radiated outward. The Aquino family had the reaction that the Dominicans had feared. His mother—the formidable Dame Theodora—came charging down to Naples in order to dissuade her son.[55] One of the reasons that the Friars were able to act so freely in the case of young Thomas was the presence of the Master General, Johannes Teutonicus, in the city. They were afraid that Thomas might be seized from them, a possibility made probable in a politically unfriendly context. Events began to move very rapidly. The Dominicans made a plan for Thomas hastily to travel to Bologna (safely in papal territory) as quickly as possible, in the company of the Master.[56] When Theodora arrived in Naples, she found her son already gone. Not to be dissuaded, she then proceeded quickly to Rome, where she missed him again. Theodora was playing the anti-Monnica to Thomas's Augustine; she had come to prevent her son from his embrace of this form of religious life, rather than confirm it. Clearly, Theodora was a noblewoman who knew how to take control of a situation. Thomas had not only deprived the family of an exceptionally good (and safe) ecclesiastical connection, he had also incurred the wrath of the emperor himself. Now was not the time to offend Frederick, who was on the verge of taking the eternal city itself, and who had ensured a nearly three-year interregnum in the papacy. Even the new pope, Innocent IV (r. 1243–54), was playing his cards close to his vest for fear of enraging Frederick further. They knew that Frederick would view Thomas's profession as a defection and a serious black mark on the once loyal house of Aquino.

A further issue had manifested itself. Historians have been puzzled by the actions of Theodora in this matter. In a normal situation, the head of the household, Landolfo, would have been the one to take action; after all, it was his interests that were most at stake. Theodora's decisive efforts have caused some scholars to claim that Landolfo was dead by this time, leaving matters in the more than capable hands of his wife.[57] Yet, some of the witnesses at the canonization claim that the Dominicans feared Landolfo, and Tocco himself says that his "parents" restored him to the order after the episode. Therefore they place his father's death in 1245.[58] I would propose a new possibility. Landolfo was alive but was incapable of functioning in his role as head of the family, because of his advanced age and possible sickness. This would explain all the available data and preserve Dame Theodora's centrality throughout the whole process.

Tocco, who was on excellent terms with the descendants of

Dame Theodora and heard the stories from the family himself, makes an attempt to put a good face on the mother's actions. It appears that Theodora was on a mission in her later life to revise and sanitize her activities in the matter. Even this effort does not obscure her high-handedness and determined stubbornness in the affair, even to the point of involving the two most powerful men in Christendom—though in terms of stubbornness, the apple doesn't fall far from the tree, as we shall see. Now in Rome, Dame Theodora knew the emperor was nearby, campaigning in Acquapendente, near Orvieto on the Via Cassia, where he could intercept Thomas. She sent an urgent message to his camp. With the emperor was Thomas's brother Rinaldo. Frederick lost no time in taking action. The emperor clearly consented to Thomas's abduction, sending Rinaldo not only aid, but one of his own inner circle, the imperial counselor Pier delle Vigne. Somewhere outside of Orvieto, the small group waylaid the party of the Dominican Master General and seized Thomas. His brother ordered him to remove the habit, but the young friar pointedly refused. They then began to tussle over it, with blows raining back and forth. Thomas defended his religious garb manfully. He was, after all, descended of a knightly family and, as the youngest brother, doubtlessly had experience dissuading older siblings from violence against his person. It is one of the few instances in his life where he became physically agitated. The habit was the symbol of his profession—it would not be taken away. Thomas won this small victory and was allowed to keep his tatty habit. The habit stood for more than simply a commitment to his religious profession. Indeed, the acceptance of the habit was, for many recipients in the new mendicant orders, a liberation from the multifarious duties of secular life.[59] These obligations were compounded for members of the aristocracy. By assuming the habit, Thomas had stunningly dissolved the bonds of all secular commitments. The concession of religious profession was one of the ways Christianity introduced a shattering gospel liberty in otherwise stratified societies, one that often upset carefully calibrated social climates.

Thomas was first conducted to Montesangiovanni, a fortified castle about half a day's ride north of Roccasecca. Thomas's brothers had an idea they wanted to try before sending him back to face their mother. Clearly Thomas could not be tempted by wealth, for he had grown up in the midst of plenty and still renounced it. It was apparent that he could not be swayed by claims of family loyalty or calls to obedience. Perhaps there was one way left. His brother Rinaldo was a minor romantic poet of some note, one of the first to write vernacular songs about amorous adventures. Perhaps if Thomas had one of these escapades, his commitment would be broken, so his brothers arranged a visit from a woman with extensive experience in such assignations. Rinaldo judged poorly. It is best here to quote one of Thomas's biographers, Bernard Gui:

> His brothers in the flesh and enemies in the spirit turned themselves to the weapons of the devil, and through the comeliness of woman sought to destroy the innocence of his soul....Therefore they let a lascivious and shameless girl in both look and action be brought in, and if she would prevail in her mission, she would overthrow that tower that our menaces and schemes and blandishments have not conquered. Let us kill the boy's soul that we might rejoice in his bodily company, let us expel the spirit of God that rules over him, that we might ruin his spirit. Such actions were conceived of by his own flesh and blood, such insults suggested by his earthly parents and his friends that he might be destroyed. So they let in a most beautiful and shameless girl into the room where he was being held alone, just like a viper with a human face, that she might ensnare the young man, and if she was able, to overthrow his disposition of chastity. So she sought to attract the innocence of the youth, now with the visage of a viper and with lustful looks and caresses, not believing herself to be in a struggle with an angel, but rather with a man. So "that power might be made perfect in weakness" (2 Cor 12:9), even though he felt the excitements in his young body, yet he quickly overmastered them, controlled by a mature and virile soul. Then the virtue of chastity and righteous anger mixed together. And that he might expel the bearer of the fire of lust, he quickly ran to the fire that was burning by chance nearby and, seizing a

firebrand for fighting off the temptress, he drove her out of his chamber. This having been done, and fired by the spirit, he etched the sign of the holy cross in the corner of the room with the tip of the brand, and threw himself on the ground in tears, that God might give him the gift of permanent continence and virginity.[60]

Not having reckoned with the firmness of Thomas's commitment, his brothers ended their efforts and sent him home to Roccasecca for Theodora to deal with.

This story has been a popular staple of Thomas's hagiography, finding its way into popular tales of his life and informing the hagiographical tradition. At the same time, however, it has seemed to faintly embarrass historians. A few have gone so far as to deny its validity. The vast majority accept its historicity and yet are quickly eager to move on to the next stages of his life.[61] For instance, Torrell, in his magisterial work, gives it precisely one parenthetical reference. It is clear that the episode is historical, and it is more than probable that it occurred at Montesangiovanni, before the party had returned to Theodora. It is unlikely that such a procedure would have been condoned by Thomas's own mother. Clearly the brothers wanted a fait accompli to present to the family. In any case, the story is a testament to Thomas's renowned virginity, a fact attested to by numerous witnesses, and an expected claim to exceptional holiness in the thirteenth century.[62] It seems that it was a temptation that never caused him trouble after that. Thomas's own confessor testified that he had never heard the saint confess carnal thoughts, and Thomas was very careful to avoid women (except his own sisters, to whom he was quite close).[63]

His family kept Thomas for a period of between one and two years. The sources are somewhat unclear on the exact duration. It is also most likely that Thomas was held at the castle of Roccasecca, under the watchful eyes of his mother, for the duration of his imprisonment, though some historians challenge that he may have been resident at Montesangiovanni for part of that time.[64] Before the episode of the prostitute there is some evidence that his brothers maltreated him, but after that he was probably kept in comfortable conditions, for he was allowed to have concourse with his family, and was permitted to receive visitors. Far from being talked out of his vocation, he convinced his sister Marotta to embrace one of her own. She later became a Benedictine nun and prioress of her convent. One can even speculate that Thomas enjoyed this time. He was alone and he had books. His biographers tell us that he read and memorized the whole Bible. I am convinced that, given his experiences with the Benedictines, he was well on his way to this achievement already. Such an accomplishment is far from unbelievable; indeed, it was probably fairly common. In an age before Google and the printing press, memories were much sharper. Given the expense and rarity of manuscript books, if one wanted a ready reference one had little choice but to memorize it. In addition, he also took the time to study Peter Lombard's *Sentences*, the fundamental theological textbook of the time. Most essentially, the venerable John of San Giuliano continued to visit him, bringing him a breviary and a new habit (which Thomas continued to insist on wearing), not to mention encouragement to persist in his vocation.[65] In the meanwhile, the Dominicans had registered a protest with the new Pope, Innocent IV. Johannes Teutonicus personally appealed to the emperor. While this was an intrepid thing to do, Johannes was indeed the injured party, having been present at the abduction.[66] In addition, his German ancestry probably gave him increased access to Frederick, and the fact that the emperor had not yet been reexcommunicated gave him the opportunity to speak. In former times Johannes and the emperor had been friends, and the Dominican had tried to hew to the papal line without unduly irritating Frederick. The emperor determined that in this case he should cover his tracks and decided that he would take some action. He ordered a few of those who had assisted the abduction arrested (though not, it seems, the ringleaders Pier delle Vigne and Rinaldo d'Aquino). It was a way of placating the pope and disclaiming responsibility. The order did not pursue legal action against Dame Theodora. After all, it had really been Frederick's remote fault and Rinaldo's proximate one. They were also permitted access to Thomas through John of San Giuliano, who knew of Thomas's commitment and likely communicated this fact to the order. Because of this the Dominicans did not press their case, hoping for an eventual end to the impasse.

Such a reaction against parents was not extraordinary in the thirteenth century. Indeed, it seemed almost required for a saint of the mendicant orders. St. Francis had stunningly denuded himself of his relations to his bourgeois father in the Bishop of Assisi's presence, renouncing his patrimony and becoming a public penitent. His follower, the noblewoman Clare, opposed her parent's plans for her marriage and effected an escape aided by a domestic servant, a story seemingly more suited to a chivalric romance than a hagiography. But she ran off to no waiting earthly bridegroom, but to Francis, who sheared off her beautiful hair and made her a bride of Christ. Thomas's confrere Peter of Verona had been born among the heretics of northern Italy and turned his back on his family so completely that he became a persecutor of their coreligionists. So Thomas, too, opposed the wishes of his parents. His family's reaction and his unbending resolve become part and parcel of the hagiographical texture of the age. Yet, Thomas's family, in the end, did waver. This was for two main reasons. In the first place, Landolfo had probably died. The partisan of the emperor had passed on, and the pope had already won his eldest son, Aimo, to the church's side. Thomas's sisters had been won over by the young man's patience and conversation. The last straw was really the excommunication of Frederick II by Pope Innocent IV at Lyons. Once this was done, it seems that the family fully swung over to the political allegiance of the pope. Thomas's own abductor, Rinaldo, would be so affected by this turn of events that he not only abandoned Frederick but participated in a conspiracy to assassinate him, an action that would lead to his own execution for treason. According to the consensus of the sources and of historians, his family simply let him go back to the Dominicans in Naples in early 1246. Yet, Tocco—contradicting his own testimony at the canonization hearings—cannot help but to include a bit of hagiographical romance. Probably taking a page out of the life of St. Clare of Assisi, he reports that at the connivance of Dame Theodora, Thomas escaped Roccasecca by climbing down a rope let out of a window.[67]

Thomas was free and able to return to his brethren at Naples. He had undergone a severe trial and had outlasted the remonstrations of his own family, imposed by force. As will be clear, Thomas is a writer who almost disappears in his work. One of his modern biographers notes that he is the opposite of Paul and Augustine, who write themselves into their works prominently.[68] Thomas is hidden, yet very occasionally one can glimpse a hint of autobiography. Throughout his career Thomas was adamant on the right of the young to elect the religious life, even against the wishes of their parents. While there are many passages from the *Summa* that are better known, they are tame in comparison to an almost throwaway comment in II-II, q. 101 a. 4. In that article on our duties in piety, Thomas himself interpolated a quotation by St. Jerome. Jerome had counseled that it is sometimes necessary to trample underfoot one's own father. Thomas added, right in the middle of Jerome's quotation, "one's own mother."[69]

His time in Roccasecca was not in vain, however. He had intensified his prayer life, and John of San Giuliano had accompanied and deepened his commitment to the Dominican order. He had immersed himself in his studies. It is, after all, hard to imprison a hermit. Still, it is difficult for some people to understand how much of a blessing it is to an intellectual to have privacy and access to literature. Thomas wasted not a moment. In a real sense his incarceration did not interrupt his studies. Indeed, his enforced enclosure only served to undergird his already set sentiments for his career. When he arrived in Naples, the order once again sent him away, this time not in hasty anticipation of familial interference, but as part of a plan for completing his education. For this he would have to be sent north, to the intellectual heart of Christendom.

Chapter 3

ON THE SHOULDERS
OF GIANTS

The Intellectual Ancestors
of Thomas Aquinas

Johannes Teutonicus took the young scholar into his party and once more they set off for the north. Historians agree that their direction was Paris, but the duration of Thomas's stay in the university city has caused much dispute.[1] Up until this point the young man had not been able to complete a full course of study, being passed from monastery school, to *studium*, to imprisonment. The resources of Naples were no longer sufficient to educate the promising student. He needed to be apprenticed to a famous Master in the north. Since he showed little interest in the law, Paris was the logical destination. While on the road, his family seems to have made a last-ditch effort to thwart his plans. Leveraging their new influence with the papacy, they seem to have persuaded Innocent IV to offer Thomas the abbacy of Montecassino, if it would dissuade him from becoming a Dominican. Not wishing to displease his new allies, the pope not only offered the abbey but—as a sop to Thomas's well-known devotion to his habit—allowed that if the young man accepted the offer, he could continue to wear the black and white clothing as the head of the Benedictine house.[2] Thomas refused point-blank. As he would several times later in life, he followed Dominic's original intention that the Preachers refuse to accept ecclesiastical honors.[3] Thomas was iron-willed in his determination to follow his new calling for the rest of his life.

Thomas was now truly freed from parental interference and commenced his wholehearted commitment to his vocation. Most modern historians now agree that Thomas pursued university studies at Paris in the period between 1245 and 1248. While at Paris—now certainly studying advanced Arts and beginning Theology—Thomas was exposed to the rough-and-tumble life of an intellectual center second to none. Many of the ideas that he had been steeped in in Naples were then spreading across the school. In the university classroom, Thomas now needed to face the active side of Dominican life and, in the midst of it, attempt to maintain a contemplative stance in the convent of Saint-Jacques. The environment of the university was a melting pot of new ideas: the very nerve center of the academic life of Christian Europe. In order to see the vast array of movements then coursing through Paris, we should pause to unpack some of the major trends of the time. After all, mature Thomism did not happen in a vacuum. Thomas appropriated what had come before him and scrutinized it with the eyes of a genius. He cooperated with other Masters, he listened, and he evolved. Too often Thomists proceed as if one day St. Dominic struck Aristotle's head with an axe, and out popped Thomas like Athena, fully grown and possessed of a Master's chair.[4] The reality is far more complicated. In order to understand Thomas, we must understand his predecessors. Scholars have estimated that there are more than 48,000 references to various authorities in the works of St. Thomas.[5] When we read his writings and come across such honorifics as "the Philosopher," "the Commentator," "the Jurist," or "the Rabbi," it is necessary to understand whom he means. All through his works we witness Thomas in the midst of a conversation with tradition, and in his intellectual development we see intellectual sparks strike off the anvil of the past. In order to understand that conversation, we need to know what that heritage was.

For centuries the West had participated in and formed an intellectual world that descended from both the Greek and the Jewish traditions. From the Jewish heritage came the sovereign textbook of the medieval schools: the Holy Bible. Collected and authorized by the church, and then translated under the expert care of St. Jerome, the Vulgate Bible was the standard reference and authority for theology in the medieval church. It was for Christians the word of God, the divine message of the Father to the human race, which pointed to the ultimate consummation of all things in Christ. The doctrine of the church was to be found in its entirety in the Bible, even if only in seed.[6] In a certain sense all other theological texts, be they the writings of the fathers or the decisions of popes and councils, derived from its message and were dedicated to explaining, developing, and defending its teachings, and to providing an authoritative interpretation.[7] Further, medieval thinkers knew that the correct reading of Scripture was rooted in the literal sense of the text; one must not build "castles in the air" of esoteric spiritual allegories.[8] Any symbolic interpretation had to be rooted in the texts themselves. It should not be surprising if this approach sounds like one later adopted by the Protestant Reformation (except for the necessity of authoritative interpretation).[9] Indeed, the primacy of Scripture is one of the things that becomes crystal clear once one becomes immersed in the writings of the Scholastics. If later thinkers, particularly in the fifteenth century, drifted from this primacy of scriptural theology, it was not the fault of the medieval doctors. All theological scholars had to begin their careers by making "cursory" commentaries on the literal sense of the scriptural text and by constructing their theologies from there. Most medieval academics, because of their frequent use of the biblical text, had likely memorized the greater part, if not the whole, of the Scriptures and could cite them at will. Thomas understood this primacy of Scripture as a theological source, and he employs its text through all his work.[10] Even in his philosophical treatises references to the Bible can be found. Thomas knows the different senses of the text and is aware of the human authorship, yet he also has a firm conviction, like all premodern theologians, of the unity of the Scriptures provided by the divine author. Because of this, Scripture is the sovereign source and fount of all his theology.

For medievals, however, the Scriptures were books of the church and were to be interpreted only within her sacred tradition. Christ had left a mandate to the apostles to rule over the Christian people. For Catholics, the popes and bishops now had inherited that role. Their determinations, whether communally taken in council or determined individually by the papacy, were normative for Christian doctrine and constituted a source for theology in their own right. Thomas was just as familiar with these sources as he was with the Bible. In addition, the works of the fathers were of prime importance to the Middle Ages. In the West, these were biased toward the Latin fathers of the church, such as Ambrose and Jerome. Later in his life, Thomas began to apprehend and appropriate the Hellenic tradition more, particularly St. John Chrysostom and St. John Damascene. Yet, for the whole of the Middle Ages the key father was St. Augustine (354–430). His comprehensive genius had solidified Western Christian theology, and it was particularly he who mediated the wisdom of the ancient pagan world.

This Greek strand of the tradition, present not only from the foundations of Christianity itself but even in the Wisdom literature of the Jewish Second Temple Period (530 BC–AD 70), would be admirably appropriated by the church fathers. When, in the sixth century BC, the Greeks began to turn away from mythological explanations to a search for the foundations of reality, they effected a revolution. This was the exaltation of humanity through reason, the characteristic that set humanity apart from all animals. The ancient Greeks—particularly following the revolution of Parmenides—had fixated upon the idea of Being as the common denominator of all reality, thus underscoring the fundamental divide between Western and Eastern philosophies. The fundamental figure was Socrates (469–399 BC), who "brought philosophy down from the clouds" by taking the perennial Greek search for excellence and applying it to human life. "What must I do to be an excellent human?" he wondered. His search led him to formulate the concept of virtue, the habitual acts whereby we become good, and vice, the habitual acts whereby we become bad. By acting in accord with our reason—which is the source of our dignity as humans—we can accomplish acts that will be in fulfillment of our human nature and so perfect ourselves according to that nature. Conversely, we can act contrary to reason, incline to disorder, and thereby become evil. Related to this was Socrates's conception of the divine, in which he approached very close to a type of monotheism, as well as his conviction of the perduring immortality of the human soul. Socrates left no written record, and so it was up to his pupil Plato (427–348 BC) to streamline and complete his thought. He accomplished this through the Socratic dialogues, a series of conversations whereby Socrates is pictured as asking questions in order to delve more deeply into truth. Plato espouses a philosophy of idealism whereby the material world is lesser and imperfect, often deceiving us. In order to reach truth we must transcend the mutable and sensible world, using our immaterial ability to reason about abstract ideas. Only then will we come into contact with the permanent things, the "forms" of reality conceived apart from their material aspects. It is for this reason that this philosophy was named Realism, for the "Ideas" themselves were the most real and enduring, as opposed to the changeable material world. As we become purified from materiality, we more nearly approach our excellence as humans. It is by firmly placing the rational power in control over our baser nature that we will come to fulfill our perfection. In abstracting from changeable material reality, we will come into contact with the eternal ideas. For example, we will know what Justice is, as it is. We will know what Truth is. In the end we will know the Good, the prime form, which many have argued is Plato's conception of Socrates's monotheistic god.[11] Plato's philosophy was so powerful and comprehensive that indeed there is much truth to Alfred North Whitehead's quip that the Western philosophical inheritance is "a series of footnotes to Plato."[12]

Plato had a brilliant student and friend named Aristotle (384–322 BC). Aristotle, in the main, agreed with many of Plato's conclusions, but had a differing interpretation concerning the means whereby we attain knowledge. He was one of the most comprehensively brilliant men in history—an expert in philosophy, natural science, biology, logic, and aesthetics. Yet it was Plato who would finally come to hold the field in the ancient world. Many looked upon Aristotle simply as a talented natural scientist, and he was gradually shifted to the margins of the intellectual world, to be consistently preserved only by the Syriac Christian tradition (the teachers of the Arabs). Thomas would aid and ground Aristotle's astonishing comeback in the West—but that is to get too far ahead in the story.

Platonic philosophy began to take root in the eastern Mediterranean, not only among the Greeks but also among the Jews.

Late biblical literature such as the Book of Sirach and the Wisdom of Solomon show clear evidence of influence by Platonic ideas. When Christianity arose, Platonism was in the air and Greek had long since become the common language of the area. Christianity, while taking its roots from the Hebrew tradition, struck deeply into Greco-Roman soil. Unlike many who argued in the past that the Greek milieu was an unwelcome add-on to early Christianity that turned it from its Hebraic purity, it has now become crystal clear that the Greco-Roman mindset is inseparable from Christianity itself.[13] Though Christianity can take root (and, indeed, has taken root) in any culture, at its most fundamental it is established upon the foundation of the three cities of Jerusalem, Athens, and Rome. To remove any of those three is to lose an essential characteristic of the Christian movement. The whole of the New Testament came to be written down within the idiom and the thought world of Koine Greek. While we see Paul tentatively interacting with Greek culture in his epistles, it becomes much clearer in Luke–Acts, in which the literary form of the Greek historical narrative is employed throughout. But in the later Johannine literature, particularly in the foundational first chapter of the Gospel of John, we see Platonism beginning to unfold in Christianity. John uses the charged term *Logos*, flatly translated as "word"—"In the beginning was the Word." To John's hearers and readers, however, that term was a powerful philosophical idea that conveyed not only "word" but also "thought," "reason" "rationale of the whole universe." John had integrated Greek philosophical language into his Gospel. However, Christianity was to be more than "Platonism for the masses," as Nietzsche dismissively described it.[14] While John uses elevating Platonic language in describing the preexistence of Christ, he drives a spear through the Platonic worldview in verse 14 of his opening chapter. The eternal Logos, rationale of the universe, the absolute Thought of the Father, "became flesh and lived among us." Christianity was to be more than disembodied Platonism, more also than the pastoral transcendence of the Hebrew God: Christ was Reason in the flesh. In this new religion, the material world could not be so easily gotten rid of, as Plato wished. Hearkening back to the Jewish tradition, everything that was created was created "good," and that included material reality. Beyond that, however, God himself re-created this earthly reality by his own immanent participation it; the one who had "emptied himself, taking the form of a slave" (Phil 2:7) and had become a human baby. It was the incarnation that set Christianity upon its distinct path, one that appreciated the respective goodnesses of *both* spiritual and material realms. Though Platonism sat somewhat uneasily with this new religious belief, still many of its metaphysical and ethical conclusions were consistent with those of the infant church: the spiritual was more noble than the material, there was one God source of all good, the soul was immortal because of the immateriality of human reason, and humans ought to act in virtuous ways (the moral theory of the Greeks nearly always matched Christianity, even if Hellenistic praxis did not). Aristotle might have provided a more amenable philosophy—Thomas was to think so 1,200 years later—but early Christianity had largely passed the Stagirite over (a nickname derived from Aristotle's hometown). The Platonic consensus reigned in the first one thousand years of the church. The subapostolic fathers, particularly those formed in Johannine Christianity, continued to live and think in Platonic terms. Of particular importance was St. Justin Martyr (ca. 100–165), who made explicit the claims of Johannine Platonism. He was a man engaged on a philosophical search for truth. He had attempted to learn from an Aristotelian philosopher but was deterred by the man's demand for a payment before teaching. One can only wonder how different the history of Western thought might have been had this Aristotelian been less venal! Justin then proceeded to a Platonist, who inspired him by the exalted Platonic doctrine of the immaterial. After this he met a Christian and converted but carried his newfound Platonism with him, using it as a tool for the refutation of paganism and for making an apologetical defense of Christianity.

From that point Neoplatonism (the Platonic movement from the second to fourth centuries AD) was the de facto philosophical background for early Christianity, in both the Greek East and the Latin West (Syriac Christianity was an exception, but one whose voice was muffled between the other two). Though some Christians were wary of philosophy as such, their backgrounds all betray an environment of Platonism, both implicitly and explicitly. Some early Christians' Platonism developed into heterodox religious movements that denied the goodness of the material outright, such as the Docetists and the Gnostics. Antimaterial dualism was indeed easier to conceive of than attempting to reconcile Plato and Christianity. This is not to say that such dualism is directly traceable to Platonism, yet his philosophy provided a habitat for such ideas to germinate. Still, orthodox Christians were always grounded by the doctrines of the bodily incarnation and resurrection, as well as their devotion to the Genesis accounts of Creation. They refused to cede the goodness of the material world, and so—while remaining Platonic in their defense of immateriality—added to it the new wine of Christian materialism. Even so, the mixture of Platonism and Christianity was always a delicate balance. Platonism, in its best form, considered the material world to be deceptive and unimportant. Such ideas fed into Christian asceticism, sometimes producing rhetoric that can appear shockingly antimaterialist.[15] Yet these statements must be understood mainly according to hyperbole and the needs for monastic order. The Christian and Platonic doctrines of the superiority of the spiritual sometimes seemed to occasion a rejection of the body. Such ideas often aided the development of doctrine, but sometimes sat uneasily with Christian orthodoxy.

As Christianity came of age in the third and fourth centuries, pagan Platonism was experiencing a golden era, under the tutelage of the brilliant Plotinus (ca. 204–70) and his student Porphyry (ca. 235–ca. 305).[16] The impetus they gave to Plato's thought gave birth to Neoplatonism. These philosophers made explicit the absolute monotheism of Plato, referring to the origin of all things as the One. Plotinus even theorized a subordinationist Trinity of sorts: the One emanates the Thought (the *nous*, or the Platonic Logos), while the Thought emanates the world spirit. Neoplatonists emphasized mysticism and contemplation of the One in a pagan analogue to Christian contemplation. I find it difficult to think that Plotinus was theorizing in a vacuum: he must have had some contact with Christian ideas; indeed, his student Porphyry wrote a comprehensive refutation of Christianity. The momentum of the Neoplatonic movement carried over into Christianity, and the post-Nicene fathers are imbued with its spirit. The Cappadocian fathers—Basil, Gregory of Nyssa, and Gregory Nazianzen—are steeped in Neoplatonic thought when they theologize about the Trinity. Yet it was Augustine who would set the seal of Neoplatonism on the West.

No thinker was more crucial for the medieval Scholastic period than St. Augustine of Hippo (354–430).[17] Augustine's discovery of the Neoplatonists complemented his conversion to the search for truth. Their philosophical arguments about immateriality convinced Augustine that God and the soul are not corporeal substances; further, they were critical for his conviction that evil is not created reality in itself, but rather the absence of right order. This philosophical conversion paved the way for his religious conversion, and for the rest of his life Augustine would weave a theology that left a deep imprint of Neoplatonism on Latin Christianity. His status as the primary patristic theological authority in the West would cement the influence of Platonic philosophy on the Middle Ages. This became truer as the original dialogues of Plato disappeared. Indeed, at the time of Thomas only the *Meno*, *Phaedo*, and *Timaeus* were available, and he did not even use the first two. All of Thomas's exposure to Platonism comes secondarily, a testament to the deep-seated influence of the philosopher on the West, and to the sufficiency of Augustine to transmit the Greek's thought.[18] It is not simply Augustine's Neoplatonic background, however; the whole of his philosophy and theology was absolutely formative for the West, and his thought was dominant for eight hundred years before the coming of Thomas Aquinas. Among Augustine's volumes of works were two comprehensive classics. The first, *Confessions*, was an autobiographical account of his own conversion, a classic of the interior life and a masterpiece of human psychology. His *City of God* was not only an extensive and exhaustive tour of Christian theology but an entire Christian philosophy of history, and it was to become a political and religious charter for the Middle Ages. His work on the Trinity and on teaching Christian doctrine was pervasive in Western thought. In particular his Christianization of the ideas of Plato was decisive. The "world of Forms," in which abstract ideas existed apart from their material exemplars, was transposed in his philosophy into the "mind of God." In order to reconcile our ability to know these abstract ideas, Augustine pioneered the thought of a divine *concursus* or illumination. God gives us the light and power to know reality abstracted from sensible things, but only with an external grace of illumination. In other words, we need the direct action of God upon our minds to know reality. These issues would later be critical during Thomas's career.[19]

Subsequent Christian thinkers continued this Platonic trend. The Christian philosopher Boethius (480–524) was a particularly ardent follower of Plato and was convinced that Aristotle could be reconciled with him. He proposed an ambitious project to translate all their works into Latin. He fell afoul of the Ostrogothic king, however, and was martyred before he had finished with even half of Aristotle's logical works. Those translations were the only ones of Aristotle's books known to the West until the 1100s. Particularly formative for Thomas was a writer known as Dionysius (sometimes spelled Denys) the Areopagite. This author, who wrote in the early sixth century, was by the late patristic and medieval period confused with Dionysius of Athens. According to tradition, this man was one of Paul's only converts at Athens (Acts 17:34) and later was ordained the first bishop of the city. This presumed apostolic connection gave the writings of Pseudo-Dionysius a staggering amount of theological authority for nearly one thousand years.[20] As a result, his theology was immensely influential in the Middle Ages. It is from Dionysius that we receive the names of the heavenly choirs of angels, and in particular the "apophatic" approach to God, or the way of negation. Since God is utterly transcendent and unknowable, we can only approach him by understanding what he is not. For example, he is not bodily, not limited, not constrained, not composed. It is only from these negations that we acquire a knowledge of what and how God really is. Dionysius represents the mystical strain of thought that would particularly affect Scholasticism in the late medieval period. Thomas offered extended commentaries on several of Dionysius's works and quoted from his corpus over a thousand times. The mysticism and Neoplatonism of Dionysius's works and their influence on Thomas has sometimes been underestimated.[21]

Still another tradition in Christianity shaped Thomas, along with all his fellow Dominicans. The Christian ascetic movement, while present from the earliest days of the church, had come into prominence in the fourth century after the legalization of Christianity. This resulted in a rapid expansion of monasticism into the world of the church. Monastic praxis and theology would be critical in the foundations of Dominican life: not only their asceticism, but their devotion to patient and meditative reading of the theological authorities of Christianity, particularly the Scriptures. The lives and practices of the desert fathers of monasticism became one of the prime sources of meditation for early Dominican life, particularly the collection known as the *Vitae Patrum*.[22] One monk in particular was to have a profound effect on the friars, and especially on Thomas. John Cassian (ca. 350–435) wrote his *Conferences* (*collationes*) in the form of a dialogue discussing the progress and challenges of the interior life.[23] It was one of the most popular spiritual books of the Middle Ages and helped to form the mystical and contemplative traditions in Christianity. Benedict ordered that excerpts of the work be read in his monasteries. It was St. Dominic's favorite book, one that he carried everywhere. Jordan of Saxony writes that "this book refined the purity of his conscience, intensified the light of his contemplation, and raised him to a high level of perfection."[24] Thomas too always kept the book with him. Tocco reports that in the midst of aridity produced by extended bouts of abstract and speculative thinking, Thomas would turn to this work for spiritual succor. "I find that when I pick up this book of devotions, it is easier to rise back to speculation, so that the affections might have expanded in devotion, and the intellect—through [the book's] merits—able to rise to higher things."[25] Here again we see traces of Thomas's religious formation among the Benedictines. Here he is able to elide the Benedictine tradition with the example of Dominic. One understands Thomas better by an examination of the things to which he was devoted. This spiritual reading was for him a type of recreation, in its fullest sense of "re-creation" of the spirit and preparation for labor. It was for the purpose of exciting his affections toward God and recharging himself to mount the heights of speculation.

Further augmenting the Benedictine tradition in the life and thought of Thomas were the works of Pope St. Gregory the Great (r. 590–604), formerly a Benedictine abbot. It was Gregory, that eminently down-to-earth Latin, who provided the praxis to go along with the advanced theology of Augustine. His two main works, *Regula Pastoralis* (the pastoral rule), and the *Moralia in Job* (Moral commentary on the Book of Job), were deeply embedded in the thought of the West. In the *Regula*, Gregory lays out a comprehensive vision for the practice of ministry in the Christian church. It became one of the most widely distributed pastoral manuals in history and is a constant presence in Thomas's writing. Gregory is particularly attentive to the *cura animarum*, the care for souls, a concept around which the entire Dominican program revolved. The second book, the *Moralia*, was one of the most extensive works of moral theology of the patristic period. In the case of these two works, Gregory provides the practical or applied theology of the Middle Ages. For moral or pastoral questions, he was the authority to examine. Thomas would have been exposed to him as well in the monastery of Montecassino, and Gregory's works of theology endured as authorities in the schools of the Middle Ages. The careful coordination of all these authorities was plain in the Dominican program, which combined the active and contemplative lives. The innovation for the friars was to hold both of those poles of the Christian life in tension, and their success reverberates to the present day.

Less influential on Thomas were the writings of the Greek fathers, with a few salient exceptions.[26] The reason for this was the chasm that grew between Latin and Greek branches of Christianity starting in the late fifth century and consummated by the Great Schism of 1054. Compounding the problem was a mutual lack of language skills. It is one of the tragedies of theology that Augustine, much like Thomas, knew little or no Greek (though the ignorance of the Latin fathers among the later Greeks is equally blameworthy). A few works were translated and continued to circulate in the West. Jerome and Rufinus provided some translations of Origen's (184–253) works, and Thomas absorbed some Origenistic thought through the medium of St. Ambrose of Milan (ca. 340–97).[27] In particular, Thomas was familiar with the Greek father's biblical commentaries. He also possessed the homilies of St. John Chrysostom (ca. 349–407) and used these extensively. There were some documents that passed under John's name (e.g., the *Opus Imperfectum in Mattheum*) but were actually Arian forgeries—though Thomas was smart enough to amend the offending passages. The Greek father who was most consequential for Thomas was St. John of Damascus, or St. John Damascene (675–749). John lived his entire life in Islamic lands, rising to a position of eminence in the government of the Caliphate. He is perhaps best known for his defense of the use of images in worship, against the iconoclastic Byzantine emperors of the eighth century. More important for Thomas, however, was his work *The Fountain of Wisdom*. This is perhaps the first attempt at creating a systematic theology in the history of the church. It was exceptionally influential in the Greek East, but its significance did not end there. Translated in the 1150s, it demonstrated to the Scholastics the possibilities of system building. Thomas would have read this Latin translation and been exposed to the richness of a summary theology that capped the Patristic period. John, the "First Scholastic," made two substantial contributions to the medieval academic world. In the first place, he introduced the use of dialectic as a process for the unfolding of theology, which served as the foundation for a discursive summary of thought, indeed the first "Summa." John was also one of the first to employ Aristotle aggressively in his works. His familiarity with the Syriac tradition aided the reincorporation of the Philosopher's thought in mainstream Christianity. The use of St. John in both East and West is a memorial to the time of the united church. Therefore, while Thomas was deprived of much of the Eastern tradition, he was still able to incorporate much of its teaching and ethos into his own works.

During the period of disorder following the collapse of the late antique Roman political system, the Benedictine monasteries preserved the learning of the West within their confines. Patiently they read, copied, and studied the works of the past until such a time as came to reignite the appetite for learning. Under Charlemagne (r. 768–814) a period of renewal commenced. Following the lead of the monk Alcuin (ca. 735–804), schools began to be established in the cathedral cities of the Frankish kingdom. Aided by many other scholars, Alcuin reestablished the primacy of solid Latin grammar and ensured a commonality of script and punctuation. Such prosaic innovations sped the dissemination of information and made possible the foundations for a Scholastic revolution. John Scotus Eriugena (ca. 815–ca. 877), benefitting from the brief renewal of the Carolingian Renaissance, translated Dionysius into Latin and communicated anew the Neoplatonic tradition. He was extremely firm in separating faith and reason, and indeed got into some trouble for asserting the superiority of the latter. Yet, in spite of the efforts of such men, the time for a sustained renaissance had not yet arrived. Europe, menaced by external enemies and by internal squabbles, needed all its wits simply to survive the ninth and tenth centuries and was unable to bring about a sustained rebirth of learning.

With the stabilization of Europe in the 1100s, the cathedral schools again took up their mission of teaching the trivium. Increasing wealth and security gave intellectuals the leisure that was necessary for an advancement of culture. The impetus of the Gregorian reform led to increased interest in the sources of the Christian faith and in its defense against its enemies, real or perceived. The work of two men in particular reflected this tendency. The first was the international scholar Anselm (ca. 1033–1109). Born in northern Italy, he later became an abbot in Normandy and ended his life as the Archbishop of Canterbury in England. Anselm represented a new wave in Christian theology. Having secured the conversion of most of Europe and enjoying a newly stabilized political situation, Christian theologians were free to do theology from the "heart of the church." Not concerned primarily with apologetics or polemics against non-Christian religions, they could begin to let their speculations roam more freely. Anselm, as one of the primary originators of Scholasticism, saw the fundamental import of both language and rationality in the work of theology, and aggressively investigated the faith using both. He is a representative of the astonishing optimism of the Scholastic moment, identified by Richard Southern.[28] While humanity was indeed morally tainted from the effects of the fall, reason could perhaps be reintegrated. The Scholastic project was to be nothing less than the reconstruction of the knowledge available to Adam in paradise, before the original sin. Anselm in particular, among all other scholars, is borne on the shoulders of such optimism. While he is convinced that we know many Christian truths through faith for certain, he is also persuaded that these—coming from the God who is reason itself—are also reasonable truths. If they are reasonable, they can not only be rationally defended, but actually proven. In his quest to do this, he attempted rational proofs of both the Trinity and the incarnation. In his famous ontological argument, which is still the subject of debate today, he asserts that the existence of God is self-evident. As soon as the definition of God is understood, it is plain that he must exist. Rarely has there ever been an argument that so lays bare philosophical presuppositions. The ontological argument would prove an effective dividing line between idealist Platonists and more empirical Aristotelians. Scotus, Descartes, and Leibniz accept it, Thomas and the Dominican theologians do not. Whatever one's philosophical position on it, Anselm's attempts are some of the most audacious intellectual efforts in the history of Christianity: a declaration that reason is a gift of God himself and to be used in the defense and exploration of the Christian faith.[29]

Anselm was later accorded the honor of canonization, but a second founder of Scholasticism received a much more ambivalent reception. Peter Abelard (1079–1142) was a brilliant student and scholar who quickly mastered the art of dialectic, or the rigorous logical analysis of arguments. Abelard possessed that characteristic arrogance that is often an unfortunate accompaniment to genius. He quickly alienated his academic Masters and set up a school where he could teach his own students. Returning to Paris, his reputation and egotism preceded him. Relying on his prestige and self-confidence, he acquired the job of tutor to Heloise, the brilliant niece of the canon Fulbert, and essentially seduced her. Because of this he received "the unkindest cut of all" and was separated from her, to spend the rest of his days as a monk. This did not alter his personality, and he spent his days taunting the other members of the house for their lack of intellectual sophistication. Eventually he made a powerful enemy in the person of St. Bernard of Clairvaux (1090–1153). In spite of Abelard's chronic condition of being in trouble with someone, he still managed to establish the logical works of Aristotle as the centerpiece of the Scholastic method. Around the time of his entrance to the monastery he published his major work, entitled *Sic et Non* (Yes and no). This book arranges authorities from the Christian faith who seem to contradict and sets them against one another. While this could be seen as scoffing at Christianity, the work gets to the heart of a central theme of medieval Scholasticism: harmonization.

It did not take a brilliant intellectual to notice that discrepancies exist within traditions. The Bible itself sometimes gives differing accounts of events; even the Gospels provide divergent timelines for the public ministry of Christ. The fathers were aware of this, and they occasionally wrote in order to untangle such thorny problems. In addition to these, over the course of a millennium councils and popes had issued hundreds upon hundreds of decisions. Many of these appeared to conflict in their interpretations of salient issues. At the same time, the implications of similar conflicts were also being felt in the Islamic and Hebrew traditions. Working from philosophical backgrounds comparable to Christianity, they too began an attempt at reconciling the varying determinations of their respective faiths. This led to remarkable projects of harmonization. Indeed, the medieval period can be called the Age of Harmony, not because of any inherent peacefulness, but because of the concerted efforts of intellectuals and artists to achieve some sort of reconciled balance, using rationality, to bring order to a disorganized whole. One could see this in the marvelous systematization of canon law in Gratian's collection in the 1130s, which, fittingly, he entitled the *Harmony of Discordant Canons*.[30] Using the principles of dialectics, he not only collected the varying decisions of the past as Abelard did but, unlike the proud Frenchman, Gratian set about attempting to bring them into understandable order. This paralleled similar efforts in the realm of civil law, with the rediscovery of the Code of Justinian and the streamlining of the public laws of Christendom. Art too saw the desire to harmonize, as mighty Romanesque and Gothic cathedrals rose across Europe, employing exact harmonic and geometric principles. Most notable was the area of music, as the miracle of polyphony was born in the cathedral of Paris under the Masters Leonin and Perotin, turning plainchant into harmonic multivoiced beauty. So profound was this movement that historian Erwin Panofsky saw the harmonics of the perfect geometric cathedral in the harmonious theological synthesis of Thomas's *Summa Theologiae*.[31] Even if his effort was not wholly convincing, it illustrated a sentiment that grounded medieval efforts, a movement toward order, unity, and balance.

An intellectual harmonization had already begun among the thinkers of the other two monotheistic faiths. Islam had conquered an area from the Atlantic seaboard to the gates of the Himalayas within one hundred years from the death of its founder in 622. Once this initial tide of aggression was over, and when both Europe and China finally repelled the Muslim armies, Islam settled down to the more difficult task of actually governing. The

Umayyad Caliphate (661–750; but until 1031 in Spain) began to stabilize the Islamic territories and started to govern as an imperial power. Since the Arab tribes had few men experienced with civil service in the maintenance of a complex empire, the Umayyads often turned to the Christian minority, which had been in power in the area for three hundred years. The Muslims appointed them as ministers (St. John Damascene was one such man who served the Caliphs in Damascus). The Abbasid Caliphate succeeded the Umayyads in 750.[32] The elaboration of Islamic culture was particularly emphasized under these rulers. During their dynasty, the first steps were taken in the intellectual renaissance of the Islamic world. They appropriated the knowledge of their subject peoples, in particular the wisdom of Christians, Jews, Zoroastrians, and Hindus, and through them acquired access to a treasury of ancient texts. Muslims became known for their skills in medicine, mathematics, and mechanics. For deeper wisdom, however, they especially turned to the Christian monks. One will recall that the Syriac Christians were often marginalized, particularly as church history is often presented as a struggle between Greek and Latin. However, the Syriacs represented a Christian religious tradition as ancient as the other two, and with a rich heritage of its own. In order to learn the wisdom of the ancient world, Muslims began to apprentice themselves to Syriac Christian masters. From them they first learned of the works of Aristotle, which had been preserved in Syriac translations from the Greek. Because of this the Islamic world encountered logic and dialectic for the first time. As Judaism and Christianity confronted the traditions of the Greeks, so, too, were the Muslims drawn into the world of rational investigation.

As a result of this there was an Islamic intellectual renaissance. This originated with the *Kalām* theologians, who began to pursue the understanding of Islamic revelation through the lens of rational analysis. As in other cases, this type of theology arose in particular as an effort to defend Islam against the attacks of Jews and Christians. Eventually this movement expanded from mere reactionary apologetics to an attempt to harmonize the whole of the Muslim system. This also led to a push to rationalize and apply Islamic law, bringing into harmony all the declarations that seemed to conflict with one another. Some thinkers began to go beyond theology and to practice pure philosophy. The movement of *Falsafa* was an attempt to understand the rational systems of the ancient pagan world, in particular those of Plato and Aristotle. The first formal Islamic philosopher was al-Kindi (801–66). His fundamental principle could just as well have been articulated by Thomas himself: "We should not be ashamed to acknowledge truth from whatever source it comes to us, even if it is brought to us by former generations and foreign peoples. For him who seeks the truth there is nothing of higher value than truth itself."[33] While not an especially original thinker, al-Kindi ensured the translation of relevant texts into Arabic and was instrumental in the creation of a philosophical vocabulary in that language. He gave rise to a stream of rationalist thought that began to discover uncomfortable problems. For example, reason brought demonstrable certitude; yet Islam claimed that some knowledge was available only through revelation. What if the conclusions of each approach were contradictory? The physician-philosopher al-Razi (865–925) illustrated one possible answer: only reason gives certain knowledge; all religions—including Islam—were therefore dangerous. One could see how such speculations could make people uneasy. This rationalism reached something of a peak with al-Farabi (ca. 872–950/951). He was perhaps the most prominent mediator of Aristotle, for his interpretations influenced all later writers, be they Islamic, Jewish, or Christian. Al-Farabi was the originator of an idea that would later cause much trouble to Thomas and cause a powerful agitation throughout the universities of Europe. He recognized both the power of al-Razi's assertions as well as Islamic claims to truth. Al-Farabi proposed that only a few can reach the pure heights of truly philosophic knowledge; therefore, religion was instituted for everyone else in order to know and do the good, not through reason but rather through peremptory divine command. This disjunction was not formally a "double truth theory"; however, it did make a claim that was unsettling to the Islamic order: the philosophers were the elites, in a certain sense "exempt" from religion. Everyone else, including the theologians, was at a lower level of knowledge.

Falsafa continued to develop, particularly among the two most brilliant Islamic thinkers. The first was Ibn-Sina (c. 980–1037; known to the Latin West as Avicenna). Like Aristotle, Avicenna was a universal genius, writing on subjects as diverse as astronomy, geology, mathematics, and poetry. Yet it was as a philosopher that he acquired his claim to fame. Like al-Farabi he understood that the fundamental purpose of metaphysics was a question of Being or existence, which is the first idea that we conceive of in our intellect. Avicenna was fundamentally Neoplatonist, arguing in support of a series of necessary emanations from God. The problem for religious monotheism is that such necessary emanations entail compulsion in God, denying his essential freedom. These emanations for Avicenna concluded with the agent or active intellect. Aristotle understood this active intellect as the power of abstraction. We abstract from concrete material things in order to rise mentally to comprehend their essential nature. For example, from our experience of a number of dogs, we abstract the essential qualities of each until we are able to conceive of a "nature" of dog: what is common to all individual dogs. Avicenna was of the opinion that this active intellect was separate from us. Yet if this power—our only essential claim to immateriality—does not belong to us personally, then perhaps the individual human possesses no individual, immortally existing soul. While this interpretation would prove problematic in the thirteenth century, Avicenna gave it a far deeper meaning. It was he who first articulated the position, usually taken to be Thomistic, of the separation of essence and existence. Thomas's first formal work, *De Ente et Essentia*, would be directly reliant upon Avicenna's ideas. Essence is the nature of a thing, while existence is the actualization of that essence in an individual reality. Human nature is an essence, but Bob and Carl are existing individual examples of that common essence. All created things are composites of essence and existence; that is, they are essences that have received a separate act of existence. Avicenna was the first to point to existence, or Being, as the fundamental subject of metaphysics, rather than essences. Yet—since such existing things are composites made up of both essence and existence—they cannot explain the "why" of their existence. In order to understand this, there must be a "necessary existent" or an existence for which it is impossible not to exist. Thomas will later develop this into his famous definition of God: the being whose essence *is* existence. In God, essence and existence are identical, whereas in all other things they are separate and composite. Avicenna's understandings would ground Thomas's own metaphysics.

Spanish-Muslim philosopher Averroes (Ibn Rushd, 1126–98)

Of deeper consequence for the history of medieval thought was Ibn-Rushd (1126–98; known to the Latins as Averroes). Averroes lived at the end of the Islamic Golden Age. Even before his time, uncomfortable Muslim theologians had been challenging the rationalism of the Islamic philosophers. Avicenna had been a pious man who had tried to avoid politically sensitive issues, but after his death many of the theologians began to attack Arab philosophy. Averroes responded to these in an exceptionally bold manner. He daringly embraced Aristotelianism at nearly every point of its disagreement with Islam. In particular he defended Aristotle's idea of the eternity of the material world and abandoned the idea of an *ex nihilo* creation. This is the idea that the universe was created from nothing and that it had a beginning in time. Averroes's position was an offense to believing Muslims (indeed to Jews and Christians as well). His robust defenses of Aristotle would cause much mischief in the world of the Christian universities. In addition, Averroes contended that both the active intellect (that power that knows immaterial realities) and the passive intellect (that power that receives intelligible forms from the active intellect) are one for all people. This drives even further home the problem of human individuality and immortality. Though it seems that, in places, Averroes affirmed the immortality of souls, still the problem remained where to locate the source of individuality.[34] He also deepened al-Farabi's meditations on the distinction between philosophy and religion. In essence he draws an absolute line between them. Philosophy is the truest form of knowledge because it gives certitude about reality. The mob will have to remain content with the signs and symbols offered by religion. Religion, for Averroes, was a useful tool for teaching the population morality. The mob lived not by reason, but by imagination. Religion provided the imagery necessary to explain to them how to live virtuously. Indeed, to put it bluntly, religion was a useful tool for keeping the mob from killing the philosophers. This aggressively utilitarian account of religion, too, would trouble the Middle Ages (and would reappear in the modern West). Yet, even in all these arguments Averroes's brilliance shines through. When the West first began to deal with Aristotle, they encountered him with Averroes as his constant companion. Thomas considered the Muslim thinker to be the finest of the Philosopher's interpreters, calling him by the honorific "the Commentator." He was a primary interlocutor for Thomas his whole life, a relationship that started as early as his time at the University of Naples.

Judaism also benefited from this attempt to use logic and dialectic to understand religion. Among many Jewish philosophers, the most noteworthy was Rabbi Moses ben Maimon, or Maimonides (1135/1138–1204). His most influential text was the *Guide for the Perplexed*, which achieved notable distribution in the Christian Middle Ages.[35] He aggressively attempted to reconcile Aristotelian philosophy with the Hebrew Testament. Yet he seems to be operating on two levels. Like Averroes, the Jewish thinker accepts biblical revelation within the context of religion, but himself pushes further with philosophy. While he makes no declaration that is similar to Averroes, nonetheless Maimonides does seem inclined in that direction. He was driven by the idea that no inherent contradiction could exist between the revelation of God in the Torah and the natural knowledge of God acquired by reason. This principle undergirded all Scholastic approaches to philosophy and theology, but often sat rather uncomfortably when confronted by seemingly opposite philosophical conjectures. Maimonides's thought and influence earned him the title "the Rabbi" from Thomas, who takes both his and the Muslim philosopher's words with utmost seriousness and uses them to substantial profit.

Both Maimonides and Averroes lived in an Islamic world that was rapidly changing. In the first place, the theologians had been attacking what they perceived to be errors in the philosophers' thought. Arguments in favor of the eternity of the world, skepticism toward revelation, and the rejection of mystical/prophetic experience in favor of rationalism drove the theologians to denounce the philosophers for unbelief. Islam, like Christianity, had begun with the premise that faith and reason were complementary and could not contradict one another. Yet as time went on, the theologians and philosophers divided into respective camps of fideism and rationalism. From the very moment of Islam's inception, it had all the tools that were available to the West both textually and conceptually to orchestrate a harmonization of faith and reason, of philosophy and theology. Indeed the Arab world had a mighty head start on Christendom in this endeavor. Yet something did not sit well from the very beginning; the theologians suspected the philosophers, who in turn derided the theologians. Both were suspect by the increasing numbers of Quranic literalists after the year 1000. Two new groups—Berbers from north Africa and Turks from the central Asian steppes—overran the older Arabic centers of culture in the 1100s, bringing with them a simplistic and literalist reading of Islamic tenets. They were uninterested in the intellectual achievements of the Golden Age. The promising project of the Islamic cultural renaissance was stunted by a combination of rampant fundamentalism, distrust of reason, new cultural forms that did not value the achievements of the Islamic mind, and finally by the derision of the philosophers themselves for the entire Islamic project. In the end Averroes was exiled, and his books purged. The Salafism of the 1100s advocated a return to a primitive Islam free from the cultural corruptions and accretions of the Islamic golden age. Salafism not only repudiated philosophy but attacked the application of reason to theology as well, not to mention the entire cultural complex of the Islamic renaissance. The attempt at a unification of faith and reason had failed so spectacularly that Islamic philosophy and theology almost ceased to exist by the 1300s, partly as a result of these fundamentalisms, and partly as a result of the radical divorce of reason from faith occasioned by Averroes.[36] Ironically, the heir of the Islamic Golden Age was Christendom.[37] The works of the prominent Islamic and Jewish philosophers made their way to Spain, along with Arabic translations of the pagan Greeks. There in the 1150s a massive project of translation began to introduce this wisdom to the West. The weighty question was whether Christianity could avoid the fate of Islam: Could it indeed hold faith and reason as complementary authorities, or would it in the end occasion a bitter split similar to the Muslim world?

SCHOLASTIC ANTECEDENTS

With the advent of the new knowledge, the Scholastic renaissance of the twelfth century gained vital momentum. Spurred by these developments, Christian thinkers began to compose many of the key works that would form the curriculum for the next several hundred years. Already Gratian's *Decretum* had begun the arduous task of harmonizing the church's unwieldy legal tradition. The most influential work on the side of the theologians had come from Peter Lombard and was entitled the *Sentences*. To understand this work is to comprehend the basic theological efforts of the Middle Ages. Peter Lombard (ca. 1096–1160) was well known to most of the consequential personages of the time. Patronized by St. Bernard of Clairvaux, he was also well acquainted with Abelard and the canons of St. Victor, and was friends with Pope Eugenius III (r. 1145–53). He became a renowned Master in Paris and ended his life as bishop of the city. His four books of *Sentences*, or determinations, were to become the standard textbook of the Middle Ages, remaining so well into the Reformation. Peter Lombard's purpose was at one with the medieval theme of harmonization. He set himself the task of reducing theology from a chaotic literature to a reasonable system. In this he went beyond Abelard, who had critically arrayed authorities against one another. Peter Lombard was more irenic and sought harmonization, more in the spirit of the age. Every major theologian studied the *Sentences* and most, including Thomas, began their careers by commenting upon it. Its strength lies not in its originality—Peter has few unique doctrines—but rather in its organization. The four books are divided into (1) the Trinity, (2) creation, (3) Christ and redemption, and (4) the sacraments. What Peter did was to compile quotations from authorities in Scripture and then match them topically with the sayings of the fathers and the decisions of popes and councils.[38] Peter did for theology what Gratian did for law. The purpose of both was the harmonization of doctrine. What Lombard accomplished was to create a field in which the most brilliant of minds could till. Far from being a work that choked off theological commentary, the *Sentences* rather allowed research to blossom, and it became one of the finest springboards for speculative theology ever composed. In the 1220s, the Master Alexander of Hales (later to become a Franciscan) was the first to order, comment, and introduce the *Sentences* into the university milieu.[39] The indispensable nature of the *Sentences* should not be underestimated. It remained the primary theological textbook long after Thomas's death.[40] The Dominican constitutions, at least from 1234, commanded that each province was obliged to provide its Parisian students with a copy of the *Sentences*. It also prescribed the Bible and the *Historia Scholastica* by Peter Comestor, another product of Scholastic synthesis that recounts biblical history and continues with commentary on the progress of the church throughout time. These three texts were the basis of early Dominican theological formation.[41]

The coming of the Dominican order meant its almost immediate penetration into the schools of medieval Europe. From their first moments it had begun to attract Masters of Law, of Arts, and of Theology. These Masters began to pave a way for subsequent generations of Dominican scholars, and in turn began a massive project of educating new Dominicans, creating an order that—for the first time in the history of the church—was dedicated to permanent study.[42] Early Dominican education was quite conservative, hewing to contemporary bans on the study of Aristotle and limiting the purview of a friar's exposure to theological works, eschewing the Arts and Medicine.[43] The purpose of study was the salvation of souls, to be achieved through the medium of preaching. As a result, many of the theological efforts of the friars were practical and reactive, and dedicated to the refutation of the theological opponents of the church. The works of the first generation of Dominicans are known from their writings in the literary genre of *Summae* (or summations). These early efforts are little known for two reasons. In the first place, Thomas's massive theological output a generation later threw them into the shadows and, second, the problem that they addressed—Catharism—was largely defeated by the year 1300. That said, the existence of these works meant that Thomas would not have to bother overmuch with theological refutations of heresy, given that his brethren had so comprehensively answered the challenges before his time. Among the better known of these are the *Summa* of Roland of Cremona, the *Summa Contra Hereticos* attributed to St. Peter of Verona, and especially the compendious *Summa* written by Moneta of Cremona in 1241.[44] This last was perhaps the single greatest intellectual achievement of the order before the time of Albert and Thomas. Further study of these early efforts would be rewarded in that the *Summa* of Moneta essentially represents the first ever *Summa de Ecclesia*—the first systematic work on ecclesiology in history.

Other Dominicans were hard at work preparing aids for theological study. Most notable in this respect is Hugh of St. Cher (ca. 1195–1263), the Dominican who would later become the order's first cardinal in 1244.[45] A professor equally comfortable teaching philosophy, theology, and law, Hugh—like Roland, Peter of Verona, and Moneta—heard the siren call of the Dominicans. Already a Parisian Master at the time of his reception into the order in 1225, he quickly rose through the ranks, becoming provincial prior of France by 1227 and prior of the convent of St. Jacques in Paris from 1233 to 1236. Hugh was one of the founders of the Scholastic method that involved bringing forward conflicting authorities that were then reconciled by argument, a style so familiar to Thomas's readers. In addition, he was one of the most comprehensive Scripture scholars of the Middle Ages, producing no fewer than three paramount works. His *Postillae* are commentaries on the whole of Scripture, one of the first enterprises to include patristic sources coupled with contemporary theological speculations. The work is a tour de force, commenting on the whole of the Bible using the four traditional senses of Scripture. Second, confronted with a barrage of divergent readings of the scriptural text (the bane of a literary culture transmitted by handwritten manuscript), Hugh spearheaded the creation of a *Correctorium*, which was an attempt to record variant readings and create a more faithful edition of the Vulgate from ancient manuscripts. His work became the predecessor to the critical editions of the sixteenth century and the eventual establishment of the Clementine Vulgate. Because Hugh was also concerned about the quality of preaching, he compiled his *Concordantia*, which was the first verbal concordance of Scripture, with topics alphabetized for ease of location. With these efforts Hugh had forged the tools for the vast expansion of theological efforts that would characterize the next one hundred years. They would prove invaluable to all future Scholastic Masters.

The libraries of the order were equipped with the books that the friars would need for their ministry. Other works that were relevant for Dominican life, besides the constitutions, were the hagiographical texts, particularly those by Jordan of Saxony and later biographers of Dominic. Through these lenses the early friars understood their own mission and strove to match the deeds of the founder and his first disciples. Later Dominican hagiography, particularly Thomas's own, would be indebted to these works, and when the historian looks at Thomas's written lives, one of the things to be aware of is their conformity to earlier hagiographical efforts. Numerous model sermon collections and "florilegia" (collections of quotations arranged topically) were of further benefit to a group dedicated to preaching and teaching, as were books of advice on how to preach (most notably by Humbert of Romans, Master General from 1254 to 1263). Such tools aided the Preachers in easily accessing texts for composing their own sermons. In the area of pastoral life, the Dominicans were almost as committed to the confessional as to the pulpit. The friars were pioneers in medieval confessional manuals; in fact, one of the first intellectual products of the order was just such a practical directory, written by the early Dominican Paul of Hungary. This effort was marked not only by theological and legal references useful for the confessional, but also by a marked pastoral stance that advised the confessor about matters that might arise, or recommendations regarding how to approach different kinds of sinners.[46] From the very beginning the Dominicans combined speculative and practical theology.

The most notable work in this confessional genre was by the brilliant Raymond of Peñafort (ca. 1175–1275, Master General 1238–40). Already a famous law Master when he entered the order, Raymond had completed a *Summa de Casibus Conscientiae* (Summa of cases of conscience) by 1225. Revising it over the next ten years, it became the standard for Dominican confessors and was constantly updated and commented upon. Even after the efforts of Thomas, later Dominicans merely elided the moral teaching of the *Secunda Secundae* of the *Summa Theologiae* into Raymond's *Summa*. This work was notable for introducing the concept of the confession as tribunal, with the priest being the judge of moral "cases." As historian Christine Ames has pointed out, this did not mean that the older model of confession as spiritual medicine—with the confessor as the physician—died out; they merely existed side by side.[47] Raymond also was charged by Pope Gregory IX (r. 1227–41) to edit a new collection of laws that would serve together with the *Decretum* of Gratian. These would be a compilation of papal decisions, called *decretals*. Raymond completed the *Liber Extra* in 1234, and it was so influential that it became normative Catholic law until 1917. Thomas would have reason to refer to this text on many occasions. What we can glean from this brief survey is that Thomas's predecessors and confreres in the order abundantly established the foundations of theological education and the tools available to the scholar. This enabled intellectuals such as Thomas to use this groundwork in order to construct a system without having to go through all the trouble of assembling the components. One needs to see all the streams that flow into a river in order better to understand its course and to be liberated from the myth of the autonomous genius. The medieval schoolmen, as Bernard of Chartres remarked in the 1100s, truly did "stand on the shoulders of giants."

THE FURTHER EDUCATION OF THOMAS

There was one teacher more than all others, however, who was critical to Thomas's formation as a scholar, a contribution recognized by all historians and theologians, even if their exact intellectual interdependence is still a subject of debate. This was Albert the German, also called Albert the Great (ca. 1200–1280). After Thomas's liberation from his family, the brethren at Naples sent him to Master Johannes Teutonicus in Rome. Thomas then accompanied Johannes to Paris for the 1246 General Chapter. The purpose of this journey was to enroll the young man in the university in order to complete his training in the arts so as to prepare him to study formal theology. The lack of documentation about this period has produced a wide variety of opinions, but it is well established that Thomas was in Paris until 1248.[48] It is also most likely that the young student finished the Arts courses, making many friends and colleagues there. It is clear from later in his life that Thomas's stalwart allies in Paris were in the school of Arts, while most of his adversaries were in Theology. He also probably completed his canonical novitiate in the French city and professed his solemn vows in the convent of Saint-Jacques. While it is not likely that the order specifically sent him to study with Albert in 1245 (as some of the sources suggest), nonetheless it was at Paris that he and Albert met. Soon thereafter, Thomas began to study under the Dominican Master, at the very least by the end of his time in the city.

Albert the Great was already a famous scholar by the time he accepted Thomas as an apprentice. Probably recruited into the order in the 1220s by Jordan of Saxony, Albert had already studied at the universities of Padua and Bologna.[49] There he became an aficionado of all things Aristotelian. This did not mean that he became fundamentally converted to Aristotelian metaphysics, but rather that he was deeply interested in all of the new texts then being translated. He was the first German Dominican to become a Regent Master (meaning an active professor) in Paris. Albert became a prime mediator of Aristotle to the Parisian community and to the rest of the Western world. He was a universal genius whose work penetrated into all the branches of science, much like Aristotle, the object of his particular interest. Many of Albert's colleagues were puzzled by the writings of the Greek pagan, and they asked him to produce some commentaries on Aristotle's works so that they would be "intelligible to the Latins."[50] In order to do just that, he spent the next twenty years on this project, writing compendiously, not simply on theology and philosophy, but also on nearly every branch of empirical and natural science. Some have even pointed to Albert (and his younger Franciscan colleague, Roger Bacon) as the founders of Western empirical science.[51] Indeed, the Dominican has become the patron saint of natural scientists in the Catholic Church. One of the reasons for this, besides natural interest and aptitude, was the renewed value placed on the senses by Aristotle. For the Greek philosopher, all of our knowledge is mediated through the senses. Only when we have sense data (called phantasms) can our minds then abstract their essential properties. It is only then that we can apprehend what Plato called natures or "ideas." Aristotle thus modified the "realism" of his teacher and posited that natures are never found apart from things themselves, and our abstraction of them is only mental. This meant that the Aristotelian revolution brought with it a renewed possibility for experimental science. Without Albert's mediation of Aristotle, it would be difficult to conceive of the coming of a scientific revolution beginning in the Renaissance. Yet, Albert had far broader interests than Thomas, whose work was almost wholly restricted to philosophy and theology. With all that said, Albert was an imperfect interpreter of Aristotle, and he often mixed Platonism in an uneasy alliance with newly rediscovered Aristotelian concepts. While he tried accurately to report the Greek's thought, Albert often felt compelled to correct it. For instance, he rejected Aristotle's arguments on the eternity of the world and had repudiated the presumedly Averroistic doctrine on the unicity of human intellect.[52] It is possible that Thomas's exposure to Aristotle and the Arabs in Naples had insulated him somewhat from Albert's rather eclectic interpretations. Thomas completed the Arts courses at the university, which probably focused on Aristotle's *Ethics* and *De Anima*.[53] In addition, Torrell proposes that he began to take Albert's theological classes in the convent of St. Jacques.[54] There he encountered Pseudo-Dionysius for the first time. Albert was lecturing on the *Celestial Hierarchies* and commissioned Thomas to become his secretary. Thomas dutifully copied Albert's lectures for publication and dissemination to the Parisian community. Recognizing his talents, Albert took a salient interest in the young man.

Albert's regency was over in 1248, the same year that the General Chapter met in Paris. The assembled friars agreed to set up a *studium generale* in the German city of Cologne.[55] A *studium generale* was essentially the medieval term for university.[56] In particular, this *studium* would be a place for advanced theological study for Dominicans, and its creation evinced the growth of the order in Northern and Eastern Europe. Cologne would be a center for the education of students from these areas. As Albert was a native German and had completed his Parisian regency, the order naturally selected him to go and found this new undertaking.

Albert requested that Thomas continue to work and study with him, and so the apprentice traveled with the Master to Cologne. There he was both a student and secretary to Albert. In a certain sense Thomas was Albert's teaching assistant, doing much of the grunt work that falls to those on the lowest rung on the academic ladder. In Germany, Thomas not only attended lectures but also compiled and edited them. He completed the publication of Albert's commentary on Dionysius and began to organize the lectures of his Master on Aristotle's *Nicomachean Ethics*. It is astonishing that almost a third of Thomas's time would have been taken up with this secretarial work.[57] So useful did Thomas find Albert's lectures on the *Ethics* that he later created a system of note cards in order to help him reference it as he completed the *Secunda Secundae* (the part of the *Summa Theologiae* that deals with moral issues).

Tocco reports that while Thomas was in Cologne, some students took to calling him the "dumb ox of Sicily."[58] Some historians seem to be uncomfortable with this story. I do not see any reason why it should not be accepted. Thomas was known for his silence and ability to focus and think abstractly. He had found a brilliant teacher in Cologne and was content to sit at his feet and learn. As a teacher, one often sees a talkative student who lacks intellectual gifts, whereas a taciturn one hands in outstanding work.

One day there was a particularly difficult lecture and another student, mistaking Thomas's silence for a lack of understanding, charitably offered to study with him. As the student was going over the lecture, he became lost in the intricacies of the argument. After a period of silence, Thomas picked up right where his confrere left off and explained the rest of the topic. The student said that he understood it far better after Thomas explained it (more clearly than Albert, the story notes). Thomas was not always silent. Occasionally Albert held practice disputations in the *studium*. These were formal debates, with presentations and defenses of difficult questions. In a certain sense they were practices that foreshadowed the later responsibility of quodlibetal questions, as we will see in the next chapter. Being impressed by Thomas's work, Albert one day decided to test him by having him hold a disputation. The theses were difficult (their subject is unreported), but Thomas maintained them stubbornly and without difficulty. Not only did Thomas lay out the relevant counterarguments (which should have been the job of a fellow disputant), he then proposed to solve all difficulties with one summation (which was Albert's job as Master). Thomas ran away with himself here. Albert admonished him, insisting that he was not simply debating, but deciding the question. Then Albert himself began to dispute with him. Thomas held his own against the assaults of the brilliant Master. It was at this point that Albert is supposed to have said, "You call him dumb ox, but one day his bellowing will be heard throughout the world."[59] As Tugwell says, it would be surprising if Albert was only then discovering Thomas's talents.[60] What we have here is likely hagiographical telescoping of the gradual maturation of Thomas's intellectual abilities under the watchful eyes of Albert. I also think that the quotation from Albert masks evidence of a youthful lack of discipline—and perhaps a glimmer of arrogance—which Thomas seems to have bridled as time went on.

Some have proposed that not only did Thomas complete his theological curriculum at Cologne, but also that Albert used him as his biblical bachelor. This meant that he began his university teaching career, somewhat like an apprentice professor, in making cursory lectures about the Bible. These were lectures intended only to educate the students in the literal meaning of a biblical text. Most scholars (pace Tugwell) are convinced that Thomas gave these cursory lectures on Jeremiah, Lamentations, and had at least begun the Book of Isaiah in Cologne. This would correspond with his beginning in Paris with the *Sentences* rather than with such scriptural summaries. In spite of the rapidity of the composition of these lectures (indeed one gets the impression of a harried professor scratching down notes just before a class begins), and although they do not plumb many spiritual depths, Torrell remarks that these are the first truly "theological" works of Thomas Aquinas.[61] We are fortunate to possess these texts from Thomas's own hand, yet a further point can be made about works he wrote personally. It is possible that Thomas did not long remain secretary to Albert, not only because of his evident brilliance, but because of his horrendous handwriting, known to history as the *littera illegibilis* (the illegible writing).[62] It is no exaggeration to say that there are few scholars in the world practiced in the paleography necessary to decipher Thomas's handwriting. In the standard study of his script, Gils states that "Saint

Thomas was a man in a hurry."[63] His handwriting stumbles all over itself as if it cannot keep up with the torrent of thoughts pouring from his mind. Thomas makes many mistakes, and there are erasures, additions, and lapses in his text. Careful scholars have demonstrated Thomas at work here. His thought did not come fully formed from some Platonic innate idea, but rather gushed forth, was sweated over, changed, modified, and augmented. Torrell suggests we can see a maturation here when compared to Thomas's later works, which exhibit more discipline.[64] Here we see the progress of a young scholar from struggle, to increasing confidence, and finally to a mastery over himself and over his thoughts.

Albert maintained a school of future luminaries of the order. In addition to Thomas, there was also Ulrich of Strasbourg, who became prior of the German province and was a faithful disciple of Albert's philosophy, and Blessed Ambrogio of Sansedoni, a Sienese by birth, who developed into one of the most renowned preachers of the order.[65] Certainly there were also less famous students, whom Thomas perhaps tutored. One of his earliest works, called *De Principiis Naturae*, is an attempt to explain change from an Aristotelian perspective.[66] Scholars propose that Thomas meant it as a guide—perhaps even crib notes—in order to unpack Albert's commentary on Aristotle's *Physics*. If this is indeed what it was, we see the first indications of what will become a primary concern of Thomas's career, to be always available to answer questions and give advice and interpretations. Some question why Thomas did not further follow the path of Albert (or Aristotle for that matter) into deeper investigation of the natural world. It was not his "cup of tea." "Thomas was profoundly uninterested in the world around him, except inasmuch as it contained books and people."[67] The purpose for all intellectual endeavor was truth, love of God, and love of neighbor. Therefore, he never forbore taking time to answer and to teach (even when the questions were inane—see his responses to the six queries of the Lector of Besançon), and he was convinced that "to lead a man from error to truth—this he considered the greatest service which one man can render another."[68] Thomas's life was not to be beholden to some ivory tower, but rather he was committed to living out the motto that his own writings would give to the order: *Contemplata aliis tradere*, "to bring the fruits of contemplation to others."

Chapter 4

THE UNIVERSITY CRUCIBLE

The Idea of a University, circa 1250

The streets of the Latin Quarter of Paris in the late 1220s would have seen one of the most diverse cross-sections of society since the time when Rome was a world capital. Young men from around the Christian world were drawn to the university, which had become famous as a center of learning in Europe. It was there that the miracle of "Scholastic humanism"—as historian R. W. Southern called it—came to pass. From a variety of linguistic, cultural, and social backgrounds students and Masters rubbed shoulders with one another. Latin united them across time and space, rooting them in the past and serving as a medium of communication that dissolved the babel of vernacular languages. From the furthest corners of the continent they came, drawn by the coruscating promises of the pursuit of truth allied to a desire for advancement. The "life of the spirit was expressed in a collective organism where tradition and creativity were linked together."[1] Yet there was a flipside to the high ideals and speculative monuments described in the last chapter. The university is not only a home of ideas, it is the dwelling of real people, living the intellectual life in close physical proximity. It is an embodied entity, made up of flesh and blood, students and professors. Hastings Rashdall, an early scholar of higher education, expressed it well when he said,

> If [a person] would see how this leaven worked in the
> eager life of the schools, he must sit in the schools, listen

to lectures and disputations, and master their rules and practices. In short, he must live in the valley and mix with the crowd before he follows the great teacher to the heights, not take his stand on the high ground and peer with casual curiosity at the insignificant life below.[2]

So one must understand the people among whom such scholars as Thomas Aquinas made their living. Just as one must pursue him into the cloister, so also must we attend to his activities in the classroom.

These students and Masters who choked the streets of Paris came from all over Christendom. As time went on, the scholars of the university coalesced into four nations: the French, the Picards, and the Normans, while a catch-all group of other peoples—mostly from Northern Europe—was simply called the "English." These divisions led to rivalries and disturbances, for, as any denizen of a university town knows, students can be rowdy. This caused irritation among the local townspeople. The stress of town-and-gown relations is nothing new. Wherever groups of young have gathered they have always provoked tension with established powers and authorities. As it was, the residents of Paris cast a wary eye on these young scholars, though grudgingly tolerating them because of the prestige and pecuniary returns that they brought with them. March of 1229 was a particularly fraught time for this strained relationship. The Carnival season (literally "farewell to meat") was and remains a time of boisterous and unrestrained behavior, particularly in Catholic countries. One only needs think of Rio de Janeiro or New Orleans to have some idea of the social dislocation that such an event betokened. The whole of the Christian population took Lent very earnestly and kept it with care, and with far more rigor than today. It was the forty-day period of preparation for the high Feast of Easter. During the Middle Ages only one meal could be taken per day. Not only was meat forbidden for the whole of the period, but so were products related to meat, such as milk, cheese, and eggs. Given the strictness of such a fast, the preparatory time was one of raucous celebration, so that one could consume as much of the forbidden food as possible. The gravity of the season was underscored because, by the 1200s, it was during that time that Christians usually made their annual confessions. As a result, a certain amount of license came to be tolerated before Ash Wednesday. Carnival was a time of general riotousness, drinking, gorging, and merriment, during which many social customs were upended. When such ingredients were added to the heady elixir of youth, the results could be explosive.

Shrove Tuesday 1229 was the last day before the full weight of the Lenten fast was imposed. Students were also well aware that the Lenten season was the heart of the academic year, the period when the preponderance of work and study was accomplished. As if they needed one, this gave them still another reason to celebrate with, let us say, extreme festivity. Matthew Paris, a Benedictine chronicler who would later be quite biased against the mendicants, relates the story of how the students had been enjoying a day out, and they came upon a tavern that "by chance" happened to have excellent wine. After what was probably excessive consumption, a disagreement grew about the bar tab. Mutual declamations descended quickly into a general fight; the students and the tavern keeper exchanged blows. The innkeeper was bested, but then called his neighbors, who attacked the students and drove them away. The chastened students retired, but the next day returned with a crowd of fellow scholars with swords. They then proceeded to maltreat the innkeeper, seize the tavern and run the taps full open, drinking their fill until they tumbled out into the streets, causing still more mayhem. The neighbors appealed to the regent, Blanche of Castile, mother of St. Louis IX. Afraid of a general riot, she ordered the police to restore order, which they did with such gusto that they began attacking students indiscriminately, leading to the death of several innocent scholars. Making things much worse was the fact that students at university, if not actually tonsured clerics, legally had the "benefit of clergy," meaning that they were exempt from the jurisdiction of secular courts. Yet, the bishop of Paris was deaf to the protests of the university. He was irritated that the school existed outside of his direct supervision and was more disposed toward the complaints of the townspeople, who supported the local church. As a result, the Masters of the university gathered together and called for a general strike, suspending the operations of the whole school until such time as the situation would be resolved.[3] Clearly, behind the actual events lay significant tension that broke out into open conflict. Such machinations set the stage for the university in the time of Thomas Aquinas.

THE IDEA OF A UNIVERSITY

In order to understand this and subsequent conflicts, many of which involved Thomas personally, the first thing that should be understood are the roots of the university itself, and in particular how it came to hold such sway against powers both secular and spiritual. Writing in the early 1280s, a German author supplied a remarkable image of the function of the intellectual classes in Christendom. "If the empire, the priesthood, and the universities work in unity then Christendom is given life, enlarged, and guided. These three are like the foundation, the walls, and the roof, which are the components of a physical church."[4] It is the cooperation of the three that will provide health and success for the Christian people. Of all of these, the universities were the newest element, so it is useful to trace some of their history and development.

The first thing to notice is that the medieval word *universitas* had nothing to do with a particular location or physical plant (or—to the shock of modern college presidents and boosters—with a sports program). The origin of our universities was, first of all, a company of students gathered around a group of Masters. As mentioned previously, it was like a human person, which is composed of body and soul. The soul of the university was the speculative life of ideas, which gave order and harmony to the body, the enfleshed people who composed it. This is all that is needed; this is the core or essence of university education. The proper name for such an institution in the Middle Ages was a *studium generale*, a term that would be standard for the Dominican order. To be such a *studium* required several key factors. Students had to come from a broad range of territories and not simply be drawn from the local towns. In addition, there had to be a location, at least temporary, where a number of Masters could form a faculty of some higher study, be it Arts, Law, Theology, or Medicine. The key concept to be drawn from *universitas* was the idea of a body of people formed together in a corporation. The corporation was a legal body that could sue and be sued and that possessed the right to govern itself.

Such private corporations were key to the functioning of medieval society and one of its most significant achievements. Further, in order to reinforce the related concept of universality, by 1200 it was normative that such bodies could be chartered only by a power that claimed universal authority, meaning either the empire or the papacy.[5]

Before such an authorization could take place, an evolution was needed from the ad hoc forms of instruction found during the times of Peter Abelard, where Masters came and went and transient bodies of students moved from place to place. In order for the formalization of what would come to be known as "universities," many steps were needed. These procedures were common to many organizations at the time, ranging from confraternities to professional guilds. In the first place, the customs that had developed orally over time had to be reduced to written statutes. A recognizable body of governing laws was necessary to achieve public legal recognition, not to mention to assure internal order. This having been done, an organization was eligible for incorporation, creating a legal person with corporate rights before the law. This was usually accompanied by the appointment of common and permanent offices to be occupied by the community's leadership. Once all of these things were attained, the final step to full public recognition was the creation and use of a common seal. Such seals were essential in the Middle Ages, as they assured the legal validity of documents in civil and ecclesiastical cases. Corporations jealously guarded them, and their symbolic value was very high indeed. One can trace all these developments in the life of the University of Paris. There was a university guild of Masters as early as the 1170s, and by the year 1200 all of the component parts had fallen into place whereby they might act as a veritable *universitas* on the public stage.

By 1210 Innocent III had issued a bull recognizing and authorizing the written constitutions of the university. Innocent himself had studied at Paris—as had most of the popes of the era—and was quite sympathetic to the burgeoning intellectual life of the schools. It is good to ask why there was a special papal predilection for the universities. Several possible reasons present themselves. In the first place, most popes were products of the schools, as were many of the men who staffed the administration of the

church. The schools bore witness to the rise of a professional clerical culture, necessary for the proper functioning of an increasingly
complex papal curia. The rise of a written culture in both law and
theology, traditionally clerical pursuits, propelled this evolution.
It was natural that those who rose to prominence in the Roman
church would be the products of the new system and would prove
themselves grateful alumni when the time came to defend their
almae matres. A further reason prevailed on the papacy. The universities of medieval Europe were possessed of a universality that
transcended national and cultural boundaries, one that spoke the
learned language of the church. As such they were fountainheads
for catholic or universal sentiment, valuable at a time when the
papacy was expanding and consolidating its authority. Beyond
that, though, the universities also needed to appeal to a universal authority for their own recognition and claims of jurisdiction.
While they could theoretically appeal to the emperor (as at the
University of Naples), not everything was under his actual jurisdiction. It was far better to appeal to a more universal source.
Most centrally, though, the reason that the papacy valued these
centers of learning was related to its privileges of exemption. Like
that extended to the religious orders, the accordance of exemption to the universities was mutually beneficial to both scholars
and papacy. The Masters acquired independence from interference from any source, while the papacy was able to expand the
purview of its authority. As it had with the orders, the exemption provoked jealousy and anger at the novel privileges of groups
such as the university corporation of Paris. The *studium generale*
enjoyed numerous privileges showered upon it by the Holy See,
and it rankled the local clergy of Paris. It not only irritated the
bishop but also particularly affected the traditional center of
ecclesiastical power in the city: the secular canons of Notre Dame
Cathedral. They would prove to be the most implacable enemies
of the university.

The key issue was the right of leadership and supervision of
the university. In the 1100s the cathedral canons had acquired the
right to appoint a chancellor of the school, who was to act as a sort
of episcopal vicar to oversee the Masters. In a very real sense, all of
the efforts of the guild of Masters between 1170 and 1230 were
to free themselves from what they perceived to be the external

interference and arbitrary authority of this officer. Even though the chancellor originally held the power to approve or deny the granting of degrees and to deprive a scholar of his Mastership, he himself was not necessarily an academic. In addition, the chancellor often behaved in a high-handed manner, repeatedly asserting his authority over the school. This exasperated the Masters to such an extent that they labored for decades to free themselves, mainly by forming a legitimate corporation that could sue on behalf of their rights. When they had achieved such recognition, they could act contrary to the chancellor's wishes. For instance, if the chancellor approved someone unsuitable for a degree, the consortium of Masters could, as a corporation, refuse to admit the candidate to their number and forbid their students from attendance at his lectures. Rashdall puts this intractable situation perfectly when he says, "Each party tried by the use of its unquestionable prerogative to nullify in practice the equally unquestionable prerogative of the other."[6] Clearly there was a confrontation coming—one that required outside mediation.

By 1212 the matter had come to a head, as the situation was quickly becoming intolerable. The Masters, having achieved the rights of a corporation, appealed to the pope. The scholarly Innocent sided almost wholly with the Masters. The chancellor retained the power to grant degrees; however, he had to do it solely on the recommendation of the guild of Masters. The rights of students and Masters were also guaranteed against the autocratic interference of the bishop, which had occasionally included imprisonment in the episcopal prison for minor infractions. The chancellor was prohibited from interfering in the internal life of the *studium* and was only to imprison students for grave offenses. In addition, in 1215 the pope sent an envoy, Robert de Courçon, in order to mediate the situation and impose the papal terms. In spite of Robert's confirmation of the school's statutes, the church of Paris continued its onslaught against the university. After Innocent's death, the local church thought it could get improved terms from Pope Honorius III (r. 1216–27), for he, unlike Innocent, was not an alumnus. In this they were much mistaken. The new pope continued his predecessor's support for the universities, reiterating Innocent's decrees in both 1219 and 1222. Honorius himself also approved a new religious order founded among the Masters of the university, called *Valle Scholarum*, or the "Valley of Scholars."[7] The canons of Paris did achieve one victory. Apparently the Masters had created a corporate seal in order to signify their status, and they had done this without authorization. The pope commanded that this seal be broken. Nothing was done for several years, and the Masters continued to act as a corporation. In 1225, however, the papal legate—Romano, Cardinal of Sant' Angelo—had arrived in the city and had begun to listen with a sympathetic ear to the established clergy of Paris in their complaints against the upstart university. Romano summarily ordered the seal destroyed. The Masters saw this as an act of war against the privileges and corporate identity of the university, which had been acting independently de facto for at least a decade. The university—Masters and students together—descended en masse to the legate's house and, with swords, started a riot. They went so far as to break down the doors, and the cardinal was saved only by the timely arrival of royal troops. Such a backdrop helps to explain the tensions in the city during the carnival of 1229 and the subsequent strike of the Masters.[8]

The corporation was as good as its word; it dissolved itself and the university was closed. The Masters scattered to the four winds, planting the seeds of scholarship in many new cities. Some went across the English Channel to Oxford and Cambridge, while others migrated to places such as Toulouse, Reims, and Angers. This caused anxiety in many hearts. The university was really one of the only attractions of Paris, which, despite being a commercial center for northern France, was at the time merely the royal seat of a small territory. The secession of the scholars deprived the city not only of revenue but also of a massive source of prestige. While the secular clergy of Paris probably congratulated themselves, the royal family was aghast and began a fateful shift in favor of the university against their own clergy. The papacy too was shocked at the secession but could do little since the events of 1225 had transpired at the end of the pontificate of a sick and elderly Honorius. That changed with the election of a vigorous, far-seeing, and competent new pope. Gregory IX (r. 1227–41) was himself no mean scholar; he had attended both Paris and Bologna. He was not only completely attuned to the rise of the universities but was also passionately attached to the new mendicant orders. He had no time for the reactionary old guard who were jealously preserving their privileges. He recalled Romano, the chief source of friction in the debate, and intervened with his personal authority. At his order the Masters returned to Paris, armed now with the most significant document in their history, the papal charter *Parens Scientiarum*.[9] The papacy confirmed the right of the corporation to strike if its privileges were ignored. The office of chancellor was reduced essentially to figurehead status; indeed, it was now ordered to follow the instructions of the Masters in granting degrees. Over the course of the century the remaining powers of the chancellor would atrophy, and the university was able to act wholly independently in accordance with its own regulations. It had truly achieved the status of a medieval corporation, indeed one of the most privileged and powerful of the time.

Another issue was swirling below the surface of these institutional events, this time an intellectual one. Since the early years of the 1100s, new works had been making their appearance in the West as a result of the closing of the intellectual renaissance of the Islamic world. The bulk of these texts were from the Aristotelian school, in the main lost from the Latin West since the fifth century. In 1128 James of Venice translated Aristotle's *Posterior Analytics*, which, when combined with the existing translation of logical works made by Boethius, completed the *Organon*, or the collection of the whole of Aristotle's corpus of works on logic. This sped the introduction of high-level dialectic to the schools. Spearheaded by Abelard, the "New Logic" became the fundamental toolbox for the Scholastic movement and created stunning possibilities for precision and comprehensive summaries that came to characterize the works of university scholars. While the risks of the exposure of revelation to Aristotelian logic had already raised the ire of some commentators, particularly monastics, the reaction was nothing compared to the controversies to come. Over the course of the twelfth and early thirteenth centuries new works began to trickle back in, particularly through Sicily and Spain. The *Physics* and much of the *Metaphysics* were available by 1200 in addition to *On the Soul* and other works on the physical sciences. These came accompanied by many Arabic commentaries, particularly by Averroes. Confusingly, these Arabic commentators had mixed in much Neoplatonism in their analysis of Aristotle.[10] Through these works scholars discerned that Aristotle and the Arabs had attempted to demonstrate certain teachings that appeared to contradict Christian revelation, for instance, the Greek's insistence on the eternity of the world, the possibility of necessary emanations in God (eclipsing his freedom), the apparent impossibility of God knowing particular created things, and the supposedly Averroistic doctrine of monopsychism (or one single intellect for all of humanity).[11] Here was something truly dangerous: the possibility that a definitive, rational proof had come to a different conclusion than a truth of the faith.

It was not long before the authorities took direct action against the issues raised by this new treasury of philosophy pouring into the schools. While warnings about Scholasticism could be found throughout the 1100s, it is in the thirteenth century that one starts to discover institutional efforts to control the dissemination of Aristotelian works. In 1210 the Council of Sens, worried by a small efflorescence of pantheist thinkers, interdicted all the works of the Philosopher at Paris. However, this prohibition only tended to be applied to the Arts faculty, who were forbidden to lecture on the texts (though not necessarily to read them). Further, the admonition only applied to the region around Paris. This led to the opportunistic University of Toulouse advertising that its scholars could continue to read Aristotle.[12] Interestingly, it was at Toulouse that the Dominicans first began to attend lectures. This also meant that the prohibition did not affect other centers of learning farther afield, such as Oxford and Naples, where study of the Philosopher proceeded apace.[13] But the difficulties presented by Aristotle, and particularly by his Arab commentators, continued to agitate the intellectual world. When Robert of Courçon imposed his statutes on the university in 1215, he made the ban more explicit. He prohibited lectures from the *Physics* and the *Metaphysics*, in addition to commentaries drawn from them—most probably referring to Averroes.[14] It named those works specifically, an implicit toleration of other studies in his logical works and from the *Ethics*. While the Dominicans repeated such condemnations in their own constitutions, this was likely a result of their desire to conform to accepted academic standards of the time and betokened no specific animus toward the Philosopher.[15] It turned out that such regulations were like putting tape on a weakened dam. Aristotle was in the air, and people continued to read him with gusto. Even among the Dominicans, the flood of brilliant Arts Masters and students who flocked to the order had been steeped in Aristotle, something already evident in Dominican works from the 1230s.[16] Indeed, Gregory IX himself relaxed the prohibitions in 1231, saying that the Philosopher's books could be studied after a commission had expurgated their errors. Such a commission never finished its work, largely because of the successful efforts of the Masters of the European schools carefully to untangle Aristotle from his Arab commentators and to understand the Philosopher from within his own context. The ineffectiveness of the prohibitions was amply demonstrated in that the Bishop of Paris himself, William of Auvergne (r. 1228–49), freely used the banned works throughout his vast corpus.[17] That the reception of Aristotle was a fait accompli is clear from the 1255 statute of the Arts faculty that did not simply permit the study of the Philosopher, but rather *prescribed* it as integral to the curriculum. This success, however, did not mean that the problems in Aristotle's thought were solved; it merely meant that they took on new definition. It would take the efforts of men such as Albert and Thomas to make them wholly palatable to the Christian world.

THE COMING OF THE MENDICANTS

Dominic had dispatched his earliest brethren to Paris at the Pentecost chapter of 1217. Soon they were also established at Bologna. The General Chapter of 1220 ordered that the annual gathering of the friars alternate between each city.[18] The Preachers set themselves up along the academic axis of Christendom from the very beginning. At first, the city received them warmly, with no indications of future tension. In exchange for the spiritual suffrages of Mass and the rights of burial, they were accorded the convent of Saint-Jacques.[19] Apparently the Secular Master John of St. Alban's aided them in this transaction and then began to teach in the priory, making Saint-Jacques a teaching college of the university. Dominicans and other students began to be educated there, and John began to produce scholars such as Jordan of Saxony, who probably was John's teaching bachelor. Between 1225 and 1226 John of St. Alban's was succeeded as Regent Master by another Secular, John of St. Giles.[20] Under his mastership, Roland of Cremona began to lecture at Paris. Roland had already been a Regent Master in Arts at Bologna when he joined the order in 1219, but he now traveled to Paris to prepare for a Mastership in Theology. Such versatile scholars were emblematic of the level of academic achievement then percolating throughout the order. It seems that for most of their first decade in Paris things went smoothly for both the university and the order, but cracks were beginning to appear.

When the friars arrived, they brought with them a new style of religious life. In the past other religious had not really affected the university much. Many monks had eschewed the bustle of urban life and, while they pursued academic work, they did it behind the walls of their monasteries. Even when a group of scholars pursued religious vocations—such as the "Valley of Scholars"—they did it as a sort of pious association, remaining outwardly like the rest of the university. For most of its history the university had been the domain of the urban and traditionally "secular" clergy. The word *secular* here merely indicates that they came from what would be called the diocesan clergy today, those who were not part of any particular religious institute. The mendicants came with new claims, particularly to the *cura animarum* or "the care of souls." For over one thousand years the pastoral care of souls was in the hands of the secular clergy. Monks, after all, fled the world, while the new canonical orders, such as the Norbertines, were bound to liturgical service at a discrete church. The mendicants were "unmoored." They roved about freely and, with a copious collection of privileges obtained from the Holy See, claimed also to have the right to supervise the care of souls: the avowed domain of the secular clergy. In particular they were preachers. Because this was their primary mission, they became quite good at it. Men from the two orders became renowned for their skill at public preaching. The power of preaching at the time was considerable. Some have called it the primary form of mass media of the age.[21] People came from miles around to hear famous preachers, who would usually go on for hours, spellbinding audiences with their dizzying array of rhetorical skills. They were charismatic, doctrinally orthodox, and sometimes apocalyptic. Preaching had been a relatively minor activity of the secular clergy. Most did it rarely, if at all, and preaching was formulaic and programmed. It is no surprise that the laity began to be drawn to the sermons of the new orders. As we have seen, everyday urban Christians were hungry for new forms of religious devotion, and the Franciscans and Dominicans provided them. The increasing popularity of auricular confession, and the expertise with which the mendicants administered it, drew in the laity (and their money) to their churches and away from their own pastors. In addition, the corporate poverty of the new orders demanded a constant supply of alms, something that the urban middle classes were more than willing to provide. While this did not itself undermine the required tithes the laity had to make to the secular clergy, it did send up warning flags. What seriously rankled the clergy was that Christians began to ask for burial in the mendicant churches in order to secure the suffrages of these holy men. Burial brought with it bequests, and it was precisely this point that raised the most hackles among the secular clergy. These often considerable endowments were now being rerouted from their traditional destination in the parish churches run by the Seculars, and being directed toward the begging friars.[22] The alacrity with which the new orders bandied about their papal exemptions no doubt aggravated the situation.[23] Resentment was beginning to build.

On March 27, 1229, the corporation of Masters declared the strike and left the city. John of St. Giles did not consent and remained teaching at Saint-Jacques. He was followed by a handful of other Masters, primarily those teaching the Franciscan students (e.g., Alexander of Hales, who himself would later become a Minorite). Lectures went on as normal at the religious houses. This in itself would not have presented much of a problem, because no one really denied that religious students could continue to receive education in their own colleges. The mendicants disdained the strike in any case. Their students, having taken vows to the religious life, probably played no part in the raucous behavior of that year's carnival—why should they bother with such a matter? But a serious problem arose when John began to admit secular students to his lectures in the house of Saint-Jacques. Perhaps he had pity on young scholars who were too poor to transfer wholesale to a different city. In any case, and by any definition, the mendicants were now strikebreakers, crossing "picket lines" in a stunning lack of solidarity with fellow Masters of the corporation. But that was only the beginning. Since Roland of Cremona was now eligible to be advanced to the rank of Master, John simply disintermediated the guild and presented Roland as a candidate to the chancellor. Eager to have an opportunity to twist the dagger in his opponents, the chancellor acquiesced, and Roland became a Regent Master of Theology in Saint-Jacques.[24] Because the guild had by then temporarily disbanded and scattered, there was little it could do. Even in its absence the chancellor still had his authority. Things grew even worse for the Seculars. In 1230 John of St. Giles, still a secular Regent Master, made a stunning gesture, but far from unusual for that time. In the middle of a sermon on poverty in the Dominican church, he stepped out of the pulpit, immediately requested vestition in the order's habit, was received, and resumed the pulpit to finish his sermon—as a Friar Preacher.[25] While the sources present this as a surprise, it was probably well planned in advance. At least the receiving prior, most probably Hugh of St. Cher, must have had previous knowledge of the plan. It was not simply a religious conversion; it was a genuine academic *coup d'état*. John brought his academic chair with him. Now the Preachers had two academic chairs at the university, a remarkable feat considering that they had only arrived a decade previously. Roland's chair would be held in the future by French Dominicans, and John's chair would be for foreign Dominicans, held by such personages as Albert, Thomas, and Meister Eckhart. Such a move was not calculated to please the Secular Masters, who gritted their teeth in provincial towns while the Dominicans were going from strength to strength.

When the professors returned in 1231, they faced a fait accompli. In spite of Dominican successes, the Masters were mostly content that papal intervention allowed their reinstatement in Paris. While they had largely triumphed, they nursed their resentment against the mendicants over the next few decades, until the battle would break out again in earnest in the 1250s. In the meantime, the friars continued to prosper. Hinnebusch estimated that with the provinces sending a new round of three students every year, each for a three-year course of study, this meant that by 1230 almost 110 students annually were being trained at Saint-Jacques.[26] Around 1236 Alexander of Hales (ca. 1185–1245), already a famous Master (and strikebreaker), formally joined the Franciscans and brought his chair to that order. It is truly astonishing how an order started by the humble man of Assisi who disdained intellectual labor had, within ten years of his death, become itself an intellectual juggernaut that produced many fine scholars.[27] In the 1230s tensions were somewhat dampened by the contributions made by mendicant academics. Alexander had introduced the *Sentences* formally into the university curriculum, while Hugh of St. Cher (ca. 1200–1263) had both produced extensive work on biblical commentaries and provided a much more reliable edition of the Vulgate Bible for academic use. Hugh had incepted as Master under Roland, thus beginning the academic genealogy of the order.

The Dominicans certainly had utilitarian reasons for sending so many students. Their constitutions required each priory (which could be as few as twelve friars) to have a Lector in theology, a resident academic whose job would be to lecture the students in each house, creating an atmosphere of continuing education. These Lectors were to be completely dedicated to the brethren, and this especially included instruction in the practical matters most necessary to the Dominican vocation, particularly preaching and confession.[28] What this meant vis-à-vis Paris was that the vast majority of Dominican students had no interest in graduating from the institution, but merely in learning for three years and then being deployed throughout Christendom for the purposes of the order. The same can be said for the Masters. Unlike the Seculars, the mendicant scholars did not make Paris their permanent home. Until 1259 (the end of Thomas's first Regency) no Dominican Master stayed at the university more than nine years.[29] They made their reputations, then bolted—as did Albert when he departed in 1248 to found a *studium generale* at Cologne. It need not be said that these new Dominican *studia* were competition for Paris. While Paris remained preeminent, the mendicants' habit of using the institution's prestige and resources to make names for themselves, only to leave to found competing institutions, impressed itself deeply on the proud Masters of the university. One needs to understand this from both sides. The Seculars were wholly committed to the university, spending their lives and their talents there. They identified with the university, with its privileges and its prestige. From their perspective, the mendicants were scholarly freeloaders, capitalizing on the riches of Paris and then abandoning it. On the other hand, the mendicants had bigger fish to fry. Their mission was a universal one, and learning was to be a means, not an end in itself. This meant that their Masters were not attached to the university as an institution; they did not attach considerable importance to its privileges, nor did they pay much attention to its governance. The Dominicans' actions from 1229 to 1231 proved this amply. From the Secular Masters' point of view, the mendicants were bad academic citizens. They lacked the fellow feeling that one was supposed to obtain in medieval corporations. They failed in the duty of solidarity. Worst of all, they enjoyed the privileges of the university without bearing its burdens. While the view of the Seculars was more limited, they did have a point. It was the mendicants themselves who were causing the initial rupture.

THOMAS RETURNS

Thomas Aquinas, then in his mid-twenties, had spent at least four years in quiet and earnest study at the *studium* of Albert the Great in Cologne. In 1251 the Master General asked Albert to send someone to Paris to be a bachelor. When the German proposed his young protégé, Master General Johannes Teutonicus hesitated. Thomas was below the age of twenty-nine, the age stipulated by the university constitutions; Thomas was probably then twenty-six or twenty-seven years old. Knowing that the conditions in Paris were beginning to deteriorate, it is easy to see why the Master General might have had his reservations. Albert knew Thomas was intellectually ready for such a task, having mentored him for nearly half a decade. He certified that the young man was accomplished enough in matters of "knowledge and uprightness of life," as was required by Robert de Courçon's statutes.[30] Later events would confirm the German doctor's foresight. Paris was quite familiar to Thomas. He had likely completed his Arts course there between 1245 and 1248, a period when tensions with the mendicants had been quiet. He made many friends among the Arts students, and they would later be some of his strongest supporters against the secular theologians. Little did Thomas know he would be stepping into a minefield. Soon after his arrival in 1251, the conflict broke into the open.

Before we descend to details, however, something should be said about the academic life of the university in terms of ranks and distinctions. We shall make use of many terms such as "Bachelor" and "Master," and it is necessary to understand precisely what such things meant in the thirteenth century. A student coming to the University of Paris in the 1240s would have started at a very young age, perhaps thirteen or fourteen. Indeed, the relative youth of many of the mostly unsupervised students led to much of the chaos endemic to the Latin quarter of Paris. These students would work through the courses in Arts, particularly grammar, logic, and rhetoric, and would later enter upon the quadrivium for about six years, with much of the emphasis being laid upon the study of dialectic and the proper way to argue, debate, organize, and refute opponents. At the age of twenty, they would either leave or choose some professional path of higher study, which could be in Law, Theology, Medicine, or some advanced Art. Since Paris was the chief theological school in Christendom, it is likely that most students who did elect higher studies would affiliate with that faculty. The Theology students would then matriculate into the Theology faculty and spend six or seven years as an auditor. Four years were dedicated to the Bible, the "sovereign textbook of the schools." Following this would be two years spent learning Peter Lombard's *Sentences*. Only when he had completed that task would a postulant appear before a board of Masters, certify his attendance at the theological classes, and supplicate for his first course. It is probable that at this time there was much weeding out of inferior candidates. If the board of Masters judged him to be suitable, he would be admitted to reading his first course, and would formally become a Bachelor (a word whose etymology is ultimately unknown, but which probably comes from local vernacular usage of someone in a low position of a hierarchy). The Bachelor was placed under the supervision of a Master. One can see analogues both to the medieval guild system and to the modern university. A student was very much like a medieval apprentice, learning the tools of his trade. The Bachelor was equivalent to a journeyman, someone who had begun to work on matters directly relating to the business in question, while the Master was an accepted, full, and governing member of the guild. To put it in modern university terms, the Bachelor (from whence we get the term *bachelor's degree*) was like a promotion to journeyman, who could then begin to craft a "masterwork" (like a dissertation) that would be assessed by a board of Masters, who alone could judge its quality and were the only ones who could raise the worthy candidate to a position of equality, or "Mastership."

Once a medieval Bachelor was created, he served at the discretion of his Master. He performed functions much like those Thomas undertook in Cologne, such as preparing notes, tutoring students, and organizing research. Further, another function of the Bachelor was to give "cursory" lectures. For one year he had to give such lectures on the Bible, and in the next year he gave a similar class on the *Sentences*. The Bachelor was now also known by the name Cursor, be it *cursor biblicus* or *cursor sententiarius*, depending on where he was in his curriculum. The Cursor had to find time during the day to offer his lectures, as the coveted morning slots were reserved to Regent Masters. These lectures were meant to go through a text rapidly, introducing it to students. Thomas may have begun cursory lectures on the Bible upon his arrival in Paris; however, many scholars adhere to the idea that he began such lectures in Cologne.[31] I agree that Thomas arrived in 1251 and probably at least continued his cursory lectures there. These lectures involved the Books of Isaiah and possibly Jeremiah. The whole purpose of these was to acquaint the young Theology students with the simple, literal sense of the texts, since feats of dialectical and allegorical interpretation were reserved for the more leisured courses of the Masters. While accomplishing all these tasks, the Bachelor also had the duty of coordinating student disputations, which were modeled on the disputations of the Masters, and had the purpose of training both students and Bachelors in the technique of refined debate.[32] In the normal course of events, in the ninth year of study (probably at the age of twenty-nine or thirty) the Bachelor was required to undergo a *Tentamen* (a "testing"), whereby the Master would propose a question, and the Bachelor would have to defend it against the most senior Bachelors. This accomplished, he then began his cursory lectures on the *Sentences*. Once they had done this for at least nine months, they were called "formed bachelors," who continued teaching as they awaited the reception of their license. Thomas, it seems, short-circuited many of these procedures. This was both because of his native intelligence and due to his order's rather cavalier attitude toward university statutes. Indeed, his rapid and early advancement probably stoked the resistance that was just about to break into open conflict.

So Thomas presented himself in Paris, and probably began teaching in the autumn of 1251. It is more likely that Thomas was called in a period of peace rather than one of strife. He served as Bachelor under the supervision of Master Elias Brunet of Bergerac, who, strangely, is nearly unknown. Thomas, who had served Albert so well, did not seem to have preserved or copied any of his new Master's writings. Indeed, he dove into his own work with relish, and we begin to see the early thought of the friar beginning to emerge. Besides his cursory lectures, which are rather standard and hurried examples of the genre, Thomas began his own "master work" with a common task: to create his own commentary on the *Sentences* of Peter Lombard. The normal method of understanding Lombard's work was through its divisions into *res et signa* (things in themselves, and their signs). Books 1–3 were about the Trinity, creation, and the incarnation—the things in themselves—while Book 4 was on the sacraments, which were signs of deeper realities. Peter employed an Augustinian distinction between *frui* (things to be enjoyed for themselves) and *uti* (things to be used as means to other ends in a rightly ordered manner). The Trinity is *frui*, creation is *uti*, the incarnation bridges the two.[33] Thomas cleverly notes a new ordering that will become a motif in his commentary and that will undergird his later work in the *Summa Theologiae*. He places God at the center of his theology, the beginning and end of all things. The structure begins with God as he is in himself, then it focuses on the Trinity and creation, and finally on the fall or the going out of all things from God: the *exitus*. The incarnation begins the turn back, followed by the moral life and the sacraments. These constitute the *reditus*: the return of all things back to God. This approach would undergird much of the rest of his work, and in it one begins to detect a stunning originality.[34] Yet while its application to the *Sentences* was new, Thomas drew from a deep tradition. Such *exitus-reditus* meditations were drawn from the Neoplatonic tradition, and were mediated through Proclus's *De Causis*, Pseudo-Dionysius, and Avicenna.[35] In addition,

Thomas also made it plain that he was going to use philosophy and use it aggressively. Aristotle is by far the most cited thinker in the *Commentary*, twice as often as Augustine. What Thomas was constructing was a theology embedded in the Augustinian tradition, but in fruitful concurrent development with novel and innovative readings of Aristotle.

A further note should be added concerning the history of the reception of Thomas's thought. The *Sentences* remained the standard university text until very late in the Middle Ages. Today Thomas's thoughts on Lombard are generally neglected; indeed, they are not yet all translated into English. They are generally seen as being wholly superseded by the more mature *Summa*. Thomas's *Commentary* was read far more than the *Summa Theologiae* until the beginning of the sixteenth century. In order to grasp the development of Thomism, much more attention needs to be paid to this significant work, perhaps Thomas's key contribution within the university tradition. As we will see, the *Summa* was really a personal and pedagogical experiment, and it was not until the commentaries of John Capreolus in the fifteenth century that the *Summa* began again to attract attention.[36] Nonetheless, the foundations of Thomism are clearly evident in this early work. His rejection of Augustinian universal hylomorphism (form and matter) is already present—for example, that angels do not possess some sort of "spiritual matter" added to their nature. In the *Commentary on the Sentences* Thomas also rejects any actuality in prime matter, reducing it to pure unformed potential. The work defends the personal individuality of the active and passive intellects against Averroes. Most significantly, it also defends the idea of the unity of substantial form in humans, or the difficult metaphysical position that the spiritual soul in man is also responsible for all animal and vegetative activities.[37] This belief in particular would lead to substantial criticism of Thomas in the future. All of these teachings are novel and, while they would certainly be refined and developed throughout his long career, are all present at the beginning. These would go on to become some of the fundamental theses of philosophical Thomism.[38]

The young scholar did more than attend to his professional duties; he also had a mission to teach and to explain. As an aid to his brethren, he produced one of the most valuable interpretive keys to his thought during this period. *De Ente et Essentia* (On

126

being and essence) is, in a certain sense, an introductory guide to his developed metaphysics. Thomas shows himself to be an attentive student of Avicenna and his breakthrough notions concerning existence.[39] In the work, Thomas had three main objectives: to define being and essence, to outline the characteristics of essence, and to discuss the relation of essence to universals.[40] Former theologians had focused primarily on essence, or the nature of a thing. This was because of their intellectual descent from Plato, who had emphasized Ideal Forms as the most real things (remember that it was for this reason that Platonists were known as "realists" in keeping with their contention that Forms or Ideas were the most "real"). To put it simply, "essence" is the answer to the question, "What is it?" Thomas elevated the notion of Being, or the act of existence, to the primary metaphysical characteristic, because for him existence was the nature of God himself. Existence, for Thomas, was not what a thing is, but rather *that* it is. Essence only became "actualized" when it had received an individual act of existence. In this he shows an early break with the Platonic tradition. Following Aristotle, Thomas was a "moderate realist." For him essence had no independent existence. It was only found in real, existing things. Once those things were encountered by the senses, then our mind could abstract and understand the essence in itself, but that was a mental existence, not a real, separate existence. But Thomas pushes his fundamental distinction further. Only in God was essence identical with existence; his being *is* the unlimited act of existence. In everything else essence and existence were separate realities: God *is* existence itself; we merely have it, we *participate* in Being. Our essence is humanity, but humanity is only realized within each of our concrete individual existences. Thomas had established existence as the fundamental crux of his metaphysics. As Tugwell succinctly put it, "The mystery of things is not what they are but that they are."[41] While Thomas's thoughts would develop further, they would evolve along the lines he set in this seminal and key work. The maturity displayed in it demonstrates not only an astonishing grasp of the thorny metaphysical problems of the previous 1,500 years; it distills and analyzes them in such a way as to pave the way for a radically new approach to the metaphysics of Being.

Once again it is essential to remember that Thomas was not working in a vacuum. When he arrived at Paris, he returned to the epicenter of the movement of ideas, while running headlong into the maelstrom of antimendicant sentiment. While the mendicants were matriculating through the university, they had apparently refused to request the official license to teach as Master from the chancellor. The ostensible reason for this was that the humility of the mendicants precluded them from petitioning for the license themselves.[42] I would suspect that the rapid development of Dominican education and its demonstrable independence from the university had caused them to neglect this essential step. A further reason was because, by 1250, the license of the chancellor had essentially become a rubber stamp. The chancellor thus decided to exercise one of his few remaining reserve powers. If the orders did not ask for the license, he saw no reason to grant it. Given the impasse, the papacy had to intervene. Pope Innocent IV (r. 1243–54) ordered the chancellor to license a candidate who had accomplished all the requirements of study, even if he did not ask for it. This disintermediated not only the chancellor, but the entire faculty of Theology. If the mendicants merely presented one of their number who had completed his theological training at their colleges, the chancellor had to accept him. The Theology Masters did not really care if the chancellor's rights were curtailed; after all, they had been pursuing that for years. But the new regulations did provide grist for their growing irritation at the papacy and its mendicant creations. It also did not help that the mendicants accepted the papal directives with no little smugness, happy in the knowledge of high-level protection to continue to do as they wished, notwithstanding the complaints of the chancellor or faculty. But the heart of the problem went deeper. The real issue was the number of chairs being aggregated by the mendicant orders. There was a limited supply of Regent Masters' chairs to go around. When the university was founded, there were only eight chairs total. By 1250, however, the total number had increased to twelve; the Franciscans held one and the Dominicans tenaciously maintained two. Supply had not kept up with demand, and the mendicants seemed not only to be hoarding any available expansion, but actively to be thumbing their noses toward the corporation in which they enjoyed the benefits of membership.

Because of all these issues, the Theology faculty decided to act. In the academic year of 1252–53 it passed a statute against the mendicants. In order to limit the acquisition of more chairs, it decreed that no religious could become part of the consortium if his order did not already have a college at Paris (which meant no newer orders, like the Carmelites, could make inroads). Further, no Bachelor could be promoted unless he had already been apprenticed to a Regent Master who was recognized by the consortium. The key statute, however, was aimed directly at the Dominicans. All religious colleges should be content with only one chair and one Master. In this way they sought definitively to deprive the Dominicans of their second chair, one that admittedly had been in a constitutionally unclear situation since John of St. Giles had brought it to the Preachers during the strike of 1229–31. Matters remained deadlocked there for almost a year, but the situation was simply tinder waiting to be set ablaze.

The spark came in the turbulent carnival atmosphere before Lent of 1253. During the festivities civil officers killed a student during in a street brawl, while some other students were imprisoned in violation of the papal bull of 1231. At least in this case it appears that the authorities were certainly in the wrong, and in response the consortium of Masters called a strike. The mendicants refused to participate. Though the right to call a strike was guaranteed by papal authority, the Franciscans and Dominicans pleaded their exemptions and appealed directly to Rome. This enraged the consortium. The mendicants would not even accept the university privileges accorded by papal decree, and indeed, as soon as there was trouble they went over the heads of the Masters back to Rome itself. When the Masters enjoined an oath to obtain justice for the slain student and the other imprisoned scholars, the mendicants again refused. For this they were formally expelled from the consortium. The friars ignored this and continued not only to teach their own students (which would have been permissible in any case) but also to accept external students and teach as if they had the plenary authority of Regent Masters. In April 1253, the university imposed an oath on all Masters to follow all the statutes of the consortium and to observe strikes. As Rashdall cannily comments, the Masters themselves compromised their position by relying too much themselves on papal grants and privileges, losing much of the self-governing character of their institution.[43] What was developing then was a contest between papal favorites—the university and the mendicants. The issue would have to be settled solely by an exercise of papal authority.

Unfortunately for the Masters, they had fallen out of favor with the papacy. The mendicants were now the apple of the pope's eye. They were the tip of the spear of orthodoxy, spreading rapidly through the Christian world and beyond. They had stood beside the pope in the life-or-death struggle with Frederick II, had served as legal and theological advisors of the highest order, and had achieved positions of trust in the church serving as inquisitors, bishops, and cardinals. The orders had no problem gaining privileges, something particularly characteristic of the Preachers. Thomas of Cantimpré, a thirteenth-century Dominican chronicler, noted this when he described Gregory IX creating a new verb just for Johannes Teutonicus. The pope was so partial to the Dominican Master General that he said to write down whatever the Master wished, then *Ego bullabo* ("I shall 'bull' it [command it]").[44] The Dominican proctors wasted no time and indeed acquired bulls commanding the readmission of the mendicants to the consortium, pending a papal decision. On July 1, 1253, Innocent IV ordered the reinstatement of the mendicant Masters. For some reason, the bishops entrusted with the mission of promulgating the bull decided simply to delegate the job to subordinates. Fatefully they selected the traditional enemies of the consortium: the canons of Notre Dame. The canons now had a powerful weapon to wreak some vengeance upon their foes. They decided to enforce the papal sanctions in one fell swoop, without any warning. One morning at Sunday Mass, the decrees were read from all pulpits in Paris, effectively suspending all the Masters and shutting down the university. Immense consternation followed as the consortium of Masters decided to resist with all its might. There is no evidence of collusion between the mendicants and the canons, but I find it difficult to believe there was none. The Dominicans had, after all, agitated for the bulls; they must have known they were coming. It is indeed possible that the Preachers had been the ones to suggest that the canons be entrusted with the delegation.

Matters were quickly coming to a head. The consortium of Masters decided that they would continue to resist and to prevent the mendicant Masters from affiliating, in spite of the papal bulls. When the academic year resumed in 1253 the Masters sent their bedels to enforce the ban. The bedel was the academic official charged with the collection of fees, the posting of decrees, and the general policing of the university body. A particularly energetic bedel appeared at the doors of Saint-Jacques, ready to publish the edict of the Masters on the doors (it should be remembered that church portals were the public message boards of the Middle Ages). He was espied by young Dominican friars. Armed with the knowledge of papal approval, they decided to take out their anger upon the person of the bedel. They pursued and accosted him, apparently to the point of drawing blood. The sight of young friars physically assaulting a university official was a sign of the serious disagreements then percolating through the city. While Thomas most probably did not participate in the assault, he was certainly present for it, and was just as certain of the rightness of the friars' cause as the rather high-spirited youths. Not even the university rector was able to publish the decree, being met with similar resistance, nor was the papal legate able to intervene. The Masters decided that they would make an appeal to all Christendom, and issued an encyclical letter to defend and explain their position in early 1254.[45] They complained in particular of the multiplication of chairs for the religious orders, while there were only nine for the secular clerks (not including the three ex officio chairs reserved for the canons of the chapter of Notre Dame). As a result, there were almost no opportunities for promotion for brilliant young secular students. This problem was compounded because secular Masters often remained in their chairs for long periods, while there was massive turnover from year to year as the religious orders advanced one after another of their students through the academic hierarchy. Further, the income of the secular Masters was limited by the fees of their students. The mendicants had a massive machinery of charity behind them, not to mention subventions from priories all over the world, that paid the way of their young scholars to come to Paris.

The university Masters were feeling increasingly isolated. In addition to their traditional enemies in the chapter and in the episcopal palace of Paris, they now had to face down the papally sponsored mendicants. The situation was made worse because the French court—traditionally a partisan of the university—had begun to patronize the mendicants. William of Tocco reports that

Thomas and King Louis IX of France had a particularly close relationship.[46] While Tocco may exaggerate the affinity of the two
men for each other, it is clear that the court as a whole had turned
in favor of the mendicants. As early as the time of Jordan of Saxony in the 1220s, Louis's mother, Blanche of Castile, had been an
avid supporter. Louis was known to use the mendicants as his
court confessors and advisors. Known for his extremely pious
nature, Louis naturally tended toward the new orders.[47] The Masters could hope for little assistance from the French throne, their
former partisans. Besides their effort at a public relations offensive
with the encyclical letter of 1254, they were also active on the
most salient front, the papal curia. Innocent IV was himself a
famous canonist and former professor of canon law. He had showered the Dominicans in particular with signs of favor, for they had
served as his intrepid ministers against the emperor, against heretics, and in the expansion of the purview of papal authority. He
had even canonized their second saint, Peter of Verona, in 1253
after an interval of only eleven months. What hope could the Masters expect from such a pontificate? They nonetheless decided to
make a last appeal to the court of final resort. In this they were led
by the ambitious secular Master William of St. Amour, who would
become the enemy par excellence of the Dominican life.[48] Almost
at once, the situation began to turn in the Seculars' favor. First,
they had new ammunition following the publication of a work
entitled *Introduction to the Eternal Gospel* by the Franciscan
Gerardo de Borgo San Donnino.[49] Using apocalyptic language, the
Introduction argued that the world had entered into the third age
of the "Eternal Gospel" of the Holy Spirit. The legalistic second
age was concluded, and the third age would appear in 1260 with
the coming dominion of new groups of holy men who would lead
the church. Much of Gerardo's work was heretical, but it also
struck a chord. It criticized older forms of ecclesial life, while lion-
izing the new and exciting religious orders. As C. H. Lawrence
evocatively said, "Gerard's essay in millennial fantasy dropped into
the Paris dispute with the explosive force of a bomb falling into a
quarrelsome duckpond."[50] Armed with this, William and his com-
rades published a condemnation and carried it with them when
they appeared before the papal curia. Unexpectedly, but strategically, the Franciscans capitulated. There had always been a rivalry

between the two orders, but this was a serious assault on mendicant solidarity. They were more exposed to attack because of the Franciscan authorship of the *Introduction* and rumors that highly placed men in the order approved of it. Yet in reality, at least as far as Paris was concerned, the Minorites had less skin in the game. They only had one chair, and so already fulfilled the Secular Masters' demand that the orders be limited to that alone. They were also less committed to the academic life, which was irreducibly central to the Dominicans. The faculty permitted the holder of the Franciscan chair, Bonaventure, to lecture, but as a pointed reminder of the Masters' renewed power, he was not admitted to the consortium.

The situation of the Friars Preachers quickly darkened. Innocent IV, near the end of his life and very possibly quite sick, heard William's report with alarm. He immediately ordered that all Masters, religious included, had to submit to the decisions of the consortium.[51] William sensed blood in the water, and went far beyond academic critique and began to denounce the mendicants wholesale. Innocent, up to that point a fierce partisan of the Dominicans and Franciscans, completely folded. He issued a bull entitled *Etsi Animarum* on November 21, 1254, that could have been utterly disastrous to the new orders.[52] Nearly all of the privileges the mendicants had obtained over the previous thirty years were summarily stripped. This bull stretched far beyond the mere academic concerns of the university and touched the very fabric of the new movements. Only the persuasive power of William coupled with increasing sickness can begin to explain this astonishing reversal of papal position. All of their exemptions to hear confessions and to preach without the permission of the local ordinaries were dissolved. The mendicants were prohibited from unlicensed celebration of the sacraments, except in cases of necessity. While the local bishop was preaching, they were forbidden to give sermons. The bull ordered them to cease requesting donations and burial bequests, a major source of income. Fully implemented, this would have spelled the end of the new orders. Apparently the leadership of the Preachers ordered the praying of the Penitential Psalms and the saying of litanies against these injunctions. These proved effective. Innocent died on December 7. Such a close coincidence between the bull and the death of Innocent led to a common saying: "Beware the litanies of the Friars Preachers."[53]

Almost overnight the winds of fortune shifted. On December 20 the former cardinal protector of the Franciscans became Pope Alexander IV (r. 1254–61). He immediately suspended enforcement of *Etsi Animarum*. The new Dominican Master General, Humbert of Romans (r. 1254–63), had been elected in the midst of the crisis. He was acutely aware of how much the friars had depended upon papal power, and now he attempted to pilot the order in a more irenic direction toward the other powers of Christendom. Humbert decided to make certain concessions, in deference to the bishops and in cooperation with the Franciscans. In this way he cleverly made the dispute about the university rather than having a "Dominicans-versus-the-world" debate.[54] Impressed by Humbert's conciliatory attitude, and having duly considered the matter, Alexander IV issued *Quasi Lignum Vitae* on April 14, 1255. He restored the privileges of the orders, clarified the limits of their prerogatives, and commanded that the two Dominican Masters be admitted to the consortium, on pain of clerical suspension. The friars were supposed to observe a strike called by two-thirds of the Masters, but this effectively meant that they could block any strike they wished.[55] William of St. Amour was shocked at these developments, for rarely had a situation deteriorated as quickly as the one he now faced. He launched a new two-pronged strategy. On one hand he turned to propaganda to whip up students and the Parisian laity against the friars, and on the other he began to spend his energies writing an intellectual defense of the rights of the university that would serve as an academic critique of the mendicant life as a whole. He was answered by the Franciscan Master Bonaventure at the same time that the Dominicans were still laboring to reenter normal university life.

In the short term, William was successful. Intellectually, he achieved a victory in that the *Introduction to the Eternal Gospel* was condemned as heretical by a commission that included the Dominican Cardinal Hugh of St. Cher. This decision particularly affected the Franciscans, who were now in the position of having to reaffirm their orthodoxy, especially since their Minister General, John of Parma (r. 1247–57), was rumored to be sympathetic to the book. William's positions were also extremely significant for the other Secular Masters, and they took a dramatic step in response to what they perceived as undue outside interference in their corporation, as well as an attack on their privileges. At the end of the summer of 1255, the university took the extraordinary step of threatening to dissolve itself. Since the injunctions were addressed to the corporation, the commands and penalties were nullified if there *was* no corporation. The Masters declared that they had no intention of depriving the friars of their own *studia*, just as long as their rights to make binding statutes on the members of their own consortium was maintained. William was active on another front as well. He whipped up popular agitation so significantly that the friars could not leave their convent for fear of being pelted with offal and rocks. He inspired Rutebeuf and other vernacular poets to write songs against the friars, portraying them in the worst possible light.[56] Partisans fired arrows against the walls of the convent. In the fall of 1255 Florent of Hesdin was set to be inaugurated as a new Dominican Regent Master. Because of the incipient threat of violence, King Louis IX had to send royal archers to protect the ceremony.[57] Thomas and his brothers were effectively confined to the convent of Saint-Jacques, continuing their studies certainly, but in the knowledge that they were an island surrounded by enemies and that their allies seemed very far away indeed.

It was at this point that Master General Humbert scored several marked public relations victories. First, he issued a common encyclical with John of Parma in 1255, emphasizing the unbreakable unity of the two orders.[58] Usually the Masters General sent these encyclicals in their own names to their own orders, so this common text indicates something genuinely serious. The irenic tenor of the letter belies the very real issues that simmered between the Franciscans and the Dominicans. However, in public they made nice and Humbert defused a serious threat from his own flank. He issued much more realistic assessments internally to the convent at Orleans in 1256 and then to the order as a whole in 1257, describing the attacks on the order at Paris as nothing less than satanic.[59] Within the privacy of the order he reinforced his own troops in the face of such virulent assaults. But it was at Pentecost 1256 that he scored his most serious victory. Knowing that the Chapter General would be held in Paris, he decided upon a risky strategy. Though the debate was then at its highest pitch, he decided to frame the chapter as a victory lap for the order. Cleverly he acquired the relics of the popular new saint Peter Martyr and made them the centerpiece of the meeting. In doing so he deflected attention from the order and toward the new martyr, symbolic of the devotion of the friars to orthodoxy and to the church. Under this aegis he invited the king, court, and church and civil authorities to venerate the new saint. Nearly the whole of the French aristocracy turned out. Louis was the guest of honor at the chapter, and the relic-hungry king acquired some choice new bones for his collection. A massive concourse of notables from both church and state honored the saint and, indirectly, covered the assembly with a halo of approval. Thomas and his brethren no doubt were present at this exposition of the relics of their fallen brother and at the chapter in which such a display had been orchestrated by Humbert.[60]

At this point William of St. Amour overplayed his hand. He had written a compendious list of charges in a book entitled *The Perils of the Last Times.*[61] In particular he put forth certain ecclesiological theories that the system of bishops and parishes found its roots in the New Testament. Conversely, the friars were extraneous to such a system and were very possibly the pseudoprophets spoken of by St. Paul (2 Tim 3:1–9) and the wandering monks called *gyrovagues* condemned by St. Benedict. This meant in particular that they should be excluded from pastoral care (and, one might mention in passing, all the income that went with it). William also particularly attacked the practice of begging, declaring that gospel poverty meant either living with possessions in common (monks) or by dignified manual labor. William did not stop there; he challenged Bonaventure in open debate. They traded barbs without a solid resolution (though Bonaventure's notion that "spiritual labor" was worthy of remuneration would later recur in antisecular defenses). William's downfall came when he decided to preach publicly the whole of the academic year on the hypocrisy of the mendicants. In particular he fell into a sort of apocalypticism of his own, declaring that these friars were the false prophets whose coming foretells the end of days. In some of these sermons he made veiled attacks on the king himself. These sealed his fate. While William had been criticized by some local prelates for his intemperance, Louis decided to remit the whole case to Rome. Astonishingly, the university assigned William to be one of the proctors to argue his own case before the papal curia. Given the recent behavior of the university, as well as the pope's partiality toward Louis and the orders, this was an act of serious obtuseness.

THOMAS THE MASTER

During all of this, Thomas had completed his probationary baccalaureate and was presented to the chancellor for the license. One can only imagine the climate in which this young scholar found himself. The life of the mind is still the life of the body, and no one knew that better than Thomas. That he could function and be so productive as an academic in the midst of such strife is a signal testimony to his abilities. One should also measure his output against the surviving work of other Dominican scholars at Paris in the 1250s. There is almost none. While this may be explained as a function of Thomas's later popularity and lack of surviving sources from his contemporaries, that does not tell the whole story. An abundant amount of work exists from Preachers in the decades before and after (and from those not present in Paris). It seems possible that Thomas alone was able to thrive in this exceptionally difficult situation. One of the most distinctive features of Thomas's character was a massive imperturbability in the face of trying circumstances. Before we examine some of Thomas's efforts as Regent Master of the foreign chair at Saint-Jacques, we should look a bit more deeply into the procedures of the university in order to see what exactly the function of this figure was.

When the chancellor certified that Thomas had completed his baccalaureate period in February of 1256, the university granted him the highest degree then awarded, the *Licentia ubique docendi*. This degree (which, though not currently terminal, survives at church institutions as the licentiate) was the most valuable acquisition that a scholar could receive from a chartered *studium generale*. This "license" was essentially the certification from the university that one had the right to teach anywhere. It gave the person the privilege of teaching or of setting up a school for himself anywhere in Christendom and certified his education at the top level of academic achievement available at the time. However, not all of those with licenses were allowed to "incept" as Regent Masters. Those who permitted that privilege were the corporation of Masters themselves. It is also good to note that, while today "professor," "doctor," and "master" have interdependent but distinct connotations, in the Middle Ages they were essentially the same.[62] Resistance to the mendicants was made worse because it was clear that Thomas was under the canonical age of thirty-five; indeed he was probably only thirty-one or thirty-two when licensed. Objections from the Secular Masters were relatively ineffectual, however, since they had previously dissolved themselves as a corporation. Thomas seems to have become somewhat of a pawn in this high-stakes game. Alexander IV wanted to use Thomas's degree as a sort of *coup de grace* that would symbolize his supremacy over the university. It appears that he sent a bull to the chancellor commanding that Thomas be given the license. The chancellor anticipated this papal intervention and, in the absence of the university Masters, exercised his right and awarded Thomas the degree. It also appears that there were other suitable candidates, but the pope and the order pushed him to the front of the line.[63] In addition to the young friar's recognized brilliance, it is possible that the pope wanted to demonstrate his authority in the matter by putting forward someone under the canonical age. Later witnesses in the canonization depositions reported that Thomas said that he was quite upset about this elevation, perhaps conscious of being advanced beyond more senior friars, and nervous that this licensure would bring down upon his person the wrath of the Secular Masters.[64] Indeed, Thomas was also acutely aware that he had not yet finished his commentary on the *Sentences*, which would not be complete until 1257.[65] William of St. Amour was also loudly declaiming against the "humility" of friars who went about accepting honors, "poor men" who bore the title "Master." Thomas was already working on a book countering William of St. Amour's arguments; in it he wrote, "It is untrue to say that the act of teaching is an honor. It is the teacher's office which is honorable. And, even if religious renounce all honors, they cannot renounce all honorable functions.... 'Honor,' to quote Aristotle, 'is the reward of virtue.'"[66] According to tradition, a vision (or perhaps a dream, following Gui) of an elderly friar who counseled him to accept dispelled Thomas's doubts.[67] The friar also gave him a theme from Psalm 103 (104) for his inaugural lecture: "You water the hills from the high places, the earth shall be filled with the fruits of your works." This tale was in circulation while Thomas was alive; it is one of the best-established stories in his biography.[68]

The inauguration or inception of a Master was a significant event in the life of a medieval university. Such an inception was distinct from the licensing by the chancellor and meant that the scholar became a Regent Master: an active professor at the university currently holding a chair. Because of an annoying nineteenth-century German predilection, professors today stand to lecture. This was not the case in the Middle Ages. The position of magisterial authority is sitting. When Christ was depicted teaching in art, he was in a seated position. Indeed, the very name *cathedral* is derived from a bishop's chair. Traditionally, when they were fulfilling their roles as official teachers, professors would do so sitting. This can still be seen when the pope reads an official declaration of canonization: he does so from the throne, or the *cathedra*. Similarly, university Masters also had magisterial powers, and all teaching was done from a chair and table on a raised platform. We still retain a vestige of this today when we speak of certain professors holding "chairs." In order for a Master to be invested with formal teaching authority, which included official lectures and the right to settle disputed questions, it was necessary for him to go through a two-day ceremony. On the day before the investiture, there was a Vespers disputation in the evening. The aspiring Master and senior Bachelors would have proposed and discussed several questions, and the proceedings were usually presided over by the novice's old Master. At the end of the debates, the presiding Master gave a commendation of Scripture, which usually devolved into a "roast" of the new candidate.[69]

The next day was the formal ceremony of "birretation." This was one of the most solemn activities at the school, and all lectures were suspended so that the full corporation of Masters could be present. The inceptor sat in the front between the representative of the chancellor and his former Master, while the fellows were arranged alongside in order of seniority. The Presiding Master then placed the biretta upon the head of the new Master, as a symbol of his authority. Rashdall makes the intriguing suggestion that this may be a relic of the old Roman method of manumission, the liberation of the scholar from the servitude of being a pupil.[70] Later there was a presentation of a Master's ring and an open book, but this particular part of the ceremony may not have been in place by the 1250s. In any case, the biretta was the symbol of magisterial authority, and gave its name to the ceremony. This was followed by the kiss of peace from all the other Masters present. This ceremony probably has roots in the ordination rituals of the church, particularly the Minor orders. At the invitation of the chancellor's delegate, the new Master was "chaired" or seated upon the magisterial cathedra and invited to begin his *principium* lecture, which, in Thomas's case, was on the text, "You have watered the mountains from the high places." This lecture was fortunately discovered in 1912 and is on the subject of the mediation of truth by the teachers of sacred doctrine. Thomas preached that the university Master indeed has a certain eminence, whom he compares here to the mountains, yet any dignity he possesses is because he has received the rain of divine wisdom from heaven. His academic position thus causes such wisdom to course over the whole earth. The speech was at the same time an affirmation of the honor of the Mastership and an effective refutation of William's false teachings regarding humility. I suspect that this ceremony was simplified in the case of Thomas. Most of the Masters would have refused to come, and so there would be no admission of Thomas to the corporation (that would have to wait until early 1257). The event was probably attended only by the chancellor's representative, Thomas's former Master, and perhaps the other Masters of the religious orders, along with their students. This was because the antimendicant furor was at its height.

Though both Thomas and Bonaventure were excluded from the consortium, they still used their considerable abilities to refute the doctrines of William of St. Amour and his partisans. In 1256, right at the beginning of his Regency, Thomas wrote "Against Those Who Attack the Religious State and Profession." This work, while polemical in tone, was mild compared with the virulence of the attacks against its author. Thomas, who had been awarded the title of Master, had also learned to master himself. Rarely was there ever a man less disconcerted by the course of events, yet even in the midst of his almost preternatural calm, he came to the defense of his beloved religious order and its rights and privileges in the church. This work carefully analyzes and dismantles the scriptural exegesis of William of St. Amour. Few indeed are the professors who have to begin their careers with a work defending their very right to teach! The work is a two-pronged defense of the rights of the new mendicant orders as well as a robust articulation of their claims to become university Masters. Thomas primarily uses Gratian's *Decretum* (the principal law book of the church) and the *Ordinary Gloss* (the authoritative commentary on Scripture). Since William bases his case primarily upon these in order to root the position of the Seculars in terms of recognized authorities, Thomas deploys them to counter his interlocutor's objections. In this he gives a preview of one of his most fundamental methodological positions:

> Sacred Scripture, since it has no science above itself, can dispute with one who denies its principles only if the opponent admits some at least of the truths obtained through divine revelation; thus we can argue with heretics from texts in Holy Writ, and against those who deny one article of faith, we can argue from another. If our opponent believes nothing of divine revelation, there is no longer any means of proving the articles of faith by reasoning, but only of answering his objections—if he has any—against faith. Since faith rests upon infallible truth, and since the contrary of a truth can never be demonstrated, it is clear that the arguments brought against faith cannot be demonstrations, but are difficulties that can be answered.[71]

It is futile to argue with an interlocutor if he does not accept your authorities. To hurl biblical proof-texts at an unbeliever is, at minimum, useless and, at most, damaging. Battle must be joined only with the weapons of the intellectual enemy. As Thomas later argues,

> Theology especially ought to use the authorities which are accepted by those against whom one disputes. If one is arguing with Jews, it is useful to adduce the authorities of the Old Testament. If one debates with Manicheans,

who reject the Old Testament, then one should use only the authorities of the New Testament: if yet one disputes with schismatics, who accept the Old and New Testaments, yet not the teachings of our Holy Doctors, like the Greeks, one should argue from the Old and New Testaments, and from those Doctors which they receive. Yet if one's interlocutors accept no authority, one must appeal to natural arguments from reason.[72]

In this debate with William, Thomas has available the full panoply of reason, Scripture, and tradition, and does not stint in using them. William had argued that the Minors and Preachers were false prophets and forerunners of Antichrist. In response, Thomas argues for the mendicant life of poverty, chastity, and obedience as the highest form of life, whereby the person sacrifices his or her human goods as an offering to God. William had asserted that the new orders only pretended to the life of the apostles because they did no manual labor. For Bonaventure and Thomas, preaching and teaching the word of God is also labor, even though these activities were not performed with one's hands. Rather, they were spiritual works of mercy, and because of that the friars were entitled to live a simple life from a modest revenue of alms. Little noticed by many commentators, Thomas's defense of the intellectual life parallels the justifications for the new professions then burgeoning throughout the European continent as a result of the commercial revolution. In the transition to a knowledge and market economy, whole new classes of professions arose that seemed to have no inherent productive value: scholars, lawyers, accountants, and the like. More conservative critics tended to suspect such vocations. Thomas here dismisses these detractors with a virile defense of the value of intellectual labor and its claim to remuneration—particularly in its highest form: the transmission of sacred doctrine.

Thomas had begun his career as a Master in the *Studium* of Saint-Jacques in an atmosphere of antimendicant agitation. Slowly the situation calmed. In June 1256, William of St. Amour had finally foundered on his own hubris. Confident in the lecture halls of the Seculars in Paris and feted in the taverns of the city by his troubadour allies, he found a frosty reception waiting for him at the papal curia. Alexander had ordered him deprived of his benefices (i.e., his income) for his stubborn refusal to admit the friars to the consortium. In October the pope condemned *De Periculis* (though significantly not as heretical), and he ordered all copies to be burned. William remained impenitent to the end and was exiled from Paris to his home village, never to return. The other Secular Masters acquiesced and reluctantly admitted Thomas and Bonaventure to the consortium, although, for the latter, it was too late. Before his admission had come through, he had been promoted to Minister General of the Franciscan order. In that role he disciplined the friars responsible for the *Eternal Gospel* and ordered friar Gerard of Borgo San Donnino into perpetual imprisonment. He had, after all, been the spark that had lit the fire at Paris and who had brought the reputation not only of his own order, but of all mendicants into disrepute. In December of 1257, *Quasi Lignum Vitae* came into full effect. Even so, in order to maintain peace, there were some remaining restrictions. The number of mendicant chairs was absolutely capped at one Franciscan and two Dominican. Secular students, by custom, generally refrained from the lectures of friars and only incepted under Seculars. Since the prescriptions of the pope only applied to the Theology faculty, the Arts faculty reserved the right to refuse entry to mendicant Masters. It is not too much to say that the animosity of the Arts faculty was broken down largely by Thomas himself, whose dedication to the philosophical sciences they particularly valued, and he apparently earned friendship and sincere admiration from the Arts Masters by the end of his life. The Theology faculty, a group that increasingly included his own Franciscan colleagues, remained implacable opponents to Thomas up to his death—and beyond.

The position of Regent Master carried with it certain responsibilities. Peter Cantor laid these out half a century earlier. The reception of the license gave the Master the obligation to lecture, to dispute, and to preach.[73] He had to lecture on the Scriptures in the coveted morning class slots. These lectures were not the "cursory" efforts of lightly going through a text's literal meaning. These were to be sustained analyses of the scriptural text, sometimes taking several years to complete the analysis of a single book. Indeed, the most ancient academic title of the schools was "Master of the Sacred Page," *Magister in Sacra Pagina* (only later in the thirteenth century did "Doctor of Sacred Theology" become common).[74] The Master would conduct the lectures seated on his platform, with students arranged in front of him, as he proceeded verse by verse through the whole of the scriptural text. These lectures generally discussed the traditional four senses: literal, allegorical, moral, and apocalyptic. They would proceed through etymological analysis, linguistic study, and the commentaries of the fathers. While this method was far removed from modern critical scriptural study, it was nonetheless deep and rigorous, imbued with an abiding sense of Scripture as the inspired word of God. During the first Parisian regency, Thomas lectured on Matthew. He was relatively unique among his contemporaries in that he focused primarily on the literal text. Usually this sense was restricted to the introductory cursory lectures of biblical Bachelors, but Thomas underscored it as the primary method of interpretation. In this he was accompanied by Roland of Cremona and Albert, yet it was Thomas's use that proved so enduring. The fathers of the Alexandrian, Platonic tradition delighted in allegorical symbolism, which, for example, sees Christ on every page of Scripture. This mystical interpretation blossomed within the church community and provided deep material for spiritual development and meditation. The straightforward Thomas recognized a limitation in this overreliance on allegory. It was possible to miss the direct sense of Scripture and to build castles of spiritual interpretation in the air. He would later write,

> Thus in the bible no confusion results, for all the senses are founded on one—the literal—from which alone can any argument be drawn, and not from those intended in allegory, as Augustine says (Epis. 48). Nevertheless, nothing of Holy Scripture perishes on account of this, since nothing necessary to faith is contained under the spiritual sense which is not elsewhere put forward by the Scripture in its literal sense.[75]

Later commentators who blamed the Middle Ages for aggressively spiritualizing interpretations of the Bible did not have Thomas to blame. When reading Thomas's scriptural commentaries, one needs to realize that most of them come from lecture notes taken by one of his scribes; these are called *reportationes*. It seems that Thomas only corrected one of his lecture *reportationes*: the commentary on the Gospel of John. In a second category were the works written or dictated by the professor himself, then corrected and fashioned into a finished product. Into this category fall the Aristotelian commentaries, as well as the "disputed questions."[76]

The second responsibility for a Master was to dispute. This usually came in the form of "disputed questions." These were extended examinations of difficult issues and often were some of the most significant speculative theology done by an academic. During this time Masters were chafing against the limitations of the lecture system, with its close textual analysis and reliance upon the explanation of existing authorities. By the 1250s the magisterial commentaries had begun to use the *Sentences* and the texts of Scripture merely as launching points for extended theological and philosophical meditations. The rise of disputed questions was the Masters' "declaration of independence" from the rigid boundaries of the classroom. This did not mean that they cast aside authorities, but rather that those authorities would now be used organically within a dialogue, rather than forming an artificial organizing principle for a monologue.[77] The disputed question came more and more to displace the formal lecture, for it offered not only more flexibility, but was more effective in training students in the arts of debate and formal reasoning. In Thomas's case his first disputed questions were those called *De Veritate* (On truth). He would hold his normal lectures in the morning and then proceed to dispute with the students in the afternoons. The *De Veritate* occupied over two years of discussions and demonstrated Thomas's vigorous academic method. The work exhibits his evolution in thinking about certain issues and is particularly valuable because the first part of the work was done in Thomas's own hand, providing rich evidence to the paleographers of the Leonine commission.[78] The scope of the work is vast, dealing with problems regarding the knowledge of God and humanity, free will and predestination, and the issue of the "Good." This work elucidates many of Thomas's novel Aristotelian views and sets up later debates on illumination and knowledge.

A second type of disputed question was the magisterial quodlibet (literally "questions about whatever"), which often dealt with issues of immediate and contemporary interest. Regent Masters alone had the right to hold them, and they were reserved to the particular work periods of Lent and Advent.[79] These were intended to be virtuoso performances, an occasion open not only to the whole university community, but to the public at large. Though the Master usually posted a list of subjects that he and his Bachelor would publicly defend, other more spontaneous questions could be added as the situation demanded (an example of such a quodlibetal dispute was the ninety-five theses that Martin Luther posted on the university message board). Such theses would have to be maintained against all comers. A public spectacle of this kind ran the risk of serious embarrassment of the Master, one that quite a few professors were reluctant to hazard. Thomas was not cowed by such a challenge and was one of the most prolific disputants of the thirteenth century (along with his later secular rival, Gerard of Abbeville). During the dispute the Bachelor would ordinarily present the theses and respond to questions. If he fell into difficulty the Master could intervene, and at the end of each quodlibet Thomas would make a "magisterial determination," summing up the thesis, weighing the arguments, and definitively settling the matter. Two sets of quodlibetal questions exist, respectively from Thomas's two Regencies at Paris. Much ink has been spilled about their chronology, which does not correspond to their numbering, but their order has now been generally agreed upon.[80] To take an example of a timely quodlibetal question, in the context of the secular-mendicant controversy, we see Thomas laying out many of the issues collected in *Contra impugnantes* in his quodlibets. A particular question arose in the 1250s about the level of authority enjoyed by the pope in formal canonizations. This was a critical question because the mendicants had experienced a spate of canonizations (Francis in 1228, Anthony in 1232, Dominic in 1234, Peter Martyr in 1252, and Clare in 1255). Some in the broader church questioned the veracity of such canonizations. This was of particular importance for Thomas, since the canonization of his brethren touched not only upon the validity of the order, but upon papal authority as well. He responded in Quodlibet IX, question 8. In it he carefully defends the right of the papacy to identify and proclaim saints, implying the infallibility of such an act (and in so doing providing one of the very first articulations of papal infallibility).[81] The quodlibets freed the Masters from the tyranny of the syllabus and a rigid focus on texts and gave them the opportunity to address matters of serious consequence in the lives of society and the church.

The new Regent Master also did not neglect what would be called in the modern university "research." Though many Masters were content simply to publish their lectures, Thomas extended his studies far beyond what was expected of the Theology faculty. He retained a lifelong interest in philosophy and consistently studied, commented upon, and sought new translations of ancient texts in nearly every field. In addition to refining his disputed questions into publishable material, he also expounded on other works. One example of his broad interests was his commentary on Boethius's *De Trinitate*. That he was the only thinker who wrote on this text during the entire century gives us an example of his catholic tastes. In particular he uses this unfinished work as an intellectual exercise to hone his metaphysical explanation of the "Good." Nearly a quarter of Thomas's works remain unfinished (most famously his *Summa Theologiae*). While this suggests a fertile mind, ready to move rapidly to new ideas and to abandon forms considered inadequate, it can also evince a certain personality type that can sustain massive intellectual effort and then suddenly lose interest in a topic, moving quickly on to another without compunction. Thomas simply had a new idea and put down his commentary on Boethius, yet did not leave behind what he had learned. Indeed, the structure of Thomas's next work, the *Summa Contra Gentiles*, is suggested by his organization and meditations on Boethius's efforts.[82]

One of the many achievements of the Leonine commission was the establishment of the fact that Thomas began the *Summa Contra Gentiles* in Paris, confirming a story told by a deponent at the canonization that he began the work by using whatever scraps of paper were at hand.[83] Indeed, the *Summa* was begun using the same parchment and ink as his commentary on Boethius.[84] This handwritten text of Thomas's is the work of a scholar with ideas pouring from his pen. It is heavily marked up and corrected, written like sparks coming off an anvil.[85] According to tradition, Thomas conceived this work as a manual for missionaries, composed at the request of Raymond of Peñafort, for intrepid Dominican missionaries penetrating far into Africa and Asia, who would be meeting Jews, Muslims, and Orthodox and Oriental Christians, not to mention pagans. It has proven a popular and enduring myth, one saint asking another for a plan for evangelical action. Unfortunately, the first reference to the story is more than fifty years after the death of both saints, merely an aside in a Dominican chronicle from Spain in the year 1313. The story is found in no contemporary sources, nor is it found in the canonization records or *vitae* of St. Thomas. By the 1250s, Dominican mission efforts were just beginning. Even then, Humbert was making complaints to the order about the lack of linguistic knowledge in Greek, Arabic, and Hebrew.[86] What we have here is a pious projection upon a document that had later proven useful for missionary efforts, which themselves had only really accelerated in the 1280s. Marie-Dominique Chenu, from a theological perspective, and René Antoine Gauthier, from an historical and paleographical one, have undercut this tradition. Both note how far the *Summa* goes beyond mere instructions for missionary success, and stress its far-reaching, deep intellectual purposes. Mere evangelism would not have required such astonishing depth of thought. It is most likely that it was Thomas's comprehensive effort to situate the new trends of pagan, Jewish, and Muslim thought then coursing through the university, particularly after the Arts faculty added Aristotle to the curriculum in 1255. The "Gentiles" are certainly people such as Aristotle, Avicenna, and Averroes, but in reality, Thomas is in dialogue with his contemporaries, particularly those in the Arts, in their shared mission of understanding and incorporating the difficult traditions they were then inheriting. The actual achievement of Thomas is often missed among these debates on purpose and method.[87] What he proposes is no less than the wholesale defense of the Catholic faith without recourse to revelation and dependent completely upon reason. While Thomas will refer to scriptural and ecclesial authorities, in this *Summa* they are probable arguments, and he reserves discussion of issues of God, creation, and Nicene Christianity to the rational argumentation employed by the philosophical tradition.

Some biographical episodes can be dated to his first Paris Regency and give us a clearer picture of Thomas at work and at play. One day he decided to take a group of students to visit the Royal Abbey of St. Denis, north of the city. There they witnessed the first example of Gothic architecture, created in marvelous geometric harmony. Scholars in the past have noted the correspondence between the beautiful and ordered system of the cathedrals with the intellectual synthesis of Thomas and the scholastics. While those meditations were a bit fanciful, they bore witness to the age of harmony. The great churches of Christendom went up at the same time that the Scholastics were undertaking their vast organization of human knowledge. They prayed in those vast churches, hearing the marvelous strains of harmonic polyphony just being introduced. In this short journey to St. Denis, Thomas shows himself completely a man of his age, not only in harmonics, but also in practice. He demonstrates devotion to two of the predilections of all medieval Christendom: relics and pilgrimages. Both of these were irreducibly critical to medieval religiosity, from the humblest layman to the most powerful king. Thomas's faith in the incarnational power of relics was of a piece with his contemporaries, and after all, an outing to the tombs of the saints was preferable to the usual preoccupations of the Parisian scholars, overturning taverns and brawling with the locals. While on the way back they crested the famous hill of Montmartre, probably with the rays of the setting sun bathing Paris, dominated by its mighty Cathedral of Notre Dame: the city of the king and of the university. The students breathed a spirit of admiration, happy to be part of the scene playing out below. A student asked Thomas, probably playfully, if he would not like to be the lord of such a scene. Tocco and Gui intimate that the pupils expected some pious and edifying response. Thomas, his mind far away from lordship or the bustling city, simply said, "I would rather have Chrysostom on Matthew."[88]

Thomas's regency, according to contemporary Dominican practice, was to end at the conclusion of the 1258–59 academic year. Thomas had the pleasure of overseeing the inception of his senior Bachelor, William of Alton, in the spring of 1259. Soon William would be succeeded by Thomas's junior Bachelor and close friend Annibaldo d'Annibaldi, later to become a cardinal. It was probably expected that Thomas would return to Italy, but the order had something particular in mind before that could transpire. It assigned him to a commission that would meet at the General Chapter of Valenciennes in 1259 in order to address the order's educational curriculum. Yet Thomas's tenure, which had begun in strife and conflict, would end in the same way. The final duty of a Master was to preach, and Thomas ended his Regency with a sermon on April 6, 1259, Palm Sunday. It would be the last formal act of his term. During the sermon the bedel of the Picard nation, a man named Guillot, got up in the middle of the homily and began haranguing Thomas with passages from William of St. Amour. Guillot was probably escorted from the church, and Pope Alexander IV decreed his excommunication two months later. But it did not seem to affect Guillot much, for in 1267 he had been promoted to bedel of the whole university (probably in recognition of his allegiances). Obviously, the old quarrel had merely gone underground. It would emerge again, bound up with the animosity of the Seculars, the rivalry of the mendicants, and the new ideas of Averroes, all leading to serious disturbances at the end of the 1260s. Thomas left Paris, but his presence would be needed again.

Chapter 5

THE ITINERANT PROFESSOR

Thomas on the Byways of Europe

The year 1259 was one of fundamental transition, both for Thomas and for his order. Forty years had elapsed since the foundation of the Preachers, and the friars had faced many challenges. Because of Dominic's constitutional vision—and the genius of the administrators who followed—the order itself was solid. The threats faced by the Preachers were mainly external. The Dominicans had weathered challenges from bishops, older monastic orders, the Franciscans, secular remonstrants, and had endured virulent opposition from the secular clergy at large. While those obstacles would not be completely surmounted for nearly a hundred years, by the end of the 1250s the Friars Preachers could look back with pride. They had a presence throughout Christendom, with around ten thousand priests and two thousand lay brothers in hundreds of priories around Europe—and beyond.[1] While these numbers were smaller than those for the Franciscans, one could say that the Dominican esprit de corps was more focused, its friars more deeply formed, and its identity more coherent. For their part, the Minorites were just beginning an enervating debate about their founder and his relationship to poverty that would continue to dog them well into the fourteenth century.[2] The Dominicans were solidly united under strong leadership and had attained positions of power and authority in the church, reaching even to the highest levels of the Roman curia. They already enjoyed two canonized saints and were members of an organization that boasted a plethora of holy men and women who would later be raised to the honors of the altar. The papacy had entrusted the friars with the most delicate roles of diplomacy and inquisition. Dominican Masters spread throughout the order, bringing with them the latest learning. These men were fresh off from their astonishing victories at the University of Paris, a triumph in which Thomas played no small part.

Thomas was just about to complete the period of his mastership. The practice of the order had been to rotate professors rapidly in and out of Paris. This process not only assured a steady supply of brilliant men for deployment throughout the order but also raised the ire of the more stable secular elements of the university. It was no reflection on Thomas that his tenure ended after only four years. Actually, that was a long time for a Dominican Master to retain his chair; his successor would only hold a one-year Regency. By 1259—and still in his early thirties—Thomas was a well-known friar, and the stories of his entrance into the Dominican order and his travails at Paris were common knowledge.[3] He was an advisor to the king of France and maintained strong relations with the Master General and with the order's other professors, particularly his old mentor, Albert the Great. Given the period of relative peace following the first mendicant controversy at the university, Humbert of Romans—perhaps the most capable Master General of the thirteenth century—was not about to rest on his laurels. It seems that he took the opportunity of the lull, combined with Thomas's cessation as Regent, to convoke a commission of five Masters who would meet at the General Chapter of Valenciennes in order to examine and make recommendations for the order's practices regarding academic work.[4] These five Masters, in addition to Albert and Thomas, were Master Bonhomme (Regent at Paris from 1248 to 1255) and Master Florent of Hesdin (Regent from 1255 to 1257), the friar whose inauguration was so tense that Louis IX had to send archers to protect the convent of Saint-Jacques from attack. The final Master was Pierre of Tarentaise, who was about to begin his Regency in the French chair in 1259 and hold it until 1264. He would later go on to be elected as Pope Innocent V in 1276. This group made up the academic aristocracy of the order. All possessed immense experience in the academic life and were acutely aware of the difficult positions in which the order often found itself. While there was representation from the whole order, the presence of three Frenchmen and the fact that all five were Parisian Masters makes it clear that the Valenciennes commission would be focused on the issues that had arisen at the epicenter of academic life. While their recommendations would apply to the whole order, the process proceeded in light of Parisian experiences.[5]

The order had been fundamentally oriented to the intellectual life from its very inception. The friars considered academics to be the essential precondition for effective preaching and the salvation of souls. At the beginning, the order's attitude was generally conservative, hewing to extant church legislation that harbored suspicion regarding natural philosophy. The primitive constitution of 1220 forbade students to study the books of the "pagans and philosophers." The General Chapter of 1228 modified this position and gave the order's authorities permission to allow access to such works.[6] Even so, it was only under the generalate of Johannes Teutonicus (r. 1241–52) that such permissions were granted widely.[7] Given this abundance of caution, it would take enormous time and effort to change the Dominican course of study. If regular study of natural philosophy was to be introduced, it would have to be made subordinate and useful to the primary aim of zeal for souls. The rapidly evolving situation would force the order's hand. The charged atmosphere of the mid-1200s anticipated issues surrounding the friars' academic formation. In the first place there was the arrival of Aristotle and his commentators. Since the 1220s an immense number of peripatetic works had become available, completely changing the face of the academy. The tide had shifted so significantly in favor of Aristotle that the bans of 1210 and 1231 were all but forgotten, and in 1255 the Arts faculty of Paris mandated the study of Aristotle in its curriculum. The Dominicans were in very real danger of being left behind in this new milieu. Albert in particular had argued that student-friars should be given greater exposure to the philosophical arts. He often hit a brick wall and had become quite exasperated at the intransigent attitude of some of his brethren, who doggedly refused to admit the Arts into the curriculum. He inveighed against the "ignorant who wish in every way to fight the use of philosophy" and who were "brute animals who blaspheme against what they do not know."[8] Albert probably chafed under the strict restrictions of the 1230s and 1240s. For example, the General Chapter of 1243 in Paris explicitly forbade the study of the Philosopher and his commentators, except by special permission. The Preachers' efforts should focus on positive theology and apologetics.[9] While Albert certainly read and commented on the books (presumably after receiving such permission), it meant that the application of philosophy to the rest of the order was severely restricted. The Bologna chapter of 1244 was even more reactionary. It ordered Lectors to avoid new opinions in their teaching and to follow more common and accepted teachings.[10] Armed with this traditional orientation, the order's leaders put off the discussion for a long time and essentially buried their heads in the sand. There was a reason for this. In the first generation, many of the famous scholars who had professed either came as Masters in the Arts, or they had affiliated as students who had already taken the Arts courses in the university. Thomas himself was a prime example: he had commenced his study of the Arts at Naples and was able to continue at Paris under the supervision of Albert himself. As the 1240s progressed, many postulants affiliated themselves before beginning formal academic training of any sort. This meant that—unlike the first generation—they had no exposure to philosophy, even accidentally. Perhaps personal experience convinced the scholars of the first generation that profane studies were dangerous. As such, an undercurrent appeared that was simply happy with an education in theology, particularly the practical science necessary for the confessional and the pulpit. In light of all this, some have tried to fashion the Valenciennes Commission as the liberator of Dominican studies, but the story is more complex. In reality, Albert's rather lonely efforts lay upon a knife's edge. Confronted with the grave disturbances at the university, many in the order would have been content to focus on "common and accepted" opinions, directed to practical ends. Had this element succeeded, the Dominicans would have ceased to lead European academic achievement; indeed, they probably would have been left far behind, even in theology.

Master General Humbert had spent no small effort on victory at the University of Paris. He had tirelessly worked to defend the intellectual life of the order. While he represented a turn of the tide away from more conservative elements, he had to tread carefully. Though he empaneled the academic committee, Humbert was balanced in his vision, knowing that any opening to natural philosophy had to serve the holy ends of the order. At the same chapter of Valenciennes, he had authorized Gerard of Frachet's *Vitas Fratrum*, which contained many cautionary stories of brethren who became too curious about secular sciences.[11] The expansion of the *studia generalia* from one to five in 1248 was the first stirring of positive intellectual developments that Humbert worked later to leverage.[12] Capitalizing on the order's traditional commitment to study, Humbert entrusted the reformation of the system to five Masters who themselves were committed to the academic world, and who were conversant with philosophy. These were no revolutionaries. On the surface, the admonitions of the Valenciennes chapter (made on the recommendation of the Masters) seem jejune and administrative.[13] The five Masters cemented the primacy of the intellectual life in the priories of the order, always keeping within the traditional context of a zeal for souls. They centralized academic supervision under the authority of the Master General, who alone was allowed to permit inception or to dismiss Dominican Masters from Paris. The committee strengthened the office of Lector in each of the convents of the order. The Lector was a sort of in-house professor who was required for each of the hundreds of priories of the order. Should a convent lack a Lector, the young men were to be transferred to another priory that had one. This prevented the needless multiplication of convents without the necessary apparatus of Dominican life and ensured that the next generation of students would be trained under the new rules. Indeed, the conventual lectures were not even to be interrupted by Mass. This is not to say that Mass was viewed as unimportant, just that it should occur at a time of the day that would not affect study. The students were to be relieved of any undue burdens that would impede their study. This probably indicated a transition away from manual labor for the professed friars: a burden transferred to the illiterate lay brothers.[14] The Lector especially was accorded a wide berth, and the fullest use of exemptions could be applied to him in order to free him for study and teaching. In a certain sense, even the conventual prior was subject to the Lector. It did not matter that he was the head of the house; all friars had to attend the lectures of the convent professor. The regulations stipulated an annual visitation to assess the quality of the lectures and the progress of the students, with punishments administered for neglect. The provinces were to direct material resources primarily to study, with special subventions for the best students to study at Paris (a recognition of the perpetually impecunious condition of Saint-Jacques).

These admonitions about funding and visitation demonstrate that a rearguard of resistance remained, opposed to the quiet efforts of Humbert and the more impatient Albert. Buried in the middle of all these directives is a short exhortation that students who lack philosophical formation in the Arts be sent to priories that have facilities to instruct them.[15] Almost universally, historians in the past have extrapolated this one-sentence admonition into a veritable revolution in Dominican studies, with some going so far as saying it established a new *ratio studiorum* for the entire order. This is one instance in which the tendency of philosophy and theology to collapse historical movements is most evident. Many otherwise careful scholars have thus telescoped the difficult transition toward natural philosophy in the order from 1240 to 1300 and find it crystallized in this one sentence from the chapter of 1259.[16] Most recently one scholar has declared, "What was up until that point basically a personal decision of Albert and Thomas, thus went on to become one of the characteristic traits of the subsequent history of the whole of Western culture."[17] Though this idea continues to be repeated, recent scholarship has demonstrated how small a step this really was.[18] What this particular admonition signals is merely that now, officially, the order was to erect schools of Aristotelian logic in the provinces that lacked them. This logical study was already well established in the order and in the broader church, having been in use for over one hundred years. There was no dangerous novelty here, but only a reinforcement of logic, taught as a preparation for the correct interpretation of theology. Masters like Albert and Thomas could certainly have hoped for greater results, but more water would have to pass under the bridge.[19] Albert continued restlessly to agitate for increased exposure to the Arts, while Thomas quietly worked with Aristotle and his commentators. All this was preparatory to the true revolution in Dominican education that would not come until after both of their deaths. It is only then that one can begin to trace the marvelous panoply of studies that would multiply in the order, made possible as a result of the patient tilling of the Parisian Masters. Dominicans would thrive in every field of medieval knowledge, from law to philosophy, from languages to the very heights of theological speculation, but only after solid and thorough foundations had been laid in the various schools of the order.

THE PROFESSOR IN THE PRIORY

After the chapter in Valenciennes, the next two years of Thomas's life are difficult to trace. It is probable that he returned to Paris in the summer of 1259 to collect his writings and effects in preparation for the long journey back to Italy. Provinces were eager to get their students and Masters back from Paris so that they could bear fruit for the order locally, and the Roman Dominicans were no exception. It is likely that Thomas tarried in Paris perhaps until late June, the end of the academic year. Then he began the arduous trip back home on foot. He may have traveled in the company of the Master General Humbert. Because of this, their progress would likely have been slow, since Humbert would have visited the Dominican priories and perhaps female convents along their route, taking the opportunity not only for hospitality but also for visitation. Thomas may have parted ways with the Master General at Strasbourg, where the 1260 General Chapter was scheduled to be held. It would have been imperative to cross the Alpine passes before winter set in (this assumes that Thomas took the mountain path, which is only speculation). In any case, the destination was likely the Dominican house at Sant' Eustorgio in Milan, the center of the Lombard province and site of the shrine of the order's famous martyr, St. Peter of Verona.[20] Thomas likely arrived in time for the Advent season, which, in the Ambrosian rite of the Milanese diocese, starts much earlier than in the Roman rite, on the Sunday after St. Martin's day (November 11). This extra time could explain how he could have preached twelve Advent sermons, some at Milan and some at Bologna. Thomas probably stayed several weeks in Milan and then finished the Advent season at San Domenico in Bologna, which is about a seven-day walk. This allows us to date the sermons to this period, rather than to his return trip to Paris in 1268 (an unlikely date because he would not have tried to traverse the Alps in winter).[21]

Many have speculated that Thomas went to the court of Alexander IV at Anagni. He may indeed have stopped there, for Alexander had been a good patron of the order and of Thomas in particular, yet there is no evidence to support this contention. I find it most plausible that Thomas would have returned to his home convent in Naples, which seems to be the consensus among recent historians.[22] This would not exclude a courtesy stop in Anagni, which lay along the *Via Latina*. After all, this road was Thomas's most likely route, since it took him near the homes of his family members and was the most direct path to Naples. It is more likely that when he returned to Naples, the order conceded to him a period without formal duties, a sort of sabbatical during which he was able to do serious work on the *Summa Contra Gentiles*. It is most likely that he revised the first fifty-three questions that he had begun in France, and then very probably completed both the rest of book 1 and the whole of book 2 in Naples.[23]

When Thomas arrived at his home priory, he could have taken on the office of conventual Lector, but this is not certain. All we know is that in 1260 the provincial chapter gathered in Naples and appointed him as Preacher General.[24] Thomas's appointment was not necessarily a declaration that he was an accomplished sermonizer.[25] Indeed—having been ordained either in France or in Germany—members of his own province would have had little time to sample his preaching. Thomas was certainly a competent preacher, as many of his surviving sermons show, but he spoke in the highly organized "new style" of the Scholastics, rather than in the vivid, sometimes revivalistic, manner of earlier mendicants.[26] The reasons for his appointment are to be found elsewhere than in his homiletic skill. "Preacher General" was one of the most coveted titles in the Order of Preachers. The constitutions accorded such men extensive powers, including automatic dispensation from many rules of the cloister.[27] They were members ex officio of the provincial chapters, and were even permitted to have their own seals (given the controversy over the seals at the University of Paris, one can see how significant a privilege this was). Their title permitted them to preach throughout the province, wherever they wished, without the constraints of being a "limiter," who could only give sermons within the administrative boundaries of one convent. The Preachers General—with their freedom of movement and action coupled with their automatic membership in the provincial chapters—formed a sort of charismatic and aristocratic authority in Dominican life, parallel to the official hierarchy of the order. The position illustrated the lengths to which the constitutions would go to preserve the initial purpose of the friars. Yet, by the 1250s, the liberty offered by the office had become in some measure abused. This is not to blame Thomas, but rather general tendencies within the order, where some sought the title for the benefits and honors it commanded.[28] The office had also morphed into a way of honoring former Regent Masters (a tendency that would continue until such Masters finally achieved similar ex officio voting rights in 1407).[29] Even given these trends, still the appointment freed Thomas from any administrative burdens, either in the convent or in the province, with the exception of yearly attendance at the chapters. Though some may have abused the freedom of the office, Thomas employed it to its fullest potential to achieve his academic plans.

For his projects Thomas also received a privilege that was then becoming common for Masters of the order: the appointment of a permanent *socius*. The position of *socius* was meant to provide a constant companion for eminent members of the order. The functions of such an assistant were partly spiritual—to serve as a permanent confessor and Mass server to the Master in question—and partly administrative. All Dominicans were to be accompanied whenever they left the convent, and the designation of a permanent *socius* would ensure that Thomas would have the same companion to accompany him on all his journeys. The choice for Thomas was a happy one. Reginald of Priverno (sometimes Piperno) was himself a trained theologian and also an accomplished secretary. In the past, historians proposed many dates for Reginald's appointment, but the truth is we have no definitive evidence. It does seem that he became Thomas's constant companion after the latter's return to Italy in 1259; however, it is at least possible that he was acquainted with Thomas in Paris and perhaps served as one of his secretaries there.[30] In a short period Reginald learned how to transcribe Thomas's illegible handwriting and to understand his various habits. It becomes quickly apparent from the sources that they became fast friends. Reginald dedicated himself to serving Thomas for the rest of his life, performing even the most menial of duties for the often distracted and forgetful Master. It helped that the two were near neighbors, as Priverno and Aquino were situated only about twenty-five miles apart, and they were probably near the same age. The service that Reginald gave during the last fifteen years of Thomas's life was a marvelous testament to Dominican humility and subordination to the primary ends of the order. It must be remembered that Reginald himself was a theologian, one who had the training to serve as a conventual Lector himself. He put his entire career on hold in solitary dedication to Thomas. Some of the most private and intimate details of Thomas's spiritual life and habits come down to us from him.

In Naples, Thomas found a convent that had changed considerably since the days of his youthful profession. When he had first arrived in the mid-1240s, there were only two friars (the others having been cast out by order of Frederick II). They worshiped in the tiny church of San Michele Arcangelo dei Morfisa, by the kind permission of the Benedictines. That tiny church had been augmented into the Church of San Domenico, consecrated by Thomas's friend Alexander IV in 1255. The monumental church of San Domenico Maggiore that one sees today was only begun in 1283 but would be completed in time to celebrate Thomas's canonization. In spite of that, the Master would have seen the prodigious progress of the building as he worked, accompanied by the ingress of new novices and bequests into the order that would lay the foundation for one of the mightiest of all Dominican priories. Progress would be slow at first, as the remnants of Hohenstaufen power were not fully driven out until 1266, but after that the friars built and grew without interruption. Thomas returned as a famous Master certainly, but also as a normal Dominican friar, ready and willing to live the conventual life.

The house at Naples was organized like the hundreds of other contemporary Dominican foundations. Friars could travel the Christian world and find a familiar home wherever they went, following identical patterns of prayer, labor, and household organization. It was St. Augustine who had conceived the idea of a group of priests who lived a common life and yet daily went out into the secular world for their ministry. Thomas had certainly had his share of contact with the world, from his turbulent family to the disturbances at Paris, yet the haven of the priory was always there wherever he went. There the friar could take time to be with those also seeking the life of perfection, in silence, sobriety, and penance, all animated by the common purpose of living out the ends of the order, an absolute dedication to study for the purpose of bringing souls to heaven. "Study and the regular life made the priory a house of prayer in which the Dominican family worshipped God, a fortress which sheltered the life of the vows, a school where silence, regularity, obedience, and consecrated purpose engendered scholars, writers, and preachers."[31] Within the house, life differed little from the monasteries of the time. Everything was minutely governed and regimented. In a world that tends to value individual liberty, such a life can seem constricting. But such regulation brings with it a certain freedom of its own: one does not have to worry about the organization of one's day, tasks are allotted, time is fixed, and everything proceeds by dint of the convent bells that ring out the parts of the horarium. Thinkers who fixate on Thomas's works rarely consider the man of flesh and blood practicing habits of the regular life that he lived on a daily basis. In order to understand Thomas one must, in a certain sense, step into the world of a thirteenth-century convent of Preachers to follow its rhythms and practices.

A Dominican convent was meant to have everything necessary to live the regular life, to attend to the needs of the brethren, and to promote the order's vision for the salvation of souls. The Dominicans grew alongside the rising urbanization of the central Middle Ages, and much of their membership was drawn from the growing bourgeoisie. While initially some of their convents were founded in marginal areas of cities, by the mid-thirteenth century both towns and convents had grown prodigiously; the mendicant houses became centers of their own neighborhoods. Because of that transition, the houses came to be located in the bustling centers of the burgeoning urban landscape. Friars, no less than other scholars, merchants, or artisans, were men of the town and they eschewed the traditional monastic predilection for the rural wilds.[32] Their ministry was critical in providing spiritual direction for a rapidly increasing population. The religious life thus came to be deployed in a radically new situation. The novel challenge of how to observe the traditional vows in such an environment was one of the pressing questions of the early order. As much as they innovated externally, in order to meet this challenge, the friars mimicked many monastic practices within their houses.[33] The internal life of a mendicant convent in many respects was identical to a more traditional Benedictine house, with a few adaptations.

Life was centered around the church, with its choir of two rows (or more) on each side. There the friars would attend the Divine Office and the conventual Mass, in addition to spending extra time for private prayer. The ceremonies would be headed by a hebdomadarian: a friar temporarily in charge of intoning and coordinating the Divine Office. A nontraveling friar with no special dispensations could easily spend upward of five to six hours a day in choral duties, even though the Dominican constitutions stipulated that the office be sung "briefly and briskly."[34] At the sound of the convent bell, rung by the sacristan, all work would immediately cease, and the friars would solemnly and silently process into choir. The schedule differed based on the seasons, with earlier prayers in summer to take advantage of the light and to avoid the heat of midday. Medieval life was much governed by weather, light, and the seasons, even in the new urban settings. The day would begin with the chanting of Matins and Lauds, back-to-back, in the dead of night. In one of the most painful of religious devotions, the friars broke their night rest, rising at midnight and celebrating the two cycles of psalms and readings, which could stretch to almost three hours, before they could return to their beds. The friars greeted daybreak with the office of Prime, sometimes as early as 6:00 a.m. Dominicans gave the morning over to work and study, a period broken for the brief prayers of Terce and Sext, about noon. During most of the year the conventual Mass followed Sext, after which the friars partook of the main meal of the day. In Lent they celebrated Mass after None (which would have been about 2:00 p.m.). During summer there was time for repose after this period, so that friars could rest during the hottest period of the day. The main evening prayer was Vespers, which could begin as early as 4:00 p.m. in winter or as late as 6:30 in summer. During the warmer months, a second, smaller meal would be taken after this hour. This would be followed immediately by Compline.

Compline was the special office of the Dominican order and had been since its very beginning. This is, in itself, strange because it is one of the shortest hours of the monastic day. It can be explained by several facts. First, the hinges of the day had traditionally been Lauds and Vespers, morning and evening prayer, and these were elaborately celebrated not only by the monasteries but by the various chapters of canons throughout the medieval cities. To celebrate these hours with a special solemnity would seem to be stepping on the toes of the older groups and stealing their thunder. Compline also bore witness to a special Dominican devotion to the Blessed Virgin Mary. During that hour the friars developed the custom of closing with a special procession of all the friars, chanting the Dominican *Salve Regina*, a haunting composition underscored by the paucity of light in the darkening chapel.[35] This was particularly appealing since the whole community would leave the choir and go into the nave of the church, where they would all turn to the altar and kneel at the verse "turn to us, most gracious advocate." Then the friars and all present would be blessed with holy water. This admission of the laity to the nave during the ritual proved very popular. The friars realized that Compline was really one of the only hours that the laity had any real chance of participating in (unless one was an enthusiast like St. Omobono of Cremona, who used to bang on the church doors to be admitted to Matins at midnight). The combination of their piety and their devotion to Mary brought the laity to Dominican churches in the evening and proved a salutary way of attracting people to support the order, without offending any of the other ecclesiastical establishments. This act of "spiritual entrepreneurship" indeed filled a gap in the market and bound the laity more closely to the Dominican order. Compline was significant for a further reason. It was one of the only hours where all of the brethren in a convent were likely to be in attendance. In addition to friars who had been out preaching or gathering alms, all those who had received dispensations from attendance at choir were required to be at Compline at this characteristically Dominican hour. Granted Thomas's status by the time he arrived in Naples, it is more than likely that he was dispensed from attendance at most of these offices. Yet, like all Dominicans, he had a special devotion to this particular set of prayers. One of the only stories in his hagiography that details him in choir for office tells of his face bathed in tears at the chanting of a versicle from Psalm 70:9, *ne proiicias nos in tempore senecutis*, "Cast us not off in the time of our old age."[36] The verse is chanted during Compline throughout the third, fourth, and fifth weeks of Lent.[37] It is likely that during his life Thomas rarely missed this most Dominican of hours. Even though he was probably exempt, there are a few instances that place Thomas at the night watch of Matins as well, waking before the bell and remaining in prayer after its conclusion.[38] A period of private silent devotion after both Compline and Lauds was a normative practice in the order at that time.[39] While these stories intend to communicate the heroic nature of Thomas's prayer life, it also indicates that he would occasionally attend hours that he was not necessarily obliged to, particularly during the very last years of his life.

Another telling indication that the Master was dispensed from many duties seems to be his habits surrounding the celebration of Mass. It was customary in the community to hold the conventual Mass after Sext and before dinner (usually around 12:30 p.m.); all nondispensed friars, novices, and lay brothers were required to attend. The hebdomadarian was on a rotation with three other friars, who served as priest, deacon, and subdeacon for the celebration of the solemn liturgy. It is likely that these offices were rotated among the older or younger members of the community who were not actively engaged in preaching or teaching, considering the amount of work and choir attendance they demanded. Still, even with this daily solemn Mass, sung by the friars, the Dominicans were a product of a society rapidly transitioning in its liturgical piety. The century saw the acceleration of the phenomenon of Low Mass, or Mass celebrated without external solemnity or singing, solely by a priest and a server. This was due to a deepening of the theology of sacrifice in the Middle Ages, whereby each Mass could be offered for a specific intention and applied to the living or to the dead. This also encouraged an increase in eucharistic devotion. These Low Masses spread at the same time as the multiplication of side altars, which one can see in older churches. Each of these semiprivate niches would be used by privately celebrating priests, for instance when St. Thomas celebrated Mass in the St. Nicholas chapel at San Domenico in Naples.[40] Reading his lives, it is plain that Thomas was very devoted to the celebration of the Eucharist and to its worship. Not only did he say a private Mass daily, served by his *socius* Reginald, but in turn he heard and served Reginald's Mass. The image of Thomas Aquinas humbly making the responses to Reginald as a mere acolyte tells us not only about Dominican life at the time, but much about the personal humility of the saint. It also reveals that Thomas and Reginald did not want to bother any of the other brothers in their duties and to return to work as swiftly as possible. It also probably meant that both were dispensed from the conventual Mass at midday. That Thomas preached occasional public sermons should not lead us to believe that he often celebrated Mass, for until very recently it was quite common for the preacher and the celebrant to be two different people. We have only one recorded instance of Thomas celebrating a public Mass. This was near the end of his life, on Passion Sunday in Naples for a number of his noble friends.[41] The Mass liturgy and office Thomas celebrated was the Dominican Rite, standardized by Humbert in 1256. It was very much like the current extraordinary form of the Roman Rite, though without its considerable Gallican accretions.[42] Differences include the preparation of the wine at the beginning of the rite, less frequent genuflections, and fewer other ritual gestures such as signs of the cross and kisses. The Dominicans today still have the option of offering the identical Mass to the one Thomas celebrated nearly eight hundred years ago. It was a streamlined, medieval, quasi-monastic rite deployed throughout the order, one that enabled the celebrant to finish a Low Mass rather quickly and return to his duties. While the rite itself was compact, that did not mean that friars took it lightly, as Thomas was known for his devotion while either celebrating or hearing Mass.[43]

Central to the life of the Dominicans, and indeed to any religious order of the time, was the chapter room. One often encounters extremely elaborate chapter halls, sometimes even exceeding the decoration one finds in the churches, for example in otherwise plain Cistercian establishments. This embellishment was representative of the priority of this chamber in the life of a community. Here the brethren conducted all their significant business. The whole assembly of professed friars would meet there regularly to debate important issues, particularly those pertaining to the whole of the religious house. While the prior could transact day-to-day affairs, he needed the consent of all the brethren for matters of import. After all, the priory, like the guild of Masters, was a corporation, and required consent for business that related to the whole house. The chapter hall was the beating heart of the regular life of the convent. There the friars would debate the merits of new postulants and, if the decision was a positive one, clothe the novices in the habit of the order. The chapter of faults also took place there. In the thirteenth century this happened on a daily basis, though by mid-century it seemed to be slipping from its traditional placement after Lauds in the dark of the night watch to a more tractable time in the morning after Prime. There the whole of the house would gather while the novices, one after the other, prostrated themselves before the prior and made public confession of lapses from the Rule. Not only that, but once the novices had confessed, anyone in the chapter who had seen them committing faults would also report publicly, especially the official known as the Circator, whose job it was to circulate around the convent and uncover offenses. After the novices had received their penances, they retired. The professed friars, no matter how senior, then proceeded to do the same exercise. Even the prior had to participate, making confession to the subprior. While many today would see this as an effort at social control, in context it was one of the most sublime schools for humility and holiness. Daily, one was held to account for infractions against the Rule and encouraged and supported by one's brethren in the quest for perfection. Its mutuality assured its utility. The Dominicans had a singular privilege regarding this practice. For them the Rule bound only under penalty of punishment, not of sin. Their public confession of these infractions would aid them in becoming better friars and more perfectly attuned to the following of Christ. One can imagine Thomas Aquinas lying prostrate at the feet of his brethren, confessing some of the faults that make it through even in the pages of his hagiography, such as his occasional temptations to vanity, his periodic bouts of inattention, and discourtesy to guests.

In terms of the governance of the religious house, everything was subject to the personal authority of the prior. The constitutions and commentaries stipulated the administration of the house in precise detail, with Humbert noting more than thirty distinct offices and functions. In order to free him for academic work, Thomas never held any of the administrative offices of the convent. In reality he probably only ever held the position of conventual Lector, whose primary function was to lecture to the friars of the house. In spite of that, it is clear that Thomas did participate in the life of the convent, in particular by attending and deliberating at the conventual chapter. Certainly after 1259 his position as Parisian Master and as a Preacher General of necessity placed him in the inner circle of the most senior and respected friars. This inner council of the house stood between the executive authority of the prior and the democratic characteristics of the conventual chapter. This council was a body of experienced friars who advised the prior on matters of importance that did not need to be laid before the whole of the community. They were the ones who offered assessments of the limiting friars who preached locally and sought alms. The council also advised the prior on the fitness of candidates for promotion to Sacred Orders. They served as an auditing team who could supervise the accounts of the house, and they performed the duty of distributing the effects and books of dead friars.[44] It seems clear from his biography that Thomas often served as such a consultor to those in authority (which could range from his own prior all the way up to the Master General), and he was strict about curtailing abuses when he gave such advice.[45]

Feasting on the "word of God" alone did not mean that the brethren did not need bodily refreshment. The refectory was the room where the brethren gathered in common for their meals. The Dominican diet of the thirteenth century was exceptionally strict. No meat at all was permitted, unless one was sick. Even then it had to be taken in a special room set aside for the purpose. Wine, as a Mediterranean staple, would have been ubiquitous at table, but always diluted in the medieval manner, and especially after the example of St. Dominic himself. As a sign of sobriety and temperance it was the habit to drink only while holding the cup with two hands. In the summer, between Easter and the Feast of the Exaltation of the Holy Cross (September 14), there were two meals per day. In the Mediterranean tradition, the main meal was the midday dinner, with a smaller refection in the evening. Sometimes there were extra courses served, due to special donations, and these were called *pitancia*, or pittances. The winter diet, which was duplicated on the many fast days of the year, was even sparser. There was only one meal, though there could be a small snack of soup, wine, and water, called a *collation*. Silence was mandatory at all meals, save for spiritual reading done by a rotation of Lectors. Two things served to mitigate this harsh regimen. The first was the power of priors to modify it. The sick were always permitted extra food, but it was common also to allow novices and the aged to take an extra meal if necessary. The second was the gradual decay of the primitive regimen. Even in the 1250s one finds an increased amount of food being served. The popularity of the Dominicans also invited large donations, which resulted in ample supplies. Unaffected by the issues surrounding Franciscan poverty, the Preachers also began to store quantities of food in the 1240s, assuring them of steady provisions. Adding to the pressures on traditional fast were the frequent receptions of guests, in whose honor the prior usually allowed increased amounts of food for the whole community. Exceptions could also be granted for those at work, such as Masters and students. It appears that Thomas usually had the privilege of taking his meals in his own room. Reginald would fetch the food, and then Thomas, absorbed in his work, would often apparently not touch much of it. It seems his *socius* also had to exercise some form of portion control, since the Master sometimes absentmindedly ate more than was good for him.[46] He had favorite foods as well, as his request for a meal of herrings in his last days demonstrates.[47] In any case he did not seem to be fastidious about his eating and was content to take what was given.

Refreshment for the body also went hand in hand with rest. The early order, perhaps out of poverty, perhaps out of lack of usable space, at first did not employ the monastic practice of individual cells. The friars were all supposed to sleep together, barracks style, in a common dormitory. This became so strictly established that only the Master General himself and the sick were allowed separate accommodations. Difficulties were often attendant upon a common sleeping place; it was surely a serious burden and one of the challenges of the common life. While medieval people had far different ideas about privacy than we, people still annoyed one another. Thomas probably stayed in such a common dormitory as long as he was a student. Like many practices in the priory, this too was meant to be a challenge to give up one's self-love and to be patient and forbearing. However, the intellectual nature of the order raised some difficulties in a community dedicated to the intellectual life. The common hall was not terribly fit as a place for serious and sustained study. For this purpose, the Dominican constitutions permitted the use of cells. Students, according to their aptitude, could be temporarily assigned to individual cells, wherein they could read, study, and sleep, as long as their progress merited for them this privilege. Even in this cell, though, privacy was not absolute. The walls did not go up to the ceiling, but rather ended just over the normal height of one's head, and usually they were without doors. In some ways they were like the study carrels of graduate students that one sees in the libraries of large research universities, semiprivate at best. Masters, being the ones most directly engaged in the central mission of the order, were generally conceded their own quarters, more private than the simple study cells. Thomas, it seems, enjoyed this privilege for most of his career, at least after his first Regency at Paris. In his biographies most events transpire in his private cell. The rooms (perhaps even two conjoined) were simple, but large enough for a bed, a writing desk, and even praying prostrate on the floor,[48] and had space at least for several people (students or secretaries).[49] It also appears that Reginald was billeted either in Thomas's room, or in one adjoining, because the much put-upon *socius* was likely to be roused by Thomas in the middle of the night after the Master had an idea, and he needed someone to take dictation.[50]

Besides rest and refreshment, the friar also needed recreation. Since the life of the monastery was characterized by silence and purpose, the rule reserved some periods for conversation and relaxation. There was a special "speaking room" established for the use of the community, where students could be found drilling one another in their studies and otherwise undertaking tasks for which speaking was necessary. In good weather, recreation could be taken outside in the productive lands attached to the priory, or at least in the cloisters. It seems that a bit more leeway was accorded to novices, given to youthful exuberance. Strict decorum was still to be observed, and recreation consisted often in the singing of religious songs, repeating lessons, or reading aloud. Very little is reported of Thomas's pastimes, but what does survive suggests that he put these periods to good use as well, and that his favorite recreational reading was the *Conferences* of St. John Cassian, a book that had been popular with Dominic as well. Thomas read it as a salve against periods of aridity brought on by sustained intellectual effort.[51] On rare occasions there could be outings, for example when Thomas took some students in Paris to see the shrine of St. Denis, north of the city.[52] Occasionally Thomas would speak freely with his students, though this was perhaps in the context of classes in his cell, rather than at recreation.[53] It seems Thomas did not generally seek out opportunities for diversion, preferring to spend his free time either in prayer in his cell or in the chapel, or in continuing to work through the break periods. Thomas could, though, combine work and recreation, and one of his favorite places in the convent was the cloister. Usually Dominican houses had two cloisters, one for the novices and one for the professed brethren. This cloister was a central courtyard, around which were doors to the many disparate rooms of the priory. The cloister was bounded on the interior by a covered arcade, usually with benches under it. In the middle there could be trees, a fountain, a well, or some other focal point. Thomas loved to pace the cloister quickly, walking with haste as he worked out thorny intellectual problems. The cloister was an oasis within the convent, and indeed within the city itself. As ancient as Western monasticism itself, the cloister was the image of the "enclosed garden": a reminder of Eden, an allegory of Mary, and a foretaste of heaven all rolled into one. Here the friars could refresh themselves in meditation and ease, while still attending to their academic business. There could be dangers to strolling there, however. One time while Thomas was visiting Bologna, where he was not well known by sight, a brother hastily approached the seemingly idle friar and commanded that he accompany him to the market. Thomas obligingly accompanied the officious friar. Upon being recognized by some people in the market, the friar was mortified, but was promptly forgiven by the Master.[54] Sometimes brothers would also come to the conventual parlor, which was the room in which they could meet and speak with guests. Thomas's fame drew many people to seek him out, but it appears that Thomas begrudged this time he had to spend away from work and was often "abstracted" even in the presence of men of consequence, such as the time he essentially ignored the Archbishop of Capua and the Cardinal-Legate of Sicily who had come to speak to him.[55]

Other rooms were more specific to their purposes. In the infirmary the sick would be taken care of and dine separately from the rest of the community. Whenever a brother needed medical attention, he was brought there, where he would be treated with considerable kind indulgence. Though some scholars have tried to emphasize how healthy Thomas was, various stories in the biographies may indicate that he was occasionally more sickly than is sometimes suggested. This was especially true at the end of his life. The sources mention that he always celebrated daily Mass, except when he was sick.[56] While this does not give us quantitative data, it at least suggests some periodic indispositions. In addition, Thomas had issues with his teeth,[57] and at least once with an ulcerous sore on his leg that required cauterization. Such an operation would have transpired within the infirmary.[58] In addition to that, according to medieval medical knowledge, the four bodily humors had to be brought into balance for living a healthy life. In particular, the spirited Sanguine nature had to be reduced into obedience. To that end the constitutions prescribed bloodletting four times a year for the whole of the community, thought to be effective in calming the passions and for overall well-being. Thomas, of course, participated in this practice and was described as abstracting himself mentally in preparation for it, being a person of great sensitivity to pain.[59] Another room that was of significant importance, particularly for the convents of northern Europe, was the calefactorium, or warming room. While there is no evidence of Thomas using it, one may imagine a denizen of southern Italy finding such a place more than useful in locations such as Cologne or Paris. Not having had a traditional novitiate, and immediately entering upon the life of a student, Thomas probably would not have had much experience with the kitchens, storerooms, and working areas of the convent. By the time he had returned to Italy, the majority of these manual tasks had devolved upon the lay brothers who affiliated themselves to the priory.[60]

Of particular importance for Thomas was one of the most essential places for academic work: the library. Each convent was provided with a special room wherein the academic resources of the monastery were kept. In a certain sense the Dominican order had been saved by books. The practice of poverty had never included the abandonment of books, and Dominic himself valued useful literature exceedingly. Books were identified as central to the entire rationale of the order. Though there was some disquiet in the early order about handling money for academic works, by the 1250s it had become common for the friars to retain capital for the purchase of useful volumes. The libraries of the thirteenth century were modest, often only occupying the far end of the dormitory or housed in cells. A record from the prior at Lucca is probably representative of most Preachers' convents. In 1263 the house boasted thirty-five books, but by 1278 the number had grown to ninety-six (this did not count the liturgical books kept separately in the sacristy).[61] The constitutions minutely regulated the collection, cataloguing, and use of books, and their acquisition was encouraged by the Masters General. Each convent would have at the very minimum a copy of the Bible with glossed commentary, the *Historia Scholastica* of Peter Comestor, the *Sentences* of Peter Lombard, and probably a copy of Gratian's *Decretum*. As the century wore on, the friars themselves added to the collection: commentaries on confession and marriage by Raymond of Peñafort, new translations of Aristotle, the works of Albert and Thomas, the revision of and commentaries on the Bible by Hugh of St. Cher, the copious works of Humbert of Romans, and the *Vitas Fratrum* of Gerald de Frachet. Books of decretals and laws would augment existing works, and even the efforts of the Friars Minor, such as Bonaventure, could be found on the shelves. Luckier convents would have solid collections of the Latin fathers, perhaps *florilegia* (collected sayings) from Christian and classical sources, and books for preaching and pastoral work. Students and particularly Masters were permitted to take books from the library, though often reference works would be chained to benches. Thomas probably did most of his reading alone in his cell, and it is likely he had begun to accumulate a personal library that belonged only to himself, reflecting his comprehensive tastes, particularly in reference to the new translations of Aristotle. Since books were so valuable and difficult to produce, the quantity of the collections was often limited. This focused the attention of the Dominicans on quality. Contained within their modest libraries was the sum of the received wisdom of Western civilization. From these modest beginnings the Friars took command of the intellectual field of Christendom. Pierre Mandonnet estimated that by 1300, no fewer than 1,550 friars were working in academic fields across the continent, and that the literary production of the Dominican order from 1220 to 1350 was greater than that of *all previous periods of human history added together.*[62] Thomas was indeed only the tip of the iceberg in one of the most extraordinary intellectual efforts of all time.

Occasionally a friar ventured out of the convent, though this was only for serious reasons. He had to have written permission from his superiors and could not travel without a *socius*. When the Dominicans traveled, they went barefoot when they were in the countryside, only donning shoes while in towns so as to distinguish themselves from certain heretical groups who did without them.[63] They were rarely permitted to ride horses, and only in exceptional circumstances and again only with written authorization. While on the road, their behavior was to be a sober example of apostolic life to all they encountered. Friars were to try to stay at religious houses, and to avoid secular inns and taverns. To travel they dressed in their normal habit of a white tunic, leather belt, and knife, all covered with a broad white scapular down front and back, complemented by a white hood. On top of this was a large black cape, or *cappa*, that was made of coarse wool, usually black, but could appear gray or even rust colored depending on local availability. It covered the chest but was open below, exposing the white of the scapular and tunic, and had its own additional hood. It was on the road that they appeared in their full formal habit, by which they became known to the people of Europe as the "Blackfriars." They became known by this dress since they wore it whenever they interacted with the laity, be it journeying, preaching, or hearing confessions.[64] This would be the clothing that Thomas himself would bear as he became one of the most widely traveled friars of the Middle Ages, repeatedly crossing back and forth to Germany, Paris, and Italy, and carrying out his different assignments and attending the various provincial and general chapters, all the while waiting upon popes, cardinals, and members of his own family. In all of these he was accompanied by the indefatigable Reginald. It has been estimated that Thomas walked nearly ten thousand miles during his journeys, the greatest part of that barefoot. Devotion to such austerities offers one of the primary indicators of the heroic sanctity of the man. Such was the quotidian life of one of the most prominent thinkers in history.

THE MIRACLE OF ORVIETO

At the confluence of the ancient regions of Latium, Tuscany, and Umbria meanders the Paglia River. Taking its source from the uplands of Mount Amiata, it courses through the borders of the three regions, only to meet the Tiber in its leisurely trip to Rome and Ostia. On its way the ancient Via Cassia bridges it—the road from Rome that stretches through the spine of Italy until finally joining the coastal Via Aurelia in the north. The fertile area drained by the rivers produced fruitful farmland and had been settled long before the Romans made their appearance. Indeed, it was a stronghold of the advanced Etruscan peoples. The ancient city of Volsinii (later corrupted to Bolsena) was one of the most prominent centers of the old Etruscan hill cities.[65] Rising from the

Orvieto, where Thomas taught 1261–65

valley of the Paglia, commanding it in both directions, is a volcanic butte of nearly seven hundred feet that dominates the plain for miles around. Settled for over three thousand years, the town of Orvieto (*urbs vetus*—the "old city"—even to the Romans) sits atop over a thousand caves dug in the soft volcanic tufa by the original inhabitants. These caves aided the process of viticulture established by the Etruscans. The sweet, golden wine of Orvieto was much sought after in the Middle Ages and—in a dryer incarnation more suited to modern palates—still is popular today. Due to its strategic location, Orvieto has occasionally played a significant role in history. Incorporated into the Republic in the third century BC, the nearly impregnable city was last conquered by Julius Caesar in his march on Rome. During the late thirteenth century, it became a favorite residence of the papacy, which richly endowed it and built a papal palace. The city was a centerpiece of Cardinal Albornoz's efforts to secure the Papal States during the 1350s in preparation for the return from Avignon; even today one can see the magnificent fortress he constructed on the eastern side of the city. In the sixteenth century, it was Orvieto that witnessed Pope Clement VII's rejection of the annulment petition of Henry VIII, an event with profound ramifications for the English-speaking world. It is also known as the city of Corpus Christi, for the feast was promulgated there, and even today Orvieto's celebration of the holiday is one of the most significant in the world.

In 1261, however, Orvieto was a backwater. While the end of the century would see the town's population rise to thirty thousand, in the mid-century it was more likely half of that. Though it was the site of one of the earliest Dominican foundations in Italy in the first half of the 1230s, it was not a remarkable convent by any stretch of the imagination.[66] The small Dominican house may have gotten a boost by the appointment of a bishop of the order to the city. In 1251 Constantine of Orvieto, known primarily as a biographer of St. Dominic, became bishop; but he reigned only five years before the pope made him legate to Constantinople in 1256. The only record we have of him favoring the convent of St. Dominic was a decree for indulgences for pilgrims to the church in honor of St. Peter of Verona in 1253.[67] Nor had the papacy of the thirteenth century yet expressed any special predilection for the city. Recognizing its strategic importance, Pope Adrian IV

(r. 1154–59) ordered it fortified, but later the city proved to be quite resistant to papal efforts, with the Cathar heresy finding a stronghold there, manifested especially in the murder of a pro-papal official, Pietro Parenzo, in 1199.[68] With all this in mind, one can certainly ask what the diffinitors of the Roman province were thinking when they gathered there for the provincial chapter on September 14, 1261, and assigned Friar Thomas, "for the remission of his sins," to the office of conventual Lector at the marginal local priory. Of course, such a statement was boilerplate for Dominican chapters when assigning and absolving brothers, meaning it enjoined a duty on them under pain of obedience (similar language would be used in his 1265 reassignment). But perhaps one can stretch believability enough to suggest that something had transpired in Naples that required Thomas's reassignment or that would help to explain the fact that the years 1259 to 1261 are the most opaque in his whole biography.

Following his election in Viterbo on August 29, 1261, Urban IV (r. 1261–64) slowly made his way north and took up residence in Orvieto for the remainder of his pontificate. He did not actually take up residence in the city until the middle of October of 1262. The friars who gathered for the provincial chapter may indeed have heard of his election by September 14, but they most certainly did not know of any plans that included the transfer of the curia to the city. If they had wanted Thomas to be present at the curia, they could easily have assigned him to Viterbo, where the curia was then in residence. Given these conditions, it was merely a happy coincidence that the papacy later came to reside in Orvieto. While it was likely that the papacy found the fortified city safer during the final acts of the wars against the Hohenstaufens, it is also likely that the new pope knew of Thomas. Urban himself had been a student at the University of Paris, was fond of the mendicants, and was probably advised by Thomas's confrere Hugh of St. Cher, who was by this time the senior cardinal bishop, second only to the pope in precedence.[69] As a testimony of his affection, one of his first acts in the city was to consecrate the friars' church of St. Dominic. While it goes too far to say that the curial relocation was due to Thomas, his presence in the city certainly did not hurt. Nonetheless, it remains that when the provincial chapter decided to appoint Thomas as conventual Lector, none of this was known.

Thomas would come as the simple lecturer to the *fratres communes*, the friars of the local convent who did not possess the aptitude for study at the provincial *studia*, much less Paris or the other *studia generalia*. We should pause to reflect upon this step. Thomas had been a Parisian Master, already becoming well known for his works. It would be like a tenured professor from a top university being assigned to teach at a community college. It could be seen as a colossal waste of talent, yet there is another way to view the episode. Thomas reacted with perfect obedience. He was a son of the church and a son of the order, who lived out such charges with humility. He received the command and went straight to work. As will be clear, the job of lecturing in basic theology and Scripture did not particularly tax Thomas, and the next four years would be some of his most productive as a writer and thinker. Perhaps the provincial chapter intended this, as a way to augment the time Thomas had in which to do his work. In a remote convent, where the only responsibility was to instruct regular students in basic subjects, the Master would be freed to continue to develop his thought. The advent of the curia was therefore unexpected but did not detract from Thomas's vision; indeed, it provided a marvelous opportunity that he would not waste.

With the arrival of Urban IV and the rest of the curia, Orvieto became—almost overnight—the center of Christendom. Estimates of the size of the papal court in the later 1200s indicate that there may have been as many as two hundred retainers and officials who served the pope himself, and perhaps as many as six hundred attached to the various other curial officials.[70] But the residence in Orvieto was also fraught. It had been a center of Cathar activity, traces of which remained into the 1250s. By that time the heresy had become linked to political Ghibellinism in the minds of many churchmen, and Urban struggled against these tendencies during his residence. But he could tolerate those difficulties because of the town's other characteristics. Its dominating position and strong fortifications were to prove exceptionally useful as the city found itself under siege between 1263 and 1264. It provided the papacy a secure base of operations upon which to build. When one visits the city today, one sees the architectural evolution that commenced during Urban IV's tenure. Most of the pontiffs for the rest of the thirteenth century would make the pleasant and well-protected city their temporary capital, constructing a palace that would house many papal occupants over the centuries. What strikes the visitor most of all is the breathtaking Italian Gothic cathedral. When Thomas and the popes arrived, they discovered the ancient cathedral of Orvieto in a dilapidated condition. As a result of papal predilection, a massive new edifice was reared that, over the next several hundred years, became one of the glories of Christian architecture. In the 1350s a chapel was added to the cathedral complex to house the Sacred Corporal—a church parament on which the host is laid at Mass—that was said to be stained with the blood of Christ. While sources on this miracle date only from the middle of the 1300s, the relic became an object of singular devotion, particularly as it was tied into the foundations of the Feast of Corpus Christi.[71] This was not the only miracle that transpired in the Umbrian hill town. When Urban came, the whole apparatus of the papal court came with him. This meant that the itinerant papal library, with some of the most precious documents in history and the core of the present Vatican Library, also arrived. With the pope traveled an army of advisors, some of them the most brilliant men in Europe at the time, such as the mathematician Giovanni Camparo of Novara, whose works on Euclid and astronomy were foundational for the development of scientific thought. Another was Marino d'Eboli, a superb diplomat, later archbishop of Capua, whom Thomas consulted on economic matters. Cardinal William de Bray, a famous mathematician, lawyer, and theologian, held a special affection for the Dominicans and requested burial in the conventual church in Orvieto, where his beautiful tomb may be seen today. Perhaps most significant among this group was Thomas's own confrere, Hugh of St. Cher, who also took up residence in the "papal" city, if not in the convent of San Domenico itself. Hugh was a constant presence in the city until his death in 1263. As Hugh's health declined, he resigned his position as chief Cardinal Bishop of Ostia and was succeeded by the eminent canonist Henry of Segusio, known to history as Hostiensis. The Master General, Humbert of Romans, was available for consultation when he was resident in the city. Thomas would also have come to know the new Master General, John of Vercelli (r. 1264–83), and they began a fruitful relationship. As Minister General of the Franciscans, Thomas's Parisian colleague Bonaventure would often have been in residence at the curia as well. Thomas also would have had the joy of seeing his favorite student, Annibaldo di Annibaldi—himself a former Parisian Master—become a cardinal and take up residence in the city in 1262. The curia was the most international and well-developed court in Christendom, and petitioners poured into Orvieto from all over the Christian world and beyond. Perhaps the most significant of these was none other than Thomas's old Master, Albert the Great. Exhausted by his charge as Bishop of Regensburg, he traveled to Italy to ask the pope for relief. Urban accepted the resignation and Albert took up residence with Thomas at San Domenico until his departure in February of 1263. While it appears he was not in Orvieto, the Dominican translator William of Moerbeke began his prodigious production of translations of Greek literature, apparently sending them to Thomas as each was completed. All of this was pure serendipity. Thomas, who a year earlier was at a marginal convent teaching introductory courses, now found himself thrust into the very epicenter of the Christian world, surrounded by colleagues and friends. The Sacred Corporal was indeed the Miracle of Orvieto, but what Thomas and his friends were able to accomplish was no less miraculous. Rarely had such a providential concentration of talent been achieved so expeditiously.

In spite of all this, to say that Thomas was "Master of the Sacred Palace" is an anachronism. This title was later developed and conferred on the official theologian of the pope, an office held by Dominicans down to the present day. The order retroactively conferred this honor upon its most famous theologian, but the office had not yet developed during Thomas's time. While there was a school attached to the papal curia (the "Sacred Palace"), it was mostly used to train younger clerics in grammar. It was not until the fourteenth century that theologians would receive appointments as personal experts and advisors to the pope. Thomas was merely the Dominican Lector in the city in which the papal court resided.[72] While it is clear that he and Urban formed a very productive partnership, he never held any formal office in the papal curia.[73] His everyday duties as a Lector in the convent of San Domenico did not occupy much of his time, but they may have provided significant grist for his later reconsiderations on the nature of theological education. Introductory lectures for Dominican students did not even rise to the level of Peter Lombard's *Sentences*. Rather, the *fratres communes* had to be schooled in the practical knowledge necessary for the confessional and the pulpit. To this end they studied handbooks, such as the *Summa* of William of Peyraut on virtues and vices, Raymond of Peñafort's legal cases on confession and marriage, and other background exegetical and historical sources, including Vincent of Beauvais's *Speculum Maius*. Thomas never developed a contempt for such introductory studies as he taught these basic texts, but rather became profoundly aware of their haphazard nature and their disjunction from one another and from the sources of Christian theology. Students learned piecemeal from examples in manuals without coming to any solid appreciation or grounding in the whole. Thomas knew very well that the "office of the wise man is to order" and so, over the course of the next half-decade, he began to devise a new method, a comprehensive analysis and presentation of the whole of the Christian faith, so as to introduce the beginner to the riches of the Catholic tradition. This would later bear fruit in his *Summa Theologiae*, reflective of his formative experiences in teaching beginner theology.

Beyond his work in the classroom, Thomas maintained a strenuous level of academic activity. It appears conclusive that the scriptural text Thomas used to lecture to the brothers was the Book of Job.[74] Thomas focused on the literal sense of the text in his discussions, for he considered that St. Gregory the Great had provided the definitive explication of the spiritual sense of the text. It is the literal sense of the text that allows Thomas to range over what he sees as the chief problem of the book: the ways divine providence manifests itself on earth, particularly in light of the suffering of the just man. Thomas takes the reader on a journey into the heart of conversion, wherein the afflicted man turns to God in his apparently unjust sufferings and has his heart brought into conjunction with the providence of God.[75] It was not coincidental that it was these same issues that he was concurrently dealing with in the *Summa Contra Gentiles*. He concluded this massive work in Orvieto. While in the town, he also maintained correspondence with his order and with the wider world. One should remember that as a Preacher General he had the authorization for a private seal with which he could exchange letters freely. Thomas showed himself an extraordinarily patient and reliable correspondent, answering questions from Dominicans and church officials throughout Christendom, on issues as varied as buying and selling on credit and the very articles of the Creed. His generosity in answering such letters is a testament to his assiduousness as a teacher, not disdaining to take time away from his systematic works in order to answer the simple questions posed by the brethren. His patience is a characteristic that comes out in all of the stories about his life. In a person becoming so quickly and justly famous, his refusal to neglect such small tasks is an exemplary witness to his character.

His stay in Orvieto also occasioned new directions and a deepening of his theology. Thomas became fascinated by the Greek fathers. Already he had immersed himself in the philosophical schools of Plato and Aristotle, who formed the backdrop of the thinking of the fathers of the church. He was already thoroughly familiar with the Latins, particularly Augustine, Jerome, and Gregory. Now it seems that events conspired to bring Thomas into more direct contact with the Greek world. Several reasons can be cited. Clearly Thomas was familiar with the papal library, and it is likely that many significant texts were available there for his consultation. There he apparently found the records of the first ecumenical councils, which he began to use with great regularity. Thomas was no Greek scholar, and it appears that he was a poor linguist all around, never really advancing beyond Latin and his southern Italian dialect.[76] For his texts he relied upon the translations that had been done in Europe since the 1100s, and in particular depended upon his Dominican brother William of Moerbeke. Another opportunity for exposure to Greek thought presented itself with the fall of the Latin Empire of Constantinople in 1261. Many of the defeated Latins were then making their way back to the West, armed with the cultural resources they had been exposed to over the previous sixty years of control. The fall of the city to Michael Palaeologos had also made more pressing the resumption of talks on healing the bitter division between Greek and Latin Christianity. Wishing to avoid papal sponsorship of a renewed attempt to reestablish Latin control, Michael made overtures to Urban IV. It appears that the pope made Thomas his close collaborator in the effort. In the first place, Urban asked him to offer an analysis of a compilation of quotations from the Greek fathers assembled by Nicholas of Durazzo, the bishop of Crotone in south Italy.[77] The problem with his collection was that many of the citations he assembled were either spurious or badly corrected by some previous Latin compiler so that they had become a caricature of the actual sentiments of the fathers. Thomas proceeded along his usual path of respect for the authority of the fathers and struggled to construe their presumed quotations in an irenic and orthodox manner. While Thomas was fighting a losing battle to make anything out of this work, he was able to arrive at some significant interpretive principles. In the first place, he notes that we must not judge historical statements according to our current level of knowledge. In particular, before doctrine became solidified by councils and decretals, the fathers spoke with more freedom and with looser intentions than later writers, and as such we need to appreciate their historical context. In an age that was notoriously uncritical (of course, according to our modern standards), this was a significant achievement. He also noted that some passages, if translated too literally, seem to alter the meaning. Therefore a translator must be attentive to the intention of the author, rather than hewing to a rigid literalism.[78] This little book of Thomas's demonstrates that even with inferior tools, he could produce something of enduring value.

Perhaps of greater significance was his *Catena Aurea*, or the "Golden Chain." Urban IV desired a commentary on the Gospels from a contemporary thinker. Interestingly, Tolomeo gives us the detail that he originally wanted Bonaventure to produce it, but the Franciscan begged off the task due to his obligations as Minister General.[79] As such the pope turned to Thomas, producing another fruit of their successful relationship. Thomas proceeded through the entirety of the Gospels, line by line, starting with St. Matthew, offering an exposition of the literal and spiritual senses of the passage, citing authorities—particularly from the fathers—while finding room to correct the erroneous interpretations of heretics. He finished the commentary on Matthew by 1264 and dedicated it to his patron, Pope Urban. It seems that Urban died before the other three Gospels were complete, for Thomas dedicated the next books to his beloved student, Annibaldo di Annibaldi, who had been a Master at Paris himself, been created a cardinal, and was resident in Orvieto. What is most significant about this effort is that—as he began working on the second Gospel, Mark—it appears that he had penetrated much more deeply into Greek theology and indeed began to evince a marked preference for it. In the text he quotes only twenty-two Latin fathers, yet he cites fifty-seven Greeks, showing special predilection for Chrysostom and Dionysius the Areopagite.[80] He is also careful to note where his sources come from, uncharacteristic for a medieval author. Indeed, it is useful to point out the astonishing amount of work put in by anonymous editors over the course of centuries who painstakingly identified all of the particular sources in medieval authors, which we now access so easily with a glance at the page. Thomas also displays the germ of critical editing when he is able to correct some of the Arian sentiment in a commentary on Matthew attributed to St. John Chrysostom (not definitively to be excluded as a forgery until the time of Erasmus in 1530). Many have noted that the *Catena* represents a key moment in Thomas's evolution, in which he becomes far deeper and more skillful in the exploitation of the fathers as a theological resource and becomes attentive in particular to the contours of Greek theology, a real *ressourcement* before the fact, anticipating some of the issues that would come to a head in the Renaissance. It is also worth noting that this was one of Thomas's most popular works, being copied and distributed all over Europe and receiving many early printed editions. It also is notable that Thomas, usually noted as a speculative theologian and philosopher, is also critical for the history of dogma, in terms of patristic and positive theology, throughout this work.[81]

In terms of the broad life of the church, the most outstanding collaboration between Pope Urban IV and Thomas was the development of the Feast of Corpus Christi.[82] The thirteenth century was the start of the golden age of eucharistic devotion, which followed hard upon the development of sacramental theology in the central Middle Ages. The definition of transubstantiation at Lateran IV in 1215, along with the multiplication of Masses, testifies to the rising tide of interest in and devotion to Christ as fully present in the Eucharist. Attacks of anti-incarnational heretics such as the Cathars also served to deepen popular piety toward the sacrament and perhaps spurred the development of the feast.[83] In the 1240s this fervor intensified, particularly focused around a group of holy women in the diocese of Liège in modern-day Belgium. By

1246 the local bishop had promulgated a feast of the Lord's body. In 1252 the Dominican Hugh of Saint-Cher, legate to Germany, extended the feast throughout his territory and carried his devotion with him when he came to Orvieto with the pope. When just a deacon, the future Pope Urban IV himself had been present for the celebrations in Liège and bore that memory with him to the Roman curia. Some historians have tried to connect the origin of the feast and its extension to the universal church to the eucharistic miracle of Bolsena. While there is no solid evidence until the 1320s (and no chronicle sources until St. Antoninus in the 1430s), some suggestive work has been done that demonstrates that there was a "Peter of Prague" (the supposed recipient of the miracle) in residence in Orvieto in 1264.[84] Of more interest perhaps is the odd record that the feast was celebrated *twice* in 1264, once on June 19 and again after the bull's promulgation. It is possible that the first feast was for the translation of the relic from Bolsena to Orvieto.[85] One would have expected its mention in the 1264 bull promulgating the feast, or an allusion in the liturgy, but, alas, there is none. It is possible that the Dominican archbishop Antoninus had elided the miracle with the promulgation of the feast and the composition of the liturgy by Thomas. It is most likely that this was a devotion that had bubbled up from below, as it were, proving broadly popular and acquiring friends at the highest levels of the church, which led to the establishment of the feast.

For his part, Thomas participated in the fruitful theological development about the Eucharist. One can certainly say that he is a beneficiary of the debates of the previous centuries and so possesses a mature medieval doctrine of the sacrament. It was even recorded that the Masters of Paris corporately submitted to his determination about the inherence of the accidents in the Eucharist (i.e., how the outward appearances are able to remain when the substance of bread and wine is gone).[86] He was also well known for his remarkable eucharistic piety. We have already seen his devotion to the Mass, but all the biographers attest to his devotion even in extraliturgical settings. For many Catholics today, the celebration of the Mass is central to their spirituality, yet in the religious orders of the church this was not always so. The older monastic orders focused their spirituality on the Divine Office and meditative reading; a community Mass with only occasional communion was simply a small part of the horarium. In addition, very few monks were priests who had direct experience of celebrating Mass and receiving frequent communion. The rise of the Franciscan and Dominican orders brought with it a lessening of the centrality of the Divine Office. Further, the Dominicans were founded as an order of priests—a genuine first in church history—at a time when daily celebrations of the Eucharist multiplied. They were perhaps best positioned to meet the rising tide of eucharistic piety. Thomas celebrated every day and heard a second Mass said by his *socius*. These were most likely low Masses, meditative and quiet, focusing on the texts of the Mass and the reality of the sacrament. Thus, Thomas communicated under both kinds daily. This was unlike nearly every Christian in the world. St. Louis of France, for example, took the Eucharist only six times a year,[87] and Lateran IV ordained that *once* a year was a sufficient minimum for the Christian people. In order to understand Thomas's later work on the Eucharist, we must understand his priestly spirituality, which revolved around the daily celebration of private Mass rather than communal liturgical celebration or the singing of the Office. Such a devotion was critical for the deepening eucharistic piety of the thirteenth century. Further, one important component of the rise in devotion to the Eucharist was the practice of elevating the sacrament after consecration for the adoration of the faithful.[88] Thomas is one of the first to have recorded a pious sentiment that he was accustomed to say at the moment, taken from the church's Prayer of Thanksgiving, the *Te Deum*, "O Christ, you are the King of Glory, the Son of the Everlasting Father."[89] His biographers relate the story of Christ speaking to Thomas through a crucifix, telling him, "You have written well, Thomas, of the sacrament of My Body."[90] Thomas's eucharistic piety while on his deathbed was also exemplary (though not unusual for the time). When taken together, these stories give a picture of eucharistic piety characteristic of the mid-1200s. Thomas is perhaps best known to the average Catholic as a result of the liturgy and office of the Feast of Corpus Christi attributed to him, particularly as the author of the common hymns used so often in Benediction of the Blessed Sacrament.

It appears that by 1264 Urban IV was ready to promote the Feast of Corpus Christi universally, an act that he would accomplish in the bull *Transiturus* of August 11 that same year. For a long

while there was much hesitation in accepting Thomas's authorship of the Office and hymns for the feast. Militating against his
authorship was the fact that it was not mentioned until the time
of Tolomeo of Lucca in the mid-1310s. Even stranger, the Dominican order did not make the feast and its octave mandatory until
1322. In addition, the composition of such exceptional poetry and
hymnody does not appear anywhere else in Thomas's works. One
could ask why this singular and astonishing example of a poetic
soul only shows up here. One scholar argues that it is possible that
Urban and Thomas were being too avant-garde in their presentation of the feast. After all, it had been a highly localized devotion in
the Low Countries. After Urban's death later in 1264, celebration
of the feast fell into abeyance. It would be over fifty years before
the papacy would resume its interest in the feast, and finally get
the Christian world to acquiesce in its celebration. What is clear
here is the limited power of the papacy in matters liturgical. The
reluctance to celebrate such a novel feast does not militate against
the genuine devotion of the Christian people, but rather speaks to
an exceptional liturgical localism and traditionalism that resented
the imposition of feasts from "above." Popes would run into many
similar problems as they attempted to insert new saints into the
calendar throughout the 1200s.[91] In terms of the Dominicans, it
should be remembered that Thomas was asked to write a feast for
the *Roman* Rite celebrated at the curia, not his own Dominican
Rite. Having just stabilized their ordo only a decade earlier, the
Preachers would not have been in any real hurry to add new feasts
and change liturgical texts. However, few would be better positioned to write such a feast than a Dominican Master, steeped not
only in theology but in the daily lived mystery of the altar.

In the first place, we must reject as unhistorical a tale that
is ignored by the professional historians and yet repeated with
frequency by popular writers. Urban did not ask Bonaventure and
Thomas to engage in a competition to design the liturgy for the
feast. I suspect this narrative was extrapolated from Urban's original intention to have Bonaventure write the *Catena Aurea*. As the
story goes, when Bonaventure heard Thomas's sublime prayers, he
quietly tore his to shreds (thus conveniently destroying any manuscript evidence!). This story arose in the atmosphere of interorder rivalry in the early modern period and was intended softly to

elevate Thomas's reputation.[92] In terms of the liturgy as it came to exist, scholars are generally satisfied that Thomas's authorship of the office and the hymn *Adoro Te* is well established.[93] Thomas was certainly present for the first two celebrations of the feast. These would have taken place in the old cathedral of Orvieto, Santa Maria Prisca, or perhaps because of the dilapidated condition of the mother church, at Sant' Andrea. With Urban's death later that year, Thomas was probably chagrined that the feast fell into disuse in Italy. It would only be resurrected long after his death. Nonetheless, Urban's institution, Thomas's liturgy, and the agglomeration of the Bolsena miracle left behind the massive edifice of the Orvieto Duomo, and a legacy that continues to this day in the devotion to the body of Christ in that city, where the streets are yearly covered in flowers for the eucharistic procession. By 1320, a sacred play was being performed every year in which an actor playing Thomas appeared at the end to write the Office and is complemented by an offstage voice like one from heaven.[94] This legacy, too, was bequeathed to the wider world, grew in popularity through the late Middle Ages, and became a centerpiece of the Catholic Reformation of the sixteenth century. It is safe to say that of all the works of Thomas, the ones that most Catholics have encountered most often are the closing lines of the *Pange Lingua*, "Tantum ergo Sacramentum," and the conclusion of *Verbum Supernum*, "O Salutaris Hostia." Many are also familiar with the operatic versions of his "Panis Angelicus," taken from the hymn *Sacris Sollemnis*. G. K. Chesterton wrote of Thomas writing hymns "like a man takes a vacation." It is strange that such a brilliant and subtle speculative theologian and philosopher could have produced astonishing poetry of such profundity. Many writers on Thomas seem not to be surprised by this, but they ought to be. Some consider it essentially a natural outflow of his spiritual life, which one can certainly discern here. However, such spiritual consolation rarely manifests itself in such a talented and enduring form. Rare is the theologian and philosopher who is also a poet; one can only cite a handful, such as St. Ephrem, Hildegard, Kierkegaard, and Nietzsche. Indeed, Thomas's crabbed and technical prose and his utter lack of interest in writing style make it even more shocking. Thomas seems indeed to have been both poet and thinker, yet for some reason he veiled the poetic talent nearly the whole of his life.[95] But even as a "one-hit wonder," Thomas's poetry continues to reverberate throughout history, down to the present.

A NEW PATH IN AN OLD CITY

Thomas's friend and patron Urban IV died in Perugia on October 2, 1264. The curia had departed from Orvieto after the initial celebration of the Feast of Corpus Christi. For Thomas it must have seemed a town quickly becoming deserted. His mentor Albert had left in 1263, the same year his friend Cardinal Hugh had died. With the curia gone, there was little left to do in Orvieto but teach the brethren and continue his frenetic writing pace. Knowing his character, Thomas probably embraced this time of peace and silence, though one can certainly sympathize with the consternation caused by the loss of such eminent colleagues, and of the prominent visitors that would inevitably come to the papal city. On February 5, 1265, the Frenchman Guy Foucois was elected as Pope Clement IV after a four-month conclave. It is possible that Thomas could have come to know the new pope in Paris, since Guy had been a secretary of King Louis IX. In any case, the pope was a legal scholar and as disposed to patronize scholarship as his predecessor had been. He also maintained good relations with the mendicant orders, knowing them as stalwart supporters of the papacy in its wars with the Hohenstaufens. Clement also knew about the fidelity of Thomas's family to the papal cause. Knowing that much of its wealth and property had been endangered on account of this loyalty, he proposed to do something for them. Clement thought he could kill two birds with one stone. He apparently offered Thomas the archbishopric of Naples, an extremely powerful and influential see, along with additional revenues from the monastery of St. Peter ad Aram.[96] The thought was that he would reward the Dominican thinker for his close collaboration with Urban and, at the same time, help his family to recover some of the wealth they had lost in the conflict. Indeed, such a promotion was far from unheard of. Dominicans had been being appointed to powerful positions in the church since the late 1220s, and many, such as Thomas's student Annibaldo, had become cardinals and patriarchs. Thomas, however, followed the example of St. Dominic, who had refused all attempts to honor him. The Master knew that he did not want the promotion for several reasons. In the first place, it would put an immense administrative burden on him, making it impossible to continue his academic work. Further, it is plain that he had no interest in the accumulation of wealth (and was perhaps a bit discomfited by the implication that he alienate church revenue to his family). Finally, the public nature of the office would probably have terrified the reserved academic, who we already know was socially awkward. Humility certainly played a part in his refusal, but so indeed did an honest assessment of his own character. He kindly refused the offer and returned to his cell.

Thomas had been working on a different project that he was near to realizing. As an ex officio member of the provincial chapters, he had probably not been remiss in reminding them of the mandates of the General Chapter of 1259 regarding the reformation of studies in the order. After all, Thomas had been one of the authors of those very admonitions. It seems little was done to set in motion any substantive reformation of curriculum or teaching. This bolsters the idea that the instructions of 1259 were but small steps in a process that would take several generations to implement completely. Many provinces, including Thomas's own, had still not complied with the injunction to set up *studia* for logic. The province of Spain had even disbanded an early *studia artium* that it had set up.[97] The province of Provence had set up a *studium* for natural philosophy in 1262, but it went forward in only fits and starts until it was erected on a firmer basis in 1271. The origins of this hesitancy are not always clear, but the most probable reason was an undercurrent in the order that opposed the introduction of philosophy. This does not mean that the opponents were anti-intellectual, but rather that such opposition arose from those who wanted to study theology alone along traditional monastic lines or who emphasized the practical side of theology, choosing to focus on the pastoral responsibilities of preaching and hearing confessions. After all, it was supposed to be the very mission of the order to go out and preach. The *Vitas Fratrum* was characteristic of such tendencies. Within that work are several stories that castigate brothers who became too vainly curious about natural philosophy. Humbert himself chastised those who pursued study without virtue. In truth, the number of truly brilliant academics was small in proportion to the size of the order, and an attempt to bring Parisian methods into the convents was bound to draw some suspicion. It would be an uphill battle for the admission of philosophy, and particularly Aristotle, inside the walls of the priories.

Thomas was certainly not one to engage in political agitation (that was more to Albert's taste), yet his experiences at Orvieto as Lector had left him with serious questions about the means for equipping friars for their mission. Simply stated, he was dissatisfied with the tools at his disposal for teaching theology to the *fratres communes*.[98] The disconnected manuals and collections that purported to introduce people to the subject lacked coherence. The curriculum was too oriented toward practical or pastoral theology for him. It gave the end without the beginning. For Thomas it was like building a castle without foundations. He wondered how preachers could handle objections when they had only memorized manuals. If there was to be a wholesale renewal of theology, it had to begin with principles and only then proceed to practice. It was not enough for Dominicans to learn how to handle themselves in the confessional and the pulpit. Rather, they had to immerse themselves in the very sources of revelation in a sustained and systematic manner. The standard collection of Peter Lombard left much to be desired. Aside from an overarching four-part structure, there was little organization in the text itself. Indeed, it was such a jumble of authorities that Joseph Pieper has called it an "Augustinian breviary."[99] While it could serve as a springboard to deeper theological issues, there was no overall organization or fundamental orientation. What was needed was harmony, that medieval intellectual principle that could be found from music to architecture to law. For Thomas—as for Aristotle—the office of the wise man was to order things, to bring them into unity and harmony that reflected the mind of the heavenly designer. Thomas needed time to experiment and to come up with a way of structuring revelation in an ordered, rational way. Since his own province was one of the laggards concerning the streamlining of education, it is likely that Thomas leaned upon the chapters to fulfill the injunctions of 1259. As a result, when Thomas went to the provincial chapter of Anagni in September of 1265, it assigned him to the Roman priory of Santa Sabina, there to create something unheard of in the order: a *studium personale*. This school would be under Thomas's complete control, he could admit or dismiss students at will, and he had the authority to teach as he saw fit. In a certain sense this was to be Thomas's experimental laboratory where all of his previous experience would come together to create his theological masterpiece: the *Summa Theologiae*.

Rome was a good choice for this undertaking. Not only was it in the heart of the province, but there one had little chance of being drawn into papal projects. This surprising fact requires some explanation. While many point to the absent Avignon papacy of the 1300s as the source of the city's decline, in reality the popes had largely abandoned Rome for nearly half a century. The curia was itinerant, spending much of its time moving from town to town. The menace of the Hohenstaufens operating from their territories in southern Italy encouraged this mobility, but even after the end of their threat in 1268 the curia continued to be peripatetic, coming to Rome only rarely. Medieval Rome was a shadow of its former glory. It had dwindled to perhaps thirty thousand residents, with little or no native industry save that of serving (and fleecing) pilgrims. The remaining citizens, however, were fiercely independent, staging various coups and uprisings over the centuries against papal rule, making it difficult for the curia to stay for any long period. In addition, the city was divided among powerful families who fortified ancient sites such as the Colosseum to dominate their neighborhoods and to engage in periodic street violence. Some order was restored in 1265 as Charles of Anjou moved to end the Hohenstaufen dynasty and occupy southern Italy. Most of the vast area enclosed by the Aurelian walls had returned to nature, and the remaining people clustered about the unruly Tiber in the flood-prone lowlands of the *Campo Marzio*, whose wandering lanes today bear witness to its medieval origins. Residence in this low-lying area also encouraged the spread of malaria, the bane of Lazio until the early part of the twentieth century. Rome, in short, was almost as much a backwater place as Orvieto, with the added demerit of fouler air. Yet it was tranquil, and on its margins was situated the convent where Dominic had established himself. Santa Sabina stood on the northern promontory of the Aventine hill, overlooking the meandering Tiber below, raised somewhat above the malevolent air of the valley. Far removed from the bustle of the medieval town, the Aventine was almost a rural oasis at this time. There Thomas would find time for unbroken concentration on his new projects.

The *studium personale* of Thomas d'Aquino was certainly unique. He probably did not even have a Bachelor under him to assist with the lectures. Indeed, the *studium* entirely ceased to exist after his departure in 1268. It seems that its sole reason for its existence was for the Master to experiment with new curriculum and texts. Reginald, now an accomplished secretary, certainly accompanied him, and it is likely that he had at least a couple of other secretaries assigned to him at this point, particularly in light of his astonishing output. We have a very probable reconstruction of his efforts and initiatives while there.[100] In the first year, Thomas attempted again to salvage some use of the traditional textbook of the schools, the *Sentences* of Peter Lombard. The happy discovery of another set of lectures on the *Sentences* in the library of Lincoln College has established that Thomas delivered his class anew in 1265–66 at Santa Sabina (confirming an observation by Ptolemy), and has also proven useful in tracing the evolution of Thomas's thought on several decisive issues.[101] Yet, at the end of the academic year, Thomas abandoned the new commentary. He unquestionably turned his back on the *Sentences* for the remainder of his life in order to begin work on a massive new effort that would focus on an ordered and harmonious recounting of dogmatic theology in its entirety: the project of the *Summa Theologiae*. While I will not go here into all of the different models proposed for the organization of the project, suffice it to say that Fr. Chenu's model of *exitus-reditus* has proven enduring. In Chenu's conception, the plan of the work over four large volumes (with the second being divided into two parts, thus I-II and II-II), is the doctrine of God in himself, followed by the going forth of all things from God, then the return of all creation to its source, with a privileged place being extended to Christ as the fundamental and irreplaceable means of that very return. Some have challenged the Neoplatonism of this circular model, but it remains in its substantial outline as the best way to explain the whole of this symphony of theology. Thomas likely lectured from his ongoing work on the *Summa* from 1266 to 1268, omitting the material that he had covered in the *Sentences* on the existence and attributes of God, since he had the same students and would not have traversed the same material. It seems safe to conclude that Thomas completed the first part in Rome before his second departure to Paris.[102]

It was normal for a Regent Master to offer two lectures (or classes) per day. It is most probable that the afternoon class for his first two years was a commentary on the *Divine Names* by (Pseudo-)Dionysius the Areopagite. This work has gained attention because of its profound Neoplatonism. Long characterized as a fundamentally Aristotelian thinker, the influence of Plato (as mediated through Augustine and Dionysius) is pervasive in the works of Thomas.[103] This was one of the first academic texts Thomas himself had encountered when he had served as Albert's teaching assistant in Cologne, and he had kept a handwritten copy of it his whole life.[104] In addition to his duties lecturing as Regent Master, Thomas also had the responsibility of conducting disputed questions on various topics. In the Roman setting, these were certainly not the dynamic debates of his Parisian tenure, but probably had two main purposes. In the first place, it was up to Thomas to choose topics to debate, so he selected fundamental theological and philosophical problems parallel to the lectures and texts he was working on, a method common among professors. Second, it was to give his students training in the art of academic debate, which enabled him to unfold the problems with greater detail and leisure. During his Roman magistracy he most probably disputed questions on the power of God (*De Potentia*), on the problem of evil (*De Malo*), and on spiritual creatures (*De Spiritualibus Creaturis*). Yet, in addition to a rearrangement of the whole of theology, Thomas chose something unexpected for his lectures in the final academic year of 1267–68. Inspired by a new translation of Aristotle's *On the Soul* by his colleague William of Moerbeke, he plunged into a lecture-commentary on the work of the Philosopher. While it was unusual for a Theology Master to lecture on a subject in the Arts, it is not so surprising as the audience. While certainly Thomas's students were not the simple *fratres communes* of Orvieto, still they only represented the upper tier of students in the Roman province. Thomas had, on his own authority, begun to offer philosophical lectures to Theology students, understanding it as a necessary preparation for academic theology.

What has been described above would certainly have occupied the time of a normal man; but Thomas assiduously worked on further projects, not directly connected to the classroom. One is a particularly charming work, too often underappreciated by Thomistic scholars, the *Compendium Theologiae*. This work was a simple—but not simplistic—abbreviation of the contents of the *Summa* arranged according to the theological virtues, the Creed, and the Ten Commandments. It was likely done at Reginald's entreaty. The *socius* had requested this shorter work for less advanced brothers. He may have sensed that the *Summa*—which Thomas had honestly but perhaps optimistically intended for "beginners"—was indeed quite advanced theology. This shorter volume would bridge the gap between the two works, and indeed has much to commend it on its own as a more meditative and, dare one say, spiritual introduction to theology. Thomas also engaged other tasks. Even on the rural Aventine he could not evade the courier, and his position as a famous theologian ensured a stream of correspondence that Thomas answered with courtesy, exactitude, and promptness. He continued to advise Master John of Vercelli on matters of import, including defending his French colleague Pierre of Tarentaise against charges of unorthodoxy. It must be said that Thomas shows some impatience with the accuser in the text, alleging that he did not properly construe Pierre's intentions. The response certainly went some way to rescuing Pierre's reputation, since the Frenchman would return to Paris as a Master and later be elected as Pope Innocent V in 1276. Another occasional letter has had perhaps more influence than it was due. Thomas wrote a letter to the king of Cyprus during this period that was intended perhaps in the literary form of a "mirror for princes." Thomas probably dispatched this letter as a courtesy to a house that was known for its devotion to the order. The king, Hugh II, would later be buried in the Dominican church in Nicosia, and his children would become major patrons of the cult of Thomas's confrere St. Peter of Verona.[105] This was probably intended as a private missive, and it seems that the intended recipient's death in 1267 meant that Thomas also left this work unfinished. It was later completed by Ptolemy of Lucca, and it became known widely. Many attempted to see in the document an organic political philosophy, but its incomplete status, as well as its underdeveloped thought in relation to Thomas's other works, should offer a caution to anyone who tries to use this as a summation of Thomistic political thought. Thomas also continued to preach periodically during this period. It appears that once in Rome he gave a series of well-received sermons during Holy Week, culminating with a homily on the resurrection on Easter Sunday. While Tocco and Calo say this was done at St. Peter's, it is more likely that these took place as St. Mary Major, as one witness testified at the canonization that he heard the story directly from Reginald.[106] It seems Thomas was a popular preacher, for he spoke in the southern Italian dialect, probably familiar enough to inhabitants of Lazio, he adjusted his sermons to fit the audience, and—perhaps most of all—his sermons were short. As he himself said in his commentary on Hebrews, short sermons "are much more acceptable, because if they are good, they are heard more eagerly, and if they are bad, the boredom does not last long."[107] It was after the Easter sermon that a woman followed him after he left the pulpit, touched the back of his habit, and was cured of a hemorrhage. Of course the parallel to the story of the woman with a flow of blood, reported in the three Synoptics, is plain. The difference here is that unlike Christ, Thomas did not turn around, but probably hastened back to the sacristy. The woman had to travel to Santa Sabina to recount the miracle, only to be received by brother Reginald and not Thomas.[108] Thomas's care in avoiding the company of women was well known and remarked upon by many witnesses.

Thomas's achievements in Rome transpired in an atmosphere of peace and quiet, until the city itself was invaded by Conradin in July of 1268. Santa Sabina was sacked and very probably the students were dispersed. The ensuing chaos presented an opportunity for the order to use Thomas in a new role. Some historians in the past asserted that Thomas spent at least a year at the papal curia in Viterbo, but there is no evidence to support this contention at all.[109] Still, a storm was brewing in the north that would see the rise of old quarrels and the development of new ones. The rise of new antimendicant sentiment again menaced the Franciscans and Dominicans at the University of Paris, while a new battle opened over the incorporation of Aristotle and his Arabic commentators. This pitted the radical Aristotelians on one side and the "new" Augustinians of the Franciscan order on the other. Thomistic principles were caught right in the middle. As a result, the order hurriedly recalled Thomas to a highly unusual second Regency in Paris, an office that he hastened to undertake before too much of the academic year of 1268–69 had transpired. It would be one of the most challenging periods in his life.

Chapter 6

"THE HOLY DOCTORS... RAISED ABOVE THE HILLS"

The Christian world in 1268 was one of outward unity masking tectonic shifts that would echo for centuries. On one hand, the papacy had emerged victorious in its half-century (or indeed multicentury) conflict with the German house of Hohenstaufen. The last claimant of the house, Conradin, was beheaded in October of that year. The popes and their Italian allies had withstood the onslaught of the German Empire. A mostly friendly regime assumed power in southern Italy with the rise of Charles of Anjou, the brother of the friend of the church, King Louis IX. Louis was nearing the end of his life, however, and Charles would experience problems in Sicily that would endanger the security of his rule. The Crusades were tailing off into obsolescence, and the last Crusader stronghold of Acre would fall in 1291. Simon de Montfort—the son of St. Dominic's close friend—saw his representative government falter in England and in 1265 he met his demise in the battle of Evesham, ushering in a consolidation of royal authority. The Reconquista in Spain had paused after the stunning victories of St. Fernando III in the 1240s, with the kingdom passing to the scholarly Alfonso X and, after him, to civil war. The papacy itself saw a series of diminishing returns for the remainder of the century. Only with difficulty could it retain control even over the city of Rome itself, as the papal court relocated from the Lateran across the Tiber to the heavily fortified Vatican in the 1270s. Worse than that, though, was the paralysis of the increasingly reduced College of Cardinals. When Thomas's friend Clement IV died a month after Conradin in November of 1268, only twenty cardinals gathered in Viterbo to select a successor. The cardinals found that the Angevins could apply just as much pressure to the church as the Hohenstaufens had. The voters were deadlocked between pro-French and pro-Italian forces, with each side possessing enough votes to block anyone from receiving the necessary two-thirds plus one. As time went on, the cardinals were locked in (hence the origin of *conclave*, "with a key") and reduced to a diet of bread and water. Though accounts differ, it seems that the magistrates of Viterbo—under pressure from Charles of Anjou, who was then present in the city—even decided to remove the roof to encourage the election. Eventually the cardinals chose Gregory X (r. 1271–76, at that time the legate to the Holy Land) but only after a three-year delay. The interregnum of 1268–71 in reality extended into 1272, since Gregory X could not return back from the east until February. This meant that Thomas and his order lacked the foundational support of the pope at the critical juncture of his second Regency in Paris. This time, Thomas and the mendicants would have to fight on their own.

This power vacuum resulted in renewed attacks. The anxieties of the 1250s had not gone away; they simply went underground. Many in Paris and beyond still nursed grievances toward the friars, and the Dominicans in particular. This mingled with new intellectual currents swirling in the center of European intellectual life and mixed in with the reactions of many who perceived threats and unorthodoxies. The consensus of recent research is that Thomas left Rome in very late summer of 1268, took the sea route, and then followed the rivers of France north.[1] This would have gotten him to Paris as soon as possible following the commencement of the academic year 1268–69.[2] Thomas's departure from Italy was likely hastened by the sacking of Rome by the remaining Hohenstaufen loyalists in July and the volatile situation in Paris that demanded his presence at the university as quickly as possible. When he arrived to resume his Regency, he had to meet challenges on no fewer than three fronts. Allies and enemies were interwoven among all the factions. On one day Thomas might be arrayed with the Franciscans against a common target, only to find the next day the Minorites attacking his other positions. He found himself crossing swords with members of his beloved Arts faculty while attending to serious threats from the ecclesiastical powers in

Paris. Even within his own order an academic backlash was building against his and Albert's efforts to incorporate Aristotle's ideas more aggressively. To maintain one's balance while all these battles raged indeed took heroic effort. One scholar commented perceptively regarding Thomas's abilities in this regard, "Thomas belonged to that race of men whose imposing calm grows in proportion to the noise and tumult around them."[3]

It was not only the ferment of academic disputes that would occupy him. Thomas also had to conduct his normal university lectures, to continue to be present at and decide disputed questions, and to supervise the formation of new Dominican bachelors. In spite of all this, this period was the most productive of his entire career in terms of sheer academic output. Here we witness a man at the very height of his academic and intellectual powers. However, such a superhuman effort did not come without a cost. Within two years of surrendering his Parisian chair, Thomas would be dead.

FIGHTING THE CHIMERA

Hesiod describes a fantastical creature in his *Theogony*, originating in Homer's *Iliad*, that manifests itself as a three-headed beast: part lion, part goat, and part snake.[4] The brutal creature was killed by the heroic Bellerophon, aided by the winged horse, Pegasus. So, too, had three rival systems arisen to challenge the nascent Thomistic synthesis in the 1260s. The heady elixir of the new Aristotle had intoxicated many young Arts Masters, particularly as mediated by his Arabic commentator Averroes. To tell the truth, Thomas had much to do with this, and indeed he was presently engaged in a comprehensive effort to read and comment on all of the extant Aristotelian literature. Particularly salient for these young Masters were three arguments that seemed to have all the persuasive power of deductive logic behind them. First, it appeared to many that Aristotle was guilty of a type of monopsychism, the conception that there was one agent—or active—intellect that was common to all people indiscriminately. The active intellect is the power that we possess to abstract the essence or nature of a thing—its deepest reality—from its existing material conditions. Part of Aristotle's argument for the immortality of the soul was that this power was necessarily immaterial, for knowledge of immaterial realities (e.g., human nature, or justice, or triangularity) demands an immaterial power. This means that, at the very least, the agent intellect did not corrupt with the rest of the body after death. His Arab commentators pushed this conclusion further. They declared that this power did not *of necessity* attach itself to an individual soul. Although the separable agent intellect does indeed survive death, that mere fact does not thereby indicate that *I* survive death in a personal way. The Arabs speculated that there was a universal agent intellect that served as the abstracting power for all humans, a position that endangered the philosophical proof for personal immortality. This has implications down the line for human anthropology, affecting such Christian essentials as the resurrection of the body and the freedom of the will. The second issue brought up by Aristotle's Arab interpreters was the issue of providence. Aristotle had defined God as subsistent thought that thinks itself (or, to put it more colloquially, "Thinking Thinking Thinking," which is actually a grammatical sentence). This presents two problems. In the first place, God can have only one proper concept: the Absolute Thought by which he contemplates himself. He has no thoughts about contingent, secondary things, for that would be injurious to his self-sufficiency. Second, it follows that God has no special knowledge of particulars outside of himself, meaning that he—being utterly self-sufficient—has no truck with inferior things, which radically undermines the Christian theory of providence. So God, beyond having nothing at all to do with the changeable world, does not even *know* it. Yet a third issue arose that was perhaps the most serious. The first two we have mentioned were essentially Arab distillations of the Philosopher's thought. The third actually came from Aristotle himself: his proofs regarding the eternity of the world. Not having any knowledge of a divine creation, the Philosopher had determined that the world was a simultaneous, eternal effect of the one eternal cause. Of course this diverged substantially from the Judeo-Christian account found in Genesis and was perhaps the single greatest challenge to the acceptance of Aristotelian ideas among Christian thinkers. The intellectual world of Christendom was entering a very dangerous phase. One should remember that a similar charged moment ended the Islamic golden age. Theologians and literalists came to distrust the radical conclusions of Muslim philosophers. The philosophers for their part began to disdain Islamic revelation, concluding that philosophy was a higher and purer form of knowledge. This led to a backlash against the philosophical life that left the Sunni world, in particular, in intellectual somnolence. The danger was that a similar "great divorce" between faith and reason would rend the Christian world.

Disquiet about Aristotle had been growing as new texts made their way to Christian Europe over the course of the early 1200s. Despite the efforts of the authorities to restrict his study, the fascination with Aristotle only grew with each passing year. By 1255 Aristotle had definitively entered the curriculum of the Arts at Paris, and men such as Albert and Thomas were pushing for his incorporation from the side of Theology. Indeed, Aristotelian logic had long been established as the foundation of the Scholastic method. All scholars used Aristotle to some extent, and many of those who opposed Aristotle on the matters in which he seemed to dissent from revelation continued to use him where he was useful in their own work. It was not so much that there were those who wanted to banish Aristotle entirely; rather, the debate was regarding the extent to which the Philosopher could be domesticated for use by Christians in the Arts or—a more delicate job this—in the service of the queen of the sciences herself, Theology. Aligning themselves among the skeptics were many of the theologians trained in older models of monastic scholarship, and this included most of the professors of the Franciscan order. In their emphasis on will and affectivity, these thinkers spurned what they considered to be the excessive intellectualism of the Aristotelians. Echoing older critiques of philosophical curiosity, they rested content in the arms of revelation. While happy to employ Aristotelian logical tools, they disdained to allow his purview to overshadow theology itself. The members of this group have been called "traditionalists" and "Augustinians," yet both of those titles are misleading. They were not traditionalists, for they too were creatively responding to changing contemporary situations. They certainly rooted themselves in a tradition that affirmed the primacy of will and therefore the biblical supremacy of charity. While this affective theology of the will certainly had many roots in St. Augustine, in many cases positions that came to be attributed to the author of the *City of God* had simply not been heard of until the thirteenth century. Situations that would have been utterly alien to the thought world of Augustine came to be attributed to the saint. One of these was the "Augustinian" doctrine of a plurality of substantial forms in humanity. This drew upon the Greek teaching that every material thing was determined by its form. The material stone of a statue was given the "form" of Caesar by the hand of an artist. Insofar as humans were concerned, many thirteenth-century thinkers could not conceive of a spiritual form that could also "inform" matter. Therefore some philosophers proposed three forms in every human, each one controlling the vegetative, sensitive, and rational faculties, respectively. Controversially, Thomas would argue for a unicity of form in the human substance, declaring that matter and spirit are principles of one totality, that is, we are one incarnational reality. In taking this position, he was not contradicting Augustine. Indeed, many have noted the increasing influence of Augustine's thought as Thomas developed his ideas in the *Summa Theologiae*.[5]

One area in which contemporary Augustinians did attempt to follow their namesake was in the idea of divine illumination. They argued that God provided direct illumination for our power of abstraction. This combined with the previous contentions of the radical Aristotelians, and some have called this position an "Avicennizing Augustinianism."[6] While our minds are capable of knowing material reality on their own, these thinkers contended that in order to know immaterial universals, God gave us a special assistance that enabled us to participate in the Divine Ideas (the Christian analogue of Plato's "World of Forms"). This external assistance is the cause of our knowing truth and our assurance of its certitude. Thomas would respond by defending the autonomy and integrity of the human mind, able to abstract on its own without external aid. In so doing, he defended the natural sufficiency and completeness of human nature. The chief upshot of this "Augustinian" philosophy—which would be laid out in exceptional detail by Duns Scotus and William of Ockham in the fourteenth century—was the primacy of the will, a result of what one scholar calls their "weak investment in moral rationality."[7] These thinkers demanded the radical dependence of all creation upon the will of God, which to them was another way of asserting the primacy of love, which is rooted in the faculty of the will. The implications of this theory in the hands of the later radical voluntarists (*voluntas* = will) would be, not to put too fine a point upon it, troublesome.[8]

The final group—who most deserve the title "reactionaries"— was most likely the reason that the order recalled Thomas to Paris.[9] The Secular party was again on the march, dredging up old arguments against the mendicants and opening new lines of attack. Following the defeat of William of Saint Amour, the situation had quieted down, yet the resentments engendered by the crisis simmered under the surface. Restrictions remained in place against the friars, even after Alexander IV's intervention. While the university was forced to admit the Friar Masters to the consortium, it made sure to limit them to three chairs only (one Franciscan and two Dominican). The consortium restricted mendicant Masters to the Theology faculty, forbade their students from incepting in the Arts, and discouraged Secular pupils from attending the lectures of the friars and absolutely forbade them to incept under them.[10] Indeed, in sullen retaliation, in the congregation of Masters the Seculars would often bring up for discussion the recall of William of Saint Amour. Because of the papal prohibition on reviewing this decision, the mendicants would have to retire and so would be prevented from engaging in the debates of the consortium. For almost a decade the matter fermented, until combat was joined again in the second half of the 1260s. William of Saint Amour, in exile since the time of Alexander, took the occasion of the election of the French Clement IV to renew his suit at the curia.[11] While Clement responded by reaffirming mendicant privileges in February of 1267, it was an indication that the fight was ready to enter a new stage. In 1267 the troublesome Picard bedel Guillot—the one excommunicated for heckling Thomas in 1259—was elected the bedel of the entire university, a shot across the bow of the mendicants if there ever was one.[12] On October 7, onetime Secular Master and former chancellor Stephen Tempier was elected Bishop of Paris. This gave the Seculars a staunch ally, and indeed the new bishop would do much to thwart the advance of Thomism and Aristotelianism in Paris.[13] The real signal for a resumption of hostilities was Clement's death in November of 1268. The three-year interregnum meant that the mendicants had no pope to turn to for their defense this time. They would be on their own until the election of a new pontiff. The

Seculars chose their moment well, for there would be no new successor of Peter for nearly three years.[14]

The chief actor in this drama on the side of the Seculars was Gerard d'Abbeville, who was a Regent Master in Theology at Paris from 1257 until his death in 1272. He was a famous and prolific Master, holding many more quodlibets than Thomas himself during his tenure. He was a rich cleric, a fact that had notable effects on his expansive defenses of the wealth of the church. He was also a benefactor to poor students (as long as they were not mendicants) and would later be considered the founder of the library of the Sorbonne.[15] As early as 1267 he was agitating against the mendicant orders, inveighing against their admission of excessively young men. This was a perennial bugbear of Gerard's partisans, who were certain that the bulk of the friars' vocations came from overimpressionable boys. The acceptance of excessively young men was not only a technical violation of canon law, it threatened social order by removing them from the supervision of their families and hindered them from coming to study with the Seculars. During his Advent quodlibet of 1268, Gerard inveighed against religious poverty, saying it violated the Aristotelian mean by veering off into a vicious extreme. He also asserted that the most perfect life was the "pastor," which not only included bishops, but every Secular priest who had the care of souls. All of this was, however, merely preparatory. Gerard was not one to shrink from controversy (indeed, scholars of every stripe demonstrated the virtue of intellectual courage at this time). Bravely, he took his case to the Franciscans themselves, and preached a sermon against evangelical poverty from the pulpit of their own church. On January 1, 1269, he extolled the examples of Constantine and Saint Sylvester (whose feast was the day before). It was a frontal attack on certain strains of Franciscanism that elevated poverty as the sine qua non of holiness. Gerard strongly intimated that this "evangelical poverty" was but cleverly concealed heresy that sought to weaken the institutional church by divesting it of possessions it had held for nearly a millennium. This attack was brazen enough, but even more so when one understands that it took place in front of the Franciscan Regent Master, John Pecham, and none other than the Minister General himself, Bonaventure. It is also possible that, already being present in the city, Thomas too would have been in attendance in the choir of the Franciscan church to hear this open assault on the orders.[16]

These would be the enemies that Thomas would face in his four years at Paris. Further complicating the matter was the fact that each of these was opposed to the others in a myriad of ways. Thomas partly supported and partly critiqued the radical Aristotelians. He railed against excessive Averroism, but at the same time retained the love and friendship of the Arts faculty, who in turn held many of the other theologians in contempt. While he and Bonaventure were united in defending the religious life of the mendicants, their relationship was increasingly strained by Thomas's commitment to Aristotelian epistemology, cosmology, and anthropology. While John Pecham would rally to the Dominicans' side in refuting Secular critiques of their regular life, in terms of his philosophical positions he was one of Thomas's most ardent critics. Gerard, for his part, though he attacked the mendicants, was a thoroughgoing "Augustinian" in theology. Alliances depended on the issues and could rapidly shift or dissolve when confronted with new challenges. This period of Thomas's life, while he was at the height of his intellectual powers, demanded careful balancing and diplomacy. Thrown back into an astonishingly difficult situation, his poised, clear, and charitable responses to all three movements admirably illuminate his remarkable character.

REGENCY RESUMED

The amount of work that Thomas accomplished during these four years was nothing short of astonishing. In spite of his magisterial responsibilities and swirling controversies, he reached the peak of his academic output, and calculations about his work are staggering. If one takes account of all Thomas's production during this time, the total comes to over four thousand pages of text. Thomas wrote the equivalent of twelve typed pages per normal work day.[17] Nor was this simply pastoral or dogmatic material, but densely and closely argued philosophical and theological work. Knowing his prodigious capacity, the order put resources at his disposal. The most notable of these was his *socius*, Reginald, who was with him the whole time, taking dictation and editing his Master's efforts.

During this period Thomas had many more secretaries. Tocco even describes him simultaneously dictating to three and even four secretaries at a time.[18] Many have pointed out that this was not unheard of for men of genius, and they mention similar stories about Julius Caesar and Napoleon. One is forced to come to the conclusion that this is not only probable, but rather a necessary precondition to understanding his productivity at the time.[19] It is even possible that there was a team of professional scribes in attendance upon Thomas in Paris. In addition, Thomas employed research aids and tools to aid in his rapid appropriation of texts, particularly those of Aristotle. An example of this is the thematic index to the *Nicomachean Ethics*, which served to organize his thoughts for composing the II-II of the *Summa*. Further contributing to his productivity was his habit of sleeping very little, a practice that tended to lead to exhaustion and that probably hastened the approach of death. At times he would doze, continuing to mumble in his sleep. Once he burned himself with a candle that he was holding because he had drifted off.[20] This taxing schedule was superhuman, and while it could be maintained for a while, it had, as we will see, long-term consequences for Thomas's work and health.

Thomas's primary obligation at Paris was always as "Master of the Sacred Page." It was his duty to expound the Scriptures, mostly to Dominican students, but I suspect that many Arts students slipped away to attend his lectures as well. When Thomas arrived, the university was on strike (as it was periodically wont to do). Yet he commenced classes immediately. This was technically legal since his lectures were primarily for his Dominican pupils. As result, the university levied no sanctions, but such an act probably added to the preexisting tensions seething through the congregation of Masters. Thomas apparently began his teaching with a commentary on St. Matthew in the academic year of 1269–70. Among other reasons, it is clear that Thomas wanted to use this Gospel as a way to blunt the critiques of the Seculars on the perfection of mendicant life.[21] He did not just wish to engage in biblical polemics. He wanted to go deeper both theologically and scripturally. To that end, he made it his primary teaching preoccupation to create a grand theological commentary on the Gospel of John, which he covered during the period from 1270 to 1272.[22] He makes clear in his prologue that he pursued the Gospel of John because it offered a greater opportunity to meditate on the divinity of Christ than did the Synoptics, which emphasized his humanity.[23] Widely recognized as his most mature and sublime theological commentary, some have suggested that this text was the equal of his more famous *Summae*. His trusty secretary Reginald recorded these lectures, which Thomas later corrected personally. The editorial contributions of his secretary have received increasing notice, particularly Reginald's augmentations from the *Catena Aurea* on John.[24] The sheer size of the work would have demanded at least two full academic years to cover. The labor of copying and editing was paid for by one of Thomas's former students, Adenulf of Anagni. Adenulf would later incept as Regent Master himself and be elected to the see of Paris in 1288. Unfortunately this partisan of Saint Thomas would die a year later. One can only speculate how a student of Thomas who had an extended tenure as Bishop of Paris could have contributed to dispelling the cloud over Thomism that had gathered by that time. The text of the Johannine commentary is deeply contemplative; it is the work of an exceptionally profound mind, genuinely encapsulating von Balthasar's notion of *théologie à genoux*, or "theology on one's knees." What Thomas offered for his second class has been a subject of controversy for a long time. This is due to the difficulty of dating the lectures he gave on the Pauline corpus. There has been increasing consensus in pushing his teaching on the Epistles back to Naples in 1272–73, but this would imply a considerable amount of writing concentrated in a short period. While I too am persuaded by the Pauline manuscript tradition emanating from Italy and not Paris, there may still be something to say about the idea that Thomas began his lectures on Romans at the end of his stint in Paris and then continued to teach Paul's letters in Naples, making corrections to the notes upon his return to Italy.[25]

Another of the duties of a Regent Master was to hold debates on disputed questions. These were extended analyses of a particular question of the moment, which the Master would expound over a period of weeks or months. While earlier scholars were persuaded that the *De Anima*, because of its anti-Averroistic content, could be attributed to the Parisian period, the experts of the Leonine commission fixed its composition at the beginning of the

Master's Roman sojourn in the mid-1260s. It is likely that Thomas was well apprised of the debates transpiring at Paris and had begun a fundamental assessment of radical Aristotelianism before his second Parisian regency. This also helps to explain how he was able so quickly to wade into the debates when he arrived. The consensus today assigns the disputed questions *De Malo* to the second Parisian period. The study of sin and evil in this work parallels the sophisticated moral reasoning then emerging in the II-II of the *Summa*. One other disputed question, an odd one, is generally dated to the end of his term in Paris. This is the *De Unione Verbi Incarnati*, or "On the Union of the Incarnate Word." This was on the vexed question concerning the number of discrete acts of being in Christ. Did Christ have a divine existence *and* a properly human existence, or did the existence of the Incarnate Word proceed only from the divine act of being? The perplexity is because Thomas argues here in favor of a primary and secondary existence, or two "acts of being" in Christ. The problem is that he also argues—in no fewer than four places, both before and after this question—that Christ only has one proper "act of being," a divine one. Thomists have debated this question from the very beginning, and it has received increased attention recently because of the rise of phenomenology in the Catholic Church. It is a critical issue because it runs along the delicate fault line between the heresies of Monophysitism (Christ has only one nature: a divine one) and Nestorianism (Christ is properly two persons: one human, one divine). The orthodox doctrine is that Christ is one divine person who has two natures, divine and human. The question remains a difficult one, not only in theology, but also for the interpretation of Thomas's own thought.[26]

Beyond the systematic disputed questions, which were the prerogative of Regent Masters and which could be developed at leisure, were the more pressing and immediately relevant quodlibetal questions. At this stage of his career, Thomas would have let his Bachelor do most of the heavy lifting, responding to the questions that could be raised by anyone in the audience. He would reserve his magisterial determination for the end of the debates. It should be noted that some Masters offered quodlibets more than others, for it was a dangerous exercise that could open them up to criticism, particularly from ambitious young students and other

Masters seeking to make a name for themselves. Thomas was quite prolific, with twelve total quodlibets, but the most productive in this field—to his credit—was his Secular rival Gerard d'Abbeville, who held no fewer than twenty. These subjects could be quite wide ranging, from traditional theological and philosophical issues to problems of morality and economics. It is generally agreed today that, somewhat awkwardly, the majority of later quodlibets come earlier. Quodlibets 7 to 11 are from Thomas's earlier regency from 1256 to 1259, while 1–6 and 12 come from this later period in Thomas's life.[27] Within these questions are 260 discrete subjects of wide-ranging concern. Parallel to this extra work of disputation, Thomas continued to make himself available for various consultations, clearly considering it as a key work of an active professor. He answered a variety of correspondence, sometimes on unexpected issues, such as medicine, astrology, and magic, and continued to make himself available for consultations by the Master of the Order, his friend John of Vercelli. The questions on the power of superiors over their subordinates, particularly in matters of secrecy, arose after the General Chapter in Paris in 1269. While Thomas did not have a seat at the chapter, a man of his stature would probably have been present. The matter was presented to a board of Masters including Thomas, who showed an independent streak by dissenting from the other experts on several points. He was also receptive to questions from outside the order, even from laymen. One letter appears to be addressed to Margaret of Constantinople, Countess of Flanders, regarding issues of governance, particularly among the Jews in her realm. She had also addressed the same questions to John Pecham, and perhaps also to Gerard d'Abbeville. For once the burden of Thomas's other duties was betrayed by a hasty and not terribly considered reply. There was nothing groundbreaking in the letter; rather it was jejune and hurried. Thomas wished that Margaret had consulted someone more apt for the task, and perhaps considered that the other respondents had already answered satisfactorily. Thomas did not add anything to the existing history of Jewish-Christian relations, and he was perhaps even more irenic toward them than many contemporaries, while repeating the established Augustinian "witness" doctrine that grudgingly tolerated Jews, but relegated them to a second-class status.[28] There is nothing in Thomas's life or work that suggests any traces of anti-Semitism; indeed, his gentle colloquy with two Jews at the castle of Cardinal Riccardo Annibaldi at Molara one Christmas is emblematic both of Thomas's kindness and of the desire to convert Jews rather than to persecute them.[29]

During this time the Master was also pursuing his purely academic research. He had already started his magnum opus, the *Summa Theologiae*, while in Rome.[30] He had just begun the I-II when he was dispatched to Paris. While there he completed the whole of the second part, finishing the I-II and likely completing the II-II. These sections can be broadly referred to under the heading of "moral theology," which, for Thomas, formed merely another component of the one science of theology, proceeding directly from the doctrine of God and creation that he had pursued in the first part. Here Thomas is at his most original and captivating. He envisions the human moral life as revolving around the practices of the virtues, subsumed under the end of happiness. He absorbs the Aristotelian concept of the virtuous mean between two vicious extremes, and then transcends it by thoroughly situating it within the sphere of revelation. We should view the II-II in the context of Christology. We can only see the planned normativity of human virtue, lost by sin, in light of Christ (this paves the way for the Third Part and counters those who have trouble seeing Christ in the plan of the *Summa*).[31] Far from being a mere repetitive commentary on the seven deadly sins, or an exposition of the Ten Commandments, the Second part sees the end of humans in the intellectual contemplation of the truth, performed in the good, and finding its fruition in love. Here Thomas counters Franciscan insistence on the primacy of the will. We must know what to love and how to love well before we can attain to the final fruition of happiness in loving contemplation. It is in the second part that his famous meditations on law and grace can be found. Many have commented on the increasing warmth of the Second Part compared to the rather dry First Part. It was no mistake that Thomas became best known after his death for the II-II, which by far was the most circulated section of his work.[32] In spite of Thomas's insistence on the primacy of the intellect, he seems to have absorbed much of the burgeoning "Augustinianism" of the thirteenth century. Perhaps this came from his confrontation with a radicalized Aristotelianism (accelerated by the condemnations of 1270), or from a deepening spiritual experience. In any case, while far from abandoning the Philosopher, Thomas had become more fully the theologian.[33] This is also the section of the *Summa* that defends the prerogatives of the religious life. This final section of II-II is reflective of the fullness of his time in Paris. He rejects the excessive Franciscan emphasis on poverty and counters the claims of the Seculars. In so doing, he claims for the mendicants— and particularly the Dominicans—the most perfect "mixed" life of contemplation and action together. The development of the Second Part fits perfectly within the contemporary concerns that Thomas encountered in the Latin Quarter in the years 1269–72.

TAKING THE FIELD

While accomplishing all of this, Thomas was engaged directly on the three fronts: against the Secular Masters, against the Radical Aristotelians (sometimes called Latin Averroists), and against the Augustinians, mainly represented by the Franciscan Masters. It will be good to take the three in this order to understand the force of Thomas's responses. We will begin with the historical reason that Thomas was recalled to Paris—the conflict about the mendicants and religious perfection. It is difficult for many who study Thomas's thought, impressed by the sophisticated theological and philosophical answers to the radical Aristotelians and Augustinians alike, that—to his contemporaries and even to his biographers fifty years later—this conflict with the Seculars was the main event of Thomas's second tenure. For his brethren and for the writers of his histories, the mendicants' very right to exist was at stake. To lose this battle would mean the eclipsing of their vision of religious perfection and reversion to a model of the church that their orders had been founded to reform. The power of the papacy, due to its extraordinary predilection for the orders, was also at stake. Thomas's stalwart and successful defense of the order's honor was much clearer at the time of his canonization in 1323 than his critiques against either of the other intellectual challenges. For many Preachers, Thomas's triumph crystallized the moment of Dominican victory, presaged by the canonization of its saints and sealed by the election of Pierre of Tarentaise as Pope Innocent V in 1276. As

Thomism struggled for life against the resurgent nominalists and voluntarists of the 1300s and the revival of Neoplatonism during the Renaissance, his vindication of the mixed religious life of the mendicants stood out as an obvious moment of victory for a besieged cause and betokened the coming of an evolved ecclesiology, insulating the Dominicans from the backlash against new orders at the Second Council of Lyons in 1274.[34] Much was at stake, and Thomas comported himself with grace and dignity, bringing the conflict with the Seculars to a satisfactory conclusion.

Unlike the earlier conflict of the 1250s, the debate was confined to the university. Notable was the lack of any substantive popular agitation of the kind that had physically endangered the Dominicans twenty years earlier. In that sense the conflict was to be fought entirely on Thomas's own ground: the life of the mind. While people in taverns still parroted the anti-mendicant ditties of Rutebeuf, they were sung more from community memory than any genuine popular agitation against the orders. Gerard and his allies would have to fight this time on entirely intellectual terrain. The new antimendicants were also deprived of their most effective weapon of the earlier fight. The charges of Joachitism disappeared, the *Eternal Gospel* had been condemned by the church and repudiated by the mendicants, and in any case the magical Joachite year of 1260 had passed without any apocalyptic result. Therefore the Secular Masters began to hew toward other well-trodden lines of attack, wherein they sought to marshal antimendicant sentiment from the broader ecclesial culture. In particular this had to do with the uses of wealth. Especially galling to them was the professed poverty of the orders, while at the same time massive bequests poured into their coffers. From one angle, this practice of the mendicants was the height of hypocrisy: loudly claiming poverty while building grand churches and convents. On another level, the seculars were being deprived of massive revenue streams, particularly from burial bequests, wherein wealth would be directed away from traditional channels (parishes and canonries) and directed toward the mendicants in exchange for prayers and memorial Masses after death. The Seculars were especially piqued by the lack of support from the laity, which they had formerly enjoyed. By the late 1260s the mendicants were part and parcel of medieval life, and the laity increasingly turned to them for preaching, confession, spiritual direction, and advice. They found them to be holy and learned, two characteristics only rarely found among the secular clergy of the time. Because of this, lay-people spoke with their wallets, patronizing the orders to the detriment of the Seculars. The Seculars considered this social reality to be a direct threat to their existence. Using the traditional ecclesiology we have already encountered in William of Saint Amour, they alleged that only bishops and pastors possessed title and mission to preach and hear confessions, and that this was a matter of divine law from which the pope could not dispense. Indeed, the more one becomes familiar with this conflict the more one sees a nascent Gallicanism that would emerge fully in the early modern period.[35] Gallicanism is the theory that each national church is independent. The pope has an overall spiritual authority, but bishops hold power directly from God and are allowed to govern their territories with absolute independence. This proto-Gallicanism runs like a theme through all the antimendicant writers. One could even allege that the papacy, formerly a partisan of the university, was directly responsible for this by its constant, unstinting predilection for the mendicants. This forced the Seculars to close ranks and refine a theory of ecclesiastical localism.

Gerard, along with his associate Nicholas of Lisieux, molded these critiques into a theological form. Gerard had composed an analogue to William's *De Periculis* in 1257 called *Contra Adversarium Perfectionis Christianae* (Against the enemy of Christian perfection) but had never published it for fear of suffering a similar fate to William. He kept it in reserve until the opportune time. With the death of Clement IV, Gerard sprang into action and published it. In this work Gerard attacks evangelical poverty as a heresy that challenged the acquisition of temporal wealth by the church. He condemned begging, using the classical formula of St. Paul, "Anyone unwilling to work should not eat" (2 Thess 3:10). He also claimed that the state of perfection that was enjoyed by the bishops of the church also extended to every level of the traditional hierarchy, that is, to all who held the office of pastor in the Christian church. Gerard not only proposed this in his monograph, but he and his partisans took the field to offer many quodlibetal questions on the nature of perfection, poverty, and ecclesiology. At this point both Thomas and the Franciscans John Pecham and

Bonaventure joined the fray, offering their own disputed questions and writing more extensive works in defense of the orders. For the Minorites, the key was to defend their doctrine of poverty. They had the advantage of Bonaventure's moderate route of Conventualism that served to check the absolutist Spirituals.[36] The popes held the property for the Franciscans, who merely used it. It was a legal fiction, but it prevented the spread of what would become the heresy of Spiritual Franciscanism, and it had the advantage of not being a wholesale condemnation of poverty. As long as the Franciscans could maintain that balance (delicate as it was), they could withstand the attacks of the Seculars. Pecham, in particular, stoutly defended the relationship between poverty and the state of perfection.

Thomas's response was more broadly directed. He was interested in dismantling the Seculars' ecclesiology, along with their erroneous conception of religious perfection. By the beginning of 1270 Thomas had composed *De Perfectione Spiritualis Vitae* (On the perfection of the spiritual life). In this work he directly attacks the Seculars, stating that only bishops are in a state of perfection. This means that no lesser offices on the hierarchical ladder are to be included. Thomas also deftly avoids controversies over poverty by claiming it only as an aid, and indeed a lesser aid, to perfection. This was perhaps a strategy of divide and conquer, for his assault on the Seculars had a secondary target: the Franciscan overemphasis on poverty, exemplified by Pecham, who was quickly turning into one of Thomas's stoutest enemies.[37] Instead of poverty, the essence of perfection for Thomas was charity, the demands of which bound all Christians regardless of public vow. Christ established the counsels of poverty, chastity, and obedience to aid those seeking a more perfect way to holiness, for they disbar the one who makes the vow from avenues that impair the search for perfection. Thomas makes it very clear that "some people are perfect, who do not have a state of perfection [i.e., religious profession], while others have the state of perfection, but are not perfect."[38] This means there could be holy laymen and evil religious, yet the religious still possessed the state that was most amenable to the acquisition of perfection. This anticipated the development of a universal call to holiness, promoted by St. Francis de Sales in the 1600s and confirmed at the Second Vatican Council. These works by Thomas and his enemies appeared hot from the forge, and within weeks after their publication rejoinders appeared, raising numerous cogent criticisms. This led to Thomas appending another six chapters in February of 1270. In the manuscript history of his text we are privileged to watch the heat of an academic debate as it unfolded.

As 1270 wore on, the Seculars appended a new charge, one that did not form part of the attack of the 1250s. They assailed the mendicants for accepting young boys into the order before they were fully formed either in temperament or in virtue. Nicholas of Lisieux in particular held a series of quodlibets against Thomas's work that first brought the charge to light. Since the age of entrance was officially eighteen, it is clear that there was some truth to the accusation. Many youths were attracted to the order and could technically take vows as young as the canonical age of fourteen. While this ensured freedom in the contracting of vows, both marriage and religious, the Seculars were onto something about maturity (something that canonists would explore in the future). It is certainly possible that the mendicants were abusing the system and drawing into their ranks men who were too young. This is particularly clear from the chronicle sources that explicitly show the Dominicans targeting students. What this sometimes meant, as we have seen, is that the entrants often had a poor grounding in the Arts and were suitable only for basic practical Theology. More troubling to the Seculars was that their primary audience— the young Arts students—were being swept up by the mendicants before they could even darken the door of a Theology Master. This was a topic that hit close to home for Thomas. Not only had he been a Benedictine oblate as a young child, he had also entered the Dominican order as a very young man. His was undoubtedly similar to the experiences of many other brethren who entered young. He began by replying in the form of quodlibets, but these quickly metamorphosed into a new defense of the religious life called *Contra Doctrinam Retrahentium a Religione* (Against those who teach that [young men] be deterred from the religious life). In this text, Thomas comes out swinging. He declares that, should the Holy Spirit inspire one to enter religion, then one should enter with haste and without familial or social considerations. Remember that Thomas was composing the section in II-II of the *Summa* on the religious life at the same time. In it he reminds the reader that sometimes even one's closest family could be a barrier to the pursuit of perfection. Thomas took the occasion to tell people to discount friends and family who tried to dissuade religious vocations.[39] He was also careful to defend the immemorial Benedictine practice of oblation, with the caveat that once the age of puberty is attained (canonically, fourteen years old for boys), then one has the capacity to make a free, solemn, binding vow—independent of one's parents—to enter the religious life.[40] Thomas reached a pitch of pique by the end of this text. He was quite clearly finished with the "pernicious teaching" of the Seculars. In a famous passage he made what some have considered the equivalent to a challenge in chivalry.[41] "If anyone wishes to contradict this, let him not babble to children, but let him write, and let him make these writings public, so that what is true may be able to be judged by intelligent people, and so that what is in error may be convicted by truth."[42] Thomas was a man of flesh and blood, and his blood was boiling as a result of this dispute. Fortitude may be displayed in numerous ways, but it is not always apparent in the intellectual life. In an age in which "intellectuals" attempt to specialize themselves out of controversy, Thomas offers a salutary lesson in bravery. He was a knight of truth who will not tolerate an injury to the honor of God. Things eventually calmed down, however, and by 1271 the storm had largely passed. A new pope had finally been elected, Gregory X, who like his predecessors was a partisan of the orders. Thomas and his Franciscan colleagues had preserved the mendicant life by their efforts, and their teaching and example would continue to fructify the universities and the church. But in such a conflict there could not but be collateral damage.

As we have seen, relations between the Dominicans and Franciscans were strained from the very beginning. Confessional historians of both orders have done their best to minimize the reality of this tension, in the name of an outward presentation of unity. Much has been made of mythical meetings between the founders of the orders; yet even these betray biases.[43] For example, in Franciscan lore Dominic was so impressed with Francis that he apparently wanted to merge their orders. There is no historical evidence for this whatsoever. There is even a distinction in the pictorial and biographical traditions. Who was it that Innocent III dreamed was holding up the Lateran church, Dominic or Francis? It is true that, at times, the two orders did cooperate, for instance in the defense of their shared mendicant prerogatives. Founded with distinct missions, they rapidly became spiritual competitors, increasingly drawing from the same supply of vocations, depending on the same lay contributions, and vying for papal attention. In the towns of Italy one can see a visible sign of this strain: mendicant houses were built on the opposite sides of each city. This was not only to try to avoid competition for alms, but also to minimize the very real tension between the orders. In the records of the Chapters General of each, there are repeated calls not to quarrel with one another and to present a united front to their common enemies. On several occasions the Masters and Ministers General issued joint letters, begging their friars to cease interorder rivalries. A privileged battlefield in this conflict was the competition over saints and sainthood. Each of the orders was exceptionally tardy in celebrating the feasts of the other order's saints and often had to be cajoled by papal pressure. Most conspicuous was the seemingly interminable dispute over the reality of Francis's stigmata, doggedly denied by the Dominicans for nearly the whole of the thirteenth century, in spite of no fewer than nine papal bulls defending it.[44] Most especially Dominicans disdained Franciscans' claims to a higher holiness based merely on their practice of poverty. The Preachers probably watched mirthfully as the Minorites tore themselves apart in controversy over it, while the delicately balanced Dominican constitution made for smooth sailing. Perhaps more irritating to the Dominicans was the excessive attention paid to the Franciscan founder, elevating him to the level of a "super" saint, or indeed, among some Minorites, an angel of the apocalypse or even a "second Christ." The Preachers responded strongly with their new saint, Peter of Verona, who had done something that Francis had not: die as a martyr.[45] Thomas too was later a subject of hagiographical papering over of differences. For example, there is no evidence of a personal friendship between him and Bonaventure, beyond the fact that they were present in Paris at the same time. Late and unreliable stories from early modern Franciscan chroniclers attempt to assert Thomas's "approval" of Bonaventure's sanctity, probably in order to speed the latter's tardy canonization in 1482.[46] One can trace a growing professional (if not personal) animosity between them during the second Regency.

Most pressing for Thomas, however, was the growing divergence, rapidly developing into open conflict, between the theology that he was practicing and the "traditional" Neoplatonic line taken by the Franciscan Masters.

For years the tension between the theological conceptions of Thomas and the Franciscans was subdued, as each was worked out independently of the other. Yet, the multiple crises of Paris in the late 1260s brought much anxiety to the surface. In the fall of 1269, the Franciscan Master Eustace of Arras relinquished his chair in favor of the young, brilliant, and acerbic John Pecham. According to reliable sources, both from the canonization hearings and the biographies, Thomas and Gerard d'Abbeville, as members of the consortium, were present for the inception of the new Master, along with the new bishop, Stephen Tempier. Seeking to make a name for himself, Pecham bravely launched a frontal assault. But it was not directed against the Seculars (to whom Pecham had repeatedly addressed himself); rather, it was launched against the radical Aristotelians in general and Thomas Aquinas in particular. Pecham castigated the doctrine of Aristotle on the eternity of the world. Aristotle had asserted that an eternal cause must have an eternal effect. This was, of course, contrary to revelation, which demanded a world created with time. Yet Thomas, careful to outline the distinctions between the fields of philosophy and theology, saw no necessary contradiction. If God had wanted an eternal universe, he could have created one. The only way to know definitively was through revelation, but that did not negate the validity of the Aristotelian proofs. This position enraged Pecham, who saw it as an affront to revelation and an indicator that Thomas—along with the radicals—was pursuing a course that would lead them down the path of Averroes. He directly attacked Thomas at his inception, employing the same counterarguments used by Bonaventure (which are not particularly persuasive). Pecham and Bonaventure were convinced that the creation of the world could be proven through reason, ironically using the same philosophical method that Pecham was then castigating. Thomas remained impassive. After the close of the first day his students reproached him for tolerating such an overt attack. The Master replied with gentleness, not wishing to embarrass a new professor on his first day. His students continued to press him, however, and so Thomas relented. At the "resumption" on the next morning, Pecham continued obstinately to maintain his thesis. Thomas benevolently and patiently explained the Franciscan's errors and the weakness of their rational proofs for creation.[47] After the confrontation, Pecham hardened in his attitude toward Thomism, as we shall see (even if he later tried to atone for his attack by calling Thomas of "good memory" and of "holy memory").[48] In response, Thomas published *De Aeternitate Mundi* (On the eternity of the world). In this work he repeats the contentions he made at the debate, defending the arguments of Aristotle as probable and delineating the respective spheres of philosophy and theology. He did this because in Franciscan thought, while philosophical methods and arguments may be useful, in reality they are all subsumed into the sovereign science of Theology, leaving no real room for an independent philosophical science. One by one Thomas refuted the arguments of Pecham and Bonaventure, which attempted to prove rationally the creation of the world with time. He makes a clear distinction between the dependence of any universe (even an eternal one) upon God and the free decision of God to create a universe in time. This debate indicated the rising tensions between Thomas's thought and the Franciscans, a chasm that would only widen after the Master's death.

The Franciscans had been cautious since the time of their foundation about the dangers of the intellectual life. Francis himself had ignored it completely, and only with great trepidation had he permitted St. Anthony of Padua to teach theology.[49] Though the Franciscans rapidly entered into the schools after the founder's death, there was always worry that such a move would diminish the spirit of prayer and ossify into a dry intellectualism. This was underscored in their devotion to voluntarism, or the primacy of the will as the seat of charity, and they came increasingly to view Thomas and the radical Aristotelians and their primacy of the intellect with grave suspicion. To them, this was accentuated by their petulant attack on the Philosopher's arguments about the eternity of the world. This problem was only preparatory for a much more serious issue: the unicity of substantial form. This was a matter of pressing concern not only for human anthropology, but for theology itself. Did the human substance have one form, or many? Following Aristotle, Thomas argued for one substantial form in the human being: the intellectual soul. For many, this was a serious problem. How could a spiritual, intellectual substance control such things as sensation and the lower bodily functions? It was safer to locate personhood in the spiritual substance and to propose lesser, material forms for the body. The Franciscans (and others)—following a spiritualizing Neoplatonism—demanded that personhood be rooted in the soul alone. In order to assure the soul's independence from bodily necessity, they proposed other forms in humanity, such as the form of "bodiliness," which existed along with the soul, thereby defending a plurality of forms in one man. This was unacceptable to Thomas. For him the human person was not the soul, but the soul and body together: the soul as form and the body as matter. This ensured the substantial unity and integrity of the individual human. Thomas was convinced that the Franciscan position undermined our essential unity. He agreed that the soul was separable and immortal, but without the body it was only an incomplete nature. He demanded an incarnational philosophy. He rejected the mind-body dualism of Plato and contemporary thinkers. He refused to be seduced by the radical separation between mind and body that would achieve new life among Descartes and the moderns. As one scholar states, "It is truly difficult to find another western thinker who is more radically antidualist than Thomas: man is not his soul, or is not primarily his soul, but is always the composite of soul and body."[50] Further, the Master rejected Bonaventure's illuminism, a doctrine with a better Augustinian pedigree. If we cannot know for ourselves without a special external assistance, then our nature is incomplete. Therefore our body and our senses are intrinsic to our process of knowing. We possess everything necessary to live according to our nature (even as Thomas recognizes the weakness wrought by sin). He is a defender of the wholeness of the human being, body and soul together. Our mind can know truth on its own, without outside help. The body is not dispensable but intrinsic to who we are; it is a genuinely "incarnational philosophy," one that parallels the efforts of his brethren to root out the staunch dualism of the contemporary Cathars. That such teachings seem quite natural to modern Catholics belies the fact that, during his time, few doctrines caused such a backlash against Thomas as these. Though such meditations about the unicity of form and Aristotelian epistemology predated

Thomas, they quickly became identified with him. In response, Pecham tried to tie his own teachings to Augustine in order to marshal the greatest Western theological authority in his favor. Augustine himself is silent on the issue of unicity, but Pecham's use of him as a stick with which to beat the Thomists established a tradition of "Augustinianism" that is only now becoming unraveled.[51] Pecham made the problem worse by raising it to the level of Christology. If there was only one substantial form (the intellectual soul) in Christ, that means that the body in the tomb was not his. Thomas replied that the principle of unity was not the soul in Christ, but the divine person, the hypostatic union.[52] The later debates gradually became very heated and were occasionally so acrimonious that even some Dominicans began to attack the Thomistic position (indeed, even Thomas's own Bachelor refused to follow the Master's teachings in this matter). The doctrine of unicity would later prove to be the chief argument against the acceptance of Thomism in the broader academic community both during Thomas's life and after his death.

What the Theology Masters (even some Dominicans) were worried about were the implications of Aristotelianism for theology. They saw arguments about epistemology and the eternity of the world as the thin end of a wedge that could dislodge traditional Christian thought. They were not wholly wrong about this. The philosophical pursuit of Aristotle had divided the Islamic intellectual world, essentially ending it. Men such as al-Farabi (d. 950/951) and Averroes had pursued reason relentlessly and, in the end, found Islam deficient. Al-Farabi had essentially rejected his Muslim faith. Averroes was cleverer though. He created a pyramidal system whereby the world was resolved into three types of people. At the bottom dwell the vast majority of people who live by their senses and impulses. This group must be ruled by a religion that sets absolute boundaries and moves their imaginations through preaching and admonition. Far fewer are the theologians. These men are beginning to live according to reason, and spend their time spinning dialectical arguments to defend the beliefs of religion. At the top of the pyramid are the pure philosophers, who have discovered the rational structure of the universe and have no need to be restrained by the tales of the religious. They especially disdain the theologians, who unhealthily mingle faith and pure reason. This does not mean that Averroes thinks that the truths of religion are false; it is just that they are mixed with popular superstition and thus cannot approach the pure path of truth that comes from reason alone. Religion teaches truth, but in a popular and diminished way. In one sense, Averroes was a religious utilitarian who saw the benefits of religion in keeping the ignorant multitudes in check and providing them with the rudiments of civilized society. One could see the appeal of such a theory. It did not dispense with religion or call it false; in fact, it was just fine for most people. Yet, for the truly brilliant, the *elite*, Averroes offered a model that was exceptionally attractive. As can be imagined, his theory engendered exceptional resistance from the Islamic theologians, who themselves were accomplished in dialectic. The war between the two groups brought about a divorce between faith and reason in the Sunni Islamic world that was sealed when both groups found themselves rejected by a novel fundamentalism brought by the North African Berbers and the Seljuk Turks. The project of aligning religion and reason, which had appeared so promising and precocious compared with contemporary Christendom, ended in total failure.

Many in Europe considered that such a divorce was being effected among the Christians. This helps to explain the trepidation that greeted the "New" Aristotle in the first half of the thirteenth century. However, constant cautions and monitions could not check the progress of the Philosopher through the schools. As we have seen, his works had already become a required component of the Arts curriculum, and Albert and Thomas were busy trolling through his corpus, in eager anticipation of every new translation that emerged from the workbench of William of Moerbeke. Along with Aristotle came those who had expounded on him throughout the tradition. Chief among these was Averroes, whom Thomas considered such a superlative interpreter of Aristotle's thought that he always used the honorific "the Commentator" when referring to him. Averroes's works had appeared in Europe by 1225 (perhaps earlier in Naples).[53] Thomas was quite familiar with the Commentator's thought and, while he admired his philosophy, was also exceptionally clear concerning not only at what points the Muslim thinker departed from Catholic thought, but also where he introduced novel interpretations foreign to Aristotle himself.

He had written extensively against some of Averroes's contentions in the *Summa Contra Gentiles* in the early 1260s. Not all Masters were as cautious or careful as Thomas in their appropriation of the thought of Aristotle and the Commentator. A group of Arts Masters formed during the 1260s embraced Averroes in a manner that far surpassed Thomas's cautious allegiance. This school, formerly called "Latin Averroism"—but more properly termed "Radical Aristotelianism"—was spearheaded by the Arts Masters Siger of Brabant (ca. 1240–ca. 1284) and Boethius of Dacia (fl. 1270). The wild popularity of Aristotle had convinced certain Arts Masters to make a practical declaration of independence from the Theology faculty (a fact that dovetailed nicely with their conceptions of university politics). To them, philosophy was a completely separate field from theology and entitled to complete freedom of speculation, even when its conclusions seemed to diverge from revelation. When they reached a determination contrary to the faith, they simply said that it was a conclusion of philosophy, and never asserted that it contradicted church teaching. In that sense they never proposed the claim that there was a "double truth." This was a slander created by their opponents that they were always careful to avoid. The real problem was that they were wholly comfortable with rational conclusions (e.g., the eternity of the world) that seemed to contradict revelation. The theologians, who had been raised in a Scholastic environment that saw faith and reason as complementary, could not tolerate this ambiguity. It was they who "created" the heresy of Averroism. The theologians were perceptive in that they detected a move toward an orthodox Averroism that would place religion in the realm of myth and focus on philosophical truth as the seat of wisdom.[54]

Siger and Boethius were both comfortable with the assertions of Averroes that appeared most audacious to the theologians. They professed not only the eternity of the world, but the independence of philosophy from theological supervision, as well as the concept of intermediate intelligences between God and us (i.e., the idea that God can only have one proper effect). Most troubling of all, though, they accepted the Averroistic doctrine of the unicity of the agent intellect. While this means that they accepted the immateriality of soul, they denied that we each possess an *individual* power whereby we abstract from sensible reality to reach truth. This agent intellect, at least for Siger, was God himself. Indeed, this was not far removed from a Bonaventurean illuminism (although at least for the Franciscan the illumination was distinct from God). The practical implications of such a theory were grave. Since the one immaterial part of us is common to all, there is no possibility of an individual immortality. Again, Siger and Boethius did not deny the theological teaching, yet they stubbornly maintained the conclusion of reason. That, to most reasonable observers, seemed to lead to a stunning contradiction. All of this began to send up warning signals to the traditional theologians. In 1266 the Franciscan Master William of Baglione made an initial remonstration against the radical Aristotelians. It was he who persuaded Bonaventure to speak out on the issue. But most pressing was the fact that William had implicated Thomas himself in the movement, accusing the Dominican of believing both in the eternity of the world and the unicity of the agent intellect.[55]

Even though this nascent anti-Aristotelianism was not the primary cause of Thomas's second Regency, it occupied a significant amount of his time. He had a very delicate task. He was absolutely committed to the utility of Aristotle (and even Averroes) in theology and philosophy and had dedicated the better part of his career to it. At the same time he recognized the danger posed by these young enthusiasts, whose near-evangelical zeal for pure philosophy could have generated a reaction from which even a properly appropriated Aristotelianism could never have recovered. Perhaps Thomas also saw the possibility of an overreaction that would see intellectualism and the Greco-Arab bias in favor of necessity overthrown in favor of a radical voluntarism and overemphasis on contingency. Such would indeed come to pass with Duns Scotus and William of Ockham in the 1300s. So Thomas had to walk a thin line—careful to correct the zealots and mollify the traditionalists as best as he could. The extraordinary thing is the highly creative route that he took. Thomas was no mere moderate, positioned between "rightist" Augustinians and "leftist" Aristotelians. In reality, his personal approach bewildered members of both camps.[56] We have already seen his creativity in *De Aeternitate Mundi*, in which in many ways he defends the radical Aristotelians. He destroys the rational arguments against the eternity of the world, while asserting that Aristotle was merely offering probable assertions (against Boethius of

Dacia, who asserted that creation ex nihilo was rationally impossible). Thomas also affirms that there is nothing intrinsically irrational about an eternal world: God could have done it that way if he had wished. He ends with the claim that creation in time is a truth that must be accepted by faith but is not *on that account* contrary to reason. The things that are established by revelation cannot contradict reason, even though they may exceed the grasp of our rational powers. In making this assertion he both safeguards the human exercise of reason and refuses to cede ground to fideism. The faith itself is rational; faith and reason go hand in hand because they have the same source, the God who cannot deceive or be deceived, and the same end, which is truth. Not only can there not be two truths (an inherent contradiction), but faith cannot truly contradict reason. In this way the Dominican defuses the contentions of the radicals yet continues to give a proper autonomy to human rationality.

The issue of the unicity of the intellect was different, however. The apparent conclusions of reason here certainly did seem to contradict some of the most basic teachings of the faith. If personal immortality was compromised, a host of other problems inevitably followed, from anthropology to moral theology. Immediately after arriving in Paris, Thomas knew he had to deal with this issue head-on. In one of his first works he takes direct aim at Siger and the "Averroists" (ironically, Thomas may have been the first to coin this term) in *De Unitate Intellectus Contra Averroistas* (On the unity of the intellect against the Averroists). In five short chapters he thoroughly dismantles the arguments of the radicals. He does this not by asserting the Christian faith dogmatically, but rather by demonstrating that Averroes's (and their) reading of Aristotle is wrong. Averroes has interpreted Aristotle badly, and in no way does the thought of the Philosopher demand a single agent intellect for all people. After thoroughly refuting the false interpretations of Averroes, Thomas returns to the doctrine of Aristotelian simplicity: the testimony of our own experiences of consciousness and unity. That our intellect is really individual and possessed by us "must be held without any doubt, not on account of the revelation of faith, as [our opponents] say, but because to deny it is to go against things patently obvious."[57] For Thomas our everyday experience was itself a source of authority (quite the opposite of the trajectory of post-Cartesian philosophy). In later history Thomas would be called the "Common Doctor," a title bearing within itself several layers of meaning. Not only was he a doctor whom all Christians could follow in common, but unlike many others, he was a staunch defender of the commonalities and events of normal human life and—like his master Aristotle—considered them normative for constructing a philosophy. Thomas is the philosopher of common sense extraordinaire. As Chesterton said,

> The Thomist stands in the broad daylight of the brotherhood of men, in their common consciousness that eggs are not hens or dreams or mere practical assumptions; but things attested by the Authority of the Senses, which is from God...."There is an Is." That is as much monkish credulity as St. Thomas asks of us at the start.[58]

As Thomas's refutation of the Arts Masters reaches its conclusion, he finishes the work with a ringing challenge, much like the end of his *Contra Retrahentes*.

> This therefore is what we have written for the destruction of the foregoing error, not using the determinations of faith, but rather the arguments and teachings of the philosophers themselves. If anyone glorying in the name of false knowledge wishes to say anything against what we have written, let him not speak in corners nor to boys who are unable to judge such difficult matters, but reply to this in writing, if he dares. For he will find that not only I, who am the least of men, but many others zealous for the truth, through whom his error will be resisted or who will correct his ignorance.[59]

Thomas the intellectual fighter returns to field again, outraged by the Averroists' failure of professional ethics.[60] He continues his practice of only using the authorities accepted by his opponents and refusing to settle anything by dogmatic assertion. He destroys them with their own arguments, and particularly cautions them against corrupting the minds of the young Arts students. It appears that Thomas had an effect on Siger of Brabant, who began to temper some of his more extreme sentiments. Dante later placed Siger in heaven with St. Thomas, an inclusion that has never ceased to surprise commentators.[61] Dante had studied under Thomas's student Remigio de' Girolami. It is possible that the poet perhaps had some otherwise unknown knowledge of Siger's later career, but there is no consensus. It should be remembered that of the three great movements that swirled around Thomas at this time, he was personally closest to the Artists, who admired him exceedingly. He was the implacable enemy of the Seculars and suffered a widening rift with the Franciscans. It was the members of the Arts faculty that remained near to him, even when many of his own Dominican brethren abandoned him.

Thomas's impassioned dialectic was not enough to mollify the traditionalists. I suspect that a concerted effort between the Seculars and the Franciscans was enough to extract a condemnation from Bishop Stephen Tempier on December 10, 1270. For perhaps a year, lists of propositions to be condemned circulated around Paris. It appears that the faculty of Theology was irritated in particular at the intrusion of the Artists on what they considered their own turf. This was made worse by the Franciscans' rather hazy awareness of the actual boundary between theology and philosophy. One can even say that Bonaventure and Pecham were busy casting doubt on whether there could even be such a thing as philosophy, properly speaking. To be fair, this sentiment was not wholly unique to them. Even Thomas considered the formal age of philosophy to be in the past and writes about it as closed. He knew that a new and more perfect science had superseded it. Yet for Thomas and Albert, unlike the Franciscans, the discoveries of the philosophers remained a treasure to be excavated, penetrated, and understood.[62] As Bonaventure approached the end of his life, it increasingly seemed to him that philosophy was dispensable and, being so, was especially dangerous when it came into apparent conflict with faith. For him it was "like mixing water in the pure wine of God."[63] When Tempier deployed the condemnations of thirteen propositions, he drew directly from the works of Boethius and especially Siger. Thomas's recent effort to reclaim some semblance of respect for Averroes and Aristotle seemed to have no effect, unless the absence of any specifically Thomistic doctrines from the list counts. It is possible that Thomas's careful unravelling of his opponent's arguments led to a clear outline for identifying heretical Averroism. The propositions condemned were carefully considered and judiciously assembled, falling into four main sections roughly corresponding to the material presented above. These included monopsychism (the singularity of the agent intellect), determinism, the eternity of the world, and God's ability to know particular individuals. None of these touches upon the substance of Thomism. Neither would they have caused such a stir if the headstrong Artists had not insisted upon wading into the world of theology, maintaining positions that they knew to be contrary to the revealed teachings of the church. Indeed, maintaining these conclusions is what eventually got them cited for heresy before the inquisition in Brabant in 1272. If they had held them as philosophical probabilities, or carefully analyzed the provenance and substance of the arguments, as Thomas had done in *De Unitate*, then there would likely have been no problems.

This was not an issue of academic freedom or of ecclesial power crushing a nascent intellectual movement but was one of hubris on the part of the Artists. Thomas, their cautious partisan, knew this, and considered that philosophy without grace was a terrible temptation. He argued that the Artists possessed a natural, but not an absolute, autonomy.[64] He was prepared to defend that. They were still subject to the claims of truth, which could be sought within the particular methodology of each science, always remembering that truth was and is absolutely one. For Thomas, faith and reason could never contradict; to say so was an absurdity. There would never be a properly philosophical conclusion that would deny a truth of faith. Therefore the argumentation was wrong or, failing that (and far more rarely), our understanding of revelation was incorrect or underdeveloped. Thomas knew that the incarnation made imperative the difficult but necessary task of maintaining faith and reason in mutual coherence.[65] He wrote (in an oblique reply to Bonaventure) that practicing philosophy was not mixing water in pure wine, but rather "of turning the water into wine" as the incarnate God-man had done.[66] Even when a teaching exceeded our grasp, that did not thereby make it irrational. Thomas's confidence in reason matched that of the early Scholastics. He knew that the approaches to faith (its "preambles") were able to be demonstrated. He asserted that probable arguments could be marshalled for indemonstrable truths. Most of all, however, he knew that the contrary of a truth could never be a true demonstration; therefore, anything asserted against the faith could be rationally answered.[67] Because he had spent twenty years coming to grips with Aristotle, he knew the possibilities of the Philosopher for the defense and promotion of doctrine, and refused to give up on him. Unlike his adversaries, Thomas was not daunted by the challenges proposed by philosophy. From his perspective, people who focused on a few wrong turns in Aristotle were missing the forest for the trees. Thomas was convinced that the system of Aristotle could be made wholly concordant with a robustly incarnational Christianity. And so that is what he set forth to prove.

By the 1270s the entire Christian world knew the Aristotelian cat was out of the bag. The last toothless protest of the papacy against study of the Greek's teachings had been in 1263. Everyone at the universities studied him, even those who were opposed to his teachings. Thomas knew that, in order to avoid the Scylla of radical Averroism and the Charybdis of traditionalist Neoplatonism, he had to undertake a thorough analysis and interpretation of the Philosopher's corpus. Albert had begun such a project years before, but he was limited by a cursory reading, trying only to get at the literal text of Aristotle, and was hampered by earlier translations that did not always give the correct sense. As we have seen, many Aristotelian works were mediated through the writings of the Arabs, who often added their own esoteric glosses to the text, while other texts had been corrupted by Neoplatonism, making it difficult to tease out the genuine sense of the Philosopher. Thomas likely felt pity for the Arts Masters and held a genuine affection for them and their students.[68] This certainly contributed to his intention to create substantive commentaries on all Aristotle's major works. Of course, since he used Aristotle so extensively, these commentaries were also the working out of his own understandings, particularly as they applied to his theological works. So the overburdened professor took on another task, one demanded neither by any of his duties as professor nor commanded by his superiors. The task of commenting on Aristotle was not even in his "field," as academics would say today. He was a theologian, not an Artist. Yet Thomas undertook this massive effort, composing no fewer than ten commentaries in the space of a few years, each occupying hundreds of pages (even though several were unfinished). This work must have occupied almost all of Thomas's "leisure time," which likely led to severe burnout in the coming years. It does not seem that these texts were based on classroom teaching, but rather represent the private efforts of an intellectual to understand and appropriate another thinker's ideas.[69]

Thomas stands in a long line of such commentators. The Arts faculty had carried out such works since the 1240s.[70] Far from being simply literal commentaries, very often Thomas uses the arguments of Aristotle as jumping-off points, augmenting the material in the corpus and refashioning it in an explicitly Christian way. Thomas is no mere commentator or expositor; rather, he creatively interacts with the material that he finds and puts the arguments into an explicitly Christian framework. This approach may irritate orthodox Aristotelians today, as indeed it discomfited the radical Averroists of his own time. Yet what it shows is the evolution of the new system that he created. The Aristotelian commentaries are the laboratory of Thomism. They show him adapting and molding, not passively receiving, the teaching of the Philosopher. For example, in the commentary on the *Ethics*, Aristotle's eudaimonism is transformed by the reality of the beatific vision. Nor does Thomas disdain to use the breakthroughs of later philosophers. Indeed, the "metaphysics of being" (an inheritance from the Neoplatonists and Avicenna) was something that would "have been entirely foreign to Aristotle."[71] Indeed, Thomas showed himself an adept textual critic, when he was the first to discover the Neoplatonic origins of the *Liber de Causis*, long attributed to Aristotle.[72] Thomas may indeed have "baptized" Aristotle, to use the popular phrase, but the man who emerged from the font appeared quite transformed by grace. Nor must one project the historical-critical mindset back to Thomas's time. He had no interest in a rigorous reconstruction of the historical intention of Aristotle, but rather creatively engaged him as if to rewrite the commentaries in such a way as to ask the question, "What would Aristotle have argued if, given his system, he was also a thirteenth-century Christian thinker?" The results are as surprising as they are unexpected. No one today would approach an academic work with that sort of methodology, but its accomplishment is undeniable. Using the forge of Aristotle, Thomas had formed a new and enduring synthesis.

One should, however, confront an enduring image about Thomas and the Scholastics here: that they were wholly without a historical sense. While they certainly did not have the critical spirit that has been the animating force of academic scholarship since the nineteenth century, they did have a similar mentality. This sense was rooted in the providential teleology of events and bound up in a theology of the incarnation. History was for them salvation history, a story that did not end with the closing of the biblical canon, but that was to endure until the end of time itself. Its philosophy was drawn from Augustine's *City of God*. In spite of Thomas's quibbles about Augustine's Platonism, it should be remembered that the shadow cast by Augustine was a long one, and we forget how fundamentally his pattern of thinking has stamped itself on the West.[73] In Thomas's case in particular, he was intimately aware of the history of philosophy and the progression of ideas.[74] He would not have been party to the divorce of modern times between a time-bound historicism and an ahistorical method of doing theology and philosophy. It would have been utterly unfamiliar to him to divide things in such a manner. Indeed, as the theologian H.-F. Dondaine wrote, "The concrete revelation of the mystery of the Trinity is robed in the revelation of the economy of salvation," and "the goal of the whole history of the world [is to] show to rational creatures the intimate glory of the divine Persons."[75] By paying attention both to historical contingency and to abstract truth, he was able to distinguish that the *Liber de Causis* was the work of a fifth-century pagan Neoplatonist, Proclus, and not Aristotle himself. In aligning himself with an incarnational view, Thomas participated in the "Scholastic humanism" of the central Middle Ages. This meant the affirmation of human nature in its independent and autonomous existence: the exaltation of humankind whose activities were embedded in the concrete realities of historical action.[76] One scholar adroitly remarks that even Thomas's most advanced theological work, the *Summa Theologiae*, is a "pedagogical cursus" of theology mapped onto the "historical cursus of God's self-disclosure."[77] Thomas evinces a constant respect for authority and tradition, as well as for reason. Good authorities should be undergirded by a solid rational structure. For instance, Thomas can both support Augustine as a significant authority and rationally attack his Platonism.[78] As chapter 3 demonstrated, Thomas is deeply embedded among a "cloud of witnesses." He is truly like Chaucer's clerk who would "rather have at his bed's head some twenty books, all bound in black or red, of Aristotle and his philosophy," for he was one who would "gladly learn and gladly teach."[79]

FINAL JOURNEY

A number of events conspired to lead Thomas away from Paris and back to Italy after the spring academic term of 1272. In the first place, Thomas had strongly refuted those who asserted the incompatibility of Aristotle and Christianity. While this drove a wedge between him and the Franciscans (and even some of his fellow friars), it earned him the friendship of many in the Arts, which resulted in a lasting devotion to his memory in that school.[80] He had also checked the radical Aristotelians, creating a defensive perimeter around his reading of the Philosopher. While Siger's and Boethius's assertions had been censured, the condemnations of 1270 did not affect Thomas directly. He and others were free to continue aggressively to pursue an Aristotelian path. Although the Arts faculty had moved beyond the immediate controversy, it remained bitterly divided. Siger and his partisans were in the minority, and a tumult arose over the election of the proctor in late 1271. This strife turned the bishop of Paris against the university, and academic politics—at least for a time—superseded doctrinal disputes. In response to Tempier's interference, the university called a strike for spring of 1272, which Thomas and the Dominicans, as was their wont, simply ignored. The friars never were very good academic citizens. Finally, Thomas had outlasted the Seculars. The efforts of Thomas, Bonaventure, and John Pecham had proved the undoing of the Theology Masters. By December of 1271 the conflict had ended, with the mendicants once again solidly woven into the fabric of the university. So secure were the orders that most of their "superstar" professors were able to be recalled to different duties away from Paris, and the elections of both a Dominican and Franciscan to the papacy over the ensuing decade underlined the mendicants' final victory. Complicating the position of the Seculars was the ending of the interminable interregnum with the election of Pope Gregory X on September 1, 1271. The resumption of papal oversight meant that the Secular position was to have a very short shelf life, because the ecclesiological vision of the papacy and the mendicants in the thirteenth century had triumphed. William of St. Amour, the old adversary, finally died in September of 1272; Gerard of Abbeville passed away on November 8 of the same year, and Nicholas of Lisieux simply disappeared from history.[81] In the spring of 1272, Thomas served at the inception of his Bachelor, Romano Orsini, probably his final academic duty. With all of these pieces falling into place, Thomas was free to return to his home province and probably departed Paris soon after Easter 1272, bringing his second Regency to a close.

Thomas's object was certainly the city of Florence. There the Roman province would hold its annual chapter, probably in mid to late June. Thomas was an ex officio member of this body by virtue of his position as Preacher General, and he would have needed to go there in any case to receive his next assignment. The province also had the privilege of holding the General Chapter in Florence, which occurred around the Feast of Pentecost, June 12 of that year. At that meeting, the assembled fathers decided to add to the number of *studia*, intent on expanding it from the initial four to six, with one in Spain and one in the Roman province.[82] It is theoretically possible that Thomas made it to Santa Maria Novella for the celebration of the chapter, but he would have had to travel swiftly to reach central Italy by that time. Thomas was also probably mindful of the repeated admonitions of the order that people who were not directly charged with the business of a General Chapter should not attend. Thomas's presence there remains speculative. Yet we do know that he was personally given the task of erecting a *studium* in theology. The order did not mean this to be the equivalent of the four great *studia*, but rather went by the unique title *studium generale theologiae*, a school subordinate to the main centers for study.[83] The entirety of the establishment as to personnel, organization, and even the location were left completely in Thomas's hands, an exceptional affirmation of the trust that the Roman province had in him (probably with the full knowledge of Master John of Vercelli, who would likely have stayed for the provincial chapter).[84] It appears Thomas knew exactly what to do.

It was natural for the professor to return to Naples. Not only was it near his ancestral lands and the site of his mother convent, it was the location of the only genuine university within the province. Increasingly Rome was being abandoned by the papacy, and chasing the nomadic curia around was difficult, not to mention dangerous to the stability necessary for an academic institution. Thomas's project was to set up a school that would become the theological *studium* of the existing university. The province had already been making preparations for such a move long before the Master's arrival. As early as 1269 the order had designated Orvieto and Naples as sites for proposed schools, and certainly administrative preparations had been taking place since that time.[85] A further advantage was the cessation of the Hohenstaufen conflicts and the accession of the Angevin King Charles I as King of Sicily. Charles was the brother of Thomas's good friend, Louis IX of France. He was eager to resurrect the university in his capital city and took advantage of the Parisian strike of 1272 to try to lure professors to his kingdom and, as a result, was able to poach at least three Masters. Thomas himself was not to be included among these. All evidence points to his assignment being the fruit of the order's needs, and Naples appears to have been his own preference as the site for the school. Apparently Charles was simply happily surprised to have such a famous Master establish his base of operations there. In recognition, Charles ordered a donation of an ounce of gold a month to the convent of San Domenico while Thomas was in residence and teaching. Such a state subvention was common and did not in any way mean that Thomas was in the employ of the king or subject to his direction.[86]

It appears that Thomas departed from Florence almost immediately after the conclusion of the chapter. He traveled through Rome, where he met his sister Theodora and consulted with her husband, Roger of San Severino, Charles's proctor in the eternal city. There he also added a member to his small retinue, Tolomeo of Lucca, a young student who would later be a significant representative of the biographical tradition concerning Thomas. By late

June they had reached the castle of Molara, the home of Cardinal Riccardo d'Annibaldi. Unfortunately the cardinal—uncle of Thomas's beloved student Annibaldo—had recently died. Both Thomas and Reginald fell sick there. They had passed through the low-lying Via Latina south of Rome, an area infested with malarial mosquitoes. It is likely that the friars had contracted a type of malaria—called Tertian fever in the sources. Thomas recovered but Reginald lingered near death. In response to this crisis, Thomas displayed a typical type of medieval piety. He happened to be carrying a relic of the Roman virgin-martyr Agnes and applied it in direct contact with the patient. For Thomas, Agnes—a popular Roman saint named in the Canon of the Mass—was the incarnation of faithful chastity, a virtue terribly important to him. After the imposition of Agnes's bones, Reginald rallied, and in thanksgiving Thomas promised to offer a banquet for the brethren in Naples every year on her January 21 feast.[87] While Thomas's income went directly to the convent, it was likely he was given access to a certain amount of it for his own disposal, for example to purchase books and parchment. Totally uninterested in personal possessions, he put his meager resources at the service of his brethren in honor of the saints. Perhaps the most brilliant man of the medieval period believed in the efficacy of relics and of saints as much as the simplest rural peasant. Such considerations should caution anyone who attempts to separate "elite" from "popular" religion.[88] The simple piety of Thomas Aquinas runs through all contemporary accounts of his life. The deepest and most abstract speculations never drew him away from incarnational Christianity, which was always "an affair of things," of bodies and bread, wine and bones, oil and water.[89] In this sense the earthy, sensible Aristotelian in him united perfectly with the grounded piety of the Christian tradition.

Thomas arrived in Naples no later than September 10, 1272, which enabled him to begin teaching immediately in the fall term of the university that year. There he assumed two simultaneous roles: Theology Professor at his home convent of San Domenico, and Regent Master at the reconstituted University of Naples.[90] Thomas barely had time to unpack because, upon his return, he was immediately plunged into family issues. Given the stature of Thomas's relatives, their affairs also spilled over into politics. These duties soaked up a good bit of his time. His brother-in-law Roger of Aquila had died at the castle of Traetto (today Minturno) and had appointed the Dominican as the executor of his will. Thomas was probably a good choice, since not only was he in the family (meaning he would be a staunch advocate for its rights), but he was also dedicated to poverty, which eliminated the possibility of exactions from and jealousy toward the beneficiaries. In order to complete his task Thomas traveled to see King Charles at Capua on September 27, who granted him the necessary faculties to dispose the estate and to place Roger's eldest son under the tutelage of Thomas's family. It appears that the two men formed a working friendship, evidenced both by Charles's warm language and his subvention of Thomas's regency.[91] Long after Thomas's death the Angevin rule in southern Italy and Sicily would run into serious difficulties, both with the locals and with the church, but during the Master's life relations seemed warm. The professor continued to intervene on behalf of his family when the occasion warranted. He was now a man with connections. On one occasion he was able to obtain a passport for his niece Francesca, which had presented a difficulty since her husband had been a partisan of the Hohenstaufens.[92] Thomas maintained very strong ties of affection with his family in his final years, and particularly toward his sisters, visiting them relatively often and enjoying their hospitality.

The Master had also been a Preacher General in the Roman province and did occasionally give sermons to the people. Compared to his university sermons, which were pitched to an audience of intellectuals, often with undercurrents of academic politics, the homilies we possess from Naples that he preached to the laity are full of piety and warmth. "Subtleties he saved for the schools," remarks Bernard Gui, "to the people he gave solid moral instruction suitable for their capacity."[93] He undertook the arduous office of Lenten preacher in 1273, delivering nearly sixty sermons to the people of Naples.[94] With certainty he preached on the petitions in the Our Father, while he also may have preached on the Creed and the Hail Mary, though where he gave the latter sermons is uncertain.[95] While the "sermons" we have today are only reports taken down by his secretaries, perhaps more valuable are the many testimonies that exist from the canonization process. No fewer than five deponents testified that they had personally attended his homilies. Even though such depositions occurred fifty years after the fact and contain some refashioning and memory lapses (for instance, dates and durations are often incorrect), they do offer a precious window into lived memory.[96] William of Tocco testified about the plentiful concourse of people who attended the Neapolitan sermons. Thomas was clearly a known quantity at this point, a man of imposing stature and recognized holiness, as well as a local boy who made good; thus it does not strain belief to think that many were in attendance for his Lenten preaching. John di Blasio, a Neapolitan judge—though he misremembers the length of Thomas's stay and the subject of the sermons—gives us the physical memory that Thomas preached with his eyes closed, an interesting characteristic to be examined later. Yet it is clear that the preaching of Thomas left an impression, and its public nature resulted in many more people being able to testify on behalf of his holiness than would have been otherwise possible.[97]

Of course, Thomas's primary mission in Naples was teaching, though there is not absolute certainty regarding which classes he offered. We know that he was not simply a conventual Lector, which meant that he did not have to teach basic theology to the brethren. As a professor, he had a broader purview. It seems that his primary class in the academic year of 1272–73 was a lecture on the Psalms. He perhaps had a three-year plan for lectures, since in that first year he only completed the first third of the Psalter, yet, given the manuscript tradition, it is more likely that Thomas commented on psalms 1–51 according to their place in the nocturnal office of Matins. In addition, some have speculated that there was a renewed effort to examine the Pauline Epistles as well, in particular Romans and the first ten chapters of First Corinthians.[98] While a few have contended that he wrote the disputed questions *De Unione Verbi Incarnati* at this time, I am inclined to agree with others that these came from an earlier stage in his career, since he alters many of his conclusions from that disputed question in the *Tertia Pars* of the *Summa*.[99] I am more sympathetic to the opinion that the second set of courses Thomas offered at this period corresponded to the topics that he was addressing in the last part of the *Summa*, which he composed at the time.

While it is unclear why Thomas chose such texts for his tenure at Naples, some have pointed to a few intriguing possibilities.

The final years of Thomas's life were focused increasingly on the incarnation of Christ. This represents a maturation in his intellectual and spiritual life. Emphasis on the humanity of Christ is a surprising but not inexplicable elision of his commitment to Aristotelianism and his deepening spirituality toward the Eucharist and of the cross (not to mention the increasing devotion to Christ's humanity in the central Middle Ages as a whole). Thomas sees in the Psalms that "everything that bears on the end of the Incarnation is expressed in this book in so clear a way that one might believe oneself face to face with the Gospel, not with prophecy."[100] It is also a deep return to his liturgical piety, with his constant meditation on the Psalms dating back to his boyhood at Montecassino. Even more directly connected to the focus on the person of Christ was the central section of his Third Part, particularly the first fifty-nine questions. Thomas, who had investigated the moral life in the II-II, now presents Christ as the normative human, the very incarnation of reason and virtue. Thomas did not organize his Christology in an abstract and speculative manner, like his philosophical sections on God in the First Part. Rather, his Christology is rooted in the gospel and in the changed valence of the world following the incarnation. Anyone who studies the texts of Thomas's last year and a half will not fall prey to the facile idea that his is a theology without Christ. Everything in his life and work led to its summation in his theology of the incarnation, in his insistence on the substantial unity of the human form, in the sufficiency of our natural powers, in his Aristotelian epistemology, in his agitation for the proper sovereignty of reason, in his definition of man as "matter articulate," and above all in his extraordinary devotion to the Holy Eucharist.[101] Twentieth-century theologians have done Thomas a service by liberating him from the dry and speculative baroque "manuals" that attempt to condense his thought into easily digestible chunks. It still remains to overcome a common gloss of Thomistic thought that limits itself to the "Five Ways," the so-called Treatise on Law, and his reputation as a mere ape of Aristotle. The recent liberation of Thomism allows us to recapture his exaltation of the natural world, of history, of humanity, and of the transcendent significance of human nature, all of which finds its proper crown in the God-Man who is Jesus Christ.

A SUDDEN CONCLUSION

Thomas's first academic year in Naples was certainly eventful, with a full slate of classes, family business, and a course of daily Lenten sermons. For years Thomas had been working at a nearly superhuman level. The summer of 1273 was probably spent continuing his Aristotelian commentaries and pushing through the *Tertia Pars*. Though it is unclear exactly what classes Thomas offered during his final term, he likely commented upon the Pauline Epistles, and worked through the section of the *Tertia Pars* that has to do with sacramental theology. Some have speculated that Thomas's course on the Eucharist was meant to complement his commentary on 1 Corinthians 11, but he was unable to reach that point.[102] To judge by the biographies, Thomas was also becoming increasingly introspective and withdrawn. This must have attracted attention in 1273, not only because of the frequency with which it is mentioned, but because Thomas had been known for his capacity for mental abstraction all his life. It seems he became even more distracted, as depicted in an episode in which his old friend Marino d'Eboli (whom Thomas had known since his days in Orvieto) had become the Archbishop of Capua. One day Marino brought a visiting cardinal-legate to see Thomas in the parlor at San Domenico. Thomas entered and sat still as a stone, making no reverence and uttering no sound. Marino attempted to make excuses for Thomas, saying that others often found him in such a state, but one can imagine the embarrassment of the archbishop and the chagrin of the legate. Eventually Marino pulled at Thomas's habit, which woke him from his reverie.[103] Such episodes were quite common in Thomas's life. He did not like needless conversations in the parlor and always preferred his cell or pacing in the cloisters by himself. Further, it appears that he spent greater time in contemplation. During the course of his Lenten Sermons, he was celebrating the Mass of Passion Sunday. At some point during the liturgy Thomas simply stopped, lost in contemplation. He was immobile until one of his brothers came up and brought him back to his senses.[104] He also seemed increasingly to be given to the shedding of tears; such was witnessed during the Lenten compline anthem *Media Vita*. Witnesses said that he wept most copiously at the line "do not reject us in our old age." He may have indeed wept at Compline, but the verse cited seems a hagiographical retrojection.[105] In any case Thomas was still occupied with administrative tasks in addition to preparing for class. On the Feast of St. Michael, September 29, 1273, Thomas made the long journey to Rome to participate in the Roman provincial chapter for the final time and, following that, he resumed his courses at San Domenico.

Classes stopped abruptly in early December of that year. It was Thomas's custom to spend time in prayer in the Church of San Domenico, which was much smaller than the mighty edifice the visitor finds today. Within the old church was a chapel dedicated to St. Nicholas. The thirteenth century had seen a multiplication of side altars due both to the rising number of private, low Masses and to the increasing demand for suffrages for the dead. It appears that this side altar was the customary place where the Master said his daily Mass before commencing his academic work. Around the Feast of St. Nicholas, December 6, Thomas had some kind of utterly transformative experience. Reginald himself, who was present and likely was the server for the Mass, is the source, though the story is mediated through several witnesses. Nothing indicates that any externally sensible thing happened during the rite. Only later did Reginald note the metamorphosis. Thomas refused to work or to teach, or to write anything further. He rebuffed Reginald several times when the *socius* tried to discover what had happened. Used to a frenetic pace of work, this was absolutely out of character for Thomas, and Reginald was likely worried. Eventually Thomas gave a somewhat curt answer to his friend's repeated questions. Bartholomew of Capua testified that he said, "All which I have written seems to me like chaff."[106] Later both Tocco and Gui would modify the statement to "All which I have written seems to me *of little worth.*" Bartholomew's more vivid word is likely the original one; most probably the biographers were uncomfortable with the strong sentiments expressed by Thomas about his work, which they considered to be on the level of genius.[107] The nature of this vision was surely mystical, but was also undoubtedly compounded by physical and mental issues. Thomas's workload was more than a normal human could bear. His pace was frenzied and his focus on his work was to the point of obsession. No one could maintain such a level of production forever. In addition, he apparently slept less and was increasingly uninterested in food. He was also burdened with secular duties, pressure from his family, and involvement at the highest levels of the church, his order, and the state. Included in any explanation of the event must be a certain type of nervous exhaustion. Some have speculated that a stroke might have been involved, and this is most definitely possible, given his inability to write, speak, or move without difficulty. The most likely diagnosis is a combination of physical and psychological collapse that led to a breakdown. It appears that Thomas was confined to bed for some period after the transformation.[108] Some Thomists have tried to draw conclusions from the nature of his intellectual work at the time, but such assertions are mostly unconvincing. Thomas may have come to a point at which he felt he had said enough. His section of the *Summa* on Christ and the Eucharist was complete; perhaps he looked at the remaining sections with a certain weariness. He was in the midst of the questions on penance, a well-tilled area in the thirteenth century. He had not withheld anything of himself in his search for God and truth. Perhaps it was simply time to be done.

After this, it appears that his superiors made an odd decision. Instead of relieving Thomas of his workload and allowing him to rest within the convent itself, the prior permitted (or perhaps commanded) him to make the long journey to his sister's castle at San Severino. Some have assumed that Thomas was the one who wanted to go see his sister; however, there is a lacuna in the manuscript recording Bartholomew's testimony. Reginald expresses surprise, but that refers to Thomas's declaration about ceasing to write.[109] After the lacuna, the text resumes with "Brother Thomas should go see his sister." I am of the opinion that this means the convent authorities ordered or asked him to go there. This becomes more likely once we see the detail that he was only able to make the journey "with much difficulty."[110] The poor, sick professor had to make a journey of nearly one hundred miles, in winter, to San Severino, near Salerno. His sister, the Countess Theodora, was much alarmed to see him upon arrival. He stumbled into the castle, dazed and confused (*stupefactus*). It seems he was bedridden for no fewer than three days. While the tradition spins this as a mystical event, it is clear that he had to be roused from the "sleep" of contemplation. Some have speculated that Thomas departed after only three days, but this is most unlikely. It is probable that Thomas remained at the castle for the Christmas season, returning to Naples sometime in January of 1274, making the same arduous hundred-mile journey again.[111]

We do not know if Thomas celebrated the Feast of St. Agnes with his brothers on January 21 a second time, but we do know that he resumed neither his teaching nor his writing. Soon after his return he received a summons that, given his condition, was probably unwelcome. Pope Gregory X had called a General Council for the French city of Lyons, to assemble on May 1, 1274. The council was to discuss general matters of church reform and to broach the topic of an attempt to regain Jerusalem; but the real focus was on the prospective reunion with the Greeks under their emperor Michael VIII Palaeologus (r. 1259–82). In order for the issues dividing the East and West to be resolved, Gregory was determined to have his best theologians present at the council. Gregory knew that Thomas had composed a work at Orvieto on the matter, the *Contra Errores Graecorum*. Therefore he commanded that Thomas present himself at the council, armed with his text. It is interesting here to pause and consider that works that made Thomas famous to his contemporaries were later seen as quite unimportant. To his Dominican brethren he was the hero of the antimendicant controversy, and to the popes he was known for his work against the Greeks (which would be treated by the tradition at times as an embarrassment). Thomas, physically sick and mentally exhausted, remained the obedient religious to the last and began to prepare for the journey of nearly one thousand miles, in the middle of winter.

With several companions Thomas began to traverse the Via Latina, a road so familiar to him from his ancestral lands and from his frequent journeys. It is possible that at this point of life he had been accorded the privilege of traveling mounted, most likely on a donkey. This would explain more clearly the seriousness of what happened next. While just north of Teano, he hit his head on a low-hanging branch. It is not clear how his companions permitted this to happen, but nonetheless he was hardly able to stand and admitted to being hurt. Most likely the blow to the head caused internal bleeding and exacerbated his previous symptoms. Proceeding on their way, it is plain that Thomas was in an ill humor, perfectly understandable under the circumstances. Reginald attempted to lighten the mood and joke with him, teasing him about the possibility of a cardinal's hat. Thomas would have none of it: "Reginald, I am unable to be of more utility to the order than in the position I currently hold." Yet his *socius* would not stop badgering him (certainly trying to lift his spirits). Thomas cut him off curtly: "Reginald, you may assure yourself that I shall never alter my current state."[112] They probably continued along the inland Via Latina, passing near Montecassino. There he probably sent a short work on predestination to his friend the abbot Bernard Ayglier. This demonstrates several things. First, that he was still able to write, even though it was a short text of only several pages. It also shows that even given his worsening health, he continued to make himself available to his friends and correspondents for opinions. In any case, the work itself is not terribly original, essentially recapitulating a Boethian doctrine of the compatibility of human liberty and divine foreknowledge, certainly not equal to his in-depth analysis of omnipotence and free will in his recent work on the Epistle to the Romans and his sections on predestination in the *Summa*.

Feeling increasingly weak, Thomas asked to be taken to his niece's castle at Maenza, which was sixty miles farther from the scene of his accident near Teano. They probably turned then to the coastal Via Appia, which would have presented a smoother path. There he took to bed and began to refuse all food. They arrived there after February 14, the beginning of Lent. Reginald and a physician tried to induce Thomas to eat something, but he refused everything.[113] At some point he asked for herrings, a food that he had evidently enjoyed in his sojourns in the north, perhaps in Cologne or Paris. Access to such fish from the northern seas was impossible in Italy. Yet a fishmonger happened by the castle. His main cargo was sardines, plentiful in the Mediterranean. While he was looking through his stock, he happened to discover herrings. Everyone present was astonished, for such fish was never seen those parts of Europe. Thomas may or may not have eaten it; the sources differ. It was one of his best-known "miracles." I would make one note, however. Since herring was never available in southern Italy, how did anyone present (all southern Italians) know what they looked like? The Atlantic herring looks remarkably like the Mediterranean pilchard sardine. Could one perhaps speculate that the fishmonger simply found some rather larger sardines in his larder and made an opportune sale? Indeed, the most thorough account of the miracle—the canonization deposition of Peter of Montesangiovanni—makes it clear that the salesman swore "that he had brought sardines and not herrings." It was Reginald—who may indeed have seen herrings before—who excitedly plucked them up and brought them to Thomas.[114] Militating against this, however, is the astonishment of the bystanders, and the degree to which the "miracle" took root in the popular mind was mentioned in the canonization enquiry fifty years afterward and made it into most of the biographies.[115] Such a prosaic miracle was emblematic of Thomas's life, lived in humility. It was one of the only miracles reported about him while he yet lived.

Thomas apparently rallied near the end of February, at least enough to attempt to continue the journey, progressing slowly up the coast of Lazio. They had not gone far when Thomas realized the end was near, and they turned aside to make their way to the Cistercian Abbey of Fossanova. We know that Thomas rode on a mule this last time for, sick as he was, he could not fulfill the letter of the Dominican constitutions, which he had observed so thoroughly. In one account the abbot of the monastery had come with some monks to offer Thomas their hospitality. Thomas decided that, as he felt the approach of death, it was more fitting that he go to meet the Lord at a religious house rather than at the home of laymen.[116] It was said that the abbot allowed Thomas to stay in his own dwelling. The spot is still preserved today, but it may be more likely that rooms were prepared in the guesthouse for the visiting friar. The monks attended him with patience and care. An entire portion of the canonization inquisition was conducted at Fossanova, where the living memory of Thomas was alive and well among the monks, giving much insight into his last days as well as into his death. He was too sick to continue his daily custom of celebrating Mass and, apparently bedridden, he requested and received viaticum and last rites. The Catholic Church was a master of the liturgy of death in terms of psychology, drama, and pedagogy. The rites were meant to bring salvation to the dying, edification to the bystanders, and comfort to all. The Cistercians made all the requisite ministrations to Thomas. His biographers did not fail to note that he was fully alert for all of them, underscoring their efficacy. His death was intended as a model for holiness. By this time some other Dominicans from Gaeta and Anagni, and even some Franciscans, had arrived (among them the Minorite bishop of Terracina). In their presence Thomas made one final, brief, and moving testimony of faith in the Eucharist, and submitted all his teachings to the judgment of Rome.[117] Tocco alone records that Thomas left a final commentary on the Song of Songs for the brethren, but none of the canonization witnesses reported that, nor is there any surviving record of such a work.[118] One can speculate that Thomas tried to repay the exceptional kindness of his hosts by speaking a bit on the book that was much appreciated in the medieval church as an allegory of the love between the soul and God, a scriptural poem that attracted the attention of many mystics. It was probably only a short allocution, and not recorded but only received and meditated upon. It was a final and private gift to the Cistercians, whose great Master St. Bernard of Clairvaux was perhaps the most famous commentator on the Canticle. Thomas survived for three days after viaticum. Besides the many Cistercians, Franciscans and perhaps nearly one hundred Dominicans had come to witness the Master's final moments. These Dominicans likely traveled from the nearby priories and perhaps even from the small foundation at the foot of Montecassino for which Thomas had interceded.[119] On the morning of Wednesday, March 7, 1274, Thomas of Aquino, not yet fifty years old, passed from this life.[120] A common medieval idiom used by chroniclers goes *ex hac luce migravit*—Thomas passed from this dim light, now "seen through a glass, darkly," to stand face-to-face in the true light of him whom the Master had spent his whole life pursuing. His death illustrates the vast chasm that has opened up between the medieval and modern worlds. For the latter, such an "end" means destruction. For Thomas, the Christian Aristotelian, "end" means nothing other than the final and definitive fulfillment of one's nature. In Thomas's end he found his true beginning, the consummation so aptly described in Song of Songs. His end was also the source of many other beginnings as well.

Chapter 7

FROM LIGHT TO LIGHT

The Death and Afterlife of
St. Thomas Aquinas

A vast chasm opens up between Thomas's medieval biographers and his modern ones at the moment of his death. Medieval commentators, on the one hand, often continue their narratives by dwelling, at considerable length, on the wonders that accompanied the development of his cult. Modern writers, on the other hand, seem faintly embarrassed by these stories. His recent biographers speed past them uncomfortably, toward the safer area of the history of Thomism. Even the excellent English translation of Bernard Gui's life simply ends with his death, recounted in chapter 43, completely ignoring another fifty-eight chapters that Gui considered to be an integral part of a hagiographical account. As I said, this bespeaks a discomfort with the miraculous that is characteristic of the post-Enlightenment world. It is also an indicator that even the best modern works on St. Thomas are, at heart, interested in his thought rather than in his broader place in medieval history. For the people who witnessed his death, and for those who made their way to his tomb, no less than for Reginald or even Thomas himself, the key component of medieval sanctity *was* miracles. Medieval people had an organic view of life as a pilgrimage that was fulfilled in immortal bliss in the presence of almighty God. When a Christian known for holiness crossed the threshold of death, he or she remained present, both to them and now to God. The incarnational focus of medieval Christianity meant that the body of the saint was no cast-off husk. Thomas's Aristotelianism coincided with popular piety far more, I would suggest, than rarefied medieval Platonism, which tended to equate the person with the soul. Thomas had argued that the soul, while bearing immortality within it, was incomplete without the body. In some mysterious way, our personhood will not be completely reconstituted until the resurrection of the body at the end of time. While Christians waited in hope for that moment, they knew that the soul's essential concomitant, the body, was still here and present to us on earth. God and the saints had left us precious "relics."[1] For God it was the real presence in the Holy Eucharist, for the saints it was their earthly remains. It is no mistake that these two were precisely the key points attacked by the medieval anti-incarnational Cathars. The very bodiliness and materiality of Christianity made it wholly different from other forms of religion. The "spiritual" was rightly superior but, in the case of humans, was inextricably united to the "material," and indeed the inferior was the very means of the sanctification of the superior: in water, bread, wine, oil, and even human bodies.

The men and women who had begun to congregate at Fossanova in the first week of March 1274 were there to witness the death of a holy man. "Precious in the sight of the LORD is the death of his faithful ones" (Ps 116:15). Christians of the Middle Ages took the moment of death with utmost seriousness. It was privileged, the last instant in which a soul in the "wayfaring" state could make its determination between heaven and hell. When the subject was already reputed as holy, men and women came to see a "good death," a topic of paramount interest to all. In Christian society it was termed *Ars Moriendi*, or "the art of dying."[2] The church had assembled an impressive liturgy to accompany the dying. This existed in a continuum that included the prayers for the dying and the three last sacraments of penance, the Eucharist, and extreme unction, continuing after the person's expiration into the funeral rites, lasting up to the burial. Indeed, it endured beyond the grave, in the celebration of memorial requiems on the month's or year's anniversary. The Christian dead were never gone. They were still members of the church, having passed from the church militant into either the church suffering in purgatory, or the church triumphant in heaven. They remained intimately "present" to the living body of believers. They were the "very special dead."[3]

Thomas realized this model of a good death. Though he had occasionally exhibited a short temper, in his last illness he was patient amid his sufferings and even expressed sorrow at being served by others when the Cistercian brothers tended his fire for him.[4] He also fulfilled the requirement of offering pious exhortations to others, in the form of his brief excursus on the Song of Songs. Even Thomas's final effort to have himself carried into a religious house was evidence of his good intentions. For Thomas, as for all medievals, physical location was itself of spiritual relevance. Not only did he fulfill the church's liturgical cycle of deathbed rituals, ensuring that his soul was "shriven" by confession and "houseled" by the Eucharist, but he also supplied ample evidence to all present that he knew exactly what he was doing, making a spontaneous confession of faith as if to underscore the meaning of the rituals. Even in his weakened state he made the final gesture of prostrating himself before the Holy Eucharist. He received the viaticum with tears, another physical manifestation of spiritual reality quickly coming to be considered part and parcel of holiness—praying for the "gift of tears." Thomas's biographers are also quick to note that, on his last full day of life, he received extreme unction and recited the responses to all the prayers himself, an emphasis that he remained of sound mind until the very end. When all of these actions were added to the already famous stories of his life—accompanied by a multiplication of personal witnesses in his final two years—the people gathered at Fossanova that winter day knew exactly what they had on their hands: a saint of God. When confronted by such a reality, medievals expected no less than miracles. People began to report such wonders from nearly the moment that Thomas died. The Cistercian subprior John of Ferentino had been a witness to Thomas's final days. After the Master died in the early hours of March 7, it probably devolved upon John to handle many of the details of the burial preparations. Before he began, he venerated Thomas's body, prostrating himself at the feet of the corpse. Having suffered from an affliction of the eyes, he applied his face directly to that of the dead man. Immediately he reported being restored to full eyesight.[5] It was to be the first of many wonders attributed to the Dominican.

Almost immediately people began to gather for the funeral, including members of Thomas's family. In reality, these were the vanguard of many pilgrimages from local residents who sought healing or protection at the monastery. According to Benedictine custom, the funeral was on the third day after death, or Friday, March 9, 1274. Many local people had assembled for the Solemn Requiem Mass, both lay and clergy. Though the Franciscan Bishop of Terracina was present, the honor of celebrating the Mass would probably have fallen to the abbot of Fossanova. It is indeed surprising that while there were many Preachers who came from local houses, no officials of the order were present. I think this is quite easily explained by the necessity of first getting the news out to the world and then having people travel to such a remote location, about equidistant from Rome and Naples, in such a short time frame.[6] It was common to have a preacher who was not the main celebrant. This was (and in some cases still is) the custom in mendicant houses. The labor of preparation and celebration of the ancient liturgy was significant, and so a division of labor freed the celebrant to focus on the rituals and the preacher to focus on the sermon. Probably as a matter of course the choice fell upon Thomas's *socius* and close friend Reginald of Priverno. Not only was he close to the deceased, but he was also a local, for his hometown was just down the road. By all accounts he delivered a marvelous sermon, but the part that stuck most in the minds of the hearers was his testimony about his Master's confessions. Though the seal of confession was as sacred then as it is now, by that time it had become customary to offer accounts of a holy person's confessions following his or her death. The confessor was the one who had intimately known the state of the penitent's soul and so, through the course of the thirteenth century, he had become the key witness at canonization depositions.[7] Reginald, who had likely heard Thomas's confessions *daily* (as a preparation for Mass) for at least ten years, told the assembled multitude that Thomas was like a little child of five regarding purity, apparently utterly free not only of sins of the flesh, but even of inclinations in that direction. He also swore that Thomas never willingly consented to a mortal sin, a contention also becoming common for saints at that time.[8]

Since the funeral was conducted in a cloistered monastery, it meant that no women, including the members of Thomas's family, were allowed to be present. They were kept outside, which probably only intensified the emotional reaction of the assembled crowd when, as a privilege, the bier was brought to the back of the church so that his niece Francesca could see the body one last time. When the monks brought the coffin into view, it became the occasion for the women to break into loud wailing and lamentation, an outpouring of emotion that was both genuine and expected, particularly in Italy.[9] Bernard Gui, with his cultured French heritage, sniffs a bit at this and adds, "as was the custom in that country." Apparently the keening was so profound that it had an effect on surrounding livestock. The mule that Thomas had arrived on broke free at the commotion and ran toward the body. Apparently upon seeing it the animal collapsed and died, an unforeseen development that redoubled the wailing and that the hagiographers turned into a pious instance of nature itself mourning the death of Thomas.[10] It was, in any case, an eventful funeral.

The second canonization inquest was held at the abbey of Fossanova and primarily sought the memory of miracle stories. The period in which modern medieval scholars have been quietly embarrassed by miracle stories has long since passed. These texts, one of the most voluminous types of sources in medieval literature, are now seen as treasure troves of social, cultural, and local history. Though usually mediated by clerical compilers and directed toward the purpose of glorifying their saints, it is in these works that the otherwise faceless multitudes of orthodox medieval laity come to the fore. We see their problems, concerns, joys, and hopes. Medieval people, rich and poor, learned and unlettered, valued miracles and miracle stories exceedingly. We would do them a disservice—no matter what one's conception of "miracle" is—if we refused to take them and their stories seriously. There is an ever-expanding body of work on miracle stories and increasing appreciation of the many insights that such narratives provide.[11]

In Thomas's case, an excellent analysis of the miracle stories has been accomplished by Le Brun-Gouanvic.[12] Her work breaks down the 145 different wonders attributed to Thomas in the canonization literature and in the early hagiography. The picture that emerges from her effort is that of Thomas as a "shrine saint": one whose cult was centered on his physical remains at Fossanova, either in terms of miracles granted directly at the tomb or as a vowed object of pilgrimage. Thomas's cult was almost entirely local. The vast majority of miracles took place either right at the abbey or within ten miles of Fossanova, with a special focus on Priverno and Sonnino. The presence of relics, paired with memories of Thomas, helped to generate some reports of wonders in Salerno and Naples. Even in Bernard Gui's compilation of miracles—finished after the canonization—there are only tentative indications of an expanding cult. A few miracles transpired in southern France to those who were involved in presenting the case to the curia, but then they would have been familiar with Thomas's case and would have been eager to promote it.[13] There is one lonely miracle from Piedmont; the rest continue to transpire in the area surrounding the abbey where Thomas's relics lay.[14] Thomas was a friend and neighbor, a patron of the locality, and he most certainly did *not* have a Europe-wide cult. This is most clearly demonstrated by the fact that even fifty years after his death, a second inquest had to be made at Fossanova for the express purpose of finding a satisfactory number of miracles to ensure canonization. Yet assessing wonders by geographical location is but one way of understanding Thomas's cult.

Besides its local nature, another factor that dominates the assembled statistics is that the wonders attributed to Thomas are granted most often to men and women of the lower classes. Nearly two-thirds of all the miracles are reported by the orthodox laboring laity, with the remainder evenly divided between the nobility and the clergy. This is somewhat surprising because a much larger representation of the first two estates is more usual in miracle accounts.[15] This breakdown of Thomas's beneficiaries coheres with his status as a local shrine saint and is underscored by the essentially rural nature of the area. Thomas also appears primarily as a healer: of sensory organs, of contagious and organic diseases, and of wounds and paralysis. This is an area where one can make a deeper analysis of miracle typology. While Le Brun-Gouanvic gives a good account of the miracles, she limits herself to a comparison with the wonders of Louis of Toulouse, a Franciscan archbishop canonized in close proximity to Thomas. When compared to other saints canonized in the fourteenth century, Thomas appears somewhat odd. Saints in other fourteenth-century sources were depicted as favoring more exceptional and astonishing miracles than those recorded for Thomas, things like resurrections of the dead and dramatic smitings for blasphemy (termed punitive or aggression miracles). Thomas has only one of the latter, perhaps because that local area was not known for heresy of any type, particularly in the later 1200s and early 1300s. It was for the punishment of a scoffing canon of Salerno who, seeing Thomas's relic, said he was "not a saint, only a Dominican." Falling ill, he was cured by repentance and by venerating the relic.[16] Only 1.3 percent of Thomas's miracles are resurrections (a total of two), whereas the average for the fourteenth-century compilations is over 10 percent. Thomas appears to have two "specialties." The first is healing paralysis or other problems with motor function. The fourteenth-century average for this type was 12.5 percent of total miracles, but Thomas's percentage was 25.5 percent. Less dramatic but still significant is his specialty in healing contagious or organic diseases (fevers, ulcers, tumors, and the like). The average calculated by Vauchez was 31.2 percent of all miracles, while for Thomas it is 40 percent. Thomas was a friend who understood and helped with the everyday struggles of his neighbors, a fact that continues the miracles that Gui appended after his canonization.[17]

Another way of comparing miracles is to look at similar saints, most especially the two Dominicans canonized prior to Thomas: Dominic (can. 1234) and Peter of Verona (can. 1253).[18] Thomas is much more like Dominic in terms of the extent of his cult. The reports of miracles for St. Dominic come almost entirely from the area of southern France, where he was best known, as well as around his tomb in Bologna. Peter, on the other hand, won international renown with his dramatic martyrdom, and his cult was diffused over all of Europe within a year of his death.[19] Dominic and Peter had different "specialities" from Thomas as well. For instance, Dominic was not seen as much of a healing saint, but was much more associated with miracles that involved the manipulation of nature, such as the production of food and wine. Peter, having fought against heresy his whole life, was known for "aggression" miracles that involved punishment for laxity or blasphemy. Strangely, people also invoked Peter to produce fertility miracles or to obtain easy childbirth. Dominic was not reported as performing any similar miracle, and Thomas only performed two, recorded after the canonization.[20] Indeed, during the whole of the remainder of the 1200s, the Dominicans did not generate any spontaneous cultic following of Thomas. He was a brilliant man of revered memory certainly, but there would be no impetus from the order to agitate for elevation to sainthood before 1318. This is not to say that there was no cult. The veneration of Thomas was a thriving example of local sanctity, the likes of which could be found throughout Christendom. Its restricted geographical nature meant nothing to his eventual canonization. Even on a local, limited scale, in the eyes of the church miracles were still miracles. The people of coastal south Lazio and the northern Campania had their patron, he was theirs and he watched over them. They venerated him and made pilgrimages to him. Famous, international saints such as the Apostles Peter and Paul were busy men. Thomas, on the other hand, was a neighbor, always ready to listen to the plaints of his friends.

Knowing how valuable it was to have a saint in one's possession was not lost on the White Monks of Fossanova. After the funeral, they interred Thomas below the high altar.[21] However, their prize was too valuable to be left in such an open location. Even before burial people were seeking relics. Reginald's detaching of Thomas's thumb for his own devotion was a prime example. Perhaps the Friars Preachers would come to take Thomas away, depriving the monastery both of the spiritual benefit of such a patron as well as the income that the local pilgrimages produced. Reginald had already begun to draft legal documents to remove the body at "an opportune time."[22] Some days later—all had departed—the monks moved the body to a back chapel dedicated to St. Stephen where it would be easier to watch over. Seven months later, Prior James of Ferentino had a dream in which Thomas asked to be moved back to his original place. While some would take this as a rebuke, the monks turned this to their advantage. This vision was to be central to the Cistercians' defense of their possession of the body. Upon being carried to Fossanova, some of Thomas's last words were "Here shall I rest." The monks turned this into a prophetic utterance. In the prior's dream he had requested burial beside the high altar. Obligingly, the Cistercians disinterred Thomas. When they opened the grave, an indescribably sweet odor filled the monastery. The sensing of similar smells often accompanied the translation of saint's bodies, and has been reported in various instances from the Middle Ages to the present day. It was an independent and communally sensed affirmation, open to all regardless of merit, that the person was indeed holy. Such a miracle shockingly altered the course of nature. Where the stench of corruption was expected, the sweet aroma of flowers came forth.[23] Once they freed the lid from the coffin, they found Thomas entirely incorrupt, still in his perfectly preserved habit (minus one thumb). Gui makes sure to note the exceptional nature of this incorruption, particularly since the second burial place was known to be deep and wet.[24] Medievals saw incorruption as a sure sign of sanctity and accompanied many (but emphatically not all) translations of saints' remains.[25] One may gauge the attitude of the monks by their choice of liturgy. Traditionally a requiem Mass would be celebrated for such a disinterment, but instead the Cistercians changed the formulary to the Mass Os Iusti, which is the proper liturgical formulary for confessor saints. As Thomas was not yet canonized this was a bit irregular, yet it demonstrates the medieval conviction that people knew saints when they saw them.

The monks of Fossanova continued to attempt to retain the body of their new saint. The recovery of the remains seemed to have been Reginald's personal project, and after his death, Dominican efforts in that direction seem to have stalled. Around 1281 the new abbot, Peter of Montesangiovanni, ordered that Thomas be raised to a new and more honored position on the Gospel side of the high altar, where an inscription can still be seen today. In 1288 Theodora of San Severino, Thomas's sister, requested a disinterment so that she could obtain his right hand as a relic and a keepsake. It was during these events, claimed Bartholomew of Capua, that Thomas's head was removed for the ostensible reason that the Cistercians could retain something of the body if it were taken from them. Yet the records of recognitions all declare that the body was still mostly incorrupt, making the accusation of decapitation somewhat odd. While Bartholomew's testimony is often valuable, it is not always reliable. In fact, I read it as an attempt to discredit the Cistercians and rejoin the battle to recover the body around the time of the canonization in 1318. In reality the Cistercians did not need any encouragement in their efforts. The news of the election of the Dominican Benedict XI in 1303 again roused their fears that they would lose their local saint. They possibly disinterred Thomas at this time and, in order to preserve his body more compactly (and to hide it if necessary), they boiled what remained and reduced it to bones, able to be kept in a much more compact casket, which Tocco viewed in 1319.[26] This story, however, does not appear until the final Dominican acquisition of the bones in 1369 and their transfer to their final resting place in Toulouse. It is possible that by the 1310s the body had decomposed so significantly that all that was left were bones, but it is equally plausible that the Cistercians did indeed render the body. Most modern Dominican commentators have expressed distaste and embarrassment regarding such proceedings, but the medieval Dominicans never seemed to have commented adversely on it. They shared the Cistercians' views on the significance of the bodies of saints. The saint's body for medievals was a privileged nexus of heaven and earth. Thomas himself would have agreed when he said, "Man is not a soul only, but something composed of soul and body."[27] Efforts to retain the body or to litigate over its possession seem odd to modern people, but if placed within the incarnational context of premodern Christianity, they become easily explicable. While there are always issues of money and power to consider, I would suggest that Thomas's cult, local as it was, brought in only a modest income to the monastery; nor were the Dominicans particularly interested in the pecuniary rewards. Both they and the Cistercians were negotiating the demands of holy place and saintly materiality, deepened by the incarnational centrality of the body of the saint of God.

BODY AND SOUL TOGETHER

One can, then, wonder what we can know about the character and traits of Thomas in life, the man who had done so much and who had lived in such a way as to earn the admiration of both friends and adversaries. All of the physical descriptions that have come down to us date from the final two years of his life and, for that reason, are probably affected by the sicknesses that multiplied during that period. Bernard Gui gives the following description of Thomas:

> He was tall and stout. He held himself erect, as men with well-ordered souls do. His complexion was wheaten, as of a temperate man. He had a large head, with a full development of the organic powers that are required for reason. He was somewhat bald. His flesh had the delicately

255

balanced texture that indicates a fine intelligence; yet
virile also, robust and ready to serve the will.[28]

Descending from Germanic Lombard stock on his father's
side, and perhaps with some Norman blood, Thomas was of a
remarkable stature for a man of southern Italy. It is clear that he
was tall and carried himself with an aristocratic bearing born of
habit. Coupled with a billowing Dominican cape, a tall man could
look imposing indeed. He was also variously described as having
a darker or a "wheaten" complexion, which may suggest lighter
colored hair with a light brown skin, perhaps darkened by many
years of exposure to the bright Italian sun.[29] One often-repeated
claim about his appearance should be more fully examined. I am
not convinced that Thomas was as overweight as he is often made
out to be. Though his biographers do remark on his size on a few
occasions, and two deponents at the canonization describe him as
"fat," these are descriptions that come from witnesses at the end
of his life, when he was increasingly sick. It is possible that at this
period his weight increased due to a more sedentary lifestyle and
possible complications from edema (called "dropsy" in the Middle Ages). It was certainly not a result of the sparse and meatless
Dominican diet. Thomas was no gourmand, and normally seemed
quite indifferent to food. The constitutions themselves forbade
meat and game. The friars' diet was entirely fish and vegetables,
taken just twice a day, and but once during penitential periods.
One can also imagine that the supply of such food in mendicant
convents often was not plentiful. In addition, he was probably one
of the most traveled men in Europe, taking his journeys almost
entirely by foot. Aside from the Masters General of the age, there
was perhaps no more widely traveled friar than Thomas. A rough
estimation has concluded that he traveled at least fifteen thousand
kilometers on foot during the course of his career. Thomas was
also known to pace quickly when thinking about a problem. All of
this leads to the speculation that his increased girth was a result
of later complications that hastened his death. Indeed, the most
repeated comment about his body, that he was "large, fat, and tall
in stature," comes not from witnesses of the living man, but rather
from the account of the disinterment of his body seven months
after his death.[30] Time in the grave could have exacerbated these

conditions in his body. I propose that Thomas's weight was an effect of only the final years of his life. Before that he was known only as tall, robust, and prompt in movement. As evidence of his advancing age, witnesses remarked that he was balding, noticeable in spite of the Dominican tonsure on his head.[31] I would make one further point. In the iconography of the saint, he is always pictured as stout. There may be a reason for this. Thomas was the third popular male Dominican saint. Artists commonly pictured Dominic as beardless, holding the lily of virginity, while they always drew Peter of Verona with a beard. Having exhausted the aesthetic possibilities of facial hair, painters were left with a conundrum: how to differentiate the third Dominican holy man in their depictions. Dominic and Peter were thin—perhaps the artists simply reinforced Thomas's girth to set him iconographically apart.

Biographers also enjoyed tying his physical attributes to his character. Tocco remarks that he had a large head (which would correspond to his large stature, and made the baldness mentioned by witnesses more prominent), but that this was an indicator of his ample use of reason.[32] Yet, at the same time, Tocco declares that he had a delicate or gentle demeanor, which the biographer traced both to his family nobility as well as to his intellectual proclivities. Such parallels between bodily attributes, aristocracy, and virtue were quite common in medieval biography. Hagiographers wrote in a universe ordered by God in "measure and number and weight" (Wis 11:20), a symbolic cosmos in which everything pointed to its final end in some way. In those terms it was natural that bodily characteristics would point to more deeply spiritual meanings. Thomas's aristocratic upbringing certainly did come through, bearing all of the good traits that such a social status indicated and apparently with few of the demerits. He was unfailingly kind and patient (with the exception of a few understandable moments of annoyance at the end). He was also courteous, that is, when he happened to notice those around him. He carried himself with excellent posture, so often remarked upon by the witnesses. His noble bearing and patience enabled him to tolerate fools gladly, and he was exceptionally long suffering in not responding to his adversaries' polemics in kind. Thomas had a youthful impetuosity that he gradually brought under control by experience and practice. One only need think of his questions to his Master as a boy, as well as his plowing through Albert's disputed question when he was yet only the equivalent of a graduate student.[33] By his own confession he had not become puffed-up and conceited by the exceptional success of his academic career, nor by the special predilection of princes and popes in his favor. At the same time, however, he did admit that from time to time he had feelings of vanity. One could speculate that these were interior feelings of pride at his success in writing and disputations against his many foes, which nevertheless he did not display openly.[34]

Above all, Thomas had an incredibly rich interior life and was content—as many academics are—to spend long periods in solitude and to cultivate silence. While his hagiographers are eager to turn this in a spiritual and mystical direction, it is clear that they are the virtues and practices proper to an intellectual. While indeed Thomas was a man of serious contemplation and devotion, fundamentally this flowed from his native disposition. To this he added a towering power for concentration, which preferred quiet intellectual productivity to the bustle of the active life. Only such an ability can account for his prodigious output. At the same time, Thomas could be distracted from his purposes by a fixation on a new topic or approach. Nearly half of his remaining works are unfinished. Of course, in some cases this was a result of his premature death, but in other instances he simply changed tack and sailed a different course. One must then balance this sustained capacity for attention with the ability simply to leave off some work or subject without needing to return to it. It was also a measure of the swiftness of his thought, for without a doubt Thomas was one of the most brilliant thinkers ever to live. He was once asked by his student Daniel of Angusta what he thanked God for most. Without a trace of self-consciousness, he answered that, by the help of the Spirit, he never read a book without understanding it nor without arriving at the most profound meaning of the text.[35] One thing we do not hear much about are Thomas's reading habits. They must have been voracious, but the biographers only insert details about his spiritual reading. It seemed that Thomas did attribute his achievements not to his natural intelligence but to the grace of God. As an Aristotelian, however, Thomas would be the first to admit that without the natural capacity, his intellect would not have been a fitting repository for the graces sent by God. Tocco recalls a sermon given by Reginald in Naples soon after the Master's funeral. Thomas's close friend relates,

> In his soul, intellect and desire somehow contained each other, the two faculties freely serving one another in such a way that each in turn took the lead: his desire, through prayer, gained access to divine realities, which then the intellect, deeply apprehending, drew into a light that kindled to greater intensity the flame of love.[36]

In spite of these advantages Thomas had intellectual weak spots. He was particularly bad about learning languages. Other than his southern Italian dialect and its close cognate, academic Latin, it appears that Thomas was utterly dependent upon others in terms of linguistic skills. He had a smattering of Greek and no Hebrew and, while such talents were uncommon among contemporaries, it nonetheless hampered his access to original theological and philosophical sources, leaving him dependent upon translators. He recognized this weakness and never ceased to seek out improved translations, particularly those of his Dominican colleague William of Moerbeke. Nonetheless, even though he had extended stays in Cologne and especially in Paris, he never learned (or bothered to learn?) the local idioms. This would have severely limited his contact with people outside the convent and the university. It would also have hindered his preaching outside academic contexts, except when he gave his popular sermons in Naples or Rome. This was perhaps a conscious choice, for any ability or facility in the local languages would have provided his superiors an opportunity to deploy him on the "front lines" as a preacher or confessor. Even when he did preach, witnesses recalled that—while he spoke with warmth and simplicity—he always preached with his eyes closed, as if not to have to engage with the audience, something he could easily avoid during the rest of the liturgy. Even when he was sought by the laity, he tried quickly to get away from them, as shown in the story of the woman who had a hemorrhage healed in Rome when she touched the back of his vestment as he was returning to the sacristy.[37] Indeed, with the sole exception of his sisters and nieces, one could say that Thomas aggressively avoided women.[38] While he certainly became known for his chastity and purity during life and after death, it is clear that Thomas worked very hard to avoid anything that might even be a near occasion of sin. Thomas certainly sought that spiritual and bodily purity that was most conducive to intellectual contemplation and for which he was later given the title "Angelic Doctor."

That title nods not only to his famous chastity, but also to his status in the Catholic Church as the "Angel of the Schools." Thomas has become the patron saint of teachers and professors. It is most instructive—particularly for those of us who occupy similar positions—to pause and meditate on just what it is that makes him such an archetype for those who try to live the life of the mind. Thomas demonstrates that the first object of a teacher's predilection should always be the student. For him, knowledge and wisdom are not goods to possess, but rather to live out and to give away. The Master expresses his solicitude for his pupils in any number of ways. His concern for students is present from the very dawn of his career as an assistant to Albert. When his fellow scholars in Cologne had discovered Thomas's acuity in penetrating the texts lectured upon by Master Albert, they began to come to him for tutoring. Always generous with his time, Thomas explained the lectures so lucidly that the Student Master marveled and told Albert of his abilities. While one can certainly criticize the mendicants as strikebreakers in 1252, another way of looking at the issue was that Thomas was above all concerned for his students who would be deprived of learning during such a cessation and considered their welfare above the concerns of the combined faculty. During a life in which very few people were close to Thomas (with the exception of Reginald, and his rather warm relations with the female members of his family) we do know that he engendered deep mutual respect and affection from those who studied under him. We know of several students to whom he was devoted, in particular Cardinal Annibaldo di Annibaldi, to whom he dedicated the second half of his *Catena Aurea*. Other students also remembered him with affection as well, such as the Florentine preacher Remigio de' Girolami, and the bishop of Paris, Adenulf of Anagni, who paid to have the *Catena* recopied in honor of his Master. Thomas generated exceptional affection even among those traditionally considered his adversaries. This is plain in the devotion of the Arts faculty and students, demonstrated by a letter to the General Chapter in 1272 asking for Thomas's reassignment to Paris, and again after his death when they requested his last Aristotelian commentaries and perhaps some of his relics. This was in spite of the grievous confrontation with the radical Aristotelians. They knew that Thomas was one of the Philosopher's stoutest defenders and, excluding the Averroism of men such as Siger and Boethius, they knew he was the best hope for their continued exploration of Aristotle.

One could make the argument that his concern for students is most of all reflected in the fact that the majority of his lectures and works are directed to teaching. While he commented on the *Sentences*—as did nearly every thirteenth-century academic—he quickly grasped how clumsy a tool it was for introducing people to fundamental dogmatic theology. Thomas was never one simply to use a text because it was the common practice, an academic lassitude that afflicted scholars then as well as now. His awareness of the shortcomings of habitual university practices paralleled his irritation at the curricular limitations of his own order, which tended to overemphasize education in pastoral and practical theology while neglecting the roots of theology itself. His entire architectonic conception of the *Summa Theologiae* was directed to overcoming weaknesses of both text and method, by developing a comprehensive plan to overhaul the educational establishment of the Preachers. The origin of this project is perhaps most telling in terms of his attitude toward learners. When the order assigned him as Lector to the convent at Orvieto, it charged him with teaching basic theology to the *fratres communes*: common friars who lived and worked at the priory and who had not exhibited any special aptitude for further study. Thomas was just then coming from the University of Paris, where he lived and worked with the most brilliant men in Europe. In Orvieto he probably encountered the equivalent of an average community college student. Not only did Thomas not betray the least annoyance at this change in his teaching station, but he also plowed into his new job with alacrity and charity. Never in his life did he ever express any frustration with the intellectual capacities of his students. It is telling that his first reaction in Orvieto was not against the students, but rather against the curriculum, which he determined was ill-serving their needs. It has been a commonplace of professors since the time of the

Greeks to complain about their students and to rail against declining standards, yet for Thomas, the problem never lies with them. Rather the defect is in the form of teaching, the content that is being delivered, or the effort put forth by the professor to ameliorate the situation. As astonishing as it is to the contemporary reader, the *Summa* is intended for novices. "The doctor of Catholic truth ought not only to instruct the proficient, but also to instruct beginners...our purpose in this work is to present what pertains to the Christian religion, in such a way that may be appropriate to the instruction of beginners."[39] Thomas surmises that the theological science was done badly for three reasons: (1) people often read works that dealt with trifling matters, (2) things are taught out of proper order, and (3) teachers introduce a needless repetition that brings weariness. The *Summa* was meant to offset those issues. Indeed, later in life, Thomas wrote an even simpler work entitled the *Compendium*, which may have been a tacit acknowledgment that even the "milk" of the *Summa* might be a little rich. Almost equally astonishing is his comprehensive effort to comment on all the extant works of Aristotle, so as to understand them as well as possible to prevent others from misunderstanding them. In this there was no professional obligation whatsoever. He was a theology professor, not a philosopher. Yet he considered a correct understanding of the Philosopher so critical for his particular historical moment in theology that he undertook this massive extra effort—the very works that the Arts faculty clamored for after his death. It was an act of nearly superhuman academic generosity. As Pieper presciently commented, "Love of truth and love of men— only the two together constitute a teacher."[40] Both therefore were necessary for a successful intellectual.

In his love for truth, Thomas was much unlike the majority of modern research professors. For him "research" or purely academic writing were secondary to his vocation. But such research, even though subordinate, was still a necessary part of who he was. In a certain sense Thomas, who considered the "mixed" life of action and contemplation as the most perfect, saw teaching and research as two sides of the same coin. He considered it absolutely and irreducibly critical to his effectiveness as a teacher and writer to be completely up to date on the current state of not simply his particular interest, but of the entirety of the university world. While such mastery of the intellectual universe has become increasingly difficult after the early modern explosion in scientific knowledge, Thomas was broadly interested enough to go well beyond all the contemporary issues in theology and philosophy and engaged (with more or less success) in the study of political theory, economics, astronomy, physics, and even biology. How unlike this is from those modern scholars who specialize themselves out of controversy! The shallowness of their intellectual approach diminishes their ability to offer broad and learned conversations of relevance to life, and consequently academia risks being increasingly divorced from the reality of the incarnate world. Because of his character, many sought out Thomas as a "public" intellectual. One Thomist coined the very apt term *disponibility* to describe his engagement beyond the walls of the academy.[41] It seems he never disdained to be of service to the pope, the curia, the Master General, or even humble Lectors of his own order from out-of-the way convents. He answered matters of pitch and moment, whether the questions were deep or inane (as they occasionally were, such as when the Lector of Besançon asked whether the hands of the baby Jesus made the stars). Regardless of interlocutor, he answered with brevity, clarity, and charity (though he did gently suggest that the Lector focus on matters of deeper substance). Such issues give evidence of the catholicity of his purview.

Thomas made it his business to be as universal as possible. Indeed, in terms of the world of Christendom of the thirteenth century, he was a "Renaissance man" before the fact. Thomas would have considered that the gravest violation of his vocation would be to become what is known as "dead wood," a term of contempt used to describe those teachers who cease to teach well or to produce research after the granting of tenure. Thomas remained constantly engaged at the highest of levels of thought throughout his life. He was aware of all the strains running through the university world, at times being engaged on no fewer than three intellectual fronts. This aspect of his career was accompanied by extraordinary intellectual bravery, a sometimes difficult idea to conceptualize. To be intellectually brave was never to cower in the face of a challenge, something that necessarily includes modifying one's own opinions when proven wrong. In particular it involves the intrepidity to stand against the academic tide and not simply to accept the nostrums of one's colleagues. Thomas never shied away from a fight, even when it meant disagreeing with friends and associates. At the same time, he always showed himself to be charitable, which is perhaps the most heroic aspect of his work. To combine the virtues of fortitude and love is a difficult task. Even when unjustly attacked, such as during John Pecham's inaugural lecture or Gerard d'Abbeville's New Year's sermon, he remained calm and collected. The few times he issued a challenge in his work it was always because he believed that students were in danger, such as in his writings against the Seculars and the Averroists during his second Regency. Even though a common format for intellectual exchange was the polemic, Thomas disdained to use it. Even in his works hammered out in the midst of controversy, where he is directly confronting opponents, he refuses to use invective or personal attack. When one considers the massive volume of his works and the thousands of pages that he wrote, his lack of animosity and his calm are staggering. In his entire career, we have only one record of his calling any idea foolish. In the question on divine simplicity in the *Summa*, he spoke of the error of "David of Dinant, who most stupidly thought that God was Prime Matter."[42] This is the only time that the Master speaks like this; it is the exception that proves the rule of his intellectual charity. Most especially pertaining to intellectual fortitude, he performed public quodlibetal questions with an impressive regularity that was matched by only a few other teachers. These were dangerous academic performances that opened the floor to all in order to challenge the authority of the Master. That Thomas held them so often is a testament to his confidence and courage.

Another key component of Thomas's work is his deep engagement with the tradition. Above all this meant Sacred Scripture, but it also included the interpretive legacy of Catholic authors, particularly Augustine and the fathers. Too often many have pictured Thomas as some sort of theological iconoclast, overthrowing the presumed certitudes of the past and replacing wholesale the venerable Platonic superstructure with an untested Aristotelian philosophy. The more deeply one is immersed in his work, the more one sees the value that he attaches to Plato and to Augustine and how he builds upon that which he has received, even if at times he is able to cast that inheritance in a new light. Joseph Pieper sums this up well:

> An analysis of that remarkable and almost inexhaustible first article of the *Quaestiones Disputatae de Veritate* demonstrates that no pat, unequivocal, textbook reply is given to the query, "what is truth?" Rather St. Thomas first developed his own ingenious interpretation, and then, with rare modesty, works it into the garland of traditional definitions of truth in a web of reciprocal illumination and confirmation. Not one of the traditional formulae is rejected entirely or accepted as exclusively valid. Though they are in no way fully concordant, he can appreciate the partial validity of each. What actually is happening here? It happens that St. Thomas is, in effect, placing himself within the stream of traditional truth nourished by the past; without claiming to give a final solution he leaves the way open for future quest and discovery as that stream flows onward toward the yet unknown.[43]

As Pieper remarks, this is indeed the very method of the Platonic dialogues. Indeed, it is only through familiarity with the depth of his appropriation of tradition that one can see where he is truly novel. Thomas had no problem with the argument from authority, though he—like his fellow medievals—considered it to be the weakest argument. Yet it was where one had to begin. He repeats Aristotle's admonition several times: "Man acquires a share of this learning, not indeed all at once, but little by little, according to the mode of his nature: and every one who learns thus must needs believe."[44] Unlike Descartes, Thomas knew that trust, not doubt, was the proper attitude of the knower and of the student, even if that is not his final destination. In his Aristotelian worldview, our very orientation to the reality of the world presented through our senses is itself necessarily a posture of trust. As one scholar remarked, "The assent of faith does not close down after making an objective act of obedience; rather, it unleashes human curiosity so that natural human intelligence and the grace of faith work in complementary fashion."[45] It was the responsibility of the professor to proceed from the foundations of authority to deeper wisdom. It would be terrible if the teacher merely cut off debate by appeal to the tradition, or even worse, of his own authority. As Thomas said himself, "If we resolve the problems posed by faith exclusively by means of authority, we will of course possess the truth—but in empty heads!"[46]

The Master certainly did not limit himself to scriptural or Catholic authorities, however. Wherever there was the possibility of finding truth he did not disdain to follow the path. Whether the interlocutor was pagan, Jewish, Muslim, or a separated Christian, he engaged with an air of virtuous studiousness, willing to be taught and drawn toward truth as a moth to light. To read Thomas is to read a sort of dialogue that crosses cultures and centuries. Within his classroom Rabbi Moses Maimonides enters into discussion with the Muslim philosopher Averroes. Plato and Aristotle again come to life and are put in contact with John Chrysostom, Dionysius, and Augustine. When one says that Thomas had a rich interior life, that is to intimate the historically impracticable congress of minds that intellectual work makes possible. What Thomas establishes is a universal school of reason where all are admitted, simply by virtue of their common humanity and shared rationality. His incarnational faith also demands the cooperation and congruence of faith with reason. It is because of Christ and his assumption of human nature that we must take thinkers from other cultures seriously. Our common possession of humanity opens the door to the rationality of dialogue, and Thomas can search the depths of non-Christian thought for the "preambles of faith." The grace that comes from God will build upon the rational foundations of all honest seekers of truth. The foundations laid by pagans, Jews, or Muslims will not be effaced or destroyed, but reformed and redirected. How different is this world from the modern academy, which fixes its attention on the new, in total disregard to what came before, and holds itself in studied disdain of the traditions of the past. As I once heard from a prescient professor, "The medievals were privileged to stand on the shoulders of giants. The academics of today are content to dance on the graves of midgets."

Thomas was also a methodological innovator. He completely reoriented theological procedure, which began a centuries-long transition from the *Sentences* to his *Summa*. Without applying anachronistic modern categories, Thomas did manifest the beginnings of a critical mentality toward sources. Even though he was firmly in the ambit of medieval biblical commentators, his insistence on focusing on the literal sense would point to new directions in Scripture scholarship. His literal focus influenced all later authors, including the key medieval exegete Nicholas of Lyra.[47] It was Thomas who discovered that the *Liber de Causis* was not a product of Aristotle, but rather came from a fifth-century Neoplatonist named Proclus. This revelation enabled him and others to begin to unravel the Neoplatonic encrustations that had grown around Aristotelian thought. His critical perception, in a sense, liberated Aristotle from shackles that had bound the Greek since the twelfth century.[48] It is known that he accepted other attributions uncritically, most notoriously the sixth-century Christian Neoplatonist who went under the pseudonym of Paul's first-century convert, Dionysius the Areopagite. Yet at the same time he was able to detect problems in texts that had otherwise been attributed to John Chrysostom. Even though he does not call the *Opus Imperfectum* pseudonymous, he clearly distinguishes it from Chrysostom's other works. He also carefully teases out the Arian sentiments and isolates them, so as to make sure that he can glean as much as possible from the text.[49] Even when confronted with false authorities, such as when he engages Greek theology in the *Contra Errores Graecorum*, he attempts to interpret them in the most charitable and orthodox manner possible. Thomas even provides principles for interpreting patristic texts that combine charity with a critical sense. He says that later teachers speak more cautiously to steer clear of heresy. On the contrary, some early fathers wrote exuberantly and before many doctrines were defined. For this reason, they are not to be ridiculed but interpreted with reverence.[50] Thomas never ceased to demand fresh and more accurate translations of pertinent works, while also making subtle comments on the qualities of translation, which should not be slavishly literal, but rather adapt the mode of expression to emphasize the intention of the author.[51] In addition, the Master ardently sought new historical sources. During his stay in Orvieto he came to know the Greek fathers much more deeply, and he also probably discovered the records of the early ecumenical councils, which were to prove essential in grounding his later Christology.[52] Underlying his whole project was the insistence on the utility of Aristotle as a prism for the philosophical and theological project. He and Albert pioneered the full integration of the Philosopher into the medieval intellectual life and, while this by no means became the sole or even dominant stream of thought, it established a school that has not been exhausted to this day.

While many of these intellectual characteristics can be broadly applied across the Scholastic world, Thomas embodied them in a special way. He had an exceptionally elevated notion of the office of the teacher of sacred doctrine in the church. For Thomas as well as for his contemporaries, the Master who taught the Catholic faith merited a special crown in heaven, similar to those accorded to martyrs and virgins.[53] Indeed, his inception lecture gives us a picture of the exalted state of the theological profession. In *Rigans Montes*, Thomas compares doctors to the mountains that take the rain from God and water the plains.[54] The professor is an intermediary established by God to communicate the mysteries of salvation. Thomas's conception of the authority of professors is very high indeed. In his Easter 1269 quodlibet he asserts that the pastors of the church are like "manual laborers" who perform the work of administering sacraments. Bishops are like the "architects" who direct the pastors. He places doctors in the class of architects as well, who "research and teach how others ought to work in the salvation of souls." He asserts that "absolutely speaking," the office of teaching is more meritorious than dedication to the active life as a secular priest. As shocking as this is, even to many modern Catholic sensibilities, it refers to the perennial tradition of the superiority of the contemplative life. "Mary has chosen the better part, which shall not be taken away from her" (Luke 10:42). Even so, should it be necessary, bishops and doctors should go to the assistance of the pastors.[55] This speaks to the prestige enjoyed not only by Masters, but indeed by the Masters of Paris, the apex of the academic aristocracy.[56] Thomas writes of the "chair" (*cathedra*) of both bishops as well as of doctors, and indeed a much deeper knowledge is demanded for the latter, for bishops do not terribly exert themselves in Scholastic knowledge.[57] Perhaps we may be in the presence of some of Thomas's self-admitted temptations toward vanity. Many have been induced, particularly in the last fifty years, to draw from these considerations a claim that theologians have a "parallel magisterium" to that enjoyed by the bishops and popes. The concept of magisterium used in this sense is a post-Tridentine ecclesiological development. The idea of parallel magisterium only arose in the climate after Vatican II. Both these facts establish the absolute anachronicity of such a claim. It is made even more absurd when one considers that the authority of the professor, for Thomas, comes not from the position itself, but from one's profession of the Catholic faith, one's participation in the Christian tradition, one's communion with the church, and one's organic living of the life of holiness. Without any of these, Thomas would have considered that a theologian had lost the prerogatives that he describes above. Yet one can see how such considerations flowed from his defense of the mendicant orders against secular ecclesiological assertions. The sublimity and authority of the professor arose from precisely this: wisdom and truth are intertwined, and for Thomas, wise men are those who rightly order things because they know the end.[58] That person is wisest who turns his attention to the end of the whole universe, and these are the metaphysicians and especially the theologians.

For the Angelic Doctor, virtue is the end of all vocations, even of the academic life. As Chenu remarked, for Thomas "the virtuous life is the empire of reason."[59] Any attempt to teach truths about God without living the life of holiness is hypocrisy, doomed to failure. If wisdom does not lead to conversion, then it is unworthy of the name. An incarnational life demands the integration of all properly human characteristics, which means a right ordering within the soul, the dominion of the soul over the body, and the subordination of both to right reason. Thomas lived and breathed the truths he taught. For him there was no divorce between thought and practice. Thomas surrounded his intellectual work with a cocoon of faith and piety. His biographers never fail to note that he always invoked God or the saints before writing, and when he encountered a difficult problem, he habitually resorted to prayer.[60] There are many people who disdain argument: the anti-intellectuals of every age. Many again are those who argue, yet have no knowledge or practice of holiness. Thomas disputed against both; he was a saintly intellectual. He knew the mind was the special gift and attribute of humanity, and therefore the Creator expects us to use it well. While one could go far on love alone, Thomas knew that our final perfection would be a perfection of intellect. The vision of God was an intellectual perception suffused with love itself.[61] In this Thomas was a faithful follower of Dominic. Long before, when Dominic and Bishop Diego were traipsing the back paths of Languedoc, they had noticed that their arguments in favor of truth were falling on deaf ears. In order to appeal to their audience, they abandoned the trappings of power and wealth, like the heretics. In so doing they married truth and holiness together, clothing their preaching with a garment of sanctity. This is what Thomas accomplished his whole life. It is what drew people to his teaching. Even when at first they did not understand it, his example and his virtue attracted them. Even his enemies spoke well of him, and those who lived with him provided copious testimony concerning his virtuous life, interwoven with his glad fulfillment of all the manifold academic duties laid upon him. In appreciating all of these considerations one can readily see how such a man became patron of the profession of teachers, particularly those who labor in the university. The study and the lecture hall became places for the cultivation of sanctity. "At the very heart of the spirituality of Thomas Aquinas rests this conviction: human understanding is a place for holiness, because the Truth is holy."[62]

THE CHARACTER OF THOMAS AQUINAS: A HYPOTHESIS

In the course of studying this figure of such imposing physical and intellectual stature, one runs into an issue that confronts anyone inquiring into the life of a saint. The majority of the sources that record stories about him are hagiographical, which means they are designed for a specific end. In the case of Thomas's hagiographers, it was to bolster his canonization and, later, to provide material for the propagation of his cult. This happened along two primary trajectories, outlined by Innocent III. In the first place the writers had to adduce and present evidence of a life of sanctity that demonstrated the habitual practice of heroic virtues. In so doing, the stories in many hagiographies begin to converge together because they present the same pattern of holiness left by Christ the exemplar. In a certain sense, the main purpose of a hagiographical life is to present their subject as another Christ. The secondary object was to offer an account of various types of postmortem miracles, duly recorded and witnessed by reputable men and women. These literary constructions and strategies do not mean that we discard hagiography, as historians of older generations once tended to do. Once we understand this superstructure it becomes easier to peer into the sources themselves to see what they can tell us about the man. To one practiced in hagiography, one begins to notice the dissonances in the symphony of virtue, or in details that suggest that we may be able to peel back a layer of piety and look underneath. In some cases the hagiography tries to "clean up" incongruities or oddities in the life, an effort that immediately attracts the gaze of the scholar. This is not to say that the authors are hiding anything, such as covering up terrible sins; no, indeed, the saints of the Christian church have gone through rigorous examinations by history, by contemporaries, by the pious, and by legal and theological experts. What I am alluding to here are human characteristics that help the reader to understand the saint as a real, living human being, rather than as a stylized figure on a saccharine holy card. If we are careful, we can catch some of the cadences of everyday life and experience some of the tensions and uncertainties that belong to contingent human existence, as we read through the lives of these holy men and women.

The reader must also be wary of projecting back modern assumptions onto historical figures. This is particularly the case in attempting to diagnose psychological characteristics. For an instance of a failed attempt in this vein, one should reference the efforts to identify medieval female mystics who experienced inedia as having anorexia nervosa.[63] It is difficult to identify medical conditions across the span of centuries and impossible to get the historical character onto the psychiatrist's couch, as it were. Occasionally, however, some symptoms crop up in the sources in such a way as to suggest plausible explanations: for instance, the many instances of "quartan fever" among medieval Italian saints suggests some form of chronic malaria. When one discerns repetitive characteristics within the context of hagiography, along with attempts by the biographers to explain such traits away in a pietistic or devotional manner, the historian should take notice. They are very likely attempting to domesticate something that does not fit in with preexisting models of holiness. What I will unfold below is a speculative attempt to try to understand some of Thomas's character. It is hypothetical and certainly open to criticism, as indeed—after I present it—I will offer weaknesses in the position as well. The picture that I draw may also be unflattering in parts. This is not done to undermine Thomas's sanctity in any way, but rather in a good-faith effort to draw closer to the man himself. I am of the opinion that many of the descriptions of events in Thomas's life in the sources are attempting to deal with uncomfortable facts that were directly tied to his intellectual idiosyncrasies. One does not need to loiter at universities for long to realize how genuinely *strange* smart people can be. Often a college campus seems to be a sort of refuge for otherwise unemployable people. This manifests itself in any number of ways: narcissism, social awkwardness, eccentric clothing choices, and the seeming cultivation of acerbity. I once knew a professor who could speak for hours on end about obscure medieval topics, and yet be at a total loss if interrupted to ask about where to eat lunch. Famous are the stories about how Albert Einstein had to be dressed by his wife every day. The mechanical behaviors of such individuals as Immanuel Kant and Isaac Newton also come to mind. Indeed, such odd conduct often seems to be in direct proportion to one's intelligence.

Today increasing attention has been paid to the spectrum of intellectual conditions that go under the title of Autism Spectrum Disorder (ASD). This spectrum is so wide that it has consistently defied a precise medical definition. It is a neurodevelopmental issue that manifests in highly distinct ways. There can be a range of intellectual outcomes, from very low IQ individuals to virtual (though limited) geniuses. The latter particular subset of ASD is often referred as "high-functioning." Many such individuals at the present day are diagnosed with a form of ASD known as Asperger's syndrome. The common traits identified with High-Functioning Autism (HFA) and Asperger's are difficulties engaging in social situations, problems with empathy and interpersonal communication, coupled with an intense focus and ability to concentrate. In many cases of Asperger's and HFA, motor and linguistic skill sets can develop normally, unlike many others on the autism spectrum. For such an amorphous diagnosis, care must always be taken. Yet

I do not think it is too much of a stretch to suggest that many characteristics of individuals in the intellectual, academic, or technological fields can often be found somewhere along the autism spectrum. This also is correlated to a 31-percent increased risk of autism among children of especially intelligent parents.[64] The number of autistic children born to academics and to people who work in Silicon Valley is truly astonishing. It is admittedly impossible to correlate Thomas's experiences with a disorder that has only really been a subject of research in the previous eighty years, but what I do want to underscore is that when his biographers attempt to remove the rough edges of Thomas's character, they betray glimpses of the man who the Master really was.

From his youth Thomas presented an almost obsessive compulsion regarding certain items. One can see this in the episode where, as a toddler, he would not give up a piece of paper that he had placed into his mouth. That this is a common gesture of infants it is very true, but note how the hagiographers mold the story, remarking that the words "Ave Maria" were on the paper, making the whole story into a premonition of his Marian devotion and future greatness.[65] What may be dismissed as an insignificant detail from childhood becomes reinforced with the story of his abduction by his brothers. It appears that Thomas acquiesced to the capture with equanimity, that is, until his brother attempted to remove his Dominican habit. It appears that he fought so strongly (the implication is physical scuffling) that in the end the brothers—who had the advantage of both numbers and weapons— were forced to accept his decision to retain his religious garb. He stubbornly refused to doff his habit during the entire period of his captivity. As noted by the biographers, of course Thomas was wholeheartedly dedicated to his religious profession, but it was his reaction to the *thing*, the habit itself, that shook the complacent youth into action.[66] This reveals a desire not for the habit and the abstract consecration represented by it, but for the regularity that the habit signifies, a comfortable material assurance of his Dominican vocation that is genuinely and inalienably his, even in the midst of unfriendly surroundings. This type of obsessive behavior can often be found in those with ASD, who can yearn for the systematic consistency of well-established practices. The rest of Thomas's life betrays this constant yearning for regularity.

The religious life offered exceptional structure and predictability, with the daily round of scheduled activities that varied only rarely. While some have tried to associate Thomas's vocation with poverty, I think the much more likely explanation is that the freedom he found in obedience and regularity drew him to the friars. In the convent, Thomas found quiet and solitude. The professor was often anguished at being called from the vale of contemplation to the life of action. In his prayer before incepting as Master, he begs for strength because he has to go among the "children of men," where truth has decayed.[67]

Difficulty at negotiating social situations is also common among those on the ASD spectrum. While describing his time at Montecassino, his biographers note that his desire for learning and contemplation meant that he had little time for the other oblate boys. He did not play with them or engage in "frivolous" conversation. He was "silent and serious." Of course, Tocco assures us that this precocity was due to his preternatural maturity and singular focus on study.[68] This is in keeping with the medieval mindset that did not romanticize childhood, but saw it as a necessary period of formation on the way to adulthood. Thomas may indeed have preferred study to the normal concourse of his age, but the attitude also suggests a standoffish boy, one who was more comfortable inside his own head than among the bustle of others. However, the religious life is no escape from the demands of society; indeed, it is the "common life" raised to a means of spiritual perfection. Thomas certainly had to negotiate the difficulties that came with living in common, which in the early generations of the order included the necessity for novices and students to sleep in common dormitories, with all of the attendant inconveniences. While it is true that the sources describe Thomas as affable and charitable, he avoided needless chatter and human interaction, even during periods intended for relaxation. He was remembered as highly reserved at recreation, and even when pressed by his brethren to come to the garden or cloister, he would demur and "retire to his cell alone with his thoughts."[69] But the religious life can also be appealing for those uncomfortable in unstructured social situations, in that it offers a crystal-clear chain of command, and defined lines of primacy and subordination. The Master-student relationship was very clear to Thomas, and he thrived on both sides of it. He was always promptly obedient to superiors, without ever desiring any of the difficult offices of command in the order. He never once sought election to the job of conventual prior, or to any position of responsibility. Such clarity of social position was reassuring. Indeed, Thomas would rather be mistaken for a simple brother than assume any position of command, as is demonstrated in the story of the friar who suborned him for market duty in Bologna, not recognizing him.[70] On no fewer than two occasions (possibly more) Thomas refused offers of promotion, once to be the powerful abbot of Montecassino,[71] and later to the position of Archbishop of Naples.[72] The hagiographers invariably note this as characteristic of humility, and it certainly was. Yet, given Thomas's disposition, he would have run from such positions of public responsibility. The amount of interpersonal contact demanded by such offices was most likely terrifying to the retiring friar. Once again, he recognized his own limitations and probably gladly refused promotion. Indeed, one of the only times in his life that Thomas became really irritated is when Reginald suggested in a joking way that the pope was about to make him cardinal at the Council of Lyons.[73] All Thomas's friendships were mediated through hierarchy, whether with his Master Albert, his various devoted students, or his secretary-*socius* Reginald. This hierarchy provided the relief of a recognizable structure, a grid upon which more easily to map human relationships.

Outside of these clearly outlined social interactions, it seems that Thomas aggressively avoided other unstructured situations. He almost never interacted with the laity voluntarily. There is no record of him ever hearing confessions or giving any sort of spiritual direction. While it is true that Thomas sang public Masses, the fixed structure and general *ad orientem* position allowed him to focus on God and not the congregation. He also occasionally preached, with power and simplicity, but one should remember that in this most direct interaction with the assembly, witnesses recalled that Thomas preached with his eyes closed.[74] The avoidance of eye contact is also a symptom of social awkwardness that often manifests itself along the autism spectrum. Thomas's lack of linguistic skill also prevented any interaction with many people who were not themselves academics or southern Italians. This general evasion of the laity was almost obsessive in the case of his avoidance of women. Ever since the unfortunate incident in his youth, he compulsively avoided women. Even in the one instance where a woman was cured of a hemorrhage during Thomas's life, it is significant that she could only touch the back of his habit as he was returning from Mass. The Master was probably hastening to avoid contact with her, in order to hurry back to the sacristy.[75] Even the warm friendships of other Dominican holy men for religious sisters (e.g., in the lives of Dominic, Jordan of Saxony, and Peter of Verona) are completely absent in Thomas's life. Interaction with the opposite sex can be one of the most awkward of all social situations, one Thomas avoided assiduously. The only women of significance in his life were his few family members (again a recognizable and easily handled social situation). When coupled with the demands of the religious life in terms of chastity, this avoidance became elevated in the hagiography into an emphasis on Thomas's supernatural virtue of virginity.

Yet for all this, Thomas chose his vocation wisely, for his order was intended from the very beginning to facilitate study. Showing his exceptional promise, the young man was probably privileged from the very beginning with private spaces to study and to work. Eventually, when he achieved the office of Master, the order accorded to him his own quarters, there to write and study in absolute silence. While the Dominicans were rooted in the common life, it appears that Thomas took advantage of the privileges of exemption, which entailed the dispensation from almost all choral duties, though he did perhaps attend Compline often out of Dominican devotion (and the fact that it was one of the shortest of the hours). He may have attended Matins; however, this was also a good hour for those who pursued contemplation. Not only was there little interaction between the friars then (for they had just come from—and were returning to—bed), but Thomas made his privacy secure by often arriving before the bell and remaining in prayer after.[76] It appears that his chief form of prayer was the Mass and private contemplation, rather than the traditional cycle of the Office. At the height of his career Thomas often ate alone as well, having meals brought to him by his faithful secretary Reginald. Dispensed from most of the communal duties, Thomas spent much of his time in private prayer or professional concerns. While it is common for intellectuals to crave solitude, it is also a common characteristic of those who lack the easy inter-personal skills of the more extroverted.

This love for seclusion is used by Thomas's biographers in a number of ways. In the first place, they interpret it as a love for contemplation. William Tocco and Bernard Gui view this as a natural inclination for prayer, "able to raise his mind to God, as if the body's burden did not exist for him."[77] Indeed, Thomas cultivated this natural tendency, using innate aptitudes both for the pursuit of holiness in prayer and for intense periods of mental abstraction. Sometimes his biographers saw Thomas's mental efforts as prayers themselves, and Gui and Tocco cast much of his intellectual life in terms of a constant prayer to God. While it is certainly true that Thomas, like many Christian intellectuals, turned to prayer on difficult points, the hagiographers seem to blur the distinction between sustained intellectual effort and the virtue of infused contemplation. On several occasions they only just stop short of claiming a type of divine inspiration for their subject. Once, for example, Reginald extracted a confession from Thomas that he had received a vision directly from Peter and Paul to help him construe a difficult passage in the Prophet Isaiah.[78] Tocco even suggests regular visits from St. Paul, who aided the Master when he was commenting on the saint's Epistles.[79] Such narrative strategies were not unusual; indeed, his biographers are much more restrained than those of Francis of Assisi, who were rapidly turning the little poor man into a second Christ. The philosopher Étienne Gilson made a more practical allusion about Thomas's inner world as it related to his work. "His *Summa Theologiae*, with its abstract clarity, its impersonal transparency, crystallized before our very eyes and for all eternity, his interior life."[80] In any case, Thomas's intellectual and spiritual life was exceptionally rich and provided ample opportunity for his biographers to present him as a paragon of mental prayer.

This very attribute became the single most common theme that runs through the biographies: Thomas's exceptional abstraction. All through the depositions and the hagiographies we see people feeling the need to offer an explanation for Thomas's sometimes shocking behavior in terms of his habitual interiority. Of course, the justifications that the biographers offered for his demeanor matched with his intellectual tasks and his devotion to prayer, yet there is something deeper to recognize. Thomas some-times simply did not register the outside world. In the first place, he was noted for his general lack of interest either about his sur-roundings or material necessities; for instance, he was remarkable for the carelessness that he exhibited in terms of things to eat and to wear. A spirit of detachment indeed, and proper to a religious man, but again it seemed to come quite naturally to a man raised in the medieval lap of luxury. This abstraction becomes clearer when we compare it with another of his characteristics. Thomas seems to have been exceptionally sensitive in terms of sensory stimulation, a common characteristic associated with ASD. He was clearly frightened of lightning and used to cross himself dur-ing thunderstorms while uttering the pious prayer "God came for us in the flesh, He died for us and rose again." This was a kind of repetitive calming mechanism used when confronted by a situa-tion outside of his control. While a fear of thunderstorms is not unusual in itself (particularly for men who had to walk on foot from place to place), this might have been a manifestation of a deeper sensitivity. All of the sources make mention that his consti-tution made him "extraordinarily sensitive," particularly to pain.[81] Thomas's extreme sensitivity, coupled with his desire for privacy and introspection, seem to indicate a man who was less than com-fortable in uncontrolled situations. He was also able to overcome such sensitivity by retreating into his abstracted interiority. Several stories mention that he was able to overcome pain by a special mental effort that effectively rendered him insensate. One time his leg needed cauterization with a hot iron. Thomas entered a state of abstraction so extreme that when the physician applied the heat, his leg did not move at all. A similar thing happened while commenting on Boethius. While he was dictating, a candle burned down to his fingers and he kept right on going. It appears that Thomas had strict control over his body. In addition, he faced what was certainly a trial for such a sensitive person: the quarterly bloodletting. According to the canons of medieval medicine, the bodily humors needed rebalancing by removing excesses, particu-larly of blood. The Dominican constitutions prescribed commu-nal bloodletting four times a year, a procedure Thomas certainly looked upon with trepidation. When the time would come around in Paris, he would enter a state of abstraction so that he would not be able to feel the pain. He clearly was able to overcome his natural tendencies toward excessive sensitivity, but their very existence demonstrates an insight into his character.

This spilled over into his public life. While no man of such reputation could remain completely isolated, Thomas was chary of his time and contacts. Witnesses remembered him as a man of courtesy and kindness, characteristics certainly instilled from his aristocratic youth. However, these descriptions struggle against the actual stories recounted about his external relations. Witnesses repeatedly describe him as absent-minded (or "abstracted") to an extraordinary degree. Gui describes it this way:

> To those who lived with him it was wonderful to see him—a man using his senses on sensible objects like anyone else—grow suddenly abstracted and rapt out of himself and human company to the divine world, as though his mind was no longer where his body happened to be.[82]

On many occasions, due to Thomas's increasing fame, visitors would appear at the convent and ask to speak to the renowned Master. The irritation of the friar comes through clearly, even in the hagiography. He would expeditiously handle the visit, give some brief edifying story, and then just get up and leave. "It did not matter who had been speaking to him....(He would) wander off absorbed in meditation."[83] Thomas would short-circuit social visits with pious platitudes, so that he could return to his work. This was the case even with visitors of stature. One day the archbishop of Capua, Marino d'Eboli, and the Cardinal Legate of Sicily came to visit Thomas. Marino had known Thomas since his days in Orvieto in the early 1260s. Out of obedience, Thomas descended from his cell to the parlor to meet the eminent guests. He did not even acknowledge the presence of the two prelates, something that offended the cardinal. Marino knew Thomas and understood his habits. The archbishop told the legate that this was nothing to wonder at and that he was frequently like this, being disinclined to speak to many persons. Marino patiently waited a few minutes, and then sharply tugged on Thomas's cloak. At once Thomas came to his senses and apologized for his behavior after bowing to the two men. His reply is telling: "I have just discovered a beautiful idea about a problem which has long occupied me!"[84] The cardinal was mollified, if not really edified, while Marino recalled the incident with mirth. Perhaps the most famous story of Thomas's absent-mindedness was the story of his dinner with Louis IX. While scholars have argued against the strict historicity of this event, it nonetheless communicates significant truths about the Master's character.[85] In the midst of the sparkling conversation at the king's table, Thomas sat immobile (as indeed he had done many times in his own refectory). At length he brought his fist down on the table and exclaimed, "That's the way to finish the heresy of the Manichees!"[86] The courteous Louis excused the friar, who had apparently advised him often in the past.[87] He called for a scribe so that Thomas would not lose his train of thought. One of the key symptoms of many forms of ASD is the failure to understand and process social cues. It seems that Thomas's awkwardness was well known to many and, while certainly a cross for him, is also a testament to the great charity extended to him by his brethren and his friends, including Louis and Marino, who—understanding the friar's dispositions—were willing to make many sacrifices in order to accommodate the theologian.

Related to this abstraction was an almost laser-like focus that could exclude much of the outside world in favor of deep and sustained reflection on intellectual problems, executed with an almost mathematical precision. He was most content by himself and spent long hours in the seclusion of his own cell, plumbing the depths of philosophy and theology. He perfectly fulfilled the injunction of Master Johannes Teutonicus, who in his 1246 encyclical called the cell a Dominican's "path to heaven."[88] As his stature grew, the order began to accord him the privilege of secretaries. Such was his ability to focus that he was able to dictate to three or even four secretaries at a time. One secretary, Evan of Tréguier, stated that Thomas even continued to dictate while resting or napping.[89] Reginald was by Thomas's side for nearly fifteen years. Thomas, it must be said, constantly importuned the patient friar, often rousting him out of bed at inconvenient hours to take dictation concerning a new idea.[90] It seems that Reginald also accompanied Thomas on his night vigils, so as to be there to be of service to him should he need it.[91] While it is certainly the nature of religious life to submit and serve, one does sometimes leave with the impression that Thomas occasionally treated people as means. This is not to suggest any type of abuse of position; rather it simply dovetails with Thomas's character, which was not itself conducive to social interaction of a normative sort. Indeed, perhaps the best evidence of Thomas's particular mental burdens come from Reginald himself. A remarkable encomium, present in both Tocco and Gui, records the exceptional devotion that the *socius* had for the Master. The passage is worth quoting in full, particularly in light of our present contentions:

> Let us remember too that he [Reginald] had to be as a nurse to his master, supplying his needs as one supplies the needs of a child, because of that frequent, nay almost continuous, absence of mind and absorption in heavenly things which rendered Thomas unable to look after his own body and needing to be protected from accidents and have his food put on his plate before him, so that he should only take what he required and avoid eating absentmindedly what might have done him harm.[92]

This is a singular paean of praise to the patient and devoted servant. One should remember that Reginald was no illiterate *conversus* or lay brother; rather, he was a fully professed priest-friar and an accomplished Master in his own right. Reginald can certainly be called one of the "hidden saints" of the church, one of that numberless multitude who accomplishes his work in humility and solitude, without question or complaint. We must admit that in many ways, Reginald made it possible for us to have Thomas at all, for it appears that the Master was neglectful of his bodily needs to the point of danger to his health (to wit, his encounter with the low-hanging branch near Fossanova).

When one marshals the available evidence, I contend that Thomas experienced some condition that would later end up on the ASD spectrum. His social awkwardness, ability to focus intensely, lack of interest in material or bodily concerns, his sensory sensitivity, and his love for discipline, order, and hierarchy are all telling symptoms of such a possible diagnosis. There are certainly claims to be made for the contrary that might undermine such a suggestion. One characteristic that would seriously compromise such a hypothesis would be evidence of humor. Almost no references to humor or joking can be found in either the stories about or the works by the Master. Some have pointed to one quodlibetal question that, in itself, is quite funny. Thomas addresses the burning issue of "what is stronger, wine, women, the king, or truth." Some have pointed out that a sense of humor could have induced Thomas to take on the question, but in his answer he gives a strictly Scholastic hierarchy devoid of any form of joking. He considers that each is powerful in its own way, but that truth is the most sublime and powerful because it rules speculative matters.[93] A real knee-slapper that; one could almost say that Thomas missed the joke entirely. It may also be objected that he was close to his family and in particular had warm relations with his female relatives. I would answer that Thomas was certainly comfortable around them, for they knew him, and they treated him far more kindly than his male relatives did, as this book has demonstrated. Further, there was no possibility of an unstructured mixing of the sexes that would produce social discomfort. Indeed, one witness reported that Thomas expressed no grief or sorrow when hearing of the death of any of his family members, but simply offered Masses and prayers for their souls.[94] Another, stronger objection was that Thomas did have genuine and warm friendships. This is absolutely true, and Thomas himself wrote strongly about the significance of such relations. Indeed, he lists companionship of that sort as one of the key remedies for sorrow (along with weeping, bathing, and sleeping).[95] Indeed, his theological model of the life of grace is friendship with God.[96] Thomas was cordial with Pope Urban IV and with Archbishop Marino d'Eboli. He had particular affection for Reginald and for many of his students, who remembered their Master warmly, in particular Annibaldo di Annibaldi, who became Master in Paris after Thomas and later became a cardinal. Once again, however, these were "hierarchical" friendships with clearly defined roles. As Thomas was faithful to Aristotle's thoughts on friendship, many of his own relations lack a quality that the Philosopher found essential: equality. As one scholar remarks, "Thomas seems to have been essentially self-sufficient."[97] Witnesses describe how Thomas was a special lover of solitude.[98] It must be said that as much as Thomas valued friends, it is difficult to say that he needed them. Thomas was much more comfortable in intellectual dialogue with his historical "friends"—Aristotle, Maimonides, Averroes, and Avicenna—whom he treated with the utmost courtesy and amiability, making every effort to understand and appropriate their thought.

What I consider the most cogent objection to the picture I am presenting is the presence of what seems to be a rich emotional life in Thomas. Thomas seems to have a very affective spirituality. This was most significantly on display in his celebration of the Mass and his devotion to the Eucharist. He would often be seen with tears in his eyes as he said Mass, and on occasion could even get lost in contemplation in the midst of the sacrifice (which again required outside intervention to bring him back to his senses).[99] To read the office of Corpus Christi is to see the depths of emotional attachment that lie beneath his intellectual presentation of the eucharistic mystery. Many of these reports come from the end of his life, for instance the Lenten Compline versicle that made him emotional. Thomas was certainly a figure open before the mystery of God and his contemplation often reduced him to tears. One should remember that we are also looking at Thomas through the hagiographer's lens, and the "gift of tears" was becoming a sine qua non of sainthood in the early fourteenth century.[100] Even given that fact, Thomas's affectivity toward the sacrament of the altar remains clear. This affectivity was unidirectional; that is, St. Thomas directed his emotional life completely to God. It was not directed toward other human persons. Thomas avoided most activities that would have brought out or cultivated emotional relationships with others and reserved his affective life directly for contemplation. In this sense, we can understand Thomas's admitted ability to "bring the fruits of contemplation to others." While certainly not an emotional preacher, the Master was able to connect with his audiences, be they academic or lay. He could bring his audience to tears, not through rhetorical fireworks, but rather through a simple communication of the truths that he had so long contemplated. He preached simply and directly, and with full confidence that it was not his words that worked upon hearts, but rather the very truth of the faith that he studied. In this sense Thomas was more of an intermediary than a participant in the emotional reaction. He continued to preach with his eyes closed and raised to heaven, and, having completed his task, retired once more to his "secret throne of contemplation."[101]

In the past such explorations would have seemed off-putting to faithful Catholics, having been accustomed to troped stories of sanctity from birth in the lives of their holy men and women. In the twentieth century, however, a renewed emphasis has appeared in the context of the genuine humanity of the saints. I am not sure if this should be characterized as a "hagiography from below" that would parallel attempts in Christology to emphasize the human nature of Jesus. In fact, like the latter efforts, they do sometimes go too far along the path of a pure naturalism. Thomas faced threats in his intellectual life from two sides. There were the aggressive naturalists, the radical Aristotelians, who wanted to prioritize the insights of pure reason, while he also contended with theological movements that prioritized grace to such an extent that they tended to dissolve our very real humanity. He fought them both. Against the "traditionalists" he argued that we were really genuine, autonomous substances, capable of acting according to our nature as rational animals without any appeal to divine intervention. These natures existed contingently, with genius, mediocrity, and defects all located within a discrete material existence. Against the radicals he insisted on the absolute necessity of grace in order to live the supernatural life intended for us by God. That grace respects who we are as contingent, human individuals. It makes possible our true friendship with God, who gives it to us with perfect foreknowledge and omnipotence, yet without injuring the freedom of our human choice in the least. For Thomas, famously, grace does not destroy nature; rather, it perfects our nature, endowing our natural abilities with the power to operate in concert with it in the supernatural order. Thomas lays this out as preparatory to his whole theological project in question 1 of the *Summa*.[102] For him it is an absolutely irreducible principle that safeguards our human nature while, at the same time, recognizing the absolute sovereignty of God. We should not be surprised that saints have had not only to struggle against temptations to sin, but even to wrestle against their own imperfect and contingent existences in the conditions of materiality. Thomas was a man who knew his weaknesses. Sometimes he struggled mightily against them, yet most of the time he avoided situations that would expose those weaknesses to challenge, which in the end is the act of a wise man. He focused on his strengths and, in opening his heart to grace, allowed God to perfect the work he had begun in placing Thomas in discrete historical, psychological, material, and geographical conditions. That Thomas may have had many of the difficult symptoms of ASD should not make one think less of him, but rather to marvel—even more than is usual—at the astonishing work he was able to accomplish. Even more so, to be amazed that, even given these conditions, he was not content to be a "floating Platonic mind," but rather to find a way to negotiate the narrow path to a life of holiness that all around him recognized and that was, at length, confirmed by the universal church.

STIRRINGS OF DEVOTION— MARSHALLING OF OPPOSITION

All saints have an afterlife, but Thomas was different. He had two. On one hand, there was a nascent, local, organic cult that slowly took root around the site of his death in Fossanova, one that we have detailed above. On the other was the continuing career of the theological and philosophical system that came to bear the name *Thomism*. While there are a few examples of overlap between the two—such as the letter from the Arts faculty discussed already—in reality they did not interact very much in the fifty years following his death. It is only much later that the "saint" and the "thinker" came to be associated together. Thomas's cult struck deep roots locally but did not expand beyond that. He was a classic type of a local civic saint in the pattern that went back to the early days of Christianity.

I think it is not too far of a stretch to say that people did not "get" Thomas. While he had warm relations with several of his students, it seems that no one followed his theology in particular after his departure from Paris. His successors in the "foreign" chair at Paris, Romano Orsini of Rome and Annibaldo di Annibaldi, did not evince any particular affinity for Thomistic principles. Reginald of Piperno, who was a theologian himself, did not show any proclivity for founding any sort of Thomist school, and contented himself merely with collecting and editing his Master's writings.[103] Indeed the only partisan of Thomas's doctrines in the early 1270s was Giles of Rome, an Augustinian.[104] It appears that Thomas made no attempt to cultivate a body of followers that would carry on his message. This was unusual since it was quite common in academic settings for famous teachers to attract youthful disciples, particularly when confronted with "novel" doctrines. One need only consider the school of "Albertans" who were devoted to the teaching of Albert in Germany (Thomas himself was tangentially a member of such a group).[105] This was partially a function of Thomas's own personality, which would have made such a coterie undesirable. There were other, external reasons for this as well. Thomas's doctrine was dense, profound, and (as the letter from the Artists attests) somewhat diffused at this time. It would take years of patient unpacking for it to be understood and received. Further, Thomas was difficult to pigeonhole. He opposed the Augustinians and the radical Aristotelians simultaneously, and found no permanent membership in any existing theological or philosophical school. It is likely that such lack of identification caused bad feelings on both sides, though it seems more pronounced on the Franciscan-Augustinian axis of opposition to Thomas's doctrines. The Master's teachings made enemies (even if his humble and quiet temperament prevented these from becoming personal). He and his order were not beloved of the university either, and the consortium of Theologians in particular bore antipathy to those whom they considered to be bad academic citizens. Of course, this was bound up with broader antimendicant sentiment beyond the walls of the university. The condemnations of 1270, while not touching Thomas's work, had been chilling at the university. In many eyes, Thomas was implicated in the doctrines of the radicals, and, as such, many were probably dissuaded from following his teaching too closely. Even in his own order there was a strong faction that was not particularly friendly to innovation. On one hand, many Masters were still faithful to the theological consensus of the 1230s to 1250s, which coalesced under the self-proclaimed "Augustinianism" of Pecham around 1270.[106] The innovations of Albert and Thomas found few partisans until the 1280s. On the other hand, there was still a definite tendency to emphasize pastoral over speculative theology. The order had focused on the active ministry since its foundation by Dominic. The intellectual efforts of the friars had been fixated on those tasks since then. Thomas's educational reimagination of Dominican studies was revolutionary, but it took a long time to take root in the order.

It is possible that, given all of these issues, Thomism may have remained a theological cul-de-sac, a brief detour in the vast stream of medieval theology. In fact, the situation worsened considerably after Thomas's death. Pecham and his confederates at Paris were riding a rising tide of triumph. They had obtained an order that effectively prevented the Arts faculty from dabbling in theology in 1272. Without any effective defenders of Thomas or Albert on the theological faculty, the consensus Augustinianism was in full control. A movement was building that would focus on a condemnation of several theses that would implicate the Master's doctrine. I will not detail the many significant theoretical issues inherent in each, but merely recount the points of conflict. In the first place, Thomas had defended the pure potency (lack of any reality) in prime matter. Prime matter was the diametric opposite of pure actuality, which is God; therefore it must lack any proper being, according to Thomas. Thomas's opponents considered that this seemed to violate the principle of divine omnipotence, in stating that God cannot make matter without form. Here is a fundamental difference between the Thomist and Franciscan schools. The Minorites gave priority to divine power rather than rationality, a position that was to have baleful effects in the history of philosophy. Thomas simply said that matter without form is a contradiction; it is impossible, and God's power cannot extend to impossibilities.[107] At the heart of the matter was the old debate on the superiority of the intellect or the will in God (and *mutatis mutandis*, in us). The second issue is related. The Franciscans were convinced that matter could not be the principle that makes us individual, for then how could we differentiate angels? To overcome this, they came up with the odd idea of "spiritual matter." Thomas dispensed with this speculation and taught that angels are individuals not because they are made so by "matter," but because each one was its own species, possessing distinct perfections from those above and below them. Once again this seemed to the Franciscans to compromise divine omnipotence by stating that God could not make two angels that shared the same species. Therefore they defended hylomorphism (the idea of a distinction between form and matter in all created things), even in angels. Perhaps most offensive to the theological consensus of the time was Thomas's doctrine of the unity of our substantial form. Among Thomas's contemporaries, most subscribed to the doctrine of a succession of forms in the developing human. This meant that we began with a vegetative form, which was succeeded by a sensitive form when we developed our sensory capabilities, and finally an intellectual form when we had achieved the developmental capability of the organs that ministered to reason. Further, the idea that the immaterial intellectual soul could control the vegetative and sensitive functions of the body seemed to be foreign to what was possible. Thomas affirmed the substantial unity of humanity in order to defend his Aristotelian thesis that it is not simply the intellect that knows, but *we* who know, in our totality.[108] He rejected the Platonic-Augustinian model of the soul, which considered the body and subintellectual processes to be less than fully human. For Plato the soul equaled the human. Thomas, however, declared the human was the wholeness of soul and body together. For Thomas, the nature of angels was spiritual, the nature of animals was material, but for humans it was *both together*. In a certain sense, after we die we are only imperfectly human, only to fully realize our humanity again after the resurrection. The long shadow of Plato had extended for over a millennium in the history of Christian thought. It was a view that sat uneasily with the essential incarnationalism of Christianity. The significance of the body in Christianity meant that faithful thinkers could not wholly dispense with it, but neither were they wholly comfortable with it. Thomas deserves the credit as the first thinker who underscored the idea that, for an integrated human nature, the body was irreducibly essential. In spite of this, out of all his ideas, this doctrine's novelty caused the greatest backlash. Many considered that this created a confusion in humanity that threatened the immortality of the soul by tying it too closely to materiality. With its venerable, if remote, pedigree from Plato and Augustine, they defended the plurality of forms with all their might.

The Franciscans led the charge against this nascent Thomism. The interorder rivalry was intense, and resentments ran far deeper than irenic statements from officials or later histories would admit. John Pecham was the key to the opposition, following the line established by Bonaventure, both refining and deepening the Franciscan position against Thomas. It is likely that the two Minorites were behind the 1270 condemnation as well.[109] Pecham had opposed Thomas in person, and it appears that Thomas treated him in a very friendly manner during the former's inception in 1270, even though he was the subject of personal attack.[110] Following Thomas's departure, in 1272 the university issued a command for the Artists not to engage in theology. The Franciscans began to interpret orthodoxy very narrowly, hewing closely to the mysticism of Bonaventure, and the Augustinianism of Pecham, all underscored by their commitment to the superiority of the will to the intellect. Yet there was a further issue. The reason that Pecham was so interested in what the Aristotelians in the faculty of the Arts were doing is that he—along with many of his contemporaries—did not have a clear vision of the distinction between philosophy and theology. For the Franciscans, philosophy was relatively unimportant, and its few uses could be elided by theology. Indeed, both Thomas and the Minorites could claim that philosophy was the "handmaid of theology," but in reality they meant different things. For Thomas philosophy was autonomous within its own sphere, a real science. While Thomas was at heart a theologian, he had no problem working in the philosophical world, a distinct study that concerned itself with rationally demonstrable data. Often he took the fruits of this study into his theology but never clouded the boundaries of either. For Thomas philosophy was independent from and indispensable for the higher science of theology. That he was able to maintain this distinction is a testament to his conviction that faith and reason could never contradict or teach contradictory truths, for they flowed from the same source, the God who cannot deceive, and had the same end, that Truth that is essentially One. For the Franciscans, philosophy was bound up with human pride and original sin, leading even powerful minds astray. Study was supposed to lead one to love and devotion. When it did not do so it should be shunned or, at the very least, rejected as not useful. This attitude led to serious reservations about the office of "philosopher" and of the school of Arts. It also cast suspicion on Thomas's teaching of a clear distinction between the two sciences and his assurance that philosophy was, and ought to be, an independent and self-sufficient science. Once again Thomas was defending the integrity of the human person, which can know on its own because of its very nature. While Thomas was keenly aware of the darkening power of sin, he was optimistic that, under the reign of grace, real progress in philosophy and theology could be made. This optimism about human nature brought him into conflict with more pessimistic models of humanity, an opinion that would stand him in poor stead with the later Protestant Reformers.

Thomas's death, Albert's waning powers (he would die in 1280), and the ascendancy of Franciscans at the curia all conspired against the progress of Thomistic views. The pope made Bonaventure a cardinal in 1273. Before his departure he gave a series of lectures, heavy with apocalyptic overtones, that contained his most bitter polemic to date against Aristotle.[111] Pecham had carried his anti-Thomist campaign to Oxford and left as his successor at Paris William de la Mare, who continued the assault on both Aristotle and Thomas. This Franciscan, between 1274 and 1276, published a *Correctorium Fratris Thomae*, a commentary intended to defuse Thomas's "novel" interpretations. Meanwhile the radical Artists seemed to dig in their heels against the imprecations of the theologians. The stage was set for a dramatic repudiation of Aristotelian principles that would inevitably implicate Thomas. A coalition of sorts had emerged that resulted in action in 1277. Another of Thomas's old adversaries, Henry of Ghent, had lined up the Secular Masters against the new teaching, and in this he was joined by his erstwhile foes, William de la Mare and Pecham (at that time resident at the Roman curia). To this they added the long and simmering animosity of Stephen Tempier, the bishop of Paris, against the Artists. In the past the three had been at each other's throats, but a presumed common enemy made strange bedfellows. I propose that these disparate interest groups were thrown together by the unwelcome and unexpected election of Pierre of Tarentaise, a Dominican and former Parisian Master, as Pope Innocent V in 1276. While he only reigned five months, it was enough to unite the anti-Aristotelian coterie to combine their forces. It is likely that Pecham influenced the new pope, John XXI (r. 1276–77), a Portuguese and former university Master of logic, to investigate matters in Paris. In the meanwhile, a sick and aged Albert made the difficult journey to Paris to try to defend his student's doctrines. Unfortunately he failed in his mission, for what appears to be progressive dementia hampered his abilities significantly.[112] Tempier likely ignored him and made ready to act. He appointed a handpicked commission of sixteen theologians to produce a list of errors. They presented Tempier with a catalog of 219 propositions drawn from all areas of philosophy and theology. Tempier—going beyond his papal remit—immediately condemned all of them. This was no surgical strike as in 1270; rather, it was a carpet bombing, and it had a chilling effect on the evolution of thought at the university. While it is clear that the radical Artists were the real focus, some of the condemned doctrines touched upon Thomas's thought. Even if he was not the direct object, his doctrine was certainly singed in the attack. It is too little noted, but Tempier promulgated the condemnations of 1277 three years *to the day* of Thomas's death on March 7.

The ill fortune of Thomas's doctrine was not yet over. By the end of March his sole defender at Paris, the Augustinian Giles of Rome, found himself denied the license to teach. Many of the young Master's doctrines were condemned, though it appears that the unfortunate scholar was merely a proxy for attacking Thomas.[113] One should not think that Tempier was focused solely on Thomas's doctrines; this was but another stage in the long simmering battle between the bishop and the university. Tempier was ready to reassert control over the Theology faculty as well as the Arts. He opportunistically allied with former foes to kill two birds with one stone: the theological "novelties" of Thomas and the excessive independence of the faculties. After driving Giles from the city, Tempier apparently wanted to start a process against Thomas directly, but cooler heads persuaded him to refer the matter to Rome. While earlier scholars suggested this was due to the influence of Albert, it is far more likely that the presence of the Dominican Master General John of Vercelli (r. 1264–83) was behind it. John was keenly aware of the precarious position in which the reputation of the order would find itself should one of its foremost theologians be censured. As a result, he worked to remove the cause against Thomas from the fractious atmosphere of Paris. The matter did not rest there, however, and the situation rapidly worsened. On March 18, 1277, the *Dominican* archbishop of Canterbury, Robert Kilwardby, issued a condemnation directed at the heart of the Thomistic doctrine of the unity of substantial form in humans.[114] As prior of the Dominicans in England and as archbishop, he had maintained a staunchly Augustinian line, allied with Pecham who himself had returned to teach at Oxford. When the Franciscan-friendly Pope Nicholas III (r. 1277–80) appointed Robert a cardinal in 1278, his successor as archbishop was none other than the virulent anti-Thomist John Pecham, who would reign over the English church from 1279 until 1292. Pecham would maintain the condemnations of Kilwardby and expand them, continuing to attack Thomism for the remainder of his life.

This opposition had a curious effect. When the 1277 condemnations were issued, two theologians arose to defend Thomas. Giles of Lessines—a French Dominican who had studied under the Master—wrote a defense of the unity of form. In all probability, this Giles was the first one to develop Thomism, rather than merely citing it.[115] He wrote a spirited refutation of Kilwardby in an aggressively polemical manner. At the same time Peter of Conflans, the Dominican archbishop of Corinth, wrote a blistering letter to Kilwardby to criticize the condemnation. The English situation was of immediate concern to the order, and in 1278 it sent two visitators to the province to try to understand the situation. Ironically it was in England, in response to these challenges, that the first substantive defenses of Thomism appeared. No fewer than four refutations of William de la Mare's *Correctorium* appeared from Oxford Dominicans (indeed, by this time the Dominicans had created the nickname *"Corruptorium" fratris Thome*, "the Corruptor of Brother Thomas," for de la Mare's work). It is thought that Kilwardby's reaction was due to the presence of a nascent Thomistic school at Oxford, a position made more likely by the quick succession of defenses of Friar Thomas. Of particular note is the case of Richard Knapwell. In the 1280s he was a Master at Oxford and found himself intellectually converted from pluralism to the Thomistic doctrine. For three years he debated dauntlessly in favor of the unicity of form, drawing the especial ire of Archbishop Pecham. Summoned before the archbishop's court, Knapwell claimed immunity based on his position as a Master and as a mendicant. Pecham was unimpressed and excommunicated the young scholar. Richard appealed to Rome, but unfortunately found himself seeking the aid of the first Franciscan pope, Nicholas IV (r. 1288–92). The new pope imposed perpetual silence on Richard, exiling him to Bologna, where shortly afterward he tragically perished. Many Dominicans have considered him a sort of martyr for the Thomistic cause.[116] Richard's prior, William of Hothum, had also locked horns with Pecham, but in a sign of support from the órder it invited William to assume a second regency at Paris in 1287 (something only accomplished before by Thomas and Pierre of Tarentaise). This likely indicated his Thomistic sympathies. In the meanwhile, French and Italian Dominicans were also awakening to Thomism, partly due to the threat to the order, but also drawn by the depth of wisdom contained therein. Friars away from England and Paris were unaffected by the condemnations, which retained a local character. The crisis served Thomism well. "Thomism took root and developed amidst controversy rather than from within a circle of supportive friends."[117] Indeed, the vast majority of early Thomists had not been students of the Master, but rather came to the controversy from without, eventually converting to the cause.

Master John of Vercelli was active in the effort to police the order and to defend the memory of Thomas. Some even suggest that the Master General had a comprehensive strategy to accomplish this.[118] I maintain that John was essentially reacting to events that were transpiring at a startling pace (e.g., the rapid transition from the euphoric reaction to the election of a Dominican pope to a series of pontiffs consistently friendly to the Franciscans). John probably did inspire Peter of Conflans to remonstrate with Robert Kilwardby. He could not intervene himself because, once consecrated a bishop, a friar or religious was neither a member of their order nor obliged to obedience to the rule. John also likely influenced the General Chapter of 1278 to send a visitation to Oxford to ensure a united Dominican front in that province in defense of Thomas. Finally, the Chapter of 1279 ordered that all members of the order treat Thomas and his work with respect, even if they did not agree with all his conclusions. After John's death, and in light of the situation at Oxford, it was necessary to circle the wagons. At the chapter of 1286 the order commanded that all Lectors and Masters teach Thomas's doctrine, at the very least as defensible. Anyone who violated the provision was to be stripped of his offices. This did not end debate about Thomas's doctrines in the order, but it did indicate a tipping point. From this point on, and accelerating by the turn of 1300, Thomism rapidly gained ground as the official Dominican teaching. There were dissenting voices, such as Durandus of Saint-Pourçain (d. 1332),[119] whose conflict with the order was only eliminated by his promotion to the office of bishop, and the odd German tradition that remained faithful to Albert while pursuing an increasingly mystical direction influenced by Pseudo-Dionysius and the Neoplatonic tradition. In spite of the solidifying of the Thomistic consensus, there is little evidence that increasing use of Thomas's works resulted in any corresponding increase growth of his cult. Indeed, his recognition as a saint of the universal church would have to come during an opportune moment, and ironically, mostly from outside of the Dominican order.

A SATISFACTORY CONCLUSION

While the consolidation of Thomistic thought continued apace, the little local cult was thriving around Thomas's grave at Fossanova. There was no official move on the part of the Dominican order to get Thomas recognized as a saint. There was little more than a few grumblings that the Cistercians possessed the body of their brother. Remigio de' Girolami, Thomas's former student and Dante's teacher, lamented the fact, "Oh, why does Fossanova keep the venerable bones? I beg that they be moved from there and be kept by the brethren [the Dominicans]."[120] Indeed, the Dominicans experienced a significant dry spell following the canonizations of their first two saints, Dominic in 1234 and Peter of Verona in 1252. In the years following Thomas's death, the order dispatched no fewer than five petitions to the Holy See requesting the opening of canonical processes for Dominican saints. None of them was for Thomas.[121] The friars proposed Ambrose Sansedoni in the 1290s, Margaret of Hungary in 1306, and Raymond of Peñafort on three separate occasions (1279, 1296–98, and 1317–18).[122] Further complicating the matter is that the Friars Preachers were not usually the ones who presented the cases for their holy men and women. Often they followed popular sentiment and institutional pressure. For instance, the early brethren in Bologna had discouraged the cult of St. Dominic, and the initial pressure to canonize

Peter of Verona came from Pope Innocent IV and the people of Milan, rather than from the Preachers. It was the devout lay official Bartholomew of Capua who had attempted to convince the Dominican Benedict XI (r. 1303–4) to initiate Thomas's cause, but the pope lived only a short time (another lost opportunity for the order in more ways than one).[123] It appears that the order was far too busy defending Thomas's orthodoxy to be bothered overmuch with the difficult and often expensive proposal of a universal cult.

All that began to change in the 1310s. The Dominican order had largely consolidated its educational and intellectual efforts in defense of Thomism. Of course this did not mean that it had wholly appropriated Thomas. It was only his early *Commentary on the Sentences* that would serve as the primary theological text until well into the fifteenth century. It does mean that the order had rooted out internal dissention and had acquired a grudging toleration from the Christian intellectual world that Thomas was, at the very least, permissible to teach. The Franciscan order maintained its active opposition to Thomas's doctrine. In 1282 it mandated that only extremely advanced students be permitted to read Thomas, and only if also studying William de la Mare's *Correctorium*. But in the meanwhile the Minorites had engaged in an enervating debate about the nature of poverty and the person of Saint Francis that had caused a veritable schism in the order. While the moderate Franciscans had succeeded in securing papal approval—largely due to the canny leadership of Bonaventure—there remained a threatening remnant later called Spirituals who claimed that Francis had demanded absolute poverty, and that such poverty was the primary means of achieving holiness.[124] The Dominicans had always been more constitutionally stable than the Franciscans, and the controversy barely touched them. However, the Spiritual Franciscans remained stubborn and presented an actively heretical challenge to the church during the first decades of the 1300s.

This matter came to a head with the election of Jacques Duèze as Pope John XXII (r. 1316–34). John XXII was a French pope during the long tenure at Avignon. While in reality the Avignon papacy was competent and relatively independent of the French monarchy, living amid the comforts of Provence and away from Rome opened it to much criticism. Much of this came from the

Spiritual Franciscans of southern France and Italy, who whipped themselves up into an increasingly apocalyptic frenzy about the end times and the need to embrace absolute poverty. For his part John XXII was devoted to St. Thomas. He may have been the first pope to have personally engaged the Master's theology. We possess volumes of Thomas's work prepared especially for this pope, complete with his handwritten notations.[125] I would speculate that the most significant teaching that attracted the pope was Thomas's balanced treatment of poverty, not as an end in itself, but rather as a means to holiness, whereby we mortify the flesh. Thomas places obedience as a higher vow and surer path to sanctity, for in it we offer something greater than the body—our own free will. Thomas examines this in detail in the *Summa* II-II, q. 186, a. 8. One can speculate that it was precisely this article that helped to propel Thomas and his cause to the forefront of John's mind, for it provided theoretical ammunition against the Spirituals. It is quite possible that John XXII canonized Thomas because of question 186. To compound John's interest, the conclave that elected him took place at the convent of the Preachers in Lyon and included three cardinals who were former members of the Order of Preachers. There the Dominican brethren offered unstinting hospitality to the cardinals for several months. It seems that John had the idea to reward the kindness of the Dominicans by offering to canonize one of their number. The Preachers probably again put forward Raymond of Peñafort's name. A compendious and well-developed dossier for his advancement already existed, for he had been proposed on three earlier occasions. Raymond's Aragonese pedigree did not align with John's Franco-Angevin proclivities (the pope himself had canonized the Franciscan archbishop Louis of Toulouse, a member of the French royal family). As a result, I agree with the scholars who contend that the initial push for Thomas's canonization came from the pope himself.[126]

As procurator for the new cause the Dominicans assigned William of Tocco, who traveled extensively around southern Italy to gather information for his biography. He presented his results to the pope in Avignon on September 13, 1318, after which John XXII opened a formal process. There are many fine studies of both canonizations of the period in general and Thomas's in particular. Briefly, an inquisition (the general name for any investigation under civil or canon law) was held at Naples in late 1319, the results of which were delivered to the pope by the indefatigable Tocco— who was at this time about seventy years old—around the turn of 1321. The pope, a canon lawyer by training, wanted to make sure that all legal forms were observed and ordered a follow-up inquisition in Fossanova. It appears that John XXII was interested in getting eyewitness testimony about the miracles that took place around the abbey and acquiring genuine evidence of cult, without which it would have been impossible to canonize Thomas. Though the aged Tocco was unable to present the final results to the curia, his work satisfied the pope. On July 16, 1323, John preached in favor of Thomas's doctrine on poverty, while praising in particular his virginity and the accomplishment of "three hundred miracles" (which is far more than are included in the official lists). A series of sermons by many other dignitaries from both within and out- side of the order followed (including a speech from King Robert of Naples),[127] all petitioning for the canonization. One of these was undertaken by John de Tixandrie, the Franciscan bishop of Lodève, who lavished extravagant praise on the Dominican.[128] De Tixandrie was a conventual voice, selected by the pope to offer the "correct" interpretation of Minorite life.[129] Still, the intermen- dicant antipathy was apparent, even if now more muted. In one manuscript from the Dominican convent of Vienna, an aggression miracle remains that describes a Franciscan Master who opposed the canonization up to the last moment. He said he would rather die than see Thomas a saint. He died.[130] Vauchez describes the Franciscan efforts to prevent recognition of St. Thomas, not sim- ply because they were opposed to his poverty doctrines, but also because his canonization would have further legitimized his teach- ings, which opposed their Masters Pecham, William de la Mare, and Bonaventure.[131] For his part, William of Tocco sedulously avoids any themes of Franciscan spirituality in his biography. Most nota- bly, however, Bernard Gui, in his postcanonization biography, cel- ebrates Thomas's victory over the Spiritual Franciscans. In this Gui precisely followed the pope's intentions in canonizing Thomas.[132] Indeed, Gui cannot resist one more gleeful turn of the dagger against the Minorites. In one of the last miracles of his collection, a Brother Luther of the Franciscan order reported a vision of Mary with Francis and Thomas appearing together. Mary crowns them both, while Francis gestures to Thomas, saying, "Believe this one, for his doctrine shall never fail."[133] Now that was an endorsement!

It was under John XXII that the long evolution of canonization proceedings reached its zenith, both legally and liturgically. Each would remain virtually unchanged for nearly seven hundred years. In both the canonizations of Louis of Toulouse and of Thomas Aquinas, the most elaborate liturgical preparations and celebrations unfolded. A formal canonization ceremony was an impressive event. On July 18, 1323, the curia, clergy, nobility, and commoners gathered in the cathedral of Notre Dame in Avignon. After the pope made his way into the church, there were petitions from the procurators and the faithful, begging the pope to enroll Thomas into the company of the saints. Then the whole congregation knelt for the invocation of the Holy Spirit in the hymn *Veni Creator Spiritus*, followed by the litany of saints. At the conclusion the pope uttered a series of prayers that he might not be permitted to err in this monumental undertaking. Following this the pope was seated on his throne (which is the position of solemn magisterial teaching). At this point the pope proclaimed the canonization formula in full pontifical regalia:

> To the honor of Almighty God, Father, Son, and Holy Spirit, and for the exaltation of the faith and the growth of the Christian religion, by the authority of the same almighty Father, Son, and Holy Spirit, of Saints Peter and Paul, and Ours, having consulted our brethren, we declare and define that Thomas of Aquino, of holy memory, is to be added to the catalog of the saints.[134]

Following this definition, the pope intoned the great thanksgiving hymn of the church, the *Te Deum*, which was then joined by the whole of the congregation. This done, the Solemn Mass began with the confession of sins, during which the friar from Roccasecca was addressed for the first time as *St*. Thomas. The Mass then followed, in the pattern of the Mass for Confessors of the faith. The pope then proclaimed a sermon that lauded the new saint. At the conclusion of the service the church was filled with lamps and candles in honor of the new saint, and a festival—funded mostly by the Angevin King Robert and the family of St. Thomas—lasted nearly a whole week.

In less than fifty years, Thomas the friar became St. Thomas Aquinas, whose feast was to be celebrated by the entire church. As was customary, a few days after the canonization, the curia released the formal bull proclaiming the news to the whole of Christendom. Under the title *Redemptionem Misit*, the bull has puzzled many subsequent Thomists who rightly see Thomas as their intellectual standard bearer. Thomas's recent biographers try to pull some isolated phrases from the bull that suggested doctrinal or intellectual interest by the pope, but it is unconvincing.[135] Some earlier scholars were convinced that the pope canonized Thomas as a teacher, with similar results.[136] Some even opine that John XXII canonized "Thomism" in the bull.[137] There is no evidence for any of this. The bull barely mentions Thomas's intellectual life and makes almost no reference to his work. In reality the bull is highly traditional, placing Thomas in the immemorial context of a saint of God, someone who lived the virtues heroically and was recognized by God in the performance of miracles. While it is certain that Thomas's teachings on poverty did indeed speed John's recognition of him, Thomas was canonized for a very simple reason. He was a man who, under the influence of grace, had lived a life of extraordinary holiness under difficult conditions. When we look at the process and at the bull itself this becomes clear. The inquisitions at Naples focused themselves on the ascertaining of Thomas's life of virtue. This focused on his ascetic practices, his prayer life, and especially his virginity. Mentions of his academic positions or tasks were invariably in the context of establishing some pattern of virtue. In other words, his academic life was accidental to his holiness, in the minds of both the deponents and the investigators. The Fossanova process was interested almost exclusively in miracles (though it also wanted to establish Thomas's exemplary death). The bull follows this pattern almost exclusively. It introduces Thomas by underscoring the stability of his religious profession, his humility, and his virginity. These become the cornerstones of the pope's arguments for his sanctity. Of course, he exercises these within the confines of the academic life, but again that is largely accidental to their accomplishment. Indeed much was being done in these medieval canonization bulls to stress that systematic virtue could be realized in any state in life, a development that would bear fruit in the period after the Reformation. The pope describes Thomas's pious death in the context of the Dominican's travels to the Lyon council, as part of his religious obedience and his submission to the Roman church in particular. John then includes nine miracles having nothing to do with the friar's biography and drawn from the local stories of Thomas's cult in the region of Fossanova. These form nearly half of the entire document. The bull finishes with a repetition of the canonization formula and a concession of indulgences for Thomas's feast day and pilgrimages to his tomb—all in all a highly traditional document. Thomas was canonized, then, not for his mind, but for his virtue and its recognition by almighty God in the form of miracles. There was no assertion of the validity of Thomas's doctrine, nor an allusion to the beatitude of the intellectual life. Thomas was a saint of the church, pure and simple, an unrepeatable creation and gift of divine grace. Anything beyond that would have to come from his disciples over the course of centuries. But Thomas's fame was fixed, and he was added to the pantheon of Christian men and women who had "run the race" and "kept the faith." Of course, people as diverse as the peasants of the Terra di Lavoro all the way to the poet Dante already knew this. Thomas was simply "a lamb of the flock that Saint Dominic leads, where one could fatten well, as long as one did not stray." The Master was one who raises "the eye of our mind"—as he did that of the Poet—"from light to light."[138]

CONCLUSION

Thomas Aquinas was a failure. Unlike many of his contemporaries and confreres, he formed no school of disciples to hand on his teachings. He left many problems and issues unresolved at his death. Indeed, many of his own tenets would be condemned in the sanctions of 1277 and 1278. His untimely demise left a philosophical vacuum that came to be occupied by voluntarists such as Duns Scotus and nominalists like William of Ockham, men whose thought would dominate the universities until the sixteenth century. Thomas had not even persuaded his own order fully to integrate philosophical studies into its curriculum, and his project of harmonizing Aristotle remained unfinished. His moderate realism was abandoned by radical individualists and Renaissance Platonists alike. His two chief works languished for years, while Peter Lombard's *Sentences* remained at the center of the curriculum of both university and order. His own *Summa Theologiae* found itself chopped up for parts, with only the more approachable practical morality of the II-II finding wide circulation in the years immediately following his death. His other intellectual achievements were respectively ignored, disputed, or mangled. Even as a saint he failed to find a universal cult, retaining only a rigidly circumscribed veneration in Lazio and Campania. His own order seemed to forget him, neglecting even to litigate for possession of his body, and not bothering to put him up for sainthood until prodded to do so by John XXII. If one were to survey the world that Thomas left in the late 1270s, it would be difficult to avoid the judgment that the Thomistic system had been but a momentarily brilliant intellectual cul-de-sac.

Yet the arc of history is long. Famous Masters who held the field during his time, such as Gerard d'Abbeville and John Pecham, have long since faded from relevance. Movements of pitch and moment, such as the secular controversy and the legitimacy of

Aristotle, disappeared largely—as became apparent—due to the patient labors of Thomas Aquinas. That Thomism became so dominant, not only in the Dominican order but also in the church at large, obscures the difficulty in appropriating the thought of the man who was to become the "Common Doctor." Slowly thinkers began to unpack his work and to understand the complex vision of reality that was Thomas's legacy. As time went on, an ever-growing number of thinkers entered into dialogue with him, as he had with the ancient world. This transpired not only within Latin Christendom, but also within the Greek East and among those of the Jewish tradition, and his work found interlocutors far beyond the walls of convent and school.[1] By the fourteenth century a vigorous Thomistic school had developed, spearheaded by the order certainly, but also extending beyond it. His canonization propelled not only his rehabilitation but also his adoption in the West as a premier interpreter of the Christian tradition. By the time of the Reformation, Thomism was one of the most robust of theological schools and significant enough to draw the ire of Martin Luther himself, who declared—with characteristic understatement—that Thomas was "the source and foundation of all heresy, all error and the obliteration of the Gospel." Protestant attacks had the effect of focusing Catholic apologists, and the Thomists were a strong force at the Council of Trent, finding that the new Jesuit order added to their adherents (if in often idiosyncratic ways). While the famous story that the council fathers placed the *Summa Theologiae* beside the Gospels themselves at the Council is untrue, it nonetheless betrays the increasing reach and significance of Thomas's thought. The reformers of the Carmelite order, for example, mapped their spirituality onto a Thomistic framework, perpetuating Thomas's influence on mystical theology. Under the Dominican Pius V (r. 1565–72), Thomas's cult became greatly expanded, as the pope declared him to be the "Angelic Doctor" and made him the first formally proclaimed doctor of the church after the church fathers.

His influence only increased from there. It was Thomas's followers who outlined concepts of natural law and human rights that tried to defend the peoples of the New World. Especially noteworthy are his followers in Spain, who formed a powerful school that advanced concepts of international law and justice that still affect the world today. His presence was ubiquitous even in Protestant writing—what one scholar refers to as the "hidden Thomism" of the seventeenth and eighteenth centuries—where thinkers would often use his ideas and methodology without citing their origins. Unfortunately, too much success can also be a problem. Thomism began to be reduced to manuals in the baroque period, intended to distill the Master's thought for presentation to seminarians. This attenuated Thomism was, ironically, exactly the approach to education that Thomas had tried to eliminate during his life. He wanted attention paid to fundamental, biblical, rooted theology, the kind that such manuals especially obscured. This created a climate for a reaction against Thomism, both inside and outside of the church.

Faced with the brutal realities of the modern world, the church was forced to retrench and reassess its mission. Seeing the inadequacy of contemporary theological and philosophical training, the far-seeing Leo XIII (r. 1878–1903) ushered in a revival of Thomism that not only saw the establishment of the Leonine commission for editing his works, but also prompted a wholesale reassessment and reacquisition of Thomistic principles. This led to a flowering of new approaches under the broad rubric of neo-Thomism—one that is far from exhausted. Yet this also occurred at the time when many new philosophies were emerging within the church and theological modernism was attempting to uproot established theology. These new approaches tended to weaken the Thomistic revival, particularly after the 1940s. In the heady atmosphere following the Second Vatican Council, Thomas was again in danger of falling into obscurity (even though he was the second most often-quoted thinker after Augustine). Though buoyed by the somewhat peculiar personalistic Thomism of St. John Paul II, the school today still finds itself in turbulent waters. Today much of the most creative work on St. Thomas is done by scholars who are not Catholic. It will be up to such thinkers, both inside and outside the church, to make sure that the failure that Thomas appeared to be after his death does not become confirmed in the modern world. Frankly, the prognosis is not good. When Thomas entered the convent at Naples, there were only two Dominicans present in the city. In the century after Thomas, a mighty foundation arose that could house nearly five hundred friars. Today, there are only four elderly friars at the site and the order is preparing to close the renowned convent of San Domenico, home of the most famous friar in the history of the Preachers.

Thomas still has much to offer. He is the prophet of intelligibility and common sense. In many ways he is the apostle of human integrity and the bearer of an optimism about the human potentiality that is only born from a profoundly incarnational outlook. As R. W. Southern put it,

> It is probably true that man has never appeared so important a being in so well-ordered and intelligible a universe as in [Thomas's] works. Man was important because he was the link between the created universe and the divine intelligence. He alone in the world of nature could understand nature. He alone could use and perfect nature in accordance with the will of God and thus achieve his full nobility.[2]

For Thomas, this could be effected only from the very heart of Christianity. Chesterton remarked upon this when he said that people "became more orthodox, when they became more rational and natural." Thomas defended the autonomy of the human person, created in God's image, and humanity's intrinsic power and ability to know and understand the rationally created universe. His incarnational empiricism paved the way for the scientific revolution as well as for modern ideas regarding human rights and dignity. Thomas elevated existence to the fundamental metaphysical category. Again, it is Chesterton who puts it so pithily: "If the morbid Renaissance intellectual is supposed to say, 'to be or not to be—that is the question,' then the massive medieval doctor does most certainly reply in a voice of thunder, 'to be—that is the answer.'" Thomas also leaves us an inheritance that teaches us the wisdom of *order* in a chaotic and disordering world. He knows that the patient task of teaching is to judge, to arrange, and to organize, to make some of the marvelous intelligibility of the divine architect comprehensible to his students. It was Thomas who could make his lecture hall and his study a place of holiness, a call to all today who live the life of the mind. For St. Thomas is completely and unhesitatingly committed to the idea that God can absolutely be found in the classroom.

APPENDIX A

Sources for a Life of Thomas Aquinas

Reconstructing the life of Thomas Aquinas does not present the kind of problems that a historian encounters in many other medieval lives. For example, the various *vitae* of Francis of Assisi are so difficult to interpret and integrate that some scholars have thrown up their hands in frustration at ever being able to find a "historical Francis."[1] This is largely due to the fact that Francis became a political and ideological football in the decades after his death, with competing visions of his life used to reinforce various stances within the church and the Franciscan order. Thomas's lives betray none of that. There seems to be no overt agenda in the unfolding of his biographical narratives, save for the presentation of his cause for canonization. No controversial issues arose inside or outside of the order regarding the meaning of his holiness or his biography, certainly none to match the virulence of opposition to his philosophy. This reinforces my position that his cult and his theological system did not interact much in the period before his canonization. Thomas was canonized in the traditional model of a holy man rather than as a teacher or a thinker. In that sense the biographies were uncontroversial.

This is not to imply that there are not interpretive issues to consider. Most of his biographical sources come nearly fifty years after his death. While this is certainly within living memory, we have to consider what such a long interval did to the memories of the witnesses, not to mention how their testimonies changed given the fact that they were being interviewed in a formal canonization process. Such testimonies are exceptionally valuable, but even when they coincide, one has to look at the intentions of the cultic promoters and the curial officials who were asking the questions and recording (and perhaps fashioning) the answers.[2] This is compounded by the reality that most deponents gave their testimony in the vernacular, which was then translated (perhaps on the spot) into Latin. Thus they can be called "literate Latinized highlights of oral vernacular narrations."[3] The witnesses were conforming their memories to established forms and patterns of holiness. Even where they corroborate one another, we have to ask how and why such details made it into their testimony (and indeed into the final written version). In particular, the historian must be attentive to dissonances among the deponents and pay special attention to direct speech that makes it through the layers of mediation. That said, however, we are fortunate to have the bulk of the depositions from both the Naples and the Fossanova processes, giving witness to the thorough process of canonization that reached its medieval zenith under Pope John XXII. These form the raw material for the present unfolding of Thomas's life, in addition to providing the grist for his medieval biographers.

Following the testimonies of the witnesses themselves, the next level of information comes in the narratives about his life and the compiled hagiographies written about him. We are, in a few instances, fortunate to have narrative sources that tell us about Thomas's life that were in circulation while he yet lived. Stories about his dramatic entrance into the order, about the conflict at Paris, and about his struggles to preach at his inception were in circulation by 1260 in the collection known as the *Vitas Fratrum*, using information that likely came from Thomas himself.[4] This collection circulated widely among the Dominicans and was critical in the order's formation of an identity in the generations after its founding. There are also some stories about Thomas in the anecdotal collection of Thomas of Cantimpré, which must be used with discretion, but he has the earliest allusion to the attempted seduction of the young Thomas.[5] Besides this we have official documents that emanated from the order and the curia and that come in the form of capitular decisions, letters of the Masters General, and papal bulls directed at the order itself.[6] The historian is also fortunate to possess the copious records of the University of Paris.[7] Thomas was quite a famous man by the end of his life, and many official documents aver to his activities. All these provide solid evidence of a framework upon which to overlay what we know in the narrative histories. These dispassionate sources are invaluable to the historian. At a further remove, however, are the hagiographies. The earliest of these are a selection of stories by Thomas's own student Tolomeo degli Fiadoni (better known as Ptolemy of Lucca). He records some of the deeds of his Master in his broader history of the church. His insights are valuable in that, while he wrote after Thomas's death, his work was completed well before the canonization, which means that it was not specifically drafted in order to outline Thomas's holiness in particular. Rather, Ptolemy embeds his stories about the Master in the context of a medieval type of "universal" history.[8]

One must wait until the mid-1300s for comprehensive biographies. The first and most important of these was the life written by William of Tocco, who revised his work no fewer than four times.[9] This work was formally intended to present Thomas for canonization. William did indeed know Thomas personally, but only at the end of the latter's life. By the late 1310s William, by then an old but still vigorous man, began to compile his life, traveling between southern Italy and Avignon to gather material. His narrative has many merits. Besides being personally familiar with his subject, he was well regarded by both the order and the curia, and so was able to negotiate the administrative hurdles. He was a southern Italian and was intimately aware of the context of the saint's sojourns in that area. In addition to that, he became a close friend of the Aquinas family, gathering many stories from them to use in his work. Most importantly from my perspective, however, was his acquaintance with Brother Reginald himself. While Reginald had died a generation before William had started to write, he communicated many of the details regarding Thomas's life in the cloister and about his manner of study and work to the Dominican community of Naples. William collected all these into his life, and the passages that have Reginald as their source are some of the most precious windows into the life of the saint. With all this said, however, William's work has demerits. His close relationship with the Aquinas family blinds him to some of their machinations as regards Thomas. As studied previously in this book, it seems that Dame Theodora spent much of the rest of her life burnishing her role in Thomas's vocation, massaging her memories and passing on these historical adjustments to her children. The hospitality and the piety of the Aquinas family in the 1310s made William feel very obligated to them. His narratives of Thomas's youth need to be read through the lens of this excessive predilection. Further than that, though, is William's lack of familiarity with either northern Europe or the issues surrounding the University of Paris. Any stories of Thomas's sojourns in Paris or Cologne need to be taken with a grain of salt. William was not a university man, and so he often confuses the policies, titles, and procedures of the academic world. In reality, William was not much of a writer at all, with one scholar commenting that his work is "very far from being a masterpiece....(It is) tediously and conventionally rhetorical."[10] Finally, although William's work is a model of the hagiographical genre, for that very reason it makes it complicated for the historian. William's task was to present Thomas as "another Christ," or one who heroically manifested the virtues and holiness that conformed him to the exemplar. In elevated language, Tocco repeatedly connects Thomas not only to Christ, but to heroic figures of the biblical and historical traditions, fitting him in as an archetype of various holy men. This method does, however, give the historian a certain insight. Whenever a comparison seems flat, it is usually the hagiographer attempting to squeeze some odd or unexpected event or practice into an established paradigm. In these weak analogies the historian can sometimes peer in to witness something that can mark off the personality of the saint himself: a half-seen vision of the real person behind the typologies.

Tocco's devotion does not discount his very real value for the life of Thomas. He personally knew St. Thomas in his last years in Naples. He was the one who was intimately familiar with the witnesses from the canonization depositions. He placed himself in a position to tell the best story of a saint that he could, given the requirements of the hagiographical genre. For that reason, the historian is deeply indebted to him, as are all subsequent biographers. Nearly contemporary to William of Tocco was one of the eminent Dominican names of the fourteenth century: Bernard Gui. Besides being an accomplished inquisitor of heresy, Gui was perhaps the most significant historian that the order had yet produced.[11] It is interesting that three of Thomas's main biographers, William of Tocco, Ptolemy of Lucca, and Bernard himself, all met by chance in Avignon in late summer of 1318. Gui was an extremely careful writer who excelled in research. His writings streamlined and clarified the history of the Dominican order and its saints. Bernard Gui wrote a biography using the first several versions of William of Tocco, streamlining the old Dominican's wording and adding some details, particularly about France, that help us to tighten up William's facts. He greatly simplified Tocco's wordy history by shearing it of pietistic excess. Gui is also familiar with the canonization records and includes details omitted by William. However, Gui adds no new narratives to William's existing structure. He does omit many stories included by William, though. The majority of these involve Italian episodes and family-specific tales, but the fact remains that there are many stories that Gui chose to omit from this abbreviated life. We still rely on William of Tocco in the main for the fullest biographical outline. The final early biography came from Peter Calo, probably about 1340.[12] It is almost entirely derivative, but the inclusion of a few details found nowhere else invites the speculation that Calo may have had some access to an independent tradition. The provenance of all the stories and miracles of St. Thomas is outlined in appendix B.

Most of the documents relevant to the life of Thomas Aquinas have been conveniently assembled, if not edited to a completely modern standard, by D. Prümmer and M. H. Laurent in various issues of the *Revue Thomiste* between 1911 and 1937.[13] These are, however, difficult to access, and even more difficult to paginate correctly over the multiple volumes. They have been handily collected in a rare edition of the *Fontes Vitae Sancti Thomae*, and these are fortunately available on the Internet. While there was a reprint done by Ferrua in 1968, it added no new critical editing or information and is, if possible, even rarer than the *Fontes Vitae Sancti Thomae*. Of most use is the modern edition (1996) of William of Tocco's works by C. le Brun-Gouanvic, who has painstakingly edited and clarified the four different versions of the biographer's works.[14] Some of the sources for St. Thomas have been translated into English by K. Foster, but this includes only Gui's life and sections of the canonization enquiries, Ptolemy, and the *Vitas Fratrum*.[15] It is not surprising that all of Thomas's sources are still untranslated, since many of his theological and philosophical works also remain only in Latin to the present day. Still a touchstone for Thomistic scholarship are the critical editions of his works ordered by Pope Leo XIII, entitled the Leonine edition.[16] This group, which is a model of historical scholarship, has been pursuing its task since 1882 and is not yet finished. The prologues to the editions are themselves treasuries of information about Thomas and his world; however, they are also very difficult to access, and still, after nearly 140 years, the editors are not completely finished with their massive task. New translations based on this definitive edition have been even slower to appear. There is still, to my mind, no wholly satisfactory English translation even of the *Summa Theologiae*, nor is there a full translation of the *Commentary on the Sentences* (though one is currently in process).

APPENDIX B

Biographical Sources

Description	Tocco	Gui	Calo	Tolomeo	Canonization Hearings	Vitas Fratrum	Location and Date	Other
Hermit makes prophecy of birth, name, and religious order	1	1	1		N62		Roccasecca	
Death of sister in lightning storm	2						Roccasecca	
Infant Thomas refuses to relinquish paper with Ave Maria on it	3	2			N90		Naples	
Thomas offered as an oblate at Montecassino[1]	4	3	3	22.20	N20, N76		Montecassino	
Thomas disdains to associate with fellow oblates, preferring to focus on God	4	3	3				Montecassino	
Thomas sent to the University of Naples from Montecassino	5	4	4				Naples	
Thomas received into order[2]	6	5	4		N76		Naples	Bull of Canonization
Theodora hastens to Naples "to confirm him in his choice"[3]	7							
Thomas abducted[4]	8	6	6		N61, N62, N76	4.17		
Thomas reads Bible, Sentences, and some of Aristotle's logical works in prison	9							
Thomas tempted by a prostitute	10	7	7		N61			Cantimpre
Thomas, imprisoned, visited by John of San Giuliano, OP[5]	11	8	8	22.21	N76			

CONTINUED

Description	Tocco	Gui	Calo	Tolomeo	Canonization Hearings	Vitas Fratrum	Location and Date	Other
Thomas leaves for Paris with Johannes Teutonicus and is apprenticed to Albert[6]	12	9	8					
Thomas refuses Abbacy of Montecassino				22.21				Cantimpre
Thomas impresses fellow students and Albert	12	9	8				Cologne	
Thomas contends with Albert in disputation	12	10	8				Cologne	
Excursus on Albert's excellence	13			22.18–19				
Thomas sent to University of Paris as Bachelor of the Sentences[7]	14	11	9				Paris	
Thomas promoted to Master	16	12	10	22.21			Paris	Chart. 1.307
Thomas visited by vision of an Old Dominican and gives Inaugural lecture	16	12	10		N49, N50, N60, N92	4.24	Paris	Bull of Canonization
Paean to Thomas's intellectual capacities[8]	15, 17	13	11					
List of Thomas's works	17	53–54						
Thomas fights the Averroists	18							
Thomas fights William of St. Amour and his partisans	19		12					
Thomas fights against the Fraticelli and apocalypticism	20							
Thomas fights against the Greek schismatics	21							
Thomas converts two Jews at castle of Molara[9]	22	14	14		N86		Molara, 1260–68	
Praise of Thomas's virtues	23							
Thomas's humility	24							
Thomas's purity revealed to a brother	28						Molara	

Description	Tocco	Gui	Calo	Tolomeo	Canonization Hearings	Vitas Fratrum	Location and Date	Other
Thomas's ease at prayer	29	15	16					
Thomas's devotion to Eucharist[10]	29	15	16					
Thomas says Mass every day, then assisted at another	29	15	16		many			Bull of Canonization
Thomas recites passage of Te Deum at elevation	58	15	28					
Constant absorption in abstraction (prayer)	17, 29, 48	15	16					
Always prayed for intellectual enlightenment	30, 24, 32	15	17		N58			
Thomas reads homilies of the fathers—Cassian for inspiration	21	15	13					
Thomas prays for enlightenment on a difficult passage in St. Paul	17	16						
Thomas receives a vision of Peter and Paul to decipher passage in Isaiah	31	16	17		N59, N93			
Thomas prays away a toothache	51	17	26		N60			
Thomas cures Reginald of a fever with a relic of St. Agnes[11]	50	18	26	23.10	N60		Molara	
Thomas has vision of Fra Romano, presses him about the vision of the blessed	45	19		23.16			Naples, 1273	
Vision of his sister, Landulph is in purgatory, Rinaldo in heaven[12]	44	20				4.24	Paris, 1259	
Vision of his brothers, Rinaldo in heaven	34, 42, 44	21			N78			
The three petitions of Thomas		22			N78			
Reginald teases Thomas about a cardinal's hat at Lyons	63				N78			

CONTINUED

Description	Tocco	Gui	Calo	Tolomeo	Canonization Hearings	Vitas Fratrum	Location and Date	Other
Our Lady appears to Thomas, confirms his teaching and chastity	32							
Thomas levitates at Salerno[13]	33	23	17				Salerno	
Thomas levitates at Naples, and crucifix asks what reward Thomas wants[14]	34	23	18		N79		Naples, 1273	
Louis IX uses Thomas as counselor	35						Paris, 1269–72	
Masters submit to Thomas's opinion on Eucharist, Christ says he wrote well of sacrament	52	24					Paris, 1269–72	
Thomas at table of St. Louis	43	25	24				1269–70, Paris	
Thomas called to meet Archbishop of Capua and Cardinal Legate of Sicily; he basically ignores them	43	25	24	23.9			Naples, 1272–73	
Thomas lost in ecstasy celebrating Passion Sunday Mass in Naples	29	26	16				Naples, 1272–73	
Thomas in tears at Lenten Compline verse in Naples	29	26					Naples, 1272–73	
Thomas has an insight into a brother's temptation	46							
Thomas at San Severino, in ecstasy for three days, renounces writing[15]	47	27	24		N79		December 6, 1273	
Thomas compared to Moses and Paul	47	27	24					STh II-II, q. 125 s. 3 ad 1 ??
Thomas abstracted during a leg cauterization	47	28	24					
Thomas does not notice a burning candle while dictating commentary on Boethius De Trinitate	47	28	24				1256–58	

Description	Tocco	Gui	Calo	Tolomeo	Canonization Hearings	Vitas Fratrum	Location and Date	Other
Thomas abstracted during quarterly bloodletting at Paris	47	28	24				Paris	
Popular preacher, southern Italian dialect, preached simply[6]	48	29	24		N58, N87			
A brother has a vision of Thomas's life and virtues	49							
Thomas brings people to tears in Holy Week, joy in resurrection	53	29	26		N75		1265–69, Holy Week, probably St. Mary Major	
Woman touches Thomas's garment, is healed of hemorrhage	53	29	26				Rome	
Thomas not made conceited by his positions	53	30	26					
Thomas accompanies a brother, who did not know him, to market in Bologna	25	31	15				Bologna, Winter 1268	
Thomas accepts dissenting views in a License exam, calmly corrects student next day[17]	26	31	15				Paris	
Says to his students that he never read a book without understanding it[18]	39	32	21					
Composition of *Catena Aurea*	17	32	22	22.24			Orvieto, 1261–63	
Composition of Corpus Christi liturgy and office				22.24			Orvieto, 1261–63	
Reginald speaks of him dictating to three secretaries at once, and even four	17	32						
Evan of Tréguier says he sometimes dictated in his sleep	17	32			N77			
Thomas strict with those in authority, but lenient with sinners	36	33	19					

CONTINUED

315

Description	Tocco	Gui	Calo	Tolomeo	Canonization Hearings	Vitas Fratrum	Location and Date	Other
Kind and charitable, a pleasure to live with	36	33	19					
Compassion for the poor[19]	36, 37	33	20					
Thomas is recognized for his judiciousness at Paris	40, 41							
Thomas would rather have Chrysostom on Matthew than whole city of Paris, after visit to relics of St. Denis	42	34	23		N78		Paris, 1269–72	
Clement IV offers him Archbishopric of Naples and revenues of St. Peter ad Aram[20]	42	34	23	22.39			Rome, 1265–68	
Physical description	38, 66	35	21		N16, N19, N42, N45, N46			
Two witnesses see a star over Thomas's head	54	36	26		N87		1273, Naples	
John of Blasio sees a devil who came to tempt Thomas	55				N70		Naples	
Thomas called by Gregory X to Lyons, falls sick at Maenza	56	37	27	23.8	N8, N19, N50, N78, N79			Bull of Canonization
Miracle of the herrings[21]	56	37	27		N2, N9, N50			
Thomas stops at Fossanova	57	38	27		N8, N49		Fossanova	
Thomas receives viaticum and dies	58	39	28	23.9	N8, N10, N15, N19, N27, N35, N49, N80		"	Bull of Canonization
Thomas's funeral at Fossanova, many visitors	62	40	30				"	
Great lament, mule that carried the bier expires[22]	62	40	30				"	
Reginald preaches, Thomas no mortal sin, like a child for purity	63, 27	41	27		N49, N58		"	Bull of Canonization
Reginald more of a nurse to Thomas (abstracted)	63	41					"	

Description	Tocco	Gui	Calo	Tolomeo	Canonization Hearings	Vitas Fratrum	Location and Date	Other
A monk sees a star fall on the monastery in a dream and then rise to heaven	59	42	29				"	
Vision of Paul of Aquila, then in Naples, sees St. Paul enter Thomas's classroom[23]	60	42	29	23.9			"	
Albert begins to weep, revelation of death of Thomas		43			N67, N82			
Albert has a vision of Augustine and Thomas in heaven					N66			
Restoration of sight to subprior John of Ferentino of Fossanova		44			N17, N51		Fossanova	
Seven months after death Thomas appears to John to chide him for moving his body to a side altar	66	44			N8, N10, N12, N52, N80		"	Bull of Canonization
Sweet fragrance at tomb	66	44			N8, N10, N12, N15, N20		"	Bull of Canonization
Body found incorrupt, Mass Os Iusti sung (for a confessor)	66	44			N8, N15, N20		"	
Thomas had expressed his desire for body brought back to Naples		45					"	
Cistercians try to retain the body[24]	67	46	31				"	
Fr. Rainerius Maturus has a vision of Thomas three days after his death	64						"	
The exact time of Thomas's death	65						"	
Vision of Albert of Brescia		51						
Canonization of Thomas		52					Avignon, 1323	
1288 Abbot Peter of Monte San Giovanni detaches hand for Theodora, body incorrupt with sweet odor	68				N20		Fossanova	

CONTINUED

317

Description	Tocco	Gui	Calo	Tolomeo	Canonization Hearings	Vitas Fratrum	Location and Date	Other
The detached hand in Salerno is mocked by Canon Matthew of Adiutorio in 1316, and he is punished[25]	69				N46, N68		Salerno	Bull of Canonization, 8
Brother in Salerno smells the heavenly odor from the hand	70				N95		"	
Master Reginald (not the socius) healed of paralysis at tomb					N9		Fossanova	
Raynald, a doctor, healed of gout at Fossanova	M1	M3			N12, N16, N21, N37, N53		"	Bull of Canonization, 6
Nicholas of Piperno, son of James Romanus, healed of paralysis in right side at Fossanova[26]	M2	M12			N36		"	
Peter Francis of Piperno, Oblate of Fossanova, delivered from obsession at tomb[27]	M3	M4			N14, N22, N24, N30, N31, N38, N55		"	Bull of Canonization, 7
Lord Nicholas Angeli of Piperno healed of arthritis of right arm at tomb	M4						"	
Thomas Paganus of Piperno healed of fever with vow of pilgrimage to tomb	M5						"	
Lord Rainerius of Babuco, monk of Fossanova, healed of fever at tomb	M6	M79					Fossanova	
Thomas, a boy of Piperno, healed of leprosy at tomb by a vision of Thomas	M7	M76						
Bartholomew of Ferentino, lay conversus of Fossanova, cured of abscess at tomb	M8	M77					Fossanova	
Poor man, crippled in the legs, healed at a vow to make a pilgrimage to tomb	M9							
Introduction to the miracles presented to John XXII for canonization	M10							

Description	Tocco	Gui	Calo	Tolomeo	Canonization Hearings	Vitas Fratrum	Location and Date	Other
Canonization procurators saved from shipwreck in Tyrrhenian Sea by the three Dominican saints	M11							
Appointment of canonization commission, Archbishop of Naples, Bishop of Viterbo, Pandulf de Sabello	M12							
Inquisitions held in Naples and Fossanova	M13							
Bartholomew of Sulmona has a vision of Thomas praying	M14							
Lord John of Adelasia, of Piperno, monk at Fossanova, cured of abscess	M16	M8			N28, N71, N72		Fossanova	
Lord John of Sclavis, monk of Fossanova, cured of abscess and fever	M17	M6			N25		"	
Lord James of Pastina, monk of Fossanova, cured of grave fever at tomb	M18						"	
James of Fresolino, called "the Red," healed of a fever when making a vow to Thomas	M19	M10			N33		"	
James of Piperno, cellarer, hurt by hail, storm stopped by Thomas	M20				F35, F36, F37, N94		"	
Emanuel de Piperno, conversus, paralyzed arm cured after an hour on tomb	M21	M31			F8, F34		"	
Leonard of Piperno, conversus carpenter, disbelieves miracles, loses use of arm, slowly cured	M22	M7			N26		"	
Peter Carellus, oblatus, has daughter cured of grave illness	M23						"	
John the Hermit cured of sleeping disorder	M24							
Nicholas de Maximo of Piperno, injures his arm fighting, promises peace and a candle, is healed	M25	M9			N29, N32, N34, N39, N57, N65			

CONTINUED

319

Description	Tocco	Gui	Calo	Tolomeo	Canonization Hearings	Vitas Fratrum	Location and Date	Other
James, son of Peter de Tibaldo, of Piperno freed from quartan fever, vows a Mass	M26	M19			N64			
Mark Brachialis of Piperno freed of a cough and vomit of blood at tomb[28]	M27	M75			F124		Fossanova	
Daughter of Nicholas of Monte San Giovanni freed of tumor of the throat with relics	M28							
Daughter of Nicholas of Monte San Giovanni freed again of a pain in the side when he prays at tomb	M29						Fossnova	
Matthew John de Leone of Piperno saved from choking by a mental prayer to Thomas	M30	M5			N23			
Petrucio of Piperno's infant daughter freed from fever after vows of pilgrimage	M31							
Little son of Matthew Capuano of Piperno healed from convulsions from a fishbone at Thomas's tomb	M32						Fossanova	
Peter Balia of Piperno cured of blindness	M33	M20			N65			
Gregory Citer of Piperno's little child cured of insomnia when laid on tomb	M34						Fossanova	
Gregory Citer of Piperno's knee healed at the shrine	M34				N71		Fossanova	
James Marcellucio of Piperno healed of a throat tumor at tomb	M35	M22			N72		Fossanova	
John of Theodino delivered from death from a water-wheel	M36	M80						
Floredensa of Piperno cured of blindness after prayers to Thomas	M37	M81						
Alexandra of Piperno cured of arm pain by the thought of Thomas's relics	M38	M83						

Description	Tocco	Gui	Calo	Tolomeo	Canonization Hearings	Vitas Fratrum	Location and Date	Other
Margaret of Piperno cured of neck pain after calling on Thomas.[29]	M39	M15			N54, N56			
John Capuricio of Sonnino cured of jaw pain after promising a pilgrimage	M40							
Theodora of Mantua from Sonnino cured of ear tumor	M41	M63			F90, F114			
Nicholas John Stephen of Sonnino promises a wax leg, and is cured of three-years suffering of ulcers	M42							
Matthew Capuricio of Sonnino cured of a fistula in the big toe after promising a pilgrimage	M43	M85						
Stephania of Roccasecca, living in the castle of Sonnino, cured of dropsy by the relics	M44	M16			N63			
Nicholas de Leone of Sonnino cured of groin pain with a vow of a barefoot pilgrimage	M45	M18			N64			
Maria of Nicholas, of Carpaneto cured of paralysis with a vow	M46	M17			N64			
Boethius Passageno of Terracina, now of Fundanus, cured of gout with vow of pilgrimage[30]	M47	M11, M86			N40, N63			
Boethius Passageno of Terracina, cured of stomach pains when he lies on the tomb	M48						Fossanova	
Peter Grasso of Naples, soldier, cured of arm pain when applied to tomb	M50	M1			N7, N40, N43, N88		"	
Rainaldus of Terracina cured of quartan fever at tomb	M49						"	
James, captain of Naples militia, healed of eye puncture by application to the tomb	M51	M2			N44, N69		"	
Cesare Bono of Naples cured of a paroxysm[31]	M52	M24			N91			

CONTINUED

Description	Tocco	Gui	Calo	Tolomeo	Canonization Hearings	Vitas Fratrum	Location and Date	Other
Archbishop of Naples cured of leg tumor at invocation of Thomas	M53	M87						
Archbishop of Naples cured of fever by invoking Thomas	M54							
Canon Matthew of Naples cured of Tertian fever while his friends make vows	M55	M13						
Thomas cures a donkey carrying the canonization materials in the Alps	M56							
Matthew of Naples's horse is saved from plunging over a precipice	M57							
Brother Landulph of Naples, OP, cured of colic at tomb		M14			N48		Fossanova	
Nicholas Meleus of Castro Pascencii cured of eye puncture by making a vow at tomb		M21			N71, N73		"	
Nobleman delivered from persecution by a vision of Thomas		M23						
Brother Martin of Apicio, OP, cured of kidney trouble in Naples		M25						
Brother Thomas of Aversa, OP, cured of neck pain by a relic of Thomas		M26			N95			
Master Matthew of Viterbo, chaplain of the Archbishop of Naples, cured of tertian fever		M27			N96, N97			
Master Matthew of Viterbo cured of his dislike of fish by a vision of Thomas		M28			N96, N97			
Peter Boccacci of Piperno cured of injuries to his face and side from a fall from a horse[32]		M29			F6, F12			
Brother Nicholas Zappi of Piperno cured of arthritis in both arms		M30			F7, F13, F82			
Gemma of Piperno cured of fever after promising a silver ex voto		M32			F10, F105			

Description	Tocco	Gui	Calo	Tolomeo	Canonization Hearings	Vitas Fratrum	Location and Date	Other
Leonard, son of Raymond Sarraceni of Piperno, cured of kidney problems		M33			F11			
Bartholomew Leonard of Piperno healed after a fall from a height		M34			F14, F15			
Brother Mark Theobald cured of a fever he had for ten days		M35			F16, F71			
Jacoba of Valdebruni cured of throat tumor at tomb		M36			F17		Fossanova	
Maria, seven-year-old daughter of Landulph of Sonnino, cured of possession		M37			F18			
Bartholomew of Sonnino cured of eye trouble at tomb		M38			F19, F20, F23, F25, F30, F33		Fossanova	
Amatus Bruni of Sonnino cured of hernia after promising silver ex voto		M39			F21, F24, F110			
Leo, three-year-old son of Crescenzio Novelli of Sonnino, cured of fever		M40			F22, F44			
Bartholomew Theobald of Sonnino cured of leg pain		M41			F26, F27, F45			
Nicholas Infancelli of Sonnino cured of abscess		M42			F28, F31, F32			
Brother Waldebrunus, conversus of Fossanova, cured of arm pain after promising silver ex voto		M43			F29, F112			
Master James of Piperno cured of leg paralysis		M44			F38, F39, F40, F41			
Nicholas Peter cured of hemorrhage		M45			F46, F47, F48			
Peter Caroli of Terracina cured of headache		M46			F49, F52, F53			
Gemma of Terracina cured of quartan fever		M47			F50, F51			

CONTINUED

Description	Tocco	Gui	Calo	Tolomeo	Canonization Hearings	Vitas Fratrum	Location and Date	Other
Nicholas of Aprutio, tailor of Terracina, cured of a tumor on the hand		M48			F54, F55, F56, F57			
Bartholomew Peter of Sermonetto cured of fever and tumors on his limbs		M49			F58, F59, F60			
Peter Caprarii of Sermonetto cured of inedia		M50			F61, F62, F63, F64			
Maria Egidio of Sermonetto cured of fever and chronic cough		M51			F65, F66, F67			
Rosa, wife of the notary James Bellini, cured of pains in head and side		M52			F68, F69, F70			
Stephen, son of Guido, healed of injuries from a fall		M53			F72, F91, F97, F106, F130			
James of Salatino cured of paralysis		M54			F73			
Sibilla, daughter of Peter of Piperno, cured of fever		M55			F74, F93			
Matthew de Voria of Piperno cured of quartan fever		M56			F75, F76, F80			
John Garini, seven years old, cured of an enlarged testicle		M57			F77, F78, F89, F92, F94			
Peter Leto, notary of Piperno, cured of abscess of the tonsils		M58			F79, F123, F128			Bull of Canonization, 9
Schimana Endebrandini cured of pain in shoulder and arm		M59			F83, F103			
Nicholas Grasso of Sermonetto cured of fever, stomach ache, and headache		M60			F84, F113			Bull of Canonization, 10
Brother Peter Crescenzio, conversus of Fossanova, cured of facial and throat tumor		M61			F85, F104			
Nicholas Picardi of Terracina cured of ringing in the ears		M62			F86, F87, F88			

Description	Tocco	Gui	Calo	Tolomeo	Canonization Hearings	Vitas Fratrum	Location and Date	Other
Johanna Christiana cured from pain of the whole body		M64			F95			
Peter, son of Lord Romite of Piperno, cured of tumors of the whole body		M65			F96, F98, F100, F131			Bull of Canonization, 14
Lady Lea Anasola cured of paralysis of shoulder and arm		M66			F99, F101, F102			
Adelasia, daughter of Gemma Rubea of Piperno, cured of abscess of the tonsils		M67			F107, F108, F109			Bull of Canonization, 12
Jacoba, wife of Peter Nicholas of Piperno, cured of fever and restored to speech		M68			F111			Bull of Canonization, 11
Blanditia Nichola, wife of Lord Gregory of Terracina, cured of fever		M69			F115			
Agnes Filippo of Castro san Lorenzo in the Valle Ferentino, cured of arm and shoulder pain		M70			F116, F122			
Nicholas Bartholomew of Piperno cured of knee pain		M71			F117, F125, F126			
Nicholas Affirmato of Piperno cured of arm and shoulder pain		M72			F118, F127			Bull of Canonization, 13
Peter Galgano of Piperno cured of contracted bones in his right arm		M73			F119, F120, F129			
Peter Hectario of Piperno cured of fever and vomiting		M74			F121, F132, F133			
Girl cured of leg paralysis[33]		M78						
Lady of Piperno given easy childbirth when girded by a belt lain on Thomas's tomb		M82			N18			
John Stephen of Sonnino cured of leg tumor		M84						

CONTINUED

325

Description	Tocco	Gui	Calo	Tolomeo	Canonization Hearings	Vitas Fratrum	Location and Date	Other
Lord Cinzio, canon of St. Peter, nuncio to pope, prays to Thomas for saving canonization materials from falling into Lake Lausanne		M88						
Lady Mary, wife of Arnold, nephew of the pope, healed of dropsy, and baby resurrected after birth		M89						
Man healed of quartan fever		M90						
James of Piperno, cured of kidney pain and blasphemy		M91						
Diatema, daughter of Nicholas, healed of a seizure		M92						
Maria Landulpho cured of possession		M93			F42, F43			
Man of Roccasecca cured of paralysis		M94						
Jordan de Marco cured of deafness		M95						
Lady Heremita cured of bodily distension		M96						
A Lady of Asturio has son cured of contracted bones		M97						
Amenita of Castro San Lorenzo cured of lethargy at Thomas's tomb		M98						
Cunizio of Naples cured of fistula		M99						
In Piedmont in Castro Tagulano, sister of an OP is raised from the dead[34]		M100					Piedmont	
Brother Luther, OM, has a vision of Francis approving Thomas's works		M101						
William of Tocco saved from shipwreck after invoking Dominic, Peter Martyr, and Thomas		M102						

APPENDIX B NOTES

1. Calo alone has the story of the boy Thomas asking, "What is God?" repeatedly.
2. Gui gets Thomas's age from Canonization, not Tocco. Gui is also the one who says Thomas Agni of Lentini received him.
3. Part of Tocco's revisionism about Theodora.
4. Tocco mentions castle of Roccasecca; Gui omits this detail.
5. Tolomeo makes the escape dramatic, with Thomas being lowered in a basket.
6. Tocco adds the detail that he studied *Ethics* under Albert.
7. Tocco mentions reluctance of Johannes Teutonicus, Albert's insistence, and the intervention of Hugh of St. Cher; Gui omits all of these.
8. Tocco and Calo use Isidore's etymology for Thomas's name: "abyss."
9. Bartholomew of Capua details that Jews were Roman and were father and son and skilled in Hebrew.
10. Gui mentions his sister Theodora; Tocco does not.
11. Tolomeo claims to have witnessed it, gives more details.
12. Sister not mentioned in Gui.
13. On way back from San Severino.
14. Bartholomew of Capua says it was the day he ended his writing.
15. Reginald says Naples, chapel of San Niccolo; Gui gets name of Theodora from canonization, not Tocco.
16. Tocco says he didn't learn any other language (because of abstraction).
17. Tocco moderates Gui, "now you've got it right."
18. Calo says student was Daniel of Angusta.
19. Tocco and Calo relate this as a sort of *noblesse oblige*, then go into praises of his family; Tocco mentions Thomas of Marsico.
20. Tocco and Calo say it was to help support his family, which had lost much money in the struggle against Frederick.
21. Tocco and Calo say he didn't eat any after all.
22. Gui's aside on loud lamentations, a "French" addition.
23. Tolomeo was at Naples for this.
24. Gui has an independent source for Reginald drawing a legal instrument to bring Thomas's body back.
25. N68 calls him Thomas de Marchia.
26. N36 hearing calls boy James, probably a reduplication from the father's name.
27. Naples sources call him a *conversus*.
28. The Fossanova process adds he was a cleric of the Church of St. Lucy in Piperno.
29. Name added by Gui.
30. Gui and Naples call him Peter of Fundanus, monk and priest of Fossanova; could be a doubled miracle in Gui.
31. Gui says William of Tocco advised him to vow to Thomas, also calls it tertian fever.
32. Gui, M29–M75 taken from second inquisition in Fossanova.
33. Gui, 76–102 collected from "worthy witnesses."
34. Missing in some Gui mss.

NOTES

CHAPTER 1

1. For an excellent overview, see P. Brown, *The Rise of Western Christendom: Triumph and Diversity, A.D. 200–1000* (Chichester, UK: Wiley-Blackwell, 2013).

2. For an introduction, see R. S. Lopez, *The Commercial Revolution of the Middle Ages: 950–1350* (Cambridge: Cambridge University Press, 1971).

3. For the story of this foundation, see T. F. X. Noble, *The Republic of St. Peter: The Birth of the Papal State, 680–825* (Philadelphia: University of Pennsylvania Press, 2010).

4. See L. C. Chiarelli, *A History of Muslim Sicily* (Venera, Malta: Midsea Books, 2011). See also A. Metcalfe, *The Muslims of Medieval Italy* (Edinburgh: Edinburgh University Press, 2009).

5. For the conquest, see G. S. Brown, *The Norman Conquest of Southern Italy and Sicily* (Jefferson, NC: McFarland, 2003); and Brown, *Age of Robert Guiscard: Southern Italy and the Northern Conquest* (London: Routledge, 2016); see also M. Chibnall, *The Normans* (London: Blackwell, 2002).

6. For Roger, see H. Houben, *Roger II of Sicily: A Ruler between East and West* (Cambridge: Cambridge University Press, 2002).

7. For Barbarossa, see J. B. Freed, *Frederick Barbarossa: The Prince and the Myth* (New Haven, CT: Yale University Press, 2017).

8. For Innocent, see *Pope Innocent III and His World.*, ed. J. C. Moore and B. Bolton (Aldershot, UK: Ashgate, 2010); J. E. Sayers, *Innocent III: Leader of Europe 1198–1216* (London: Longman, 1997); and J. C. Moore, *Pope Innocent III: (1160/61–1216); To Root Up and to Plant* (Notre Dame, IN: University of Notre Dame Press, 2009); also still useful is H. Tillmann, *Pope Innocent III* (Amsterdam: North-Holland, 1980).

9. For Frederick, see D. Abulafia, *Frederick II: A Medieval Emperor* (London: Pimlico, 2002).

10. *The Liber Augustalis, or, Constitutions of Melfi, Promulgated by the Emperor Frederick II for the Kingdom of Sicily in 1231*, ed. and trans. J. M. Powell (Syracuse, NY: Syracuse University Press, 1971).

11. For these developments, see W. Ullmann, *The Growth of Papal Government in the Middle Ages: A Study in the Ideological Relation of Clerical to Lay Power* (London: Methuen, 1970); C. Morris, *The Papal Monarchy: The Western Church from 1050 to 1250*, Oxford History of the Christian Church, ed. H. Chadwick and O. Chadwick (Oxford: Clarendon Press, 1991); I. S. Robinson, *The Papacy, 1073–1198: Continuity and Innovation*, Cambridge Medieval Textbooks (Cambridge: Cambridge University Press, 1991).

12. For this movement, see M. Lambert, *Medieval Heresy: Popular Movements from the Gregorian Reform to the Reformation* (Oxford: Blackwell, 1997), 36–38, esp. n3.

13. The foundational work for this is H. Grundmann, *Religious Movements in the Middle Ages: The Historical Links between Heresy, the Mendicant Orders, and the Women's Religious Movement in the Twelfth and Thirteenth Century, with the Historical Foundations of German Mysticism*, trans. Steven Rowan and Robert E. Lerner (Notre Dame, IN: University of Notre Dame Press, 2005, original 1935).

14. See the fine analysis in R. W. Southern, *Scholastic Humanism and the Unification of Europe* (Oxford: Blackwell, 2002).

15. For an overview of Bernard's extraordinary career, see G. R. Evans, *Bernard of Clairvaux* (New York: Oxford University Press, 2000).

16. For the history of lay penitential movements, see A. Thompson, *Cities of God: The Religion of the Italian Communes 1125–1325* (State College: Pennsylvania State University Press, 2006), 69–102; and for Dominicans particularly, Thompson, *Dominican Brothers: Conversi, Lay, and Cooperator Friars* (Chicago: New Priory Press, 2017).

17. C. Berman argues that these changes were evolutionary rather than revolutionary and were only in place by the 1170s and 1180: *The Cistercian Evolution: The Invention of a Religious Order in Twelfth-Century Europe* (Philadelphia: University of Pennsylvania

Press, 2000). I believe them to have been far more original than she gives them credit for.

18. See the intriguing study in L. Little, *Religious Poverty and the Profit Economy in Medieval Europe* (Ithaca, NY: Cornell University Press, 1994).

19. The image of Mary and Martha as standard bearers for the contemplative and active life ran very deeply in medieval society. Mary "has chosen the better part" (Luke 10:42), that is, the life of cloistered contemplation, while Martha chose the lesser, active life. This model was not only Christian but was also deeply rooted in the teachings of Plato, Aristotle, and Cicero. The life of the mind, being superior to the body, was ipso facto superior to bodily activities. This did not mean that the active life was bad, or that within it it was impossible to be saved. Rather, it meant that those who chose the active life were choosing a *less good* path.

20. J. Dalarun, *Robert of Arbrissel: Sex, Sin, and Salvation in the Middle Ages*, trans. B. Venarde (Washington, DC: Catholic University of America Press, 2006). Interestingly, Fontevrault maintained the attraction of both male and female devotees, as it was a double monastery: men lived in one community and women in the other, with both under the authority of an abbess.

21. A. W. van den Hurk, *Norbert of Gennep and His Order (Norbert Van Gennep En Zijn Orde)* (Apeldoorn: Altiora-Averbode, 1984); an older hagiographical biography is L. T. Anderson, *Saint Norbert of Xanten: A Second St. Paul* (Dublin: Gill, 1955). See also the commentary in T. J. Antry and C. Neel, *Norbert and Early Norbertine Spirituality* (New York: Paulist Press, 2007).

22. A path traced by R. I. Moore in his *The Origins of European Dissent* (Toronto: University of Toronto Press, 2005).

23. R. Wilken, *The Spirit of Early Christianity: Seeking the Face of God* (New Haven, CT: Yale University Press, 2005), 261. He goes on, "At the center of Christian worship is a material, palpable thing, the consecrated bread and wine, through water one is joined to the church, and through things, the Holy Cross, the rock of Calvary, the sacred tomb, God accomplished the salvation of the world."

24. This ritual was called *Endura*, and was very rare, though a logical outcome of Cathar belief. When employed, it was usually only engaged in while at the point of death. For a comprehensive

overview of Catharism, see the magisterial work of G. Rotten-wöhrer, *Die Katharer: was sie glaubten, wie sie lebten* (Ostfildern: Thorbecke, 2007); for the *Endura*, see pp. 237–38.

25. M. Pegg has repeatedly argued that characterizations of Cathar belief are largely idealized and intellectualized. See his "On Cathars, Albigenses and Good Men," *Journal of Medieval History* 27, no. 2 (2001): 181–95; in this he follows the outlines developed by R. I. Moore and reaffirmed in Moore's *War on Heresy: Faith and Power in Medieval Europe* (London: Profile Books, 2014). This view is too extreme; Catharism was far more than a clerical invention. It may not have been as systematic as many churchmen thought; nonetheless, it really existed.

26. The literature on the Cathars is extensive; see, for example, A. Dondaine, "La hierarchie Cathare in Italie," *AFP* 19 (1949): 280–312; and Dondaine, "Le Manuel de l'Inquisiteur," *AFP* 27 (1947): 85–194; A. Borst, *Die Katharer* (Stuttgart: Hiersemann, 1953); R. Manselli, *Studi sulle eresi del secolo XII* (Rome: Istituto storico per il Medio Evo, 1953); W. L. Wakefield, *Heresy, Crusade, and Inquisition in Southern France, 1100–1250* (Berkeley: University of California Press, 1974); and the essays in *The Concept of Heresy in the Middle Ages (11th–13th c.)* (Louvain: University Press, 1976); more recently, see M. Lambert, *The Cathars* (Oxford: Blackwells, 1998, rev. 2007); and G. Rottenwöhrer, *Der Katharismus*, 4 vols. in 6 (Bad Honnef, 1982).

27. For Waldensianism as a movement, see G. Merlo, *Valdesi e valdismi medievali: itinerari e proposte di ricerca* (Turin: Claudiana, 1984); and, more recently, G. Audisio, *The Waldensian Dissent: Persecution and Survival, ca. 1170–1570* (Cambridge: Cambridge University Press, 1999); and E. Cameron, *Waldenses: Rejections of Holy Church in Medieval Europe* (Oxford: Blackwell, 2000).

28. Weisheipl, 5. For Thomas's genealogy, see F. Scandone, *La vita, la famiglia e la patria di S. Tommaso* (Rome: Società tipografica A. Manuzio, 1924), with the correctives in W. Pocino, *Roccasecca patria di San Tommaso d'Aquino: Documentazione storico-bibliographica* (Rome, 1974).

29. This is a contested question. I side with Weisheipl and Mandonnet that Theodora was a second wife, as it seems safe to conclude from the existence of three sons far older than the other children, against Jean-Pierre Torrell, "La pratique pastorale d'un

théologien du XIIIe siècle: Thomas d'Aquin prédicateur," *Revue Thomiste* 82 (1982): 3.

30. Weisheipl, 6.

31. Weisheipl, 6; Torrell, "La pratique pastorale," 2–3.

32. Indeed, it is probable that this Rinaldo is the composer of vernacular songs mentioned with approval by Dante himself in *De Vulgari Eloquentia*, I. c, 12, see Scandone, "La Vita." Cf. Weisheipl, 7.

33. This is recorded in the *Vitas Fratrum*, which dates to before 1259. See *VF*, 215. Repeated in William de Tocco, *L'histoire de saint Thomas d'Aquin*, ed. C. Le Brun-Gouanvic (Paris: Cerf, 2005), 44, and Gui, 1911–37, c. 21. Gui omits that it was a vision of Marotta.

34. For an in-depth discussion of the problems identifying the factions, see D. Medici, S. Raveggi, M. Tarassi, and P. Parenti, *Ghibellini, guelfi e popolo grasso*, Biblioteca di storia 26 (Florence, 1978).

35. The consensus has been 1224 or 1225. Tugwell, 210, argues for 1226, I think unconvincingly. G. Abate, "Intorno alla cronologia di San Tommaso," *Miscellanea Franciscana* 50 (1950): 231–47; and C.J. Vansteenkiste in *Rassegna di Letteratura tomista* 24 (1991): 11–12. Both argue based on Thomas's young age when advanced to the Mastership; I do not find it convincing. As A. Oliva, OP, points out, not only would this be out of step with the nearest biographies, but we must not place too much faith in the University of Paris following every one of its policies to the letter: *Les débuts de l'enseignement de Thomas d'Aquin et sa conception de la Sacra Doctrina: Édition du prologue de son commentaire des Sentences de Pierre Lombard*, Bibliothèque Thomiste 58 (Paris: J. Vrin, 2006), 202n53.

36. Torrell, "La pratique pastorale," 1.

37. Weisheipl and Torrell omit the story, but Tugwell (201, esp. n15) gives it some attention. Gui, ch. 1; Tocco, *L'histoire de saint Thomas*, ch. 1; Calo, 17–55, ch. 1; Naples, ch. 62 (testimony of Tocco himself, who says he got it from Catherine, Thomas's niece). Indeed, there was some evidence of a local tradition in Roccasecca. There is a church dedicated to Thomas halfway up from the village to the castle. Local lore suggested that this had been the site of the hermit's residence. M. Räsänen, *Thomas Aquinas's Relics as Focus for Conflict and Cult in the Late Middle Ages: The*

Restless Corpse (Amsterdam: Amsterdam University Press, 2017), 174. Most likely, this is an *ex post facto* retrojection from the story back to the town, which sought to maximize its connection with the saint.

38. Tocco, *L'histoire de saint Thomas*, 2.

39. Weisheipl, 9.

40. Tocco, *L'histoire de saint Thomas*, 3, states that his nurse made frequent recourse to this stratagem to quiet him.

41. This was not an unusual strategy; one of Thomas's fellow students, Ambrose Sansedoni of Siena, had a small cult after his death in 1287. Apparently as a toddler, whenever he would see a book, he would have a tantrum until it was handed to him, even though he could not read. Such hagiographical "prophecies" are rather common. See "Legenda maior," AA. ss. April III 864. For a commentary on this episode, see Alessandro Barbero, *Un santo in famiglia: vocazione religiosa e resistenze sociali nell'agiografia latina medievale* (Turin: Rosenberg & Sellier, 1991), 248–51 at 237.

42. For an excellent introduction to hagiography and its audience and purposes, see T. J. Heffernan, *Sacred Biography* (Oxford: Oxford University Press, 1988), esp. chs. 1 and 2.

43. H. de Lubac, *Exégèse Médiéval: Les quatre sens de l'Écriture*, 4 vols. (Paris, Aubier, 1959–64). The first two volumes are translated in H. de Lubac. *Medieval Exegesis*, trans. M. Sebanc, 2 vols (Grand Rapids: Eerdmans, 1998).

44. Tocco, *L'histoire de saint Thomas*, 3. Omitted by Gui. Only Weisheipl considers the story; Tugwell and Torrell ignore it. Tocco had good connections with the family, and other than what can be seen as providential preservation, it is certainly not unbelievable.

CHAPTER 2

1. The likely date for his entrance would be between the signing of the treaty of San Germano, July 23, 1230, and May 3, 1231; J. -P. Torrell, *Aquinas's Summa: Background, Structure, and Reception* (Washington, DC: Catholic University of America Press, 2012), 4.

2. Benedict, *Rule*, ch. 59.

Notes

3. The first record of this story comes from Bartholomew of Capua (1248–1329)—a witness at the 1319 canonization inquiry—who states that he heard it from Thomas's first Dominican brethren in Naples. Bartholomew testifies that he frequented the priory as a young man, and had seen Thomas, certainly during his latter days in Naples in 1272–74. Canonization Enquiry, Naples, n. 76, cf. Foster, 106. His biographers only say he was sent for education, to learn the rule and his letters. It was probably a conflation with Innocent IV's offer in 1244 to make Thomas abbot, in order to defuse the tension with his family.

The first record of this story comes from Bartholomew, from between the signing of the treaty of San Germano, July 23, 1230 and May 3, 1231; Torrell, *Aquinas's Summa*, 4.

4. Landolfo was not innocent of such designs: in 1217 he had attempted to place a son from his first marriage in an ecclesiastical preferment. Torrell, *Aquinas's Summa*, 4n22.

5. Torrell, *Aquinas's Summa*, 4; Weisheipl, 10.

6. D. Turner, *Thomas Aquinas: A Portrait* (New Haven, CT: Yale University Press, 2014).

7. F. Avagliano, "Erasmus v. Montecassino," in *Lexikon des Mittelalters*, 10 vols. (Stuttgart: Metzler, [1977]–1999), vol. 3, cols. 2095–96.

8. E. Kantorowicz, *Kaiser Friedrich der Zweite*, vol. 2, *Ergänzungsband* (Berlin: Georg Bondi, 1931), 268.

9. For a classic work on this form of education, see J. Leclercq, *The Love of Learning and the Desire for God: A Study of Monastic Culture* (New York: Fordham University Press, 1982).

10. R. W. Southern, *Scholastic Humanism and the Unification of Europe* (Oxford: Blackwell, 1995).

11. Calo, ch. 3, 1:18. Weisheipl and Torrell both ignore this story, and both habitually discount Calo's contributions. Tugwell allows the possibility of its truth, for Calo—though very much a compiler—does sometimes have insights that were missed in other near-contemporary biographies.

12. For this conception of "youthful maturity," see M. Goodich, "The Childhood and Adolescence of the Saint: Childhood and Adolescence among the Thirteenth-Century Saints," in his Variorum edition: *Lives and Miracles of the Saints: Studies in Medieval Latin Hagiography* (Aldershot, UK: Ashgate/Variorum, 2004).

13. A possibility suggested by C. le Brun-Gouanvic, ed., *Ystoria sancti Thome de Aquino de Guillaume de Tocco (1323)* (Toronto: Pontifical Institute of Mediaeval Studies, 1996), 101n13.

14. For this, see A. Fidora, "Augustine to Aquinas (Latin-Christian Authors)," in *The Oxford Handbook of Aquinas*, ed. B. Davies and E. Stump (Oxford: Oxford University Press, 2014), 51. For Erasmus's influence at Naples, see T. Leccisotti, "Magister Erasmus," *Bullettino dell'Istituto storico italiano* XLVII (1932): 209–315.

15. Weisheipl, 13–14. For a history of the institution, see F. Torraca, *Storia della Università di Napoli* (Napoli: Istituto Italiano per gli Studi Storici, 1993).

16. F. Delle Donne, "Per scientiarum haustum et seminarium doctrinarum: Storia della *Studium* di Napoli in età sveva," *Quaderni del Centro di Studi normanno-svevi* 3 (Bari: Adda, 2010).

17. Weisheipl, 16.

18. For this, see G. Verbeke, "S. Thomas et le stoïcisme," *Miscellanea Medievalia, Berlin* 1 (1962): 48–68, and Verbeke, *The Presence of Stoicism in Medieval Philosophy* (Washington, DC: Catholic University of America Press, 1983).

19. As found in the syllogism (argument): (A) Socrates is a man, (B) all men are mortal, therefore (C) Socrates is mortal.

20. For Peter, see M. Dunne, "Peter of Ireland, the University of Naples and Thomas Aquinas' Early Education," *Yearbook of the Irish Philosophical Society* (2006): 84–96. M. B. Crowe, "Peter of Ireland: Aquinas's Teacher of the Artes Liberales," *Arts Libéraux et Philosophie au Moyen Age* (Paris: 1969). The identification of Peter as Thomas's teacher is disputed by A. Robiglio, but I accept Dunne's counterarguments; from his testimony, Bataillon and Gauthier were also convinced of Peter's Mastership. For the debate, see Porro, 4.

21. Torrell, *Aquinas's Summa*, 8.

22. Tugwell, 203. One of the problems with the reception of Aristotle was that earlier commentators like Proclus had lumped him into a syncretic Neoplatonism. It took a long time and careful work to pry apart this amalgam.

23. For Dominic, see M.- H. Vicaire, *Saint Dominic and His Times*, trans. Kathleen Pond (New York: McGraw-Hill, 1964). This is to be read in conjunction with S. Tugwell's work: *Scripta de*

Notes

Sancto Dominico, ed. S. Tugwell. Monumenta Ordinis Praedicatorum Historica 27 (Rome: Institutum Historicum Ordinis Fratrum Praedicatorum, 1998); as well as his series, "Notes on the Life of St. Dominic," *AFP*, 65–68.

24. Jordan, *Libellus*, 15. Some historians discount this story, but I see no reason to reject it. There was nothing miraculous about the tale; Dominic would have had almost no experience of heresy before his first journey, and the discovery and confrontation in a personal manner would have affected him deeply. While Master Jordan of Saxony may be concentrating several episodes into one, or overstating the speed of the innkeeper's conversion, nonetheless Dominic began to experience heresy, personally, for the first time here, and it changed his life.

25. Stephen of Bourbon, edited in A. Lecoy de la Marche, *Anecdotes historiques, légendes et apologues. Tirés du recueil inédit d'Étienne de Bourbon, dominicain du XIIIe siècle*, Société de l'Histoire de France 185 (Paris, 1877), 83; trans. S. Tugwell, *Early Dominicans*, 89. Though this story comes from a later source (ca. 1260), recent scholarship suggests this as the most likely motivator for Diego.

26. S. Tugwell marks this as the key turning point of the mission of the legates: Simon Tugwell, "Notes on the Life of St. Dominic," *AFP* 73 (2003): 103.

27. Stephen of Bourbon, n. 83 SDL, 16. William of Puylaurens, a secular cleric, spoke in a similar way about the foundation.

28. A. Lappin, "From Osma to Bologna, from Canons to Friars, from the Preaching to the Preachers: The Dominican Path towards Mendicancy," in *The Origin, Development, and Refinement of Medieval Religious Mendicancies*, ed. D. S. Prudlo (Leiden: Brill, 2011), 31–58.

29. On Durandus, see R. Rouse and M. Rouse, "The Schools and the Waldensians: A New Work by Durand of Huesca," in *Christendom and Its Discontents*, ed. S. L. Waugh and P. D. Diehl (New York: Cambridge University Press, 1996), 86–111.

30. Innocent first makes this distinction in his letter to the Humiliati of Milan, "Incumbit nobis," June 7, 1201. Text in *Veterum Humiliatorum Monumenta*, vol. 2, ed. G. Tiraboschi (Milan, 1767), 133–34. This does not imply that the laity stopped all doctrinal preaching, see A. Thompson, *Cities of God: The Religious Life of the*

Italian Communes, 1150–1350 (University Park, PA: Penn State Press, 2005), 88–89.

31. J. Sumption, *The Albigensian Crusade* (London: Faber, 2000). See also L. W. Marvin, *The Occitan War: A Military and Political History of the Albigensian Crusade, 1209–1218* (Cambridge: Cambridge University Press, 2009).

32. Rom 8:18.

33. Matt 16:26.

34. For Francis, see particularly A. Thompson, *Francis of Assisi: A New Biography* (Ithaca, NY: Cornell University Press, 2012).

35. 2 Thess 3:10.

36. For discussions of Dominican constitutional order, see E. Barker, *The Dominican Order and Convocation: A Study of the Growth of Representation in the Church during the Thirteenth Century* (Oxford: Clarendon Press, 1913); G. R. Galbraith, *The Constitution of the Dominican Order: 1216–1360* (New York: Longman's, 1925); D. Knowles, *From Pachomius to Ignatius: A Study in the Constitutional History of the Religious Orders* (Oxford: Clarendon Press, 1966); all with the correctives in the series by S. Tugwell, "The Evolution of Dominican Structures of Government," *AFP* 69–72, 75.

37. The office of Preacher General was one bestowed by the provincial chapter for application within the province itself. See H.C. Scheeben, "Prediger und Generalprediger im Dominikanerorden des 13. Jahrhunderts," *AFP* 31 (1961): 112–41; R. F. Bennett, *The Early Dominicans: Studies in Thirteenth Century Dominican History* (Cambridge: Cambridge University Press, 1937), 80–82, 157–58; G. R. Galbraith, *The Constitution of the Dominican Order: 1216–1360* (New York, 1925), 168–74. For an explanation of the roles and duties of the Preacher General, see Humbert of Romans, "De officiis," in *Opera de Vita Regulari*, ed. J. J. Berthier, 2 vols. (Rome, 1888), 2:32–34, 356, 414.

38. V. J. Koudelka and R. J. Loenertz, eds., *Monumenta Diplomatica S. Dominici* (Domenicano, 1966), 71, 76.

39. Koudelka and Loenertz, *Monumenta Diplomatica*, 77.

40. *Libellus*, 47.

41. For vocations among students and professors, see Hinnebusch, 1:312–17.

42. *VF*, 83. Also recorded in Dominic's canonization proceedings, *Acta canonizationis sancti Dominici*, ed. A. Walz, Monumenta Ordinis Fratrum Praedicatorum Historica 16 (Rome: Institutum Historicum Fratrum Praedicatorum, 1935), 154 (Bologna Process, deposition of Esteban de España, no. 36).

43. For Jordan's particular success among students, see Hinnebusch, 1:314–15.

44. Augustine, *Confessions*, 5.14.

45. Both Chenu and Torrell overemphasize this as a factor in Thomas's conversion. See the place of poverty in the lives of early Dominican saints in my "Mendicancy among the Early Saints of the Begging Orders," in *The Origin, Development, and Refinement of Medieval Religious Mendicancies*, ed. D. S. Prudlo (Boston: Brill, 2011), 85–116.

46. STh, II-II, q. 186, a. 8.

47. Tugwell, 203.

48. See above.

49. The precise date has perplexed historians. Gui, the canonization documents (citing knowledge of John of San Giuliano), and the bull itself say that he entered before the age of puberty. In the Middle Ages, puberty was dated to age fourteen. This would put Thomas in the order almost from the moment he arrived in Naples in 1239. No orders were supposed to profess anyone before the age of eighteen, but this was almost universally ignored at this time. Tocco corrects this to "as a young man," and Tolomeo posits age sixteen. I believe Tugwell is correct when he says the elderly John had confused his acquaintance with Thomas with Thomas's actual date of profession. Tugwell, 204.

50. Mulchahey, 79.

51. Tugwell avoids the question by placing Thomas's profession in 1242 or 1243, a position rejected by most. Torrell doubts that it was Johannes because the fourth version of Tocco includes the information on Agni. Agni was perhaps more famous than Johannes in 1323, and it could be because Tocco simply relies on Neapolitan sources. Gui simply copied Tocco in that instance. In addition, the bold initiative to abscond with the young friar and the stories about his capture put Johannes at the forefront. I am inclined to give new life to Mandonnet's hypothesis and suggest

Thomas's profession at the hands of the Master General himself. Torrell, *Aquinas's Summa*, 8.

52. At that time, given the poverty of the order, various shades, including dark red, were sometimes seen in the habit.

53. A salient criticism of the new orders by secular priests and the old orders was that they took impressionable young men and pressed them into the orders before full maturity. For this see Michael Goodich, *Vita Perfecta: The Ideal of Sainthood in the Thirteenth Century* (Stuttgart: A. Hiersemann, 1982), 94–99.

54. It is also interesting to note that Innocent IV promulgated a bull *requiring* a year's novitiate for the mendicants a month after Thomas's abduction. While the issue had been percolating for a long time, perhaps Thomas's vestition and flight were related. Hinnebusch, 296.

55. Gui, 161–263, ch. 6, follows Tocco, ch. 8, who was a devotee of Dame Theodora and abetted her attempts to sanitize her place in her son's history. Indeed, Tocco presents the unbelievable tale that his mother came storming to Naples to "celebrate" her son's religious profession in the begging friars.

56. Mandonnet suggests that the party was traveling to Perugia, instead of Bologna or Paris, but that makes no sense, either in terms of destination or choice of road: Acquapendente is on the wrong side of Lake Trasimeno to be on the road to Perugia. Not only this, but the papal curia was not in residence there till much later. P. Mandonnet, "Thomas d'Aquin novice prêcheur, 1244–1246," *Revue Thomiste* 8 (1924): 247n1.

57. Historians who adhere to the position that Landolfo was dead are Mandonnet, Walz, and Weisheipl.

58. Torrell came around to this position, following Laurent and Tugwell. See Torrell, *Aquinas's Summa*, 9n40.

59. Some of this has been ably discussed in M. Räsänen, "Family vs. Order: Saint Thomas Aquinas' Dominican Habit in the Narrative Tradition of the Order," in *Identity and Alterity in Hagiography and Cult of Saints (Proceedings of the 2nd Hagiography Conference Organised by Croatian Hagiography Association 'Hagiotheca' Held in Split, 28–31 May 2008)*, ed. A. Marinkovi and T. Vedriš, Bibliotheca Hagiotheca, Series Colloquia, vol. 1 (Zagreb: Hagiotheca, 2010), 201–18. She also aptly comments on the use of this story in the 1250s, when mendicants were accused

of "abducting" impressionable youth and affiliating them to the order. What Gerald de Frachet does is deftly reverse this story. The Dominicans do not violate law and custom; rather, it is the seculars who are doing so in trying to prevent a free religious vocation, p. 209.

60. Gui, 7. Translation my own.

61. The story appears as early as the 1250s in Thomas of Cantimpre. Tocco swears to it at the canonization hearings, saying he heard the story from Robert of Sezze, who heard it from Reginald, Thomas's close associate. It most emphatically did *not* come from the material descended from Theodora. It was incorporated in all Thomas's lives. See the commentary in Tugwell, 206.

62. See André Vauchez, *Sainthood in the Later Middle Ages* (Cambridge: Cambridge University Press, 2005), 356–59.

63. No fewer than eight deponents testified to Thomas's virginity at the Naples inquisition. Tugwell, 206n78.

64. Weisheipl and Torrell argue for Roccasecca. Le Brun-Gouanvic argues in *Ystoria sancti Thome*, 108n22, that he was kept mostly at San Giovanni. Tugwell seems to argue for an extended stay at Montesangiovanni and then at Roccasecca, Tugwell, 205.

65. Gui, 8; Tocco, 11; Calo, 8.

66. There is no formal biography of Johannes Teutonicus (also known as John of Wildeshausen); see D. A. Mortier, *Histoire des maitres généraux de l'ordre des frères Prècheurs*, vol. 1 (Paris: Vrin, 1903).

67. Tocco, 12. Tocco is unrelenting in attempting to rehabilitate Dame Theodora. Why would she have to connive to let Thomas escape from her own castle, when she herself had been responsible for his capture and imprisonment for over a year? Tocco's indebtedness to—and excessive consideration for—the family of Aquino explains this attempt to burnish the image of the matriarch.

68. Turner, *Thomas Aquinas*, 4.

69. H. D. Saffrey, "Un panégyrique inédit de S. Thomas d'Aquin par Josse Clichtove," in *Ordo sapientiae et amoris*, ed. C. -J. Pinto de Oliveira, OP (Fribourg: 1993), 540; cf. Torrell, *Aquinas's Summa*, 17n83.

CHAPTER 3

1. For the controversy, see J.-P. Torrell, *Aquinas's Summa: Background, Structure, and Reception* (Washington, DC: Catholic University of America Press, 2012), 19–20. Even though some scholars favor the idea of a longer stay in Germany, the sojourn in Paris seems secure for several reasons: (1) Paris was the only *studium generale* in the order until 1248, (2) St. Albert was likely in Paris until 1248, (3) the Parisian Masters letter of 1274 suggests that it was there that he received his first formation, and (4) the majority of the biographers agree on Paris, including the very early Gerard de Frachet, with only the really dissenting voice being Tolomeo of Lucca.

2. This story is not found in most of the original biographies but is in the near contemporary Thomas of Cantimpré, *De Apibus* 1. I., cap. xx. Tugwell, 207–8, and Torrell, *Aquinas's Summa*, 14, accept the story as probable. The story is also recounted in Tolomeo of Lucca, *Historia Ecclesiastica Nova*, in *S. Thomae Aquinatis vitae fontes precipuae* (Alba: Edizioni Domenicane, 1968), 23.21. One would not expect this in the Tocco material in any case, as again it reflected poorly on the family. In reality, it was also probably not included because it reflected a bit poorly on Innocent IV as well. The device of allowing Thomas to retain the Preacher's habit as head of a Benedictine house is rather farcical and somewhat offensive to both orders, and indeed rather an insult to Thomas's own vocation and intelligence.

3. *Libellus*, 34.

4. With apologies to Peter Stone and Sherman Edwards, from the lyrics of *1776*.

5. H. Daniel-Rops, *Cathedral and Crusade*, trans. J. Warrington (London: J. M. Dent & Sons, 1963), 331.

6. STh II-II, q. 5, a. 3; Commentary on John, II.21, Lecture 6, 2656.

7. For an excellent assessment of the Bible among the Scholastics, see R. W. Southern's chapter "The Sovereign Textbook of the Schools," in *Scholastic Humanism and the Unification of Europe*, vol. 1 (Oxford: Blackwell, 1994), esp. 102–13.

8. STh I, q. 1, a. 10.

9. A distinction should be made between the "material sufficiency" of Scripture, which would have been embraced by the medievals, and the "formal sufficiency" of the Reformers. The former means that while all divine truth is contained in seed in the Scriptures, it is unfolded and made clear by the authoritative teaching of the church. The latter makes the Bible so plain and clear that no authoritative interpreter is needed. In reality, sharp distinctions between Scripture and tradition were thrown into relief only in the sixteenth century.

10. In recent years, there has been a welcome and renewed interest in Thomas's scriptural theology; one only wishes that the scriptural theology of all the Scholastics had been exposed to such wide-ranging study. See P. Roszak and J. Vijgen, eds., *Reading Sacred Scripture with Thomas Aquinas: Hermeneutical Tools, Theological Questions and New Perspectives* (Turnhout: Brepols, 2015).

11. Two excellent introductions to Hellenic philosophy are A. H. Armstrong, *An Introduction to Ancient Philosophy* (Lanham, MD: Rowman & Littlefield, 1989); and F. C. Copleston, *A History of Philosophy*, vol. 1, *Greece and Rome* (London: Burns, Oates & Washbourne, 1956).

12. A. N. Whitehead, *Process and Reality* (Riverside, NJ: Free Press, 1978), 39.

13. For examples, see the works of Adolf Harnack and Karl Barth, and correctives such as R. L. Wilken's *The Spirit of Early Christian Thought* (New Haven, CT: Yale University Press, 2003); the work of Benedict XVI is also significant here, particularly his *Regensburg Address* of September 12, 2006.

14. F. Nietzsche, *Beyond Good and Evil*, preface.

15. For a perceptive account of this, see P. Brown, *The Body and Society: Men, Women and Sexual Renunciation in Early Christianity* (New York: Columbia University Press, 2008).

16. For Plotinus, see L. P. Gerson, *The Cambridge Companion to Plotinus* (Cambridge: Cambridge University Press, 2006).

17. The best introduction to Augustine is still P. Brown, *Augustine of Hippo*, 45th anniversary edition (Berkeley: University of California Press, 2013).

18. For this, in particular, see R. J. Henle, *Saint Thomas and Platonism: A Study of the Plato and Platonic Texts in the Writings of Saint Thomas* (The Hague: M. Nijhoff, 1956).

19. While many Thomists in the past tried to draw attention to the (real) differences between the two thinkers, in reality Thomas remains profoundly Augustinian, a fact receiving increasing attention. See M. Dauphinais, M. Levering, and B. David, eds., *Aquinas the Augustinian* (Washington, DC: Catholic University of America Press, 2007).

20. Thomas, as we shall see with the *Elements of Theology* of Proclus, was not completely uncritical. He had doubts about the authenticity of Pseudo-Dionysius; see I. Hausherr, "Doutes au sujet de divin Denys," *Orientalia Christiana Periodica* 2 (1936): 484–90.

21. For an introduction, see F. O'Rourke, *Pseudo-Dionysius and the Metaphysics of Aquinas* (Notre Dame, IN: University of Notre Dame Press, 2005).

22. For this, see A. Boureau, "Vitae fratrum, Vitae patrum. L'ordre dominicain et le modèle des pères du désert au XIIIe s," *Mélanges de l'ecole française de Rome: Moyen âge—temps modernes* 99, no. 1 (1987): 79–100; and J. Van Engen, "Dominic and the Brothers: Vita as Life-Forming Exempla in the Order of Preachers," in *Christ among the Medieval Dominicans,* ed. K. Emery Jr. and J. Wawrykow (Notre Dame, IN: Notre Dame University Press, 1993), 7–25. When the Dominicans began to record their own history and tell stories about their holy ones, the *Vitae Patrum* provided the pattern.

23. For Cassian, see C. Stewart, *Cassian the Monk* (New York: Oxford University Press, 1998). John Cassian, *John Cassian, The Conferences,* ed. B. Ramsey (New York: Paulist Press, 1997). Cassian may be more familiar to Thomistic scholars from accusations about his supposed semi-Pelagianism. Such debates are far into the future, postdating Thomas himself by centuries, coming during the *de Auxiliis* controversy around 1600.

24. "Hic liber ad arduam conscientie puritatem, ad multam comtemplationis lucem, ad magnum eum perfectionis apicem gratia suffragante provexit." *Libellus,* 13.

25. Tocco, ch. 22.

26. In his later years he came more into contact with the Greek tradition, we shall examine that below. For the rise of influential Greek theologians in the medieval West, see M. -D. Chenu, *La théologie au douzième siècle* (Paris, 1957), 273–322.

27. While not traditionally counted among the church fathers due to concerns that postdated his death by centuries, Origen was venerated as a saint and a martyr. He was certainly one of the most brilliant thinkers of the early church. Pope Benedict XVI treated him as a church father as well; see his General Audiences of April 25 and May 2, 2007.

28. R. W. Southern, *Scholastic Humanism and the Unification of Europe* (Oxford, UK: Blackwell, 2001).

29. For Anselm, see Southern, *Saint Anselm and His Biographer: A Study of Monastic Life and Thought, 1059–C.1130* (Cambridge: Cambridge University Press, 1966).

30. For an interpretation of this, see S. Kuttner, *Harmony from Dissonance: An Interpretation of Medieval Canon Law* (Latrobe, PA: St. Vincent Archabbey Press, 1960).

31. E. Panofsky, *Gothic Architecture and Scholasticism: An Inquiry into the Analogy of the Arts, Philosophy, and Religion in the Middle Ages* (New York: Plume, 1974).

32. An excellent overall history is A. Hourani, *A History of the Arab Peoples* (London: Faber and Faber, 2013).

33. Cf. Hourani, *A History of the Arab Peoples*, 76.

34. Torrell, *Aquinas's Summa*, 192n55.

35. G. Hasselhoff, "Maimonides in the Latin Middle Ages: An Introductory Survey," *Jewish Studies Quarterly* 9, no. 1 (2002): 1–20.

36. A rationalist tradition was, however, kept alive among the Shi'a of Persia, but it had little effect on the Sunni majority until the twentieth century.

37. David Burrell comments that Western Christendom was more familiar with Islamic and Jewish philosophy at this period than Muslims and Jews themselves. D. Burrell, "Aquinas and Islamic and Jewish Thinkers," in *The Cambridge Companion to Aquinas*, ed. Norman Kretzmann and Eleonore Stump (Cambridge: Cambridge University Press, 2009), 61.

38. Peter Lombard was key to the mediation of Augustine to the Scholastic world; Josef Pieper called the *Sentences* an "Augustinian breviary," with over one thousand texts taken from the Latin theologian. Josef Pieper, *Scholasticism: Personalities and Problems of Medieval Philosophy* (South Bend, IN: St. Augustine's Press, 2001), 98.

39. Porro, 27. It is possible that it was Alexander who subdivided it into the four familiar divisions.

40. Indeed, it was not until the 1313 General Chapter at Metz that it was first permissible to comment on Thomas's *Summa* alongside the *Sentences*. L. Boyle, "The Setting of the Summa Theologiae," in *Aquinas's Summa Theologiae: Critical Essays*, ed. Brian Davies (Lanham, MD: Rowman & Littlefield, 2005), 17. The *Sentences* was so universal that it was studied far beyond *studia generalia* and the universities: Mulchahey, xii.

41. Mulchahey, 47; Torrell, *Aquinas's Summa*, 40–41.

42. Mulchahey, 39–46.

43. Mulchahey, 54.

44. For Moneta, see Moneta of Cremona, *Adversus Catharos et Valdenses libri quinque*, ed. T. Ricchini (Rome, 1743). I am currently editing Peter of Verona's *Summa*, which will appear in the Oxford Medium Aevum series.

45. Remarkably little work has been done on this axial figure. For an introduction, see *Hugues de Saint-Cher († 1263), bibliste et théologien*, ed. L. -J. Bataillon, G. Dahan, and P. -M. Gy, Centre d'études du Saulchoir, Actes du colloque 13–15 mars 2000 (Brepols: Turnhout, 2004).

46. Mulchahey, 530–32. For Paul, see M. Johnson. "La 'Summa de poenitentia' attribuita a Paolo Ungaro," in *L'origine dell'Ordine dei Predicatori e l'Università di Bologna*, Collana "Philosophia" 32, ed. Giovanni Bertuzzi, OP (Bologna: Edizioni Studio Domenicano, 2006), 136–45.

47. C. Ames, *Righteous Persecution: Inquisition, Dominicans, and Christianity in the Middle Ages* (Philadelphia: University of Pennsylvania Press, 2013), esp. ch. 4.

48. Torrell, *Aquinas's Summa*, 18–24.

49. For Albert's biography, see Tugwell, 3–39.

50. Cf. Weisheipl, 41.

51. For the medieval origins of science, see D. C. Lindberg, *The Beginnings of Western Science: The European Scientific Tradition in Philosophical, Religious, and Institutional Context, 600 B.C. to A.D. 1450* (Chicago: University of Chicago Press, 1994).

52. Though indeed, given recent research, Albert may be one of the theologians who actually *constructed* a fallacious reading of Averroes in this case. Torrell, *Aquinas's Summa*, 192–93.

53. Tugwell, 208.

54. Torrell, *Aquinas's Summa*, 24.

55. The friars also set up *studia* in England, Provence, and Lombardy, a clear indicator of the growth of studies in the order. *Acta*, 1248 Paris, 41.

56. Rashdall, 6.

57. From estimates by Gauthier, see Torrell, *Aquinas's Summa*, 25n29.

58. Tocco, 13, Gui, 9.

59. Tocco, 12.

60. Tugwell, 209.

61. Torrell, *Aquinas's Summa*, 29. See also J. -P. Torrell and D. Bouthillier, "Quand saint Thomas méditait sur le prophète Isaïe," *Revue Thomiste* 90 (1990): 5–47.

62. Torrell, *Aquinas's Summa*, 28–29n42.

63. P.-M. Gils, "S. Thomas écrivain," Leonine Edition, vol. 50:175–209.

64. Torrell, *Aquinas's Summa*, 94–95.

65. Tugwell, 11.

66. Tugwell, 210; Torrell, *Aquinas's Summa*, 349.

67. Tugwell, 212.

68. Pieper, *Scholasticism*, 23.

CHAPTER 4

1. M.-D. Chenu, *Aquinas and His Role in Theology* (Collegeville, MN: Liturgical Press, 2002), 18.

2. Rashdall, 1:xxxv.

3. For the events of Lent 1229, see Rashdall, 1:334–36.

4. "Hiis si quidem tribus, scilicet sacerdotio imperio et studio, tanquam tribus virtutibus, videlicet vitali naturali et animali, sancta ecclesia katholica spiritualiter vivificatur augmentatur et regitur. Hiis etiam tribus, tanquam fundamento pariete et tecto, eadem ecclesia quasi materialiter perficitur." Jordan of Osnabrück, *De prerogativa Romani Imperii*, see I. 2 n1.

5. Jordan, *De prerogativa*, I. 5–7.

6. Jordan, *De prerogativa*, I. 306.

7. C. Guyon, *Les Écoliers du Christ: l'ordre canonial du Val des Écoliers, 1201–1539* (Saint-Étienne: CERCOR, 1998).

8. Guyon, *Les Écoliers du Christ*, I. 317.

9. Chart., 1:79. [April 13, 1231].

10. For an overview of this process, see A. Maurer, *Medieval Philosophy* (Toronto: Pontifical Inst. of Medieval Studies, 1982), 86–87. For a detailed treatment, see F. Van Steenberghen, *Aristotle in the West: The Origins of Latin Aristotelianism*, 2nd ed. (Louvain: Nauwelaerts, 1970).

11. R. McInerny, *Saint Thomas Aquinas* (Boston: Twayne Publishers, 1977), 32.

12. McInerny, *Saint Thomas Aquinas*, 33.

13. Maurer, *Medieval Philosophy*, 89.

14. Rashdall, 357.

15. Mulchahey, 55–56.

16. E.g., see the use of Aristotle in the *Summa Contra Hereticos* of Peter of Verona, ca. 1235–38. Peter cites passages from *Metaphysics, Physics, On Generation and Corruption, Meteorology, De Anima, De Generatione Animalium, De Caelo et Mundo,* and *De Causis* (actually by Proclus, but attributed to Aristotle at the time).

17. Rashdall, 358.

18. Acta Cap. Gen. I. 1 (Bologna, 1220).

19. Rashdall, 1:372, esp. n3. Chart. I, n42.

20. Formerly these two Johns were confused with one person; see E. T. Brett, *Humbert of Romans: His Life and Views of Thirteenth-Century Society* (Toronto: Pontifical Institute for Medieval Studies, 2000), 11.

21. For this, see the essays in C. Muessing, ed., *Preacher, Sermon, and Audience in the Middle Ages* (Leiden: Brill, 2002). For the power of charismatic preaching in the early 1200s, see A. Thompson, *Revival Preachers and Politics in Thirteenth-Century Italy: The Great Devotion of 1233* (Oxford: Clarendon, 1992).

22. For consideration of these points, see Humbert of Romans, S. Tugwell, ed., *Humberti de Romanis Legendae Sancti Dominici* (Rome: Institutum Historicum Ordinis Fratrum Praedicatorum, 2008), 14–17.

23. While an exceptionally partial source, Matthew Paris, the Benedictine chronicler, gives a representative sampling of complaints

against the early Dominicans: arrogance, extravagance in building, perpetual conflict with Minorites, extortionate behavior at
the bedsides of the dying, unbecoming activities in confession of
women, and agitations at Paris. Tugwell collects these references,
Humberti de Romanis, 14. Each probably had some justification
behind it; similar claims surface in the miracle stories of Dominican saints. See D. Prudlo, *The Martyred Inquisitor: The Life and Cult
of Peter of Verona* (Aldershot, UK: Ashgate, 2008), 165–67.

24. Hinnebusch, 2:36–39.

25. The story is taken from the English Dominican Nicholas
Trivet, *Annales sex regum Angliae, 1135–1307*, ed. T. Hogg (London, 1845).

26. Hinnebusch, 2:39. Mulchahey, xiii.

27. For Francis's attitudes to intellectual labor, see A. Thompson, *Francis of Assisi: A New Biography* (Ithaca, NY: Cornell University Press, 2012), 106–12.

28. L. Boyle, "The Setting of the Summa Theologiae," in
Aquinas's Summa Theologiae: Critical Essays, ed. Brian Davies
(Lanham, MD: Rowman & Littlefield, 2005), 3, citing Humbert of
Romans.

29. Brett, *Humbert of Romans*, 14.

30. "In scientia et vita," Tocco repeats the passage verbatim in
his life, Tocco, 14. "Nullus recipiatur parisius ad lectiones sollemp-
nes vel ad predicationis, nisi probate vite fuerit et scientie" *Chart.*
1. 79, n20, cf. Porro, 26.

31. See Tugwell, 211n130, and Torrell, 26 for the controversy.

32. Rashdall, 1:450.

33. W. J. Hankey, *God in Himself: Aquinas' Doctrine of God as
Expounded in the Summa Theologiae* (Oxford: Oxford University
Press, 2004), 22.

34. It was Chenu who really drew attention to these patterns
in Thomas's thought. M. -D. Chenu, *Toward Understanding Saint
Thomas*, trans. A. -M. Landry and D. Hughes (Chicago: Henry
Regnery, 1964), 297–322.

35. Porro, 28.

36. Chenu, *Toward Understanding Saint Thomas*, 273.

37. Porro, 51.

38. For an attempt at providing the outline of a definition of *Thomism*, see R. Cessario, *A Short History of Thomism* (Washington, DC: The Catholic University of America Press, 2005), 22.

39. For the classic study on Avicenna in St. Thomas, see C. Vansteenkiste, "Avicenna citaten bij S. Thomas," *Tijdschrift voor Filosofie* 15 (1953): 437–507.

40. Porro, 12.

41. Tugwell, 212.

42. Rashdall, 1:376.

43. Rashdall, 1:377–91.

44. Thomas Cantimpré, *Miraculorum et exemplorum memorabilium sui temporis. Libri duo* (Douai, 1597), 573. Cf. D. Mortier, *Histoire des maîtres généraux de l'Ordre des frères prêcheurs*, 8 vols. (Paris: A. Picard, 1902–1920), 2:330.

45. *Chart.* I. no. 230.

46. Tocco, 35, 43.

47. For this see, M. -M. Dufeil, "Le roi Louis dans la querelle des mendiants et séculiers," in *Septième centenaire de la mort de saint Louis: actes des colloques de Royaumont et de Paris, 21–27 mai 1970* (Paris: Belles Lettres, 1976).

48. For William in particular, see Dufeil, *Guillaume De Saint-Amour et la Polémique Universitaire Parisienne, 1250–1259* (Paris: A. et J. Picard, 1972).

49. There was a persistent tradition that a Dominican had been responsible for it. See A. Traver, "The Forging of an Intellectual Defense of Mendicancy in the Medieval University," in *The Origin, Development, and Refinement of Medieval Religious Mendicancies*, ed. D. Prudlo (Leiden: Brill, 2011), 161n23.

50. C. H. Lawrence, *Friars: The Impact of the Mendicant Orders on Medieval Society* (London: I.B. Tauris & Company, Limited, 2013), 155.

51. E. T. Brett, *Humbert of Romans: His Life and Views of Thirteenth-Century Society* (Toronto: Pontifical Institute of Medieval Studies, 1984), 20–24.

52. *Chart.* I. no. 240, 267–70.

53. "Tunc dicere ceperunt cardinales et prelati: – Cavete a letaniis fratrum predicatorum." The earliest witness for this story is the early fourteenth-century Milanese Dominican chronicler

Galvano Fiamma; see G. Odetto, "La cronica maggiore dell'ordine domenicano di Galvano Fiamma," *AFP* 10, no. 69 (1950): 41.

54. Brett, *Humbert of Romans*, 24–26.

55. Mortier was convinced that Humbert had no knowledge of this, but Brett argues that he did and made this conciliation as the best deal he could get. I do disagree with Brett, who says that *Quasi* was simply a defense of papal prerogative. It was certainly that, but also betrayed a significant affection for the friars. Brett, *Humbert of Romans*, 35.

56. P. Szittya, *The Antifraternal Tradition in Medieval Literature* (Princeton, NJ: Princeton University Press, 1986).

57. Porro, 56.

58. [Encyclical of John of Parma and Humbert of Romans, 1255]. B. M. Reichert, ed., *Litterae encyclicae magistrorum generalium Ordinis praedicatorum ab anno 1233 usque ad annum 1376*, MOPH 5 (Rome: Typographia polyglotta S.C. de propaganda fide, 1900), 25–31.

59. [Letter of Humbert of Romans to convent at Orleans, 1256], in Reichert, *Litterae encyclicae magistrorum generalium*, 31–38; [Encyclical of Humbert of Romans to the Dominican Order, 1256], 43–46.

60. *Chart.*, 1. 317–19.

61. William of Saint-Amour, *De periculis novissimorum temporum*, ed. and trans. Guy Geltner (Paris: Peeters, 2008).

62. Though "Doctor" was generally used mostly in Law faculties. Rashdall, 19. The use of "Doctor" for physician only came into general use in the early modern period. It is primarily an academic title related to the Latin *Docere*—to teach.

63. Torrell, 50.

64. Tocco, 16; Naples, 64.

65. Weisheipl, 94.

66. *Contra Impugnantes Dei cultum et Religionem*. In *An Apology for the Religious Orders*, trans. J. Procter (London: Sands, 1902), 73–74.

67. This is one of the most popular and enduring scenes in Thomas's hagiography. Many Dominicans attributed the vision to St. Dominic himself, but this is not found in the sources. Tocco, 16; Gui, 12; Calo, 10; Naples, 49, 50, 92; *VF* 4.24.

68. Three different traditions of sources confirm the story, including the *Vitas Fratrum*, which would have been in circulation within three years of the vision; see Foster, 69n33.

69. Rashdall, 285–87.

70. Rashdall, 285.

71. STh, 1.1.8.

72. Quodlibet IV, q. 9, a. 3, translation my own.

73. Torrell, 54n2.

74. Weisheipl, 110.

75. STh 1.1.10 ad 1.

76. Weisheipl, 117–18.

77. Chenu, 133.

78. See the excellent discussion in Torrell, 59–67, 334–35.

79. Porro, 89. For the quodlibet tradition in particular, see J. Wippel. "Quodlibetal Questions, Chiefly in Theology Faculties," *Les questions disputées et les questions quodlibétiques dans les Facultés de théologie, de droit et de médecine*, ed. Bernardo C. Bazàn (Turnhout: Brepols, 1985); J. Hamesse, "Theological Quaestiones Quodlibetales," in *Theological Quodlibeta in the Middle Ages: The Thirteenth Century*, ed. C. D. Schabel, Brill's Companions to the Christian Tradition 1 (Leiden: Brill, 2006).

80. See the table in Torrell, 211.

81. For an analysis of this debate, see D. Prudlo, *Certain Sainthood: Canonization and the Origins of Papal Infallibility in the Medieval Church* (Ithaca, NY: Cornell University Press, 2015). This includes the translation of Quod. IX, q. 8.

82. Torrell, 107–8.

83. Naples, 66.

84. Torrell, 101. This was discovered by Gauthier.

85. The text is Vat. Lat. 9850, exhaustively commented on in R.-A. Gauthier, *Introduction à Saint Thomas d'Aquin*, Somme contre les Gentils (Paris: Éditions Universitaires, 1993).

86. [Encyclical letter of Humbert of Romans, 1256]. Reichert, *Litterae encyclicae magistrorum generalium*, 38–42.

87. In order to trace the different interpretations of the work's purpose, see Torrell, 104–7. For the work, see especially B. Davies, *Thomas Aquinas's Summa Contra Gentiles: A Guide and Commentary* (Oxford: Oxford University Press, 2016).

88. Walz and Foster inexplicably place this event in his second regency, 1269–72. This makes no sense, as he clearly has both the *Homilies* of John Chrysostom, and the pseudo-Johannine *Opus Imperfectum in Mattheum* for his Parisian commentary on Matthew, as well as his *Catena Aurea* written a few years later. The absence of miraculous imagery, the quotidian nature of the details (in spite of the hagiographers' labored efforts to turn it into a story of love of poverty), and its presence in all the biographies make it clear that not only is the story historical, but it dates from the middle of his first Regency, probably around 1257. This was after the quarrel with the seculars had died down, and before he had begun his lectures on Matthew.

CHAPTER 5

1. Hinnebusch corrects Mandonnet's numbers, 1:331. Hinnebusch estimates three thousand lay brothers, but A. Thompson corrects this down to two thousand.

2. For this, see D. Burr, *The Spiritual Franciscans: From Protest to Persecution in the Century after Saint Francis* (University Park: Pennsylvania State University Press, 2003).

3. This was a result of the composition and distribution of Gérard de Frachet's *Vitas Fratrum* (*VF*), a history of the order compiled and released in 1260. An older translation of the *Vitas Fratrum* is Gérard de Frachet, *Lives of the Brethren of the Order of Preachers: 1206–1259*, trans. Placid Conway, OP (London: 1924). See also Simon Tugwell, "L'Evolution des *Vitae Fratrum*," *Cahiers de Fanjeaux* 36 (2001).

4. This is the opinion of M. -H. Laurent, *Le bienheureux Innocent V (Pierre de Tarentaise) et son temps*, Studi e testi 129 (Vatican City, 1947), 46–51.

5. The critical work for Dominican education is Mulchahey.

6. The 1228 chapter was quite important, for it was a "Generalissimum" chapter, a "Most General Chapter." This was a special kind of chapter in which the legislation was immediately effective, without the necessity for approval by two subsequent chapters. It was intended to be extraordinary, and it is a testimony to the

strength of the Dominican constitution that only two were ever necessary. Hinnebusch, 1:179.

7. Hinnebusch, 1:55–60.

8. Albert the Great, "Commentarii in epistolas B. Dionysii areopagiticae," *Opera Omnia*, ed. A. Borgnet (Paris: Vives, 1890–1895), 14:910. Cf. Porro, 120. Mulchahey speculates that the first of these references could have been directed against William of Saint Amour, however the second seems definitely directed at his own brethren. Mulchahey, 225n127 and 226n128.

9. *Acta Cap. Gen.* 1. 26 (Paris, 1243). This repeats the admonishment on students from the Dominican constitutions (de studentibus, c. 14) that they were not to study the works of the pagans and philosophers. They might briefly consult them, but they were not permitted formally to study the Arts.

10. *Acta Cap. Gen.* 1. 29 (Bologna, 1244).

11. Mulchahey, 234.

12. *Acta Cap. Gen.* 1. 41 (Paris, 1248).

13. The chapter also saw the establishment of one of Humbert's most prescient schemes: the study of languages for the purposes of evangelization and apologetics. A *studium* for Arabic was to be set up in Barcelona. Humbert had consistently called for Greek and Hebrew study as well.

14. While the professed friars never did the sort of heavy manual labor associated with the monastic orders, they did perform household work, such as porter, infirmarian, cellarer, and cook, which probably became transferred to the lay brethren. I thank A. Thompson for this observation.

15. All the legislation called for by the Commission of the Five Masters is in *Acta Cap. Gen.* 1. 98–100 (Valenciennes, 1259).

16. Even otherwise exacting historians have fallen into this fallacy, such as Weisheipl and Hinnebusch; even Torrell does not completely free himself from it.

17. Porro, 120.

18. Mulchahey, 222–30.

19. Mulchahey especially sees 1259 and the origin of a three-tiered Scholastic system for the order: priory schools to teach the normal brethren basic theology, province-wide intermediate schools in logic to introduce natural philosophy to advanced students, and

a fully developed Arts course designed for the elite at the *studia generalia* of the order. Mulchahey, 232–33.

20. An epitaph to Peter, "Praeco Lucerna" is attributed to Thomas, but was most likely not by him.

21. Tugwell, 211.

22. See the discussion in Torrell, 99.

23. Torrell, 101–4.

24. *Fontes*, 582.

25. Torrell admits "he was not a master of this art." See his "La pratique pastorale dún théologien du XIIIe siècle. Thomas d'Aquin prédicateur," *Revue Thomiste* 82 (1982): 213–45.

26. For comparisons and descriptions of the different styles, see Mulchahey, 403; also A. Thompson, *Revival Preachers and Politics in Thirteenth-Century Italy: The Great Devotion of 1233* (Oxford: Clarendon Press, 1992), 17–24.

27. H.C. Scheeben, "Prediger und Generalprediger im Dominikanerorden des 13. Jahrhunderts," *AFP* 31 (1961): 112–41. Also see G. R. Galbraith, *The Constitution of the Dominican Order: 1216–1360* (New York, 1925), 168–74. For an explanation of the roles and duties of the Preacher General, see Humbert of Romans, "De officiis," in *Opera de Vita Regulari*, ed. J. J. Berthier, 2 vols. (Rome, 1888), 2:356, 414.

28. Indeed, there was a movement seriously to curtail or even abolish the office in 1255 and 1256, but it came to nothing, See R. F. Bennett, *The Early Dominicans: Studies in Thirteenth-Century Dominican History* (Cambridge: Cambridge University Press, 1937), 157.

29. Hinnebusch, 1:185.

30. Tugwell, 306nn131–32. Some of the proposed dates are 1259, 1260, and 1265, with the last being certainly too late.

31. Hinnebusch, 1:339.

32. Most scholars, including Le Goff and Lawrence, follow the traditional ascription of urbanity to the Friars; however there have been some more recent challenges. See E. Gustafson, "How Urban Was Urban for the Mendicants in Tuscany?," in *Medieval Urban Planning: The Monastery and beyond*, ed. M. Abel (Newcastle upon Tyne: Cambridge Scholars Publishing, 2017), 148–73. His conclusion shows that Franciscans also founded many rural or

suburban priories, but the traditional model of Dominican urban-ism remains.

33. For this, see D. Prudlo, "Monastic Prescriptions in the Mendicant Rules: An Examination of Hagiographical Exemplar-ity," in *Shaping Stability: The Normation and Formation of Religious Life in the Middle Ages*, ed. Krijn Pansters (Turnhout: Brepols, 2016).

34. *Primitive Constitutions*, 1.4, in *Dominic: Biographical Documents*, ed. Francis C. Lehner, OP (Washington, DC: Thomist Press, 1964), 216.

35. Jordan of Saxony instituted the singing of the *Salve*, and the practice quickly spread. *Libellus*, 120. The procession was cer-tainly in place by the time of Humbert's *Ordo* in 1256.

36. Tocco, 29, Gui, 26. This episode comes from Thomas's sojourn in Naples 1272–74.

37. *Completorii libellus juxta ritum S. Ordinis Praedicatorum* (Romae: S. Sabinae, 1949), 51–52. This episode comes from the end of Thomas's career, from the antiphon "In the midst of life we are in death." Thomas may have sensed the approaching conclu-sion of his own life and became particularly moved by the chant.

38. These occur in the context of two stories of him levitat-ing in prayer, Gui, 23; Tocco, 33, 34; Calo, 17, 18.

39. Hinnebusch, 1:352.

40. Naples, testimony of Bartholomew of Capua, *Fontes*, 376–77.

41. Tocco adds the detail that there were many knights at the Mass, one Gui omits. Tocco, 29, Gui, 26.

42. For the Dominican Rite, see W. M. Bonniwell. *A History of the Dominican Liturgy, 1215–1945* (New York: Joseph F. Wag-ner, 1945). Another notable difference in the Dominican Low Mass was the preparation of the chalice at the beginning of the rite. A mention should also be made of the wonderful resources and studies compiled recently by A. Thompson, OP, who is a mar-velous custodian of the uses of the Order.

43. Thomas's thought was deeply informed by the liturgy; see L. G. Walsh, "Liturgy in the Theology of St. Thomas," *Thomist* 38 (1974): 557–83.

44. Hinnebusch, 1:346.

45. Tocco, 36; Gui, 33; Calo, 19.

46. Tocco, 63; Gui, 41.

47. Tocco, 56; Gui, 37; Calo, 27; Naples, 2, 9, 50.

48. Gui, 15.

49. Tocco, 17; Gui, 32.

50. Tocco, 50; Gui, 18.

51. Tocco, 21; Gui, 15; Calo, 13.

52. Tocco, 42; Gui, 24; Calo, 33.

53. Tocco, 39; Gui, 32; Calo, 21.

54. Tocco, 15; Gui, 31; Calo, 15.

55. Tocco, 43; Gui, 25; Calo, 24.

56. Tocco, 29; Gui, 15; Calo, 16.

57. Tocco, 51; Gui, 17; Calo, 26.

58. Tocco, 47; Gui, 28; Calo, 24.

59. Tocco, 47; Gui, 28; Calo, 24. For issues concerning sickness and bloodletting, see A. Montford, *Health, Sickness, Medicine and the Friars in the Thirteenth and Fourteenth Centuries* (Aldershot, UK: Ashgate, 2004).

60. For these brethren, see A. Thompson, *Dominican Brothers: Conversi, Lay, and Cooperator Friars* (Chicago: New Priory Press, 2017).

61. Hinnebusch, 2:196.

62. Bennett, *The Early Dominicans*, 63. A glance at the four volumes of the *Scriptores Ordinis Praedicatorum* demonstrates how truly broad and deep was Dominican learning of the first centuries of the order.

63. Hinnebusch, 1:341.

64. For the habit, see Hinnebusch, 1:340–43; supplemented by S. Tugwell, *Bernardi Guidonis Scripta De Sancto Dominico*, Corpus Hagiographicum Sancti Dominici (Romae: Institutum historicum ordinis fratrum praedicatorum, 1998), 209ff.

65. It appears the modern town of Bolsena, though derived from the old "Volsinii," was only settled by the Romans. While scholars are in dispute about where the original Volsinii actually was, the strongest candidate is Orvieto.

66. The convent was one of the first dedicated to *Saint* Dominic. This means that the foundation happened in or after 1234, the year of his canonization.

67. For Constantine, see T. Kaeppeli, *Scriptores ordinis Praedicatorum*, 1:292–94.

68. For a study of Orvieto in this period, see C. Lansing, *Power and Purity: Cathar Heresy in Medieval Italy* (Oxford: Oxford University Press, 2001).

69. Hugh did however return to his traditional title, Cardinal of Santa Sabina, probably during 1262.

70. C. Lansing, *Power and Purity*, 161.

71. For the relic and the feast, see I. Levy, I. Christopher, G. Macy, and K. Van Ausdall, eds., *A Companion to the Eucharist in the Middle Ages* (Leiden: Brill, 2012); G. Freni. "The Reliquary of the Holy Corporal in the Cathedral of Orvieto: Patronage and Politics," in *Art, Politics, and Civic Religion in Central Italy, 1261–1352: Essays by Postgraduate Students at the Courtauld Institute of Art*, ed. J. Cannon and B. Williamson (Milton: Taylor and Francis, 2017); and M. Rubin, *Corpus Christi: The Eucharist in Late Medieval Culture* (Cambridge: Cambridge University Press, 1991).

72. The phrase that became used later in the 1200s was *Lector Romanae Curiae*, but that did not indicate direct attachment to the curia, but merely being a Lector in a religious house where the curia then was in attendance. In only that sense was Thomas a *Lector Romanae Curiae*; E. Panella, "Il 'lector romanae curiae' nelle cronache conventuali domenicane del XIII-XIV secolo," *Comité international du vocabulaire des institutions et de la communication intellectuelles au moyen âge* 5 (1992): 130–39. Compare Mulcahey, 291.

73. This discussion went on for a very long time among the Dominicans largely because of interorder jealousies of the early modern period, during which each order claimed historically implausible titles and privileges. The most famous of these is the extreme efforts of the Carmelite order to claim the prophet Elijah as their founder. For a thorough examination of the issue, see Weisheipl, 153–63.

74. Torrell, 120.

75. See the new translation of this work in Thomas Aquinas, *Commentary on the Book of Job*, trans. Brian Mullady, OP (Lander, WY: Aquinas Institute for the Study of Sacred Doctrine, 2016).

76. Thomas only preached in Latin and his native tongue and was dependent on others for translations of texts. William of Tocco testifies that Thomas was unable to learn any other language because of his "abstraction." Tocco, 48; Gui, 29; Calo, 24.

Notes

77. South Italy had been part of Magna Graecia in ancient times and was heavily colonized by the Greeks. A large population of Greek speakers, who celebrated the Greek rites, lived there. Indeed even today there are Greek-Catholic communities there that continue to testify to the long duration of Greek settlement in Italy.

78. Weisheipl, 169–70.

79. "Duo evangelia glossanda dimiserit, sed excusans se [Bonaventure] propter officium, quod habebat, quia Magister generalis erat, Doctor sanctus Frater Thomas supplevit." Lucca, *Historia Ecclesiastica Nova*, in *S. Thomae Aquinatis vitae fontes precipuae* (Alba: Edizioni Domenicane, 1968), 22.24.

80. Weisheipl, 173.

81. C. Spicq, *Esquisse d'une histoire de l'exégèse latine au Moyen Age* (Paris: Vrin, 1944), 307; compare Torrell, 137.

82. For the feast and its devotion, see M. Rubin, *Corpus Christi: The Eucharist in Late Medieval Culture* (Cambridge: Cambridge University Press, 1991).

83. Lansing, *Power and Purity*, 162.

84. Lansing, *Power and Purity*, 164–65.

85. For this work, see J. Polc, "Il miracolo di Bolsena e Pietro de Praga: Un'ipotesi," *Rivista di storia della chiesa in Italia* 45, no. 2 (1991): 437–49.

86. Tocco, 52; Gui, 24. It is possible that this story is merely a conflation of different quodlibetal questions settled by Thomas, meant to underscore Thomas's authority in the schools.

87. J. Le Goff, *Saint Louis*, trans. G. E. Gollrad (Notre Dame, IN: University of Notre Dame Press, 2009), 626.

88. This gesture had been gaining popularity since the late 1100s, due to the confluence of several factors: the increasing precision regarding the moment of transubstantiation, the eagerness of the faithful to see the sacrament, and the desire to have a liturgical exclamation point against antisacramental heretics, Rubin, *Corpus Christi*, 55.

89. Tocco, 29; Gui, 15; Calo, 16.

90. This story is not recorded in the canonization hearings, and is only included in Tocco's later revisions; however, Tocco is careful to give its provenance, declaring that he heard it personally from a Brother Martin of San Maximin, whose veracity he says is

unquestionable, in addition to many other brothers who witnessed the same thing. It is possible that this story was not reported since no canonization proceedings were held in France. Tocco, 52; Gui, 24. It is also possible that this story was a doublet, repeating a previous story where Thomas had a vision in the chapel of Saint Nicholas in Naples. See Torrell, 284–86.

91. Weisheipl, 180–85.

92. The Franciscans often did the same thing. As Thomas was known as the "Angelic Doctor," the Franciscans intimated that meant that he was represented by the lowest order of angels in the Dionysian hierarchy, perhaps because of Thomas's earthy Aristotelianism. Bonaventure thereafter became known as the "Seraphic" doctor, giving him the name of the highest category of angels. Indeed, the best biography we currently have of Bonaventure, which is included in the Quaracchi edition of his works, remarks that we know nothing of Bonaventure during the period of the composition of the office. "Ab anno 1263 usque ad annum 1265 sequitur hiatus in gestis S. Bonaventurae, cum desnint documenta certa," in *Doctoris seraphici S. Bonaventurae opera omnia*, 10 vols., ed. The Fathers of the Collegii S. Bonaventura (Florence: Quaracchi, 1882–1902), 10:56. The historical precis does not even mention the Corpus Christi story; it is a Dominican invention.

93. See the discussion in Weisheipl, 180–85; and Torrell, 129–36. The definitive study is P.-M. Gy, "L'Office du Corpus Christi, oeuvre de S. Thomas d'Aquin," in *La liturgie dans l'histoire* (Paris: Cerf, 1993), 223–45.

94. Vincenzo di Bartholomaeis, *Laude drammatiche e rappresentazioni sacre* (Florence, 1943), 1:368–81. Cf. Lansing, *Power and Purity*, 165.

95. It is perhaps for this reason that one sonnet in Italian was attributed to him, and a handful of other Latin poems, but it is unlikely that he wrote any of them.

96. The story is repeated in all the sources, Tocco, 42; Gui, 34; Calo, 23; Tolomeo, *Historia Ecclesiastica Nova*, 22.39.

97. Mulchahey, 233.

98. This is the conclusion of L. Boyle, "The Setting of the Summa Theologiae," in *Aquinas's Summa Theologiae: Critical Essays*, ed. Brian Davies (Lanham, MD: Rowman & Littlefield, 2005), 1–24.

99. J. Pieper, *Scholasticism: Personalities and Problems of Medieval Philosophy* (South Bend, IN: St. Augustine's Press, 2001).

100. See Boyle, "The Setting of the *Summa Theologiae*," and Mulchahey, 277–306.

101. Ptolemy, 23.15. First noted in H. -F. Dondaine, *"Alia lectura fratris Thome? (Super I. Sent.),"* *Medieval Studies* 42 (1980): 308–36, and confirmed in Boyle, "The Setting of the *Summa Theologiae*," 11–14.

102. Torrell, 146.

103. The foundational study is R. J. Henle, *Saint Thomas and Platonism* (The Hague: Martinus Nijhoff, 1956). Increased attention to Thomas's Platonism has been slow, but steadily building.

104. Mulchahey, 292.

105. Prudlo, *The Martyred Inquisitor*, 142–43.

106. Foster, 74n70.

107. *Commentary on Hebrews*, Lect. 3; cf. Foster, 74n68.

108. Tocco, 48; Calo, 24; Gui, 29; Naples, 75.

109. Torrell, 180.

CHAPTER 6

1. This finds support in a record of Thomas performing a miracle at sea, Tocco, 38, 321.

2. See the summary in Torrell, 178–80.

3. J. Pieper, *The Silence of St. Thomas: Three Essays* (South Bend, IN: St. Augustine's Press, 1999), 15.

4. Hesiod, *Theogony*, 319.

5. L. Elders, "Les citations de saint Augustin dans la *Somme Théologique* de saint Thomas d'Aquin," *Doctor Communis* 40 (1987): 115–67.

6. Porro, 245.

7. Marie-Dominique Chenu, *Aquinas and His Role in Theology* (Collegeville, MN: Liturgical Press, 2002), 112.

8. R. Weaver, *Ideas Have Consequences* (Chicago: University of Chicago Press, 2013 [1948]).

9. Torrell summarizes the reasons well, 182–84. Mandonnet and many non-Dominicans assume it was to face the Averroists,

but since Weisheipl there has been a consensus that the Seculars were the primary reason.

10. Rashdall, 1:391.

11. Weisheipl, 264.

12. Porro, 116.

13. Porro, 242.

14. The best introductions for this period of conflict are U. Horst, *Evangelische Armut und Kirche: Thomas von Aquin und die Armutskontroversen des 13. und beginnenden 14. Jahrhunderts* (Berlin: Akademie Verlag, 1992); and A. Traver, "The Forging of an Intellectual Defense of Mendicancy in the Medieval University," in *The Origin, Development, and Refinement of Medieval Religious Mendicancies*, ed. D. Prudlo (Leiden: Brill, 2011).

15. For Gerard, see Torrell, 84n41.

16. Later authors have established to my satisfaction that Thomas was in Paris from the fall of 1268, Torrell 179–82, against Weisheipl, 266.

17. Torrell, 240–41.

18. Tocco, 17.

19. A. Dondaine, *Secrétaires de Saint Thomas* (Rome: Editori di S. Tommaso, S. Sabina, 1956).

20. Tocco, 30.

21. Torrell, 56.

22. See M. -D. Philippe, ed., *Saint Thomas d'Aquin: Commentaire sur l'Evangile de saint Jean*, 3 vols. (Versailles: Buxy, 1981–1987). Also see the translation: M. Levering, F. Larcher, J. Weisheipl, D. Keating, eds., *Commentary on the Gospel of John*, 3 vols. (Washington, DC: Catholic University of America Press, 2010).

23. St. Thomas, *Lectura super Ioannem*, prologue. "Sic ergo ex praemissis colligitur materia huius Evangelii; quia cum Evangelistae alii tractent principaliter mysteria humanitatis Christi, Ioannes specialiter et praecipue divinitatem Christi in Evangelio suo insinuat." He later demonstrates a fine historical sense when he discusses the context of the composition of John, when the apostle faced off against Docetists and Ebionite heretics, thus influencing the gospel's content.

24. See Torrell, 199, esp. n7.

25. For the controversy, see Torrell, 250–57.

26. For a modern theologian who sees Thomas's "one existence" position as Monophysite, see J. Galot, *The Person of Christ: Covenant between God and Man; A Theological Insight*, trans. A. Bouchard (Chicago: Franciscan Herald Press, 1984). For an in-depth analysis, see A. Patfoort, *L'unité d'être dans le Christ d'après S. Thomas: a la croisée de l'ontologie et de la christologie* (Paris: Desclée, 1971).

27. See the very useful table in Torrell, 211.

28. Porro, 353. See also the conclusions of J. B. Hood, *Aquinas and the Jews* (Philadelphia: University of Pennsylvania Press, 1995).

29. This is not to deny that there were strenuous Dominican efforts against Jews, but once again, it was directed toward their conversion of religion, rather than hatred for a "race" (itself a wildly anachronistic term here). See J. Cohen, *The Friars and the Jews: The Evolution of Medieval Anti-Judaism* (Ithaca, NY: Cornell University Press, 1982), with salutary correctives in Hood, *Aquinas and the Jews*; R. Chazan, *Barcelona and Beyond: The Disputation of 1263 and Its Aftermath* (Berkeley: University of California Press, 1992); and R. Vose, *Dominicans, Muslims, and Jews in the Medieval Crown of Aragon* (Cambridge: Cambridge University Press, 2009).

30. See: J. -P. Torrell, *Aquinas's Summa: Background, Structure, and Reception* (Washington, DC: Catholic University of America Press, 2012).

31. Denys Turner, *Thomas Aquinas: A Portrait* (New Haven, CT: Yale University Press, 2014), 187.

32. L. Boyle, "The Setting of the Summa Theologiae," in *Aquinas's Summa Theologiae: Critical Essays*, ed. Brian Davies (Lanham, MD: Rowman & Littlefield, 2005), 16.

33. Weisheipl tracks these different trends, 244–45.

34. At this council, all new orders were suppressed, with the exception of the Franciscans and Dominicans (the Carmelites and Augustinian friars were placed on probation).

35. Both Rashdall, 1:393–95, and Torrell, 81, note this in passing. See also K. Schleyer, *Anfänge des Gallikanismus im 13. jahrhundert: Der Widerstand des französischen Klerus gegen die Privilegierung der Bettelorden* (Berlin: Verlag dr. Emil Ebering, 1937); also, J. Ratzinger, "Der Einfluss des Bettelordensstreites auf die Entwicklung der Lehre vom päpstlichen Universalprimat, unter

besonderer Berücksichtigung des heiligen Bonaventura," in *Theologie in Geschichte und Gegenwart*, eds. J. Auer and H. Volk (Munich: K. Zink, 1957); and Y. Congar, *Aspects ecclésiologiques de la querelle entre mendiants et séculiers dans la seconde moitié du XIIIe siècle et le début du XIVe* (Paris: J. Vrin, 1962).

36. Though the terms *conventual* and *spiritual* are anachronistic, they merely serve to distinguish the two sides here in this debate.

37. Tugwell, 229.

38. Thomas, *De perfectione spiritualis vitae*, 15. Cf. Weisheipl, 267.

39. STh II-II, q. 101, a. 4.

40. Quodlibet 4, a. 23.

41. See E. Synan, "St. Thomas Aquinas and the Profession of Arms," *Medieval Studies* 50 (1988): 404–37.

42. *Contra retrahentes*, 16, conclusion. "Si quis his contradicere voluerit, non coram pueris garriat, sed scribat, et scripturam proponat in publico; ut ab intelligentibus diiudicari possit quid verum sit, et hoc quod erroneum est, auctoritate veritatis confutetur."

43. See A. Thompson, *Francis of Assisi: A New Biography* (Ithaca, NY: Cornell University Press, 2012), 240–42. Thompson is now convinced that the two did have a passing acquaintance at the Franciscan Pentecost chapter of 1218.

44. For a history of this controversy, see A. Vauchez, "The Stigmata of St. Francis and Its Medieval Detractors," *Greyfriars Review* 13, no. 1 (1999): 61–89. For a broader overview, see O. Schmucki, *The Stigmata of St. Francis of Assisi: A Critical Investigation in the Light of Thirteenth-Century Sources*, trans. C. F. Connors (St. Bonaventure, NY: Franciscan Institute, 1991); for another view of the sources, see C. Frugoni, *Francesco e l'invenzione delle stimmate: Una storia per parole e immagini fino a Bonaventura e Giotto* (Turin: G. Einaudi, 1993). See Thompson's recent comments in his *Francis of Assisi*, 391–93.

45. The history of the interorder rivalry has yet to be written. I make some preliminary comments in *The Martyred Inquisitor*, 118–25.

46. For instance, Luke Wadding, the early seventeenth-century Franciscan historian, wrote two stories about the relationship. One was that Thomas visited Bonaventure while the latter was writing

his life of Francis. Thomas quietly withdraws, saying, "Let us leave a saint to write about a saint." This was dated to Paris in 1262, when we know Thomas was in Orvieto. Later, Wadding states that Thomas wanted to see Bonaventure's library, from whence he acquired such wonderful knowledge. Bonaventure showed him the cross. Luke Wadding, *Annales Minorum seu trium Ordinum a S. Francisco insitutorum*, 8 vols. (Rome, 1632), 138–39, 1260 c. 18 and 1260 c. 20. Another story dates from the time of the push for Bonaventure's canonization from the Dutch chronicle of Johannes Haghen, wherein Thomas had a vision of the wounded Christ pouring his blood into Bonaventure's mouth. *Doctoris seraphici S. Bonaventurae opera omnia*, ed. The Fathers of the Collegii S. Bonaventura, 10 vols. (Florence: Quaracchi, 1882–1902), 10:54n2. These stores were all likely devised to further Bonaventure's cause in Rome. Thomas's modern Dominican biographers are silent about these stories, including that of the contest at Corpus Christi. It seems they believe them unhistorical, but do not wish to say so.

47. Testimony of Bartholomew of Capua, 77. Tocco greatly enlarges and embellishes the story, 26. Neither Bartholomew nor Tocco were university men, and so some of the details are confused, but historians are in consensus as to the facts related above.

48. Chart., 517, 518, 523. Cf. Torrell, 184n20.

49. Thompson, *Francis of Assisi*, 112.

50. Porro, 242.

51. The issue is very complex, but the footnote in Torrell, 189n42, referring to R. Zavalloni's work is the best summary of the current state of the question.

52. If I may make a speculation, Tocco writes of Thomas's confuting Pecham's positions by means of a church council, which has never been identified. Is it possible that the debate on the second day expanded from the eternity of the world to the plurality of forms, and when Thomas defended his position that the hypostatic union was the principle of unity, perhaps he was referring to conciliar condemnations of Apollinarianism at Constantinople I?

53. Torrell, 192n53.

54. For a review of the debates, see R. Imbach, "L'averroisme latin du XIIIe siècle," in *Gli Studi di filosofia medievale fra Otto e*

Novecento, ed. R. Imbach and A. Maierú (Rome: Edizioni di storia e letteratura, 1991), 191–208.

55. Tugwell, 226; I. Brady, "Background to the Condemnation of 1270: Master William of Baglione, O.F.M.," *Franciscan Studies* 30 (1970): 5–48.

56. Porro, 371–72.

57. "Relinquitur igitur hoc absque omni dubitatione tenendum, non propter revelationem fidei, ut ipsi dicunt, sed quia hoc subtrahere est niti contra manifeste apparentia." *De Unitate*, IV, 2.

58. G. K. Chesterton, *St. Thomas Aquinas: The Dumb Ox* (New York: Sheed & Ward, 1933).

59. "Haec igitur sunt quae in destructionem praedicti erroris conscripsimus, non per documenta fidei, sed per ipsorum philosophorum rationes et dicta. Si quis autem gloriabundus de falsi nominis scientia, velit contra haec quae scripsimus aliquid dicere, non loquatur in angulis nec coram pueris qui nesciunt de tam arduis iudicare; sed contra hoc scriptum rescribat, si audet; et inveniet non solum me, qui aliorum sum minimus, sed multos alios veritatis zelatores, per quos eius errori resistetur, vel ignorantiae consuletur." *De Unitate*, V, conclusion.

60. Turner, *Thomas Aquinas*, 92.

61. Dante, *Paradiso*, X, 133–38.

62. Porro, 47, 302.

63. Bonaventure, cf. Chenu, *Aquinas and His Role*, 28. See J. Ratzinger, *The Theology of History in Saint Bonaventure*, trans. Z. Hayes (Chicago: Franciscan Herald Press, 1971). It is likely Bonaventure was behind these attacks of Pecham.

64. Porro, 279.

65. Chenu, *Aquinas and His Role*, 28.

66. Chenu, *Aquinas and His Role*, 28.

67. SCG, I. c. 9; STh, I. I. 8.

68. Weisheipl, 280–81.

69. Torrell, 228.

70. Torrell, 238.

71. Torrell, 238.

72. See V. Guagliardo, C. Hess, and R. Taylor, eds., *Commentary on the "Book of Causes,"* Thomas Aquinas in Translation 1 (Washington, DC: The Catholic University of America Press, 1996), x.

73. As the liberal Protestant historical theologian Adolf von Harnack put it, "Even today we live by Augustine, by his thought and his spirit; it is said that we are the sons of the Renaissance and the Reformation, but both one and the other depend upon him."

74. For this, see especially R. Henle, *Saint Thomas and Platonism: A Study of the Plato and Platonic Texts in the Writings of Saint Thomas* (The Hague: M. Nijhoff, 1956), 309–12.

75. Cf. Torrell, *Saint Thomas Aquinas: Spiritual Master*, trans. Robert Royal, rev. ed. (Washington, DC: Catholic University of America Press, 2005), 63, 100.

76. Chenu, *Aquinas and His Role*, 28.

77. Turner, *Thomas Aquinas*, 103.

78. Guagliardo and others, *"Book of Causes,"* xxiv.

79. Chaucer, *The Canterbury Tales*, general prologue, 295–97, 310.

80. The Arts faculty made an ultimately unsuccessful petition to the General Chapter at Florence in 1272 to keep Thomas at Paris; Torrell, 248–49, esp. n5.

81. A. Traver, "The Forging of an Intellectual Defense of Mendicancy in the Medieval University," in *The Origin, Development, and Refinement of Medieval Religious Mendicancies*, ed. D. Prudlo (Leiden: Brill, 2011), 157–96.

82. Weisheipl, 294.

83. Mulchahey, 307–9. She notes how the Order struggled with academic terminology for its schools throughout the thirteenth century.

84. MOPH 20, 39.

85. Torrell, 248.

86. Mulchahey, 308–9.

87. Tolomeo says he was an eyewitness of this event, *Historia Ecclesiastica Nova*, in *S. Thomae Aquinatis vitae fontes precipuae* (Alba: Edizioni Domenicane, 1968), 23.10. It occurs in every biography; Tocco, 50; Gui, 161–263; Calo, 26.

88. I fully concur with Peter Brown's dismantling of David Hume's unfortunate two-tiered model of religious life that can be found throughout the philosopher's works; see especially the first chapters of Brown, *The Cult of the Saints: Its Rise and Function in Latin Christianity* (Chicago: University of Chicago Press, 1981).

89. See R. Wilken, *The Spirit of Early Christian Thought* (New Haven, CT: Yale University Press, 2005), 40.

90. Mulchahey, 309.

91. For Charles and Thomas, see Weisheipl, 298–300.

92. The classic study of Thomas's family is F. Scandone, *La vita, la famiglia e la patria di S. Tommaso* (Rome: Società tipografica A. Manuzio, 1924).

93. Gui, 29. For Thomas's preaching, see also Tocco, 48–53; Calo, 24, 26; Naples, 58, 70, 87, 88, 93.

94. For an analysis of this preaching cycle, see P. Mandonnet, *Le Carême de Saint Thomas d'Aquin à Naples (1273)* (Roma: Società tipografica A. Manuzio, 1924).

95. Torrell, 358.

96. For recent comments on Thomas's preaching, see A. Oliva, "Philosophie et théologie en prédication chez Thomas d'Aquin," *Revue des sciences philosophiques et théologiques* 97, no. 2 (2013): 397–444.

97. For these witnesses, see Naples, 58, 70, 88, 93.

98. Mulchahey, 286–306.

99. Torrell, 318–19. Against Mulchahey.

100. Prooemium in *Postilla super Psalmos*; cf. Torrell, 259.

101. See Turner, *Thomas Aquinas*, 187, 222, 262.

102. Mulchahey.

103. Tocco, 43; Gui, 25; Calo, 24; Tolomeo, *Historia Ecclesiastica Nova*, 23.9.

104. Tocco, 29; Gui, 26; Calo, 16.

105. Tocco, 29; Gui, 26.

106. "Quia omnia que scripsi videntur mihi palee." Bartholomew of Capua, Naples, 79.

107. Both use the word "modica" in place of "palee." Tocco, 47; Gui, 27. Bartholomew's account is also more likely because he heard it personally from Reginald, and since both Tocco and Gui are confused about the location of the vision, marking San Severino as the place of the transformation.

108. Weisheipl, 323; Naples, 87.

109. Naples, 79; *Fontes*, 377.

110. Naples, 79, "cum difficultate magna."

111. Torrell, 290.

112. Naples, 78.

113. The myth that Thomas was poisoned at the order of Charles of Anjou, perpetuated by no less a person than Dante, has repeatedly proven unreliable, and has been rejected by all reputable historians. See Weisheipl, 328–29; Torrell, 293–94.

114. Naples, 50.

115. Tocco, 56; Gui, 37; Calo, 27; Naples, 9 and 50.

116. Naples, 8, 49, 80; Tocco, 57.

117. Naples, 49.

118. Tocco, 57.

119. Weisheipl, 327.

120. For the importance of the moment of death to hagiography, see Michel Lauwers, "La mort et le corps de saints: la scène de la mort dans les Vitae du haut Moyen Age," *Moyen âge* 94, no. 1 (1988): 21–50.

CHAPTER 7

1. See R. Bartlett, *Why Can the Dead Do Such Great Things?* (Princeton, NJ: Princeton University Press, 2015).

2. For some considerations, particularly in medieval Italy, see A. Thompson, *Cities of God: The Religion of the Italian Communes, 1125–1325* (University Park, PA: Penn State University Press, 2005), esp. 381–418; and C. Lansing, *Passion and Order: Restraint of Grief in the Medieval Italian Communes* (Ithaca, NY: Cornell University Press, 2008).

3. The expression is Peter Brown's. See his *The Cult of the Saints: Its Rise and Function in Latin Christianity* (Chicago: University of Chicago Press, 1981), ch. 4.

4. Tocco, 57; Gui, 38; Calo, 27; Naples, 8, 49. There is a possibility that the hagiographers are "checking boxes" in these stories in order to establish the certainty of a "good death." Measuring them against the canonization depositions leads to the conclusion that the reports are largely accurate, even though deponents themselves can tend to hew toward established rhetorical types. See M. Goodich, *Miracles and Wonders: The Development of the Concept of Miracle, 1150–1350* (Aldershot, UK: Ashgate, 2007), 4–5.

5. Tocco, 61; Naples, 17 and 51.

6. Weisheipl, 329.

7. This was true at least as early as the canonization of Omobono in 1199.

8. Tocco, 27, 63; Gui, 41; Calo, 27; Naples, 49, 58.

9. This was a tradition known as the *Corrotto* or *Pianto*: the lament. See Lansing, *Passion and Order*, 61–65, 97–98, 150–52; Thompson, *Cities of God*, 399–402, 418.

10. Tocco, 62; Gui, 40; Calo, 30.

11. Statistical breakdowns of miracle stories have become more common. Representative efforts include H. C. Kee, *Miracle in the Early Christian World* (New Haven, CT: Yale University Press, 1983); for early Christianity: P. -A. Sigal, *L'Homme et le miracle dans la France médiévale* (Paris: Cerf, 1985); for the eleventh and twelfth centuries: A. Thompson *Revival Preachers and Politics in Thirteenth-Century Italy: The Great Devotion of 1233* (Oxford: Clarendon, 1992), 114–17; and André Vauchez, *Sainthood in the Later Middle Ages* (Cambridge: Cambridge University Press, 2005), 427–77. See also *Miracles in Medieval Canonization Processes: Structures, Functions, and Methodologies*, ed. Christian Krötzl and Sari Katajala-Peltomaa, International Medieval Research 23 (Turnhout: Brepols, 2018); and the forthcoming *Brill Companion to Medieval Miracle Collections* (Leiden, Brill, 2019).

12. Tocco, 45–60.

13. Gui, 88, 102. Tocco reported the healing of a donkey carrying canonization materials in France as well, 56.

14. Gui, 100.

15. Alhough, during the fourteenth and fifteenth centuries, there was a marked turn toward more representation in miracles stories from deponents from the lower classes. See S. Katajala-Petlomaa, "Narrative Strategies in the Depositions: Gender, Family, and Devotion," in Krötzl and Katajala-Peltomaa, *Miracles in Medieval Canonization Processes*, 233.

16. Naples, 46.

17. Gui, 76–102.

18. For these comparisons, see my "As primeiras canonizações dominicanas: construindo uma nova santidade," in *Proceedings of the 2nd International Seminar on Medieval Hagiography*, July 2015, ed. I. Texeira (Porto Alegre, 2017), and my forthcoming "Miracles and the Canonizations of Dominican Saints," in *Brill Companion to Medieval Miracle Collections*.

Notes

19. In this case, Peter is more akin to the martyr Thomas Becket than to his Dominican confreres. See D. Prudlo, "Martyrs on the Move: The Spread of the Cults of Thomas of Canterbury and Peter of Verona," in *Peregrinations* 3, no. 2 (Summer 2011).

20. Gui, M82, M89. See D. Prudlo, "Women, Wives, and Mystics: The Unexpected Patronage of a Dominican Martyr," *Journal of the History of Sexuality* 21, no. 3 (May 2012): 313–24.

21. The history of the vagaries of Thomas's relics can be found in C. Douais, *Les reliques de saint Thomas d'Aquin. Textes originaux* (Paris: Vve C. Poussielgue, 1903); and most recently in M. Räsänen, *Thomas Aquinas's Relics as Focus for Conflict and Cult in the Late Middle Ages: The Restless Corpse* (Amsterdam: Amsterdam University Press, 2017).

22. Gui, 45. This information is unique to Gui. It is possible he knew of such instruments, or it may be a stratagem to underscore the Dominican claim in the 1320s to possession of the saint's body.

23. For recent meditations on this, reported in many saint's stories, see Martin Roch, "The 'Odor of Sanctity': Defining Identity and Alterity in the Early Middle Ages (Fifth to Ninth century)," in *Identity and Alterity in Hagiography and the Cult of Saints*, ed. Ana Marinković and Trpimir Vedriš (Zagreb: Hagiotheca, 2008).

24. Gui elaborates on the fact as testified by Bartholomew of Capua, Naples, 10. Bartholomew does seem quite confused about the various disinterments, however. See Foster, 125n76.

25. In the Eastern Orthodox tradition, incorruption is often seen as a sine qua non of sanctity.

26. Naples, 65.

27. STh, I 75.3.

28. Ferrua, 170n106.

29. "Coloris triticei, ad temperatae ejus complexionis indicium." Tocco, 38, abbreviated in Gui, 35.

30. "Grossum, pingue, et magnum," Tocco, 66.

31. Naples, 16, 18, 46.

32. Tocco, 38.

33. Tocco, 12; Gui, 10; Calo, 8.

34. The remembrance is recorded in the sources as direct speech; it seems to have come through in some discussions with his students late in life. Tocco, 53; Gui, 30; Calo, 26.

35. Tocco, 39; Gui, 32; Calo, 21. It is Peter Calo who gives the student's name. In some few instances Calo seems to have access to alternate traditions about Thomas.

36. Tocco, 30; cf. Foster, 70n44.

37. Tocco, 53; Gui, 29; Calo, 26.

38. In spite of this practice, in his thought he had a quite balanced view of men and women. See C. Capelle, *Thomas d'Aquin féministe?* (Paris, 1982), and C. J. Pinto de Oliveira, "Homme et femme dans l'anthropologie de Thomas d'Aquin," in *Humain à l'image de Dieu*, ed. Pierre Bühler (Geneva: Labor et Fides, 1989), 165–90. Cf. Torrell, *Saint Thomas Aquinas: Spiritual Master*, trans. Robert Royal, rev. ed. (Washington, DC: Catholic University of America Press, 2005), 87n18.

39. STh, prologue.

40. J. Pieper, *The Silence of St. Thomas* (South Bend, IN: St. Augustine's Press, 1999), 23.

41. R. McInerny, *Saint Thomas Aquinas* (Boston: Twayne Publishers, 1977), 127.

42. "Sed tertius error fuit David de Dinando, qui stultissime posuit Deum esse primam materiam." STh. I. q. 3, a. 8.

43. Pieper, *The Silence of St. Thomas*, 84.

44. STh II-II, 2, 3.

45. M.-D. Chenu, *Aquinas and His Role in Theology* (Collegeville, MN: Liturgical Press, 2002), 26.

46. Quodlibet IV, a. 16 (1271); cf. Chenu, *Aquinas and His Role in Theology*, 26.

47. Torrell, *Saint Thomas Aquinas: Spiritual Master*, 58.

48. For this, see V. A. Guagliardo, C. R. Hess, and R. C. Taylor, eds., *Commentary on the "Book of Causes,"* Thomas Aquinas in Translation 1 (Washington, DC: The Catholic University of America Press, 1996), introduction.

49. J. Van Banning, "Saint Thomas et l'*Opus Imperfectum in Matthaeum*," *Studi Tomistici* 17 (1982): 73–85.

50. Porro, 182.

51. See the prologue of the *Contra Errores Graecorum*; also M. D. Jordan, "Theological Exegesis and Aquinas's Treatise against the Greeks," *Church History* 56 (1987): 445–56.

52. See P. -M. Gy, "La documentation sacramentaire de Thomas d'Aquin. Quelle connaissance S. Thomas a-t-il de la tradition ancienne

et patristique?," *Revue des sciences philosophiques et théologiques* 80 (1996): 19–36; G. Emery, "Le photinisme et ses précurseurs chez saint Thomas, Cérinthe, les Ébionites, Paul de Samosate et Photin," *Revue Théologique* 95 (1995): 371–98; and Emery, "Saint Thomas et l'Orient chrétien," *Nova et Vetera* 74, no. 4 (1999): 19–36.

53. Repeating similar sentiments of other contemporaries, Thomas says, "Non tamen omne accidentale praemium est aureola, sed praemium de operibus perfectionis, quibus homo maxime Christo conformatur secundum perfectam victoriam." *Scriptum super Sententiis*, lib. 4, d. 49, q.5, a. 2, qc. 1, ad 3 in Opera Omnia, 7.2 (Parma: 1857), 1236. Thomas distinguishes the *aureolae*, or rewards for special works (an accessory joy in heaven), from the *aurea*, the essential reward possessed by all the blessed in heaven. In the considerations Thomas often combines the office of Preacher and Doctor, seeing them in essential symbiosis. The most comprehensive works on the subject are A. Volpato, "Il tema agiografico della triplice aureola nei secoli XIII–XV," *Culto dei santi, istituzioni e classi sociali in età preindustriale*, ed. S. B. Gajano and L. Sebastiani (L'Aquila, 1984), 511–25; and E. Hall and H. Uhr, "Aureola Super Auream: Crowns and Related Symbols of Special Distinction for Saints in Late Gothic and Renaissance Iconography," *Art Bulletin* 67, no. 4 (1985): 567–603.

54. Thomas, as well as everyone up to the nineteenth century, uses the title *Doctor* to describe those with academic degrees. It was not applied to the medical profession until very recently.

55. Quodlibet I, q. 7, a. 2. See the comments on this text in Torrell, *Saint Thomas Aquinas: Spiritual Master*, 210–12 and Porro, 311.

56. For this, see E. Marmursztejn, *L'autorité des maîtres: scolastique, normes et société au XIIIe siècle* (Paris: Les Belles Lettres, 2007), esp. ch. 1.

57. *Contra Impugnantes*, 2.1; cf. Torrell, *Saint Thomas Aquinas: Spiritual Master*, 212.

58. Porro, 123.

59. Chenu, *Aquinas and His Role in Theology*, 105.

60. Tocco, 17, 31; Gui, 15, 16; Calo, 17; Naples, 59.

61. McInerny, *Saint Thomas Aquinas*, 171.

62. Chenu, *Aquinas and His Role in Theology*, 31.

63. See R. M. Bell, *Holy Anorexia* (Chicago: University of Chicago Press, 1985); and a much more productive model in C. W. Bynum, *Holy Feast and Holy Fast: The Religious Significance of Food to Medieval Women* (Berkeley: University of California Press, 1987).

64. H. Furfaro, "Children of Smart Fathers Have Higher Risk of Autism," *Scientific American*, May 14, 2017.

65. Tocco, 3; Gui, 2.

66. Tocco, 8; Gui, 6; Calo, 6; Naples, 61, 62, 76; *VF* 4.17.

67. Tocco, 16; cf. Chenu, *Aquinas and His Role in Theology*, 45.

68. Tocco, 4; Gui, 3; Calo, 3.

69. Naples, 87.

70. Tocco, 25; Gui, 31; Calo, 15.

71. Tolomeo of Lucca, *Historia Ecclesiastica Nova*, in *S. Thomae Aquinatis vitae fontes precipuae* (Alba: Edizioni Domenicane, 1968), 21.23.

72. Tocco, 42; Gui, 34; Calo, 23; Tolomeo, *Historia Ecclesiastica Nova*, 22.39.

73. The story originates in the testimony of Bartholomew of Capua, who corroborates it with other eyewitnesses, Naples, 78. Tocco, 63, tries to temper Thomas's reaction. The story is not mentioned in later biographies, perhaps because it displayed Thomas's irritation. Reginald could occasionally irritate Thomas by prying into his mystical experiences.

74. Naples, 70. Tugwell suggests those who came to hear him preach were drawn more by Thomas's fame than his skill, Tugwell, 107. See Naples, 87.

75. Tocco, 53; Gui, 29; Calo, 26.

76. Gui, 23; Tocco, 33, 34; Calo, 17, 18.

77. Gui, 15; Tocco, 28; Gui, 16.

78. Tocco, 31; Gui, 16; Calo, 17.

79. Tocco, 17.

80. E. Gilson, *The Christian Philosophy of St. Thomas Aquinas*, trans. L. K. Shook (New York, 1956), 376; cf. Torrell, *Saint Thomas Aquinas: Spiritual Master*, 21.

81. Tocco, 47; Gui, 28; Calo, 24.

82. Gui, 25.

83. Gui, 15.

84. Tocco, 43.

Notes

85. Tugwell, 341n583, agrees with Gauthier, *Saint Thomas d'Aquin, Somme contre les gentils: introduction* (Paris: Editions universitaires, 1993), 17n25. It is clear that Thomas was referring neither to the *Summa Contra Gentiles* or the *Prima Pars* of the *Summa Theologiae*. I think Tocco is misreporting an actual event, and "Manichees" served as a convenient placeholder for some rival system. Thomas wrote nothing systematic on the Cathars, who had been thoroughly answered by his brethren of a previous generation.

86. Tocco, 43; Gui, 25; Calo, 24.

87. Tocco, 35.

88. "Cella placeat, qua venitur ad celum," Johannes Teutonicus, [Encyclical of 1246 to the Order], *Litterae encyclicae magistrorum generalium Ordinis Praedicatorum ab anno 1233 usque ad annum 1376*, ed. B. M. Reichert, MOPH 5, 9.

89. Tocco, 17; Gui, 32; Naples, 77.

90. Tocco, 31; Gui, 16; Calo, 17; Naples, 59.

91. Tocco, 27, 33; Gui, 23, 27; Calo, 17, 24; Naples, 79.

92. Tocco, 63; Gui, 41.

93. Quodlibet 12, a. 20.

94. Naples, 81.

95. I-II, q. 38. Unfortunately for one of Thomas's most "popular quotations" repeated on numerous Internet memes, Thomas does not mention a "glass of good wine" here as a solvent for sorrow.

96. Denys Turner, *Thomas Aquinas: A Portrait* (New Haven, CT: Yale University Press, 2014), 211.

97. Tugwell, 262. Is not "essentially self-sufficient" the very etymology of "autism?"

98. Naples, 42, 81.

99. Tocco, 29; Gui, 26; Calo, 16.

100. Tocco, 41n30; See also Vauchez, *Sainthood*, 512–14.

101. G. K. Chesterton, *St. Thomas Aquinas: The Dumb Ox* (New York: Sheed & Ward, 1933), 34.

102. I, q. 8, ad. 2.

103. The foundational study for the history of Thomism immediately after his death is F. J. Roensch, *Early Thomistic School* (Dubuque, IA: Priory Press, 1964). Also quite useful is R. Cessario,

A Short History of Thomism (Washington, DC: The Catholic University of America Press, 2005).

104. Tugwell, 232.

105. Cessario, *A Short History of Thomism*, 53.

106. Roensch, *Early Thomistic School*, 170–73.

107. As C. S. Lewis put it in *The Problem of Pain* (New York: Simon & Schuster, 1996), 26, "Meaningless combinations of words do not suddenly acquire meaning simply because we prefix to them the two other words, 'God can.' It remains true that all things are possible with God: the intrinsic impossibilities are not things but nonentities. It is no more possible for God than for the weakest of His creatures to carry out both of two mutually exclusive alternatives; not because His power meets an obstacle, but because nonsense remains nonsense even when we talk it about God."

108. For a good, brief account of Thomas's thought on this matter, see Armand Maurer, *Medieval Philosophy*, 2nd ed. (Toronto: PIMS, 1982), 179–82.

109. Roensch, *Early Thomistic School*, 11.

110. Tocco, 26; Gui, 31; Calo, 15; Tugwell, 230.

111. Torrell, *Saint Thomas Aquinas: Spiritual Master*, 298. See J. Ratzinger, *The Theology of History in Saint Bonaventure*, trans. Z. Hayes (Chicago: Franciscan Herald Press, 1971).

112. Roensch speculates that Albert's intervention prevented an outright condemnation of Thomas by name, but there is no evidence to support this, while the balance of testimony testifies to Albert's failing abilities. Roensch, *Early Thomistic School*, 12.

113. Torrell, *Saint Thomas Aquinas: Spiritual Master*, 301.

114. R. Hissette has suggested that Robert was not reflexively anti-Thomist, but it is clear he was completely conservative in theology and opposed in particular to the unicity of form in humans. *Enquête sur les 219 articles condamnés à Paris le 7 mars 1277* (Louvain: Publications universitaires, 1977). Hissette is indispensable for this period. See also E. M. F. Sommer-Seckendorff, *Studies in the Life of Robert Kilwardby, O.P.* (Rome: Institutum historicum ff. praedicatorum Romae ad S. Sabinae, 1937); and J. F. Silva, *Robert Kilwardby on the Human Soul: Plurality of Forms and Censorship in the Thirteenth Century* (Leiden: Brill, 2012).

115. Roensch, *Early Thomistic School*, 89.

116. Cessario, *A Short History of Thomism*, 46.

117. Cessario, *A Short History of Thomism*, 40.

118. Torrell, *Saint Thomas Aquinas: Spiritual Master*, 309.

119. For an overview, see E. Lowe, *The Contested Theological Authority of Thomas Aquinas* (New York: Routledge, 2003), which should be read carefully in conjunction with the review by R. L. Friedman in *The Medieval Review* (2004).

120. "Heu nova cur Fossa/ tenet hec venerabilis ossa?/ Obsecro tollantur,/ a fratribus hec teneantur," probably composed in the 1310s. Räsänen, *The Restless Corpse*, 12.

121. Weisheipl, following Walz, is convinced that the creation of the new province of the *Regno* of Sicily and Naples in 1294 was instrumental for forwarding Thomas's cause. While it would have been good for the new province to cultivate a patron, it should be remembered that the older Roman province did not have a canonized saint either, nor is there any evidence of any interest in Thomas's cult until the provincial chapter of September 1317. If an impetus did come from the new province, it was posterior to the actions of John XXII. Torrell, *Saint Thomas Aquinas: Spiritual Master*, 318; and, Weisheipl, 344.

122. Vauchez, *Sainthood*, 72–73.

123. Naples, 80.

124. This controversy is expertly analyzed in D. Burr, *The Spiritual Franciscans: From Protest to Persecution in the Century after Saint Francis* (University Park: Pennsylvania State University Press, 2003).

125. A. Dondaine, "La Collection des oeuvres de saint Thomas dite de Jean XXII et Jaquet Maci," *Scriptorium* 29 (1975): 127–52.

126. Weisheipl, 34.

127. Robert and John XXII had a very close relationship. See S. Kelly, *The New Solomon: Robert of Naples (1309–1343) and Fourteenth-Century Kingship* (Leiden: Brill, 2003), 74–81.

128. Mentioned in the personal reminiscences of one Friar Bentius, who left a memorial of the week of canonization. *Fontes*, 517.

129. Räsänen, *The Restless Corpse*, 47.

130. M. Grabmann, "Hagiographische Texte in einer HS. des kirchenhist. Seminars der Univ. Munchen," *AFP* 19 (1949): 379–82.

131. Dominicans would return the favor in agitating against Bonaventure's elevation. He would not be canonized until 1482

by Sixtus IV, the former Minister General of the Minorites. See A. Vauchez, "Les canonisations de S. Thomas et de S. Bonaventure: Pourquoi deux siècles d'écart?," in *1274—Année Charnière, Mutations et Continuités*, ed. M. Mollat du Jourdin (Lyon: Centre National de la Recherche Scientifique, 1978), 753–67, translated in "The Canonizations of St. Thomas and St. Bonaventure: Why a Two-Century Gap Between Them?," trans. E. Hagman, *Greyfriars Review* 12, no. 2 (1998).

132. Räsänen, *The Restless Corpse*, 49.

133. Gui, 101.

134. See "Ordo Romanus XIV," Patrologia Latina 78, cols. 1258. "Ad honorem Dei omnipotentis Patris et Filii et Spiritus Sancti, et exaltationem fidei et christianae religionis augmentum, auctoritate ipsius omnipotentis Patris et Filii et Spiritus Sancti, beatorum Petri et Pauli et nostra, de fratrum nostrorum consilio decernimus et definimus bonae memoriae N...sanctorum catalogo ascribendum." Ordo Romanus XIV was composed at the curia of John XXII.

135. Torrell, *Saint Thomas Aquinas: Spiritual Master*, 321–22.

136. Pieper, *The Silence of St. Thomas*, 36.

137. Turner, *Thomas Aquinas*, 34.

138. Dante, *Paradiso*, Canto X: 94–96, 121–22.

CONCLUSION

1. For Thomas's popularity in the Christian East, see M. Plested, *Orthodox Readings of Aquinas* (Oxford: Oxford University Press, 2012). For Jewish engagement with him, see Porro, 401.

2. R. W. Southern, *Medieval Humanism and Other Studies* (Oxford: Blackwell, 1984), 50.

APPENDIX A

1. For this saint, see particularly A. Thompson, *Francis of Assisi: A New Biography* (Ithaca, NY: Cornell University Press, 2012).

Notes

2. For discussions of this fashioning, see J. Kuuliala, "Proving Misfortune, Proving Sainthood: Reconstructing Physical Impairment in Fourteenth-Century Miracle Testimonies," in *Miracles in Medieval Canonization Processes: Structures, Functions, and Methodologies*, ed. C. Krötzl and S. Katajala-Peltomaa, International Medieval Research 23 (Turnhout: Brepols, 2018), 201. For interpretive issues in hagiography more broadly considered, see T. J. Heffernan, *Sacred Biography* (Oxford: Oxford University Press, 1988).

3. S. Katajala-Peltomaa, "Narrative Strategies in the Depositions: Gender, Family, and Devotion," in Krötzl and Katajala-Peltomaa, *Miracles in Medieval Canonization Processes*, 228.

4. *VF*. The material on Saint Thomas can be found in chapter 4, sections 17 and 24. Translated in Gérard de Frachet, *Lives of the Brethren of the Order of Preachers, 1206–1259*, trans. P. Conway, OP (London: Burns, Oates and Washbourne Ltd., 1924). Should be read in conjunction with S. Tugwell, "L'Evolution des Vitae Fratrum," *Cahiers de Fanjeaux* 36 (2001): 415–18.

5. Thomas of Cantimpré, *Bonum universale de apibus* (Douai, 1605), Book I, c. 20, 79.

6. *Acta Cap. Gen.*, 1:1220–1303; *Acta Capitulorum Provincialium: Provinciae Romanae 1243–1344*, ed. Th. Kaeppeli and A. Dondaine, MOPH 20 (Rome: In domo generalitia, 1920); *Litterae Encyclicae Magistrorum ab Anno 1233 Usque ad Annum 1376*, ed. B. M. Reichert, OP, MOPH 5 (Rome: Institutum Historicum Ordinis Fratrum Praedicatorum, 1900); and *Bullarium Ordinis Fratrum Praedicatorum*, ed. T. Ripoll, 7 vols. (Rome: Ex Typographia Hieronymi Mainardi, 1759).

7. Chart. Some of these have been translated in *University Records and Life in the Middle Ages*, ed. and trans. Lynn Thorndike (New York: Octagon Books, 1971, 1944).

8. There is no modern edition of Ptolemy. Ptolemy of Lucca, *Historia Ecclesiastica*, ed. L. Muratori, Rerum Italicarum Scriptores 11 (Milan, 1724). The material on Saint Thomas can be found from 22.17 to 23.16. The pertinent material is translated in Foster, 127–39. For Ptolemy, see J. M. Blythe, *The Life and Works of Tolomeo Fiadoni (Ptolemy of Lucca)* (Turnhout: Brepols, 2009).

9. For William, see the commentary in Foster, 6–9.

10. Foster, 9.

11. For Gui, see the commentary in *Bernard Gui: Scripta de Sancto Domenico*, ed. Simon Tugwell, MOPH 27 (Rome: Institutum Historicum Ordinis Fratrum Praedicatorum, 1998).

12. For Calo, see the commentary in *Miracula Sancti Dominici Mandato Magistri Berengarii Collecta, Petri Calo Legendae Sancti Dominici*, ed. S. Tugwell, MOPH 26 (Rome, 1997).

13. *Fontes*, in fascicles of *Revue Thomiste* (1911–1937). A previous edition of the lives can be found in Acta Sanctorum, *Martii 1*, March 7, 655–747.

14. Tocco. This edition has been translated into French: William de Tocco, *L'histoire de saint Thomas d'Aquin*, ed. C. Le Brun-Gouanvic (Paris: Cerf, 2005).

15. See Foster, who betrays sincere irritation at William of Tocco's style, and as a result the fundamental biography of Thomas is only translated in snippets.

16. [Leonine Commission], *Sancti Thomae de Aquino: Opera omnia iussu Leonis XIII P. M. edita*, 50 vols. (Rome: 1882–).

BIBLIOGRAPHY

PRIMARY

Original

Acta Capitulorum Generalium Ordinis Praedicatorum. Edited by B. M. Reichert, OP. Vol 1:1220–1303. MOPH 3. Rome: In domo generalitia, 1898.

Acta Capitulorum Provincialium: Provinciae Romanae 1243–1344. Edited by Th. Kaeppeli and A. Dondaine. MOPH 20. Rome: In domo generalitia, 1920.

Acta Sanctorum, Martii 1. March 7. 655–747.

Bullarium Franciscanum Romanorum Pontificum: constitutiones, epistolas, ac diplomata continens Tribus Ordinibus Minorum, Clarissarum, et Poenitentium a seraphico patriarcha Sancto Francisco institutis concessa ab illorum exordio ad nostra usque tempora. Edited by G. G. Sbaralea. 4 vols. 1759; Assisi: Edizioni Porziuncola, 1983.

Bullarium Ordinis Fratrum Praedicatorum. 7 vols. Edited by T. Ripoll. Rome: Ex Typographia Hieronymi Mainardi, 1759.

Chartularium Universitatis Parisiensis. Edited by H. Denifle, OP. Paris: ex typis fratrum Delalain, 1899.

Codex Constitutionum Quas Summi. Pontifices Ediderunt in. Solemni. Canonizatione Sanctorum a Johanne XV ad Benedictum XIII sive ab A.D. 993 ad A.D. 1729. Edited by G. Fontanini. Rome: ex typographia Rev. Camerae apostolicae, 1729.

Constitutiones Antiquae Ord. Frat. Praedicatorum. Edited by H. C. Scheeben. Analecta sacri ordinis fratrum Praedicatorum 2. Rome: In domo generalitia, 1895.

Fontes vitae sancti Thomae. Edited by D. Prümmer and M. H. Laurent in fascicles of *Revue Thomiste* (1911–37).

381

Gérard de Frachet, OP. *Vitae Fratrum Ordinis Praedicatorum.* Edited by B. M. Reichert, OP. MOPH 1. Louvain: Charpentier, 1896.

Humbert of Romans. *Opera de Vita Regulari.* Edited by J. J. Berthier. 2 vols. Rome: Typis A. Befani, 1888.

[Leonine Commission]. *Sancti Thomae de Aquino: Opera omnia iussu Leonis XIII P. M. edita.* 50 vols. Rome: 1882–.

Litterae Encyclicae Magistrorum ab Anno 1233 Usque ad Annum 1376. Edited by B. M. Reichert, OP. MOPH 5. Rome: Institutum Historicum Ordinis Fratrum Praedicatorum, 1900.

S[ancti] Thomae Aquinatis vitae fontes praecipuae (sic). Edited by A. Ferrua. Alba: Edizioni domenicane, 1968.

Scriptores Ordinis Praedicatorum Medii Aevi. Edited by T. Kaeppeli, OP. 4 vols. Rome: Polyglottis Vaticanis, 1970.

William of Saint-Amour. *De periculis novissimorum temporum.* Edited by G. Geltner. Dallas Medieval Texts and Translations 8. Louvain, 2008.

———. *The Opuscula of William of Saint-Amour.* Edited by Andrew Traver. Münster, 2003.

Ystoria sancti Thome de Aquino de Guillaume de Tocco (1323). Edited by C. Le Brun-Gouanvic. Toronto: Pontifical Institute of Mediaeval Studies, 1996.

Translations

Commentary on the "Book of Causes." Edited by Vincent A. Guagliardo, Charles R. Hess, and Richard C. Taylor. Thomas Aquinas in Translation 1. Washington, DC: The Catholic University of America Press, 1996.

The De Malo of Thomas Aquinas. Edited and translated by Richard J. Regan. Oxford: Oxford University Press, 2001.

Gérard de Frachet. *Lives of the Brethren of the Order of Preachers, 1206–1259.* Translated by Placid Conway, OP. London: Burns, Oates and Washbourne Ltd., 1924.

The Life of Saint Thomas Aquinas. Biographical Documents. Translated and edited by K. Foster. London: Longmans, Green & Co; Helicon Press: Baltimore, 1959.

Summa Contra Gentiles. Notre Dame, IN: University of Notre Dame Press, 1955; 2009.

William de Tocco. *L'histoire de saint Thomas d'Aquin*. Edited by C. Le Brun-Gouanvic. Paris: Cerf, 2005.

SECONDARY

Abulafia, David. *Frederick II: A Medieval Emperor*. New York: Oxford University Press, 1992.

―――. *The Western Mediterranean Kingdoms 1200–1500: The Struggle for Dominion*. London: Longman, 1997.

Anderson, James. "Was St. Thomas a Philosopher?" *New Scholasticism* 38 (1964).

Anzulewicz, Henryk, and Norbert Winkler. *De quindecim problematibus: Über die fünfzehn Streitfragen: Lateinisch-Deutsch: Nach dem Text der Edition Coloniensis*. Freiburg im Br: Herder, 2010.

Ashley, Benedict M. *The Dominicans*. Religious Order Series 3. Collegeville, MN: Liturgical Press, 1990.

Barbero, Alessandro. *Un santo in famiglia: vocazione religiosa e resistenze sociali nell'agiografia latina medievale*. Turin: Rosenberg & Sellier, 1991.

Batallion, Louis-Jacques. "La predicazione dei religiosi mendicanti del secolo xiii nell'Italia centrale." *Mélanges de l'école française de Rome: Moyen âge—temps modernes* 89 (1977): 691–94.

Bazàn, Bernardo C. *Les Questions disputées et les questions quodlibétiques dans les facultés de théologie, de droit et de médecine*. Turnhout, Belgium: Brepols, 1985.

Bennett, R. F. *The Early Dominicans: Studies in Thirteenth-Century Dominican History*. Cambridge: Cambridge University Press, 1937.

Bianchi, Luca. *Pour une histoire de la "double vérité."* Paris: Vrin, 2008.

Blythe, James M. *The Life and Works of Tolomeo Fiadoni (Ptolemy of Lucca)*. Turnhout: Brepols, 2009.

Bonniwell, William. *A History of the Dominican Liturgy*. New York City: Wagner, 1944.

Boureau, Alain. "Vitae fratrum, Vitae patrum. L'ordre dominicain et le modèle des pères du désert au XIIIe s." *Mélanges de l'ecole française de Rome: Moyen âge—temps modernes* 99, no. 1 (1987): 79–100.

Boyle, Leonard. "The Setting of the *Summa Theologiae.*" In *Aquinas's Summa Theologiae: Critical Essays*, edited by Brian Davies, 1–24. Lanham, MD: Rowman & Littlefield, 2005.

Brett, Edward Tracy. *Humbert of Romans: His Life and Views of Thirteenth-Century Society.* Toronto: Pontifical Institute for Medieval Studies, 2000.

Burr, David. *The Spiritual Franciscans: From Protest to Persecution in the Century after Saint Francis.* University Park: University of Pennsylvania Press, 2001.

Canetti, Luigi. *L'invenzione della memoria. Il culto e l'immagine di Domenico nella storia dei primi frati Predicatori.* Biblioteca di Medioevo latino 19. Spoleto-Florence: CISAM-SISMEL, 1996.

Cessario, Romanus. *A Short History of Thomism.* Washington, DC: Catholic University of America Press, 2005.

Chenu, Marie-Dominique. *Aquinas and His Role in Theology.* Translated by Paul Philibert, OP. Collegeville, MN: Liturgical Press, 2002.

———. *Toward Understanding Saint Thomas.* Translated by A.-M. Landry and D. Hughes. Chicago: Henry Regnery, 1964.

Chroust, Anton-Hermann. *Aristotle: New Light on His Life and on Some of His Lost Works.* 2 vols. London: Routledge & K. Paul, 1973.

Cobban, Alan B. *The Medieval Universities: Their Development and Organization.* New York: Harper & Row, 1975.

Congar, Yves. *Aspects ecclésiologiques de la querelle entre mendiants et séculiers dans la seconde moitié du XIIIe siècle et le début du XIVe.* Paris: J. Vrin, 1962.

Crowe, Michael Bertram. "Peter of Ireland: Aquinas's Teacher of the *Artes Liberales.*" *Arts Libéraux et Philosophie au Moyen Age.* Paris: 1969.

Dauphinais, M., M. Levering, and B. David, eds. *Aquinas the Augustinian.* Washington, DC: Catholic University of America Press, 2007.

Davies, Brian. *Thomas Aquinas's Summa Contra Gentiles: A Guide and Commentary.* Oxford: Oxford University Press, 2016.

Bibliography

———. *Thomas Aquinas's Summa Theologiae: A Guide and Commentary*. Oxford: Oxford University Press, 2014.

———. *The Thought of Thomas Aquinas*. Oxford: Clarendon Press, 2009.

Di Meglio, Rosalba. *Ordini mendicanti, monarchia e dinamiche politico-sociali nella Napoli dei secoli XIII–XV*. Raleigh, NC: Aonia, 2013.

Dondaine, Antonie. "La Collection des oeuvres de saint Thomas dite de Jean XXII et Jaquet Maci," *Scriptorium* 29 (1975): 127–52.

———. *Secrétaires de Saint Thomas*. Rome: Santa Sabina, 1956.

Douais, Celestin. *Les reliques de saint Thomas d'Aquin. Textes originaux*. Paris: Vve C. Poussielgue, 1903.

Douie, Decima Langworthy. *The Conflict between the Seculars and the Mendicants at the University of Paris in the Thirteenth Century. A Paper Read to the Aquinas Society...on 22nd June, 1949*. London: 1954.

Dubreil-Arcin, Agnès. *Vies de saints, légendes de soi: L'écriture hagiographique dominicaine jusqu'au Speculum sanctorale de Bernard Gui († 1331)*. Hagiologia 7. Turnhout: Brepols, 2011.

Dufeil, M.-M. *Guillaume De Saint-Amour et la Polémique Universitaire Parisienne, 1250–1259*. Paris: A. et J. Picard, 1972.

Emery, Gilles, and Matthew Levering, eds. *Aristotle in Aquinas's Theology*. Oxford: Oxford University Press, 2015.

Freed, John B. *The Friars and German Society in the Thirteenth Century*. Cambridge, MA: The Mediaeval Academy of America, 1977.

Gauthier, René Antoine. *Saint Thomas d'Aquin, Somme contre les gentils: introduction*. Paris: Editions universitaires, 1993.

Gersh, Stephen. *Κίνησις Ἀκίνητος: A Study of Spiritual Motion in the Philosophy of Proclus*. Leiden: E.J. Brill, 1973.

Glorieux, Palemon. *La littérature quodlibétique*. 2 vols. Paris: Vrin, 1925.

Golinelli, P. "Hagiographie et cultes civiques dans l'Italie du nord." In *Cultures italiennes: (XIIe – XVe siècle)*, edited by Gian Mario Anselmi and Isabelle Heullant-Donat. Paris: Éd. du Cerf, 2000.

Grabmann, M. "Hagiographische Texte in einer HS. des kirchenhist. Seminars der Univ. München." *AFP* 19 (1949): 379–82.

Grundmann, Herbert. *Religious Movements in the Middle Ages.* Translated by Steven Rowan. Notre Dame, IN: University of Notre Dame Press, 1995.

Hamesse, J. "Theological *Quaestiones Quodlibetalies.*" In *Theological Quodlibeta in the Middle Ages: The Thirteenth Century,* edited by Christopher David Schabel. Brill's Companions to the Christian Tradition 1. Leiden: Brill, 2006.

Hankey, W. J. *God in Himself: Aquinas' Doctrine of God as Expounded in the Summa Theologiae.* Oxford: Oxford University Press, 2004.

Heffernan, Thomas J. *Sacred Biography.* Oxford: Oxford University Press, 1988.

Henle, R. J. *Saint Thomas and Platonism: A Study of the Plato and Platonic Texts in the Writings of Saint Thomas.* The Hague: M. Nijhoff, 1956.

Hinnebusch, William A. *The History of the Dominican Order.* 2 vols. Staten Island, NY: Alba House, 1966–73.

Hood, John Y. B. *Aquinas and the Jews.* Philadelphia: University of Pennsylvania Press, 2017.

Horst, Ulrich. *The Dominicans and the Pope: Papal Teaching Authority in the Medieval and Early Modern Tradition.* Translated by James D. Mixson. Notre Dame, IN: University of Notre Dame Press, 2006.

———. *Unfehlbarkeit und geschichte.* Mainz: Matthias Grünewald Verlag, 1982.

Janz, Denis. *Luther on Thomas Aquinas: The Angelic Doctor in the Thought of the Reformer.* Veröffentlichungen des Instituts für Europäische Geschichte Mainz 140. Abteilung für Abendländische Religionsgeschichte. Stuttgart: Franz Steiner Verlag Wiesbaden, 1989.

Jordan, Mark D. *The Alleged Aristotelianism of Thomas Aquinas.* Toronto: Pontifical Institute of Medieval Studies, 1992.

Kelly, Samantha. *The New Solomon: Robert of Naples (1309–1343) and Fourteenth-Century Kingship.* Leiden: Brill, 2003.

Kretzmann, Norman, and Eleonore Stump. *The Cambridge Companion to Aquinas.* Cambridge: Cambridge Univ. Press, 2009.

Lauwers, Michel. "La mort et le corps de saints: la scène de la mort dans les Vitae du haut Moyen Age." *Moyen âge* 94, no. 1 (1988): 21–50.

Bibliography

Lawrence, C. H. *Friars: The Impact of the Mendicant Orders on Medieval Society*. London: I.B. Tauris & Company, 2013.

Maierù, Alfonso. *University Training in Medieval Europe*. Translated by Darleen Pryds. New York: Brill, 1994.

Mandonnet, P. "La Canonisation de Saint Thomas d'Aquin 18 Juillet 1323." *Année Dominicaine* (1923): 1–48.

———. "Thomas d'Aquin novice prêcheur, 1244–1246." *Revue Thomiste* 8–9 (1924–25).

Marmursztejn, Elsa. *L'autorité des maîtres: scolastique, normes et société au XIIIe siècle*. Paris: Les Belles Lettres, 2007.

Maurer, Armand. *Medieval Philosophy*. 2nd ed. Toronto: PIMS, 1982.

McCabe, Herbert. *God Matters*. London: Continuum, 2010.

McCool, Gerald A. *The Neo-Thomists*. Marquette Studies in Philosophy 3. Milwaukee: Marquette University Press, 1994.

McInerny, Ralph. *Saint Thomas Aquinas*. Boston: Twayne Publishers, 1977.

Meersseman, Gilles Gerard. "'In libris gentilium non studeant.' L'étude des classiques interdite aux clercs au moyen âge." *Italia medioevale e umanistica* 1 (1958): 1–13.

Mulchahey, M. Michèle. *"First the Bow Is Bent in Study…": Dominican Education before 1350*. Toronto: Pontifical Institute of Medieval Studies, 1998.

O'Rourke, Fran. *Pseudo-Dionysius and the Metaphysics of Aquinas*. Notre Dame, IN: University of Notre Dame Press, 2005.

Pieper, Josef. *Scholasticism: Personalities and Problems of Medieval Philosophy*. South Bend, IN: St. Augustine's Press, 2001.

———. *The Silence of St. Thomas: Three Essays*. South Bend, IN: St. Augustine's Press, 1999.

Plested, Marcus. *Orthodox Readings of Aquinas*. Oxford: Oxford University Press, 2012.

Räsänen, Marika. "Family vs. Order: Saint Thomas Aquinas' Dominican Habit in the Narrative Tradition of the Order." In *Identity and Alterity in Hagiography and Cult of Saints (Proceedings of the 2nd Hagiography Conference Organised by Croatian Hagiography Association "Hagiotheca" Held in Split, 28–31 May 2008)*, edited by Ana Marinković and Trpimir Vedriš, 201–18. Bibliotheca Hagiotheca, Series Colloquia, vol. 1. Zagreb: Hagiotheca, 2010.

————. "The Memory of St. Thomas Aquinas in Orvieto in the Late Middle Ages." In *Relics, Identity, and Memory in Medieval Europe*, edited by Marika Räsänen, Gritje Hartmann, and Earl Jeffrey Richards. Turnhout: Brepols, 2016.

————. *Thomas Aquinas's Relics as Focus for Conflict and Cult in the Late Middle Ages: The Restless Corpse*. Amsterdam: Amsterdam University Press, 2017.

Ratzinger, Joseph. "Der Einfluss des Bettelordensstreites auf die Entwicklung der Lehre vom päpstlichen Universalprimat, unter besonderer Berücksichtigung des heiligen Bonaventura." In *Theologie in Geschichte und Gegenwart*, edited by J. Auer and H. Volk. Munich: K. Zink, 1957.

Reltgen-Tallon, Anne. "L'historiographie des Dominicains du Midi: une mémoire originale?" In *L'ordre des Prêcheurs et son histoire en France méridionale*. Toulouse, Privat, 2001. *Cahiers de Fanjeaux* 36:395–414.

Robiglio, A.A. "Tommaso d'Aquino tra morte e canonizzazione." In *Letture e interpretazioni di Tommaso d'Aquino oggi: cantieri aperti: atti del convegno internazionale di studio (Milano 12–13 settembre 2005)*. Edited by Alessandro Ghisalberti. Torino: Istituto di filosofia S. Tommaso d'Aquino, 2006.

Roch, Martin. "The 'Odor of Sanctity': Defining Identity and Alterity in the Early Middle Ages (Fifth to Ninth Century)." In *Identity and Alterity in Hagiography and the Cult of Saints*, edited by Ana Marinković and Trpimir Vedriš. Zagreb: Hagiotheca, 2008.

Roensch, Frederick J. *Early Thomistic School*. Dubuque, IA: Priory Press, 1964.

Rottenwöhrer, Gerhard. *Die Katharer: Was sie glaubten, wie sie lebten*. Ostfildern: Thorbecke, 2007.

Rubin, Miri. *Corpus Christi: The Eucharist in Late Medieval Culture*. Cambridge: Cambridge University Press, 1991.

Schabel, Christopher, ed. *Theological Quodlibeta in the Middle Ages, Vol. 1. The Thirteenth Century*. Leiden: Brill, 2006.

Sigal, Pierre-André. "La mort des saints dans les Vies et les procès de canonisation du Midi de la France (XIe–XIVe siècle)." In *La mort et l'au-delà en France méridionale (XIIe–XVe siècle)*. *Cahiers de Fanjeaux* 33 (1998): 17–40.

Bibliography

Silva, J. F. *Robert Kilwardby on the Human Soul: Plurality of Forms and Censorship in the Thirteenth Century.* Leiden: Brill, 2012.

Sommer-Seckendorff, E. M. F. *Studies in the Life of Robert Kilwardby, OP.* Rome: Institutum historicum ff. praedicatorum Romae ad S. Sabinae, 1937.

Southern, R.W. *Medieval Humanism and Other Studies.* Oxford: Blackwell, 1984.

Teeuwen, Mariken. *The Vocabulary of Intellectual Life in the Middle Ages.* Etudes sur le Vocabulaire intellectuel du Moyen Age 10. Turnhout: Brepols, 2003.

Thompson, Augustine. *Cities of God: The Religion of the Italian Communes 1125–1325.* State College: Pennsylvania State University Press, 2006.

———. *Francis of Assisi: A New Biography.* Ithaca, NY: Cornell University Press, 2012.

———. *Revival Preachers and Politics in Thirteenth-Century Italy: The Great Devotion of 1233.* Oxford: Clarendon Press, 1992.

Tilatti, A. "La cattura di Tommaso d'Aquino da parte dei parenti." In *Ovidio Capitani: quaranta anni per la storia medioevale,* edited by M. C. De Matteis, 345–57. Bologna, 2003.

Torrell, J.-P. *Aquinas's Summa: Background, Structure, and Reception.* Washington, DC: Catholic University of America Press, 2012.

———. "La pratique pastorale d'un théologien du XIIIe siècle. Thomas d'Aquin prédicateur." *Revue Thomiste* 82 (1982): 213–45.

———. *Saint Thomas Aquinas.* 2 vols. Translated by Robert Royal. Washington, DC: Catholic University of America Press, 2015.

Torrell, Jean-Pierre, and D. Bouthillier. "Quand saint Thomas méditait sur le prophète Isaïe." *Revue Thomiste* 90 (1990): 5–47.

Traver, Andrew. "The Forging of an Intellectual Defense of Mendicancy in the Medieval University." In *The Origin, Development, and Refinement of Medieval Religious Mendicancies,* ed. Donald S. Prudlo, 157–96. Leiden: Brill, 2011.

Tugwell, Simon. *Albert and Thomas: Selected Writings.* Mahwah, NJ: Paulist Press, 1988.

———, ed. *Scripta de Sancto Domenico.* MOPH 27. Rome: Institutum Historicum Ordinis Fratrum Praedicatorum, 1998.

Turner, Denys. *Thomas Aquinas: A Portrait*. New Haven, CT: Yale University Press, 2014.

Van Riet, G. La. "'*Somme contre les Gentils*' et la polémique islamochrétienne." In *Aquinas and Problems of His Time*, edited by G. Verbeke and D. Verhelst, 150–60. Leuven University Press: The Hague, 1976.

Van Steenberghen, F. *Aristotle in the West: The Origins of Latin Aristotelianism*. 2nd ed. Louvain: Nauwelaerts, 1970.

——. *La Philosophie au XIIIe Siècle*. 2nd ed. Philosophes Médiévaux 28. Louvain-la-Neuve: Institut supérieur de philosophie, 1991.

——. *Thomas Aquinas and Radical Aristotelianism*. Washington, DC: Catholic University of America Press, 1980.

Vansteenkiste, C. "Avicenna citaten bij S. Thomas." *Tijdschrift voor Filosofie* 15 (1953): 437–507.

——. "Il Liber de Causis negli scritti di San Tommaso." *Angelicum* 35 (1958): 325–74.

Vauchez, André. "Les canonisations de S. Thomas et de S. Bonaventure: Pourquoi deux siècles d'écart?" In *1274 – Année Charnière, Mutations et Continuités*, edited by M. Mollat du Jourdin, 753–67. Lyon: Centre National de la Recherche Scientifique, 1978.

——. "The Canonizations of St. Thomas and St. Bonaventure: Why a Two-Century Gap between Them?" Translated by E. Hagman. *Greyfriars Review* 12, no. 2 (1998).

——. *Sainthood in the Later Middle Ages*. Cambridge: Cambridge University Press, 2005.

Vicaire, M.-H. "L'Homme que fut saint Thomas." In *L'anthropologie de saint Thomas: Conférences organisées par la Faculté de théologie et la Société philosophique de Fribourg à l'occasion du 7e centenaire de la mort de saint Thomas d'Aquin*, 7–34. Fribourg: Éditions universitaires, 1974.

Walz, Angelus. *Compendium Historiae Ordinis Praedicatorum*. Rome: Herder, 1930.

——." Papst Johannes XXII. Und Thomas von Aquin. Zur Geschichte der Heiligsprechung des Aquinaten." In *St. Thomas Aquinas 1274–1974. Commemorative Studies*. 2 vols., 1:29–47. Toronto: Pontifical Institute of Medieval Studies, 1974.

Bibliography

Weisheipl, James. *Friar Thomas d'Aquino: His Life, Thought, and Work*. New York: Doubleday, 1974.

Wetzstein, Thomas. *Heilige vor Gericht: Das Kanonisationsverfahren im europäischen Spätmittelalter*. Cologne: Böhlau Verlag, 2004.

Wippel, J. "Quodlibetal Questions, Chiefly in Theology Faculties." In *Les questions disputées et les questions quodlibétiques dans les Facultés de théologie, de droit et de médecine*, edited by Bernardo C. Bazàn. Turnhout: Brepols, 1985.

Wohlman, Avital. *Thomas d'Aquin et Maïmonide: un dialogue exemplaire*. Paris: Cerf, 2007.

INDEX

Index

Index

Index